The old red sandstone; or, New walks in an old field.
To which is appended a series of geological papers,
read before the Royal physical society of Edinburgh

Hugh Miller

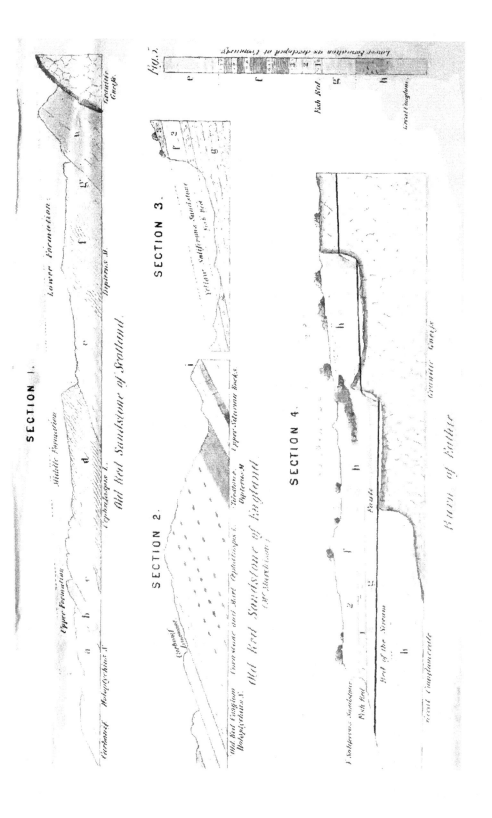

SECTION 1.

Old Red Sandstone of Scotland.

SECTION 2.

Old Red Sandstone of England.
(Sir R. Murchison.)

SECTION 3.

SECTION 4.

River of Kittlen.

THE

OLD RED SANDSTONE;

OR,

NEW WALKS IN AN OLD FIELD.

TO WHICH IS APPENDED

A SERIES OF GEOLOGICAL PAPERS,

READ BEFORE THE

ROYAL PHYSICAL SOCIETY OF EDINBURGH.

BY

HUGH MILLER, LL.D.,

AUTHOR OF "THE FOOTPRINTS OF THE CREATOR,"
"THE TESTIMONY OF THE ROCKS," ETC. ETC.

ILLUSTRATED WITH NUMEROUS ENGRAVINGS.

A NEW, IMPROVED, AND ENLARGED EDITION.

BOSTON:
GOULD AND LINCOLN,
59 WASHINGTON STREET.
NEW YORK: SHELDON, BLAKEMAN & CO.
CINCINNATI: GEORGE S. BLANCHARD.
1858.

STEREOTYPED AT THE BOSTON STEREOTYPE FOUNDRY.

———

Printed by G. C. Rand & Co. No. 3 Cornhill.

AMERICAN PUBLISHERS' NOTICE

TO THE

NEW AND ENLARGED EDITION.

"Hugh Miller's 'Old Red Sandstone,' to a beginner, is worth a thousand didactic treatises," said Sir Roderick Impey Murchison in his Address before the British Geological Society. "No geologist can peruse it without instruction and delight," said Professor Benjamin Silliman in his American Journal of Science. Of the work thus commended by the highest authorities on both sides of the Atlantic, the American publishers now have the pleasure of presenting to the public a new and greatly improved edition.

Geology is emphatically a growing science, and in the hands of no master did it ever grow more rapidly, or to better purpose, than in Hugh Miller's It thus happened that as edition after edition of his work was called for, he had new facts, new arguments, and new conclusions, wherewith to enrich its pages. Some of these were presented in the prefaces to the successive editions, others were incorporated with the text, and others took the form of notes. Since Mr. Miller's death, a new edition has been given to the public by Mrs Miller, with a preface from her own pen, notes by other hands, additional plates, and a large amount of new matter selected from Mr Miller's unpublished writings. The present American edition is re-printed from that; but, to avoid encumbering the volume, the substance of what is important in the several prefaces alluded to, is incorporated with this.

"The Old Red Sandstone" was Hugh Miller's first geological work, and was first published in 1841 In 1842, a second edition was called for. This contained about fifteen pages of new matter, referring chiefly to the least known portion of the Old Red system — that middle formation to which the organisms of Balruddery and Carmyle belong. A print (Plate XI.) illustrative of this portion of the work was also added, and one or two conjectures were made to give place to the facts at which they pointed.

A third edition was issued in 1846. In the preface to that edition, Mr. Miller announced that the bold prediction made by him in the first, — that the ichthyolites of the Old Red Sandstone would be found at least equal to those of all the geological formations united, at the death of Cuvier, — was already more than fulfilled. For, while Cuvier had enumerated but ninety-two species of fossil fishes in all, Agassiz had already, in 1846, enumerated one hundred and five in the Old Red Sandstone alone, — a formation which had been regarded as poorer in organisms than any other The catalogue of species in that formation, as determined and arranged by Agassiz, was given in this edition. Many additions to the volume in the form of notes were also made, and in several instances the text was modified It had been stated in the first two editions that a gradual increase of size was observable in the progress of ichthyolitic life, and that the Old Red System exhibited, in its successive formations, this gradation of bulk, beginning with an age of dwarfs, and ending with an age of giants. When the third edition was issued, it had been ascertained that there were giants among the dwarfs, the remains of one of the largest fishes found anywhere in the system had been discovered in its lowest formation. By the positive proof thus furnished, Mr. Miller was convinced that the theory of a gradual progression in size, from the earlier to the later Palæozoic formations, though based originally on no inconsiderable amount of negative evidence, must be permitted to drop

The fourth, fifth, and sixth editions were mainly if not wholly reprints of the third. The *seventh*, which has just been issued under the supervision of Mrs Miller, and is re-printed in the present volume, contains large and interesting additions. While the text and notes of Mr Miller are preserved without the slightest change or revision, some notes have been appended by a friend of Mrs Miller, with the view of drawing attention to whatever modifications of opinion he may himself have recorded in his later works, or may have been known to express verbally in conversation with his friends In addition to these, three or four notes have been furnished by the Rev. W S. Symonds, who is described as a well-known geologist intimately acquainted with the Silurian and Old Red of his own neighborhood in the south-west of England. Several new figures have also been added, taken either from specimens in Mr Miller's own unique collection, or from those in the possession of others, which it is known he had asked permission to copy. These present the fossils to which they relate in new and striking aspects They are those on Plates ix., x., xii., and xiv., and on pages 54 and 267.

But the most important additions to the volume are from the pen of Hugh Miller himself They consist of the Geological Papers read by him before the Royal Physical Society of Edinburgh. These papers have been selected by Mrs. Miller from the mass of her husband's unpublished writings, and, while they add greatly to the size of the volume, they add to its value no less. In each and all, the characteristics of their author's genius are abundantly displayed. The first paper presents a succinct summary of those evidences drawn from geology in favor of *revealed* religion, which it formed the chief portion of his peculiar mission to originate and establish. In the second is given a sketch of the early progress of general geologic knowledge in Scotland, together with a delightful account of his exploration of the valley of the Girvan It is germane to the subject of the twelfth chapter of "The Old Red Sandstone." The paper on the Marbles of Assynt furnishes fine illustrations of Mr. Miller's sagacity as a geologist, and of his unrivalled powers of description. The concluding paper presents a comprehensive survey of the Fossiliferous Deposits of Scotland

In preparing this volume for the press, the publishers have varied in some few instances from the arrangement of the Edinburgh edition. The four new plates which in that edition were appended to the Notes, have, with a view to convenience in this, been distributed through the body of the work at the points where they seemed most properly to belong. This arrangement made it necessary to renumber the old plates One of the new cuts has been connected with a note in which it is specifically mentioned; and several footnotes, most of them by Mr. Symonds, have been transferred from the body of the work to the "Notes" at the end. These changes, it is believed, constitute a decided improvement. With the exception of these, and the abridgment of the multiplied prefaces, the present edition is a reprint of the new Edinburgh edition.

Boston, April, 1858

TO

RODERICK IMPEY MURCHISON, Esq., F. R. S., Etc.,

PRESIDENT OF THE GEOLOGICAL SOCIETY.

In the autumn of last year, I sat down to write a few geological sketches for a newspaper; the accumulated facts of twenty years crowded upon me as I wrote, and the few sketches have expanded into a volume. Permit me, honored Sir, to dedicate this volume to you. Its imperfections are doubtless many, for it has been produced under many disadvantages, but it is not the men best qualified to decide regarding it whose criticisms I fear most; and I am especially desirous to bring it under your notice, as of all geologists the most thoroughly acquainted with those ancient formations which it professes partially to describe. I am, besides, desirous it should be known, and this, I trust, from other motives than those of vanity, that, when prosecuting my humble researches in obscurity and solitude, the present President of the Geological Society did not deem it beneath him to evince an interest in the results to which they led, and to encourage and assist the inquirer with his advice. Accept, honored Sir, my sincere thanks for your kindness.

Smith, the father of English Geology, loved to remark that he had been born upon the Oolite — the formation whose various deposits he was the first to distinguish and describe, and from which, as from the meridian line of the geographer, the geological scale has been graduated on both sides. I

(vii)

have thought of the circumstance when, on visiting in my native district the birthplace of the author of the *Silurian System*, I found it situated among the more ancient fossiliferous rocks of the north of Scotland — the Lower Formation of the Old Red Sandstone spreading out beneath and around it, and the first-formed deposit of the system, the Great Conglomerate, rising high on the neighboring hills. It is unquestionably no slight advantage to be placed, at that early stage of life, when the mind collects its facts with greatest avidity, and the curiosity is most active, in localities where there is much to attract observation that has escaped the notice of others. Like the gentleman whom I have now the honor of addressing, I too was born on the Old Red Sandstone, and first broke ground as an inquirer into geological fact in a formation scarce at all known to the geologist, and in which there still remains much for future discoverers to examine and describe. Hence an acquaintance, I am afraid all too slight, with phenomena which, if intrinsically of interest, may be found to have also the interest of novelty to recommend them, and with organisms which, though among the most ancient of things in their relation to the world's history, will be pronounced new by the geological reader in their relation to human knowledge. Hence, too, my present opportunity of subscribing myself, as the writer of a volume on the Old Red Sandstone,

   Honored Sir,

     With sincere gratitude and respect,

       Your obedient humble Servant,

          HUGH MILLER.

EDINBURGH, *May* 1, 1841.

AUTHOR'S PREFACE.

NEARLY one third of the present volume appeared a few months ago in the form of a series of sketches in the *Witness* newspaper A portion of the first chapter was submitted to the public a year or two earlier, in *Chambers's Edinburgh Journal* The rest, amounting to about two thirds of the whole, appears for the first time.

Every such work has its defects. The faults of the present volume — faults all too obvious, I am afraid — would have been probably fewer had the writer enjoyed greater leisure. Some of them, however, seem scarce separable from the nature of the subject: there are others for which, from their opposite character, I shall have to apologize in turn to opposite classes of readers My facts would, in most instances, have lain closer had I written for geologists exclusively, and there would have been less reference to familiar phenomena. And had I written for only general readers, my descriptions of hitherto undescribed organisms, and the deposits of little-known localities, would have occupied fewer pages, and would have been thrown off with, perhaps, less regard to minute detail than to pictorial effect. May I crave, while addressing myself, now to the one class, and now to the other, the alternate forbearance of each?

Such is the state of progression in geological science, that the geologist who stands still for but a very little, must be content to find himself left behind. Nay, so rapid is the progress, that scarce a geological work passes through the press in which some of the statements of the earlier pages have not to be modified, restricted, or extended in the concluding ones. The present volume shares, in this respect, in what seems the common lot. In describing the *Coccosteus,* the reader will find it stated that the creature, unlike its contemporary the *Pterichthys,* was unfurnished with arms. Ere arriving at such a conclusion, I had carefully examined at least a hundred different *Coccostei ;* but the positive evidence of one specimen outweighs the negative evidence of a hundred; and I have just learned from a friend in the north, (Mr. Patrick Duff, of Elgin,) that a *Coccosteus* lately found at Lethen-bar, and now in the possession of Lady Gordon Cumming, of Altyre, is furnished with what seem uncouth, paddle-shaped arms, that project from the head.*   All that I

* As these paddle-shaped arms have not been introduced by Agassiz into his restoration of the *Coccosteus,* their existence, at least *as arms,* must still be regarded as problematical   There can be no doubt,

have given of the creature, however, will be found true to the actual type ; and that parts should have been omitted will surprise no one who remembers that many hundred belemnites had been figured and described ere a specimen turned up in which the horny prolongation, with its enclosed ink-bag, was found attached to the calcareous spindle ; and that even yet, after many thousand trilobites have been carefully examined, it remains a question with the oryctologist, whether this crustacean of the earliest periods was furnished with legs, or creeped on an abdominal foot, like the snail.

I owe to the kindness of Mr. Robertson, Inverugie, the specimen figured in Plate V., fig. 7, containing shells of the only species yet discovered in the Old Red Sandstone of Scotland. They occur in the Lower Formation of the system, in a quarry near Kirkwald, in which the specimen figured, with several others of the same kind, was found by Mr. Robertson, in the year 1834. In referring to this shell, page 90, I have spoken of it as a delicate bivalve, much resembling a *Venus ;* drawing my illustration, naturally enough, when describing the shell of an ocean deposit, rather from among marine, than fluviatile testacea. I have since submitted it to Mr. Murchison, who has obligingly written me that he " can find no one to say more regarding it than that it is

---

however, that they existed *as plates* of very peculiar form, and greatly resembling paddles, and that they served in the economy of the animal some still unaccounted for purpose.

very like a *Cyclas*." He adds, however, that it must be an ocean production notwithstanding, seeing that all its contemporaries in England, Scotland, and Russia, whether shells or fish, are unequivocally marine.

With the exception of two of the figures in Plate X., the figures of the *Cephalaspis* and the *Holoptychius*, and one of the sections in the Frontispiece, section 2, all the prints of the volume are originals. To Mr. Daniel Alexander, of Edinburgh, — a gentleman, who to the skill and taste of the superior artist, adds no small portion of the knowledge of the practical geologist, — I am indebted for several of the drawings; that of fig. 2 in Plate V., fig. 1 in Plate VI., fig. 2 in Plate VIII., and figs. 3 and 4 in plate X. I am indebted to another friend for fig. 1, in Plate VII. Whatever defects may be discovered in any of the others, must be attributed to the untaught efforts of the writer, all unfamiliar, hitherto, with the pencil, and with by much too little leisure to acquaint himself with it now.

CONTENTS.

CHAPTER I.

CHAPTER II.

b

CHAPTER III

CHAPTER IV.

CHAPTER V.

CHAPTER VI.

CHAPTER VII.

CHAPTER VIII.

CHAPTER IX.

CHAPTER X.

CHAPTER XI.

CHAPTER XII.

CHAPTER XIII.

CHAPTER XIV.

EXPLANATIONS OF THE SECTIONS AND PLATES.

SECTION I.

REPRESENTS the Old Red System of Scotland from its upper beds of Yellow Quartzose Sandstone to its Great Conglomerate base. *a.* Quartzose Yellow Sandstone. *b.* Impure concretionary limestone enclosing masses of chert. *c.* Red and variegated sandstones and conglomerate. These three deposits constitute an upper formation of the system, characterized by its peculiar group of fossils. (See Chapter IX.) *d.* Deposit of gray fissile sandstone which constitutes the middle formation of the system, characterized also by its peculiar organic group. (See Chapter VIII) *e.* Red and variegated sandstones, undistinguishable often in their mineral character from the upper sandstones, *c*, but in general less gritty, and containing fewer pebbles. *f* Bituminous schists. *g.* Coarse gritty sandstone. *h.* Great Conglomerate. These four beds compose a lower formation of the system, more strikingly marked by its peculiar organisms than even the other two (See Chapters II. III. IV. and V) In the section this lower formation is represented as we find it developed in Caithness and Orkney In fig 5 it is represented as developed in Cromarty, where, though the fossils are identical with those of the more northern localities, at least one of the deposits, *f*, is mineralogically different — alternating beds of sandstone and clay, these last enclosing limestone nodules, taking the place of the bituminous schists.

SECTION II.

The Old Red System of England and Wales, as given in the general Section of Mr Murchison, with the Silurian Rocks beneath and the carboniferous limestone above i The point in the geological scale at which vertebrated existences first appear. The three Old Red Sandstone formations of this section correspond in their characteristic fossils with those of Scotland, but the proportions in which they are developed are widely different   The tilestones seem a comparatively narrow stripe in the system in England ; the answering formation in Scotland, e, f, g, h, is of such enormous thickness, that it has been held by very superior geologists to contain three distinct formations — e, the New Red Sandstone, f, a representative of the Coal Measures, and g, h, the Old Red Sandstone.

SECTION III.

Interesting case of extensive denudation from existing causes on the northern shore of the Moray Frith. (See pages 198 and 199.) The figures and letters which mark the various beds correspond with those of fig. 5, and of the following section. The "fish-bed," No. 1, represents what the reader will find described in pp. 221–225 as the "platform of sudden death."

SECTION IV.

Illustration of a fault in the Burn of Eathie, Cromartyshire. (See pages 201 and 205.)

PLATE I. — Fig. 1, Restoration of upper side of the elongated species of *Pterichthys*, (*P oblongus*,) referred to in page 47. Fig. 2, *Pterichthys Milleri*. Fig. 3, Part of tail of elongated species, showing portions of the original covering of rhomboidal scales. Fig. 4, Tubercles of *Pterichthys* magnified.

PLATE II. — Fig. 2, Restoration of under side of *Pterichthys oblongus*. Fig. 1, A second specimen of *Pterichthys Milleri*. Fig. 3, Portion of wing, natural size.

PLATE III — Fig. 1, *Coccosteus cuspidatus*. Fig. 2, Impression of inner surface of large dorsal plate. Fig. 3, Abdominal lozenge-shaped plate. Fig. 4, Portion of jaw, with teeth.

PLATE IV. — Fig. 1, Restoration of *Osteolepis major* Fig. 2, Scales from the upper part of the body magnified. Fig. 3, Large defensive scale which runs laterally along all the single fins Fig. 4, Under side of scale, showing the attaching bar. Fig. 5, Enamelled and punctulated jaw of the creature. Fig. 6, Magnified portion of fin, showing the enamelled and punctulated rays.

PLATE V. — Fig. 1, *Dipterus macrolepidotus*. This figure serves merely to show the place of the fins and the general outline of the ichthyolite. All the specimens the writer has hitherto examined fail to show the minuter details. Fig. 2, *Glyptolepis leptopterus*. Fig. 3, Single scale of the creature, showing its rustic style of ornament. Fig. 4, Scale with a nail-like attachment. Fig. 5, Under side of scale. Fig. 6, Magnified portion of fin Fig 7, Shells of the Old Red Sandstone.

PLATE VI. — Fig. 1, *Cheirolepis Cummingiæ*. Fig. 2, Magnified scales. Fig. 3, Magnified portion of fin.

PLATE VII.—Fig. 1, *Cheiracanthus microlepidotus*. Fig. 2, Magnified scales. Figs. 3, 4, 5, 6, 7, 8, Vegetable impressions of the Old Red Sandstone.

PLATE VIII.—Fig. 1, *Diplacanthus longispinus*. Fig. 2, *Diplacanthus striatus*. Fig. 3, Magnified scales of fig 1. Fig. 4, Spine of fig. 2, slightly magnified.

PLATE IX.—Restoration of *Coccosteus*, incomplete, found in Mr. Miller's Museum after his death. (Seventh Edinburgh edition, 1858.)

PLATE X.—Restoration of *Cephalaspis*, from several specimens lately found in Forfarshire. (Seventh Edinburgh edition, 1858.)

PLATE XI.—Fig. 1, One of the tail flaps of the gigantic Crustacean of Forfarshire. Fig. 2, Reticulated markings of Carmylie

PLATE XII —*Parka decipiens*, from a specimen in the private collection of Lord Kinnaird, at Rossie Priory. (Seventh Edinburgh edition, 1858.)

PLATE XIII.—Fig. 1, *Cephalaspis Lyellii*, copied from Lyell's *Elements of Geology*. Fig. 2, *Holoptychius Nobilissimus*, copied on a greatly reduced scale from Murchison's *Silurian System*. Fig. 3, Scale of *Holoptychius*, natural size. Fig. 4, Tooth of ditto, also natural size. These last drawn from specimens in the collection of Mr. Patrick Duff, of Elgin.

PLATE XIV.—Figure of a *Holoptychius*, found some time ago in Dura Den, Fifeshire, and now in the possession of a private collector in Dundee. (Seventh Edinburgh edition, 1858.)

NEW WALKS IN AN OLD FIELD;

OR,

THE OLD RED SANDSTONE.

CHAPTER I.

The Working-man's True Policy. — His only Mode of acquiring
Power. — The Exercise of the Faculties essential to Enjoyment —
No necessary Connection between Labor and Unhappiness. — Narrative. — Scenes in a Quarry. — The two dead Birds. — Landscape. —
Ripple Markings on a Sandstone Slab. — Boulder Stones. — Inference derived from their water-worn Appearance. — Sea-coast Section — My first discovered Fossil. — Lias Deposit on the Shores of
the Moray Frith. — Belemnite — Result of the Experience of half
a Lifetime of Toil. — Advantages of a Wandering Profession in
Connection with the Geology of a Country. — Geological Opportunities of the Stone-Mason. — Design of the present Work

My advice to young working-men, desirous of bettering
their circumstances, and adding to the amount of their enjoyment, is a very simple one. Do not seek happiness in
what is misnamed pleasure ; seek it rather in what is termed
study. Keep your consciences clear, your curiosity fresh,
and embrace every opportunity of cultivating your minds.
You will gain nothing by attending Chartist meetings. The
fellows who speak nonsense with fluency at these assemblies,
and deem their nonsense eloquence, are totally unable to help
either you or themselves ; or, if they do succeed in helping

1

themselves, it will be all at your expense. Leave them to
harangue unheeded, and set yourselves to occupy your leisure hours in making yourselves wiser men. Learn to make
a right use of your eyes: the commonest things are worth
looking at — even stones and weeds, and the most familiar
animals. Read good books, not forgetting the best of all :
there is more true philosophy in the Bible than in every work
of every sceptic that ever wrote ; and we would be all miserable creatures without it, and none more miserable than
you. You are jealous of the upper classes ; and perhaps it
is too true that, with some good, you have received much
evil at their hands. It must be confessed they have hitherto
been doing comparatively little for you, and a great deal for
themselves. But upper and lower classes there must be, so
long as the world lasts ; and there is only one way in which
your jealousy of them can be well directed. Do not let them
get ahead of you in intelligence It would be alike unwise
and unjust to attempt casting them down to your own level,
and no class would suffer more in the attempt than yourselves ; for you would only be clearing the way, at an immense expense of blood, and under a tremendous pressure
of misery, for another and perhaps worse aristocracy, with
some second Cromwell or Napoleon at their head. Society,
however, is in a state of continual flux . some in the upper
classes are from time to time going down, and some of you
from time to time mounting up to take their places — always
the more steady and intelligent among you, remember; and
if all your minds were cultivated, not merely intellectually,
but morally also, you would find yourselves, as a body, in
the possession of a power which every charter in the world
could not confer upon you, and which all the tyranny or injustice of the world could not withstand.

I intended, however, to speak rather of the pleasure to be derived, by even the humblest, in the pursuit of knowledge, than of the power with which knowledge in the masses is invariably accompanied. For it is surely of greater importance that men should receive accessions to their own happiness, than to the influence which they exert over other men. There is none of the intellectual, and none of the moral faculties, the exercise of which does not lead to enjoyment. nay, it is chiefly in the active employment of these that all enjoyment consists; and hence it is that happiness bears so little reference to station It is a truth which has been often told, but very little heeded or little calculated upon, that though one nobleman may be happier than another, and one laborer happier than another, yet it cannot be at all premised of their respective orders, that the one is in any degree happier than the other. Simple as the fact may seem, if universally recognized, it would save a great deal of useless discontent, and a great deal of envy. Will my humbler readers permit me at once to illustrate this subject, and to introduce the chapters which follow, by a piece of simple narrative ? I wish to show them how possible it is to enjoy much happiness in very mean employments. Cowper tells us that labor, though the primal curse, " has been softened into mercy ; " and I think that, even had he not done so, I would have found out the fact for myself.

It was twenty years, last February, since I set out a little before sunrise to make my first acquaintance with a life of labor and restraint, and I have rarely had a heavier heart than on that morning. I was but a slim, loose-jointed boy at the time — fond of the pretty intangibilities of romance, and of dreaming when broad awake ; and, woful change ! I was now going to work at what Burns has instanced in his " Twa

Dogs " as one of the most disagreeable of all employments —
to work in a quarry. Bating the passing uneasiness occasioned by a few gloomy anticipations, the portion of my life
which had already gone by had been happy beyond the common lot. I had been a wanderer among rocks and woods —
a reader of curious books when I could get them — a gleaner
of old traditionary stories ; and now I was going to exchange
all my day-dreams, and all my amusements, for the kind of
life in which men toil every day that they may be enabled to
eat, and eat every day that they may be enabled to toil !

The quarry in which I wrought lay on the southern shore
of a noble inland bay, or frith, rather, with a little clear stream
on the one side, and a thick fir wood on the other. It had
been opened in the Old Red Sandstone of the district, and
was overtopped by a huge bank of diluvial clay, which rose
over it in some places to the height of nearly thirty feet, and
which at this time was rent and shivered, wherever it presented an open front to the weather, by a recent frost. A
heap of loose fragments, which had fallen from above,
blocked up the face of the quarry, and my first employment
was to clear them away. The friction of the shovel soon
blistered my hands ; but the pain was by no means very
severe, and I wrought hard and willingly, that I might see
how the huge strata below, which presented so firm and unbroken a frontage, were to be torn up and removed. Picks,
and wedges, and levers were applied by my brother-workmen ; and simple and rude as I had been accustomed to regard these implements, I found I had much to learn in the
way of using them. They all proved inefficient, however ;
and the workmen had to bore into one of the inferior strata,
and employ gunpowder. The process was new to me, and I
deemed it a highly amusing one it had the merit, too, of

being attended with some such degree of danger as a boating or rock excursion, and had thus an interest independent of its novelty. We had a few capital shots: the fragments flew in every direction; and an immense mass of the diluvium came toppling down, bearing with it two dead birds, that in a recent storm had crept into one of the deeper fissures, to die in the shelter I felt a new interest in examining them. The one was a pretty cock goldfinch, with its hood of vermilion, and its wings inlaid with the gold to which it owes its name, as unsoiled and smooth as if it had been preserved for a museum. The other, a somewhat rarer bird, of the woodpecker tribe, was variegated with light blue and a grayish yellow. I was engaged in admiring the poor little things, more disposed to be sentimental, perhaps, than if I had been ten years older, and thinking of the contrast between the warmth and jollity of their green summer haunts, and the cold and darkness of their last retreat, when I heard our employer bidding the workmen lay by their tools. I looked up, and saw the sun sinking behind the thick fir wood beside us, and the long, dark shadows of the trees stretching downwards towards the shore.

This was no very formidable beginning of the course of life I had so much dreaded. To be sure, my hands were a little sore, and I felt nearly as much fatigued as if I had been climbing among the rocks; but I had wrought and been useful, and had yet enjoyed the day fully as much as usual. It was no small matter, too, that the evening, converted, by a rare transmutation, into the delicious "blink of rest" which Burns so truthfully describes, was all my own. I was as light of heart next morning as any of my brother-workmen. There had been a smart frost during the night, and the rime lay white on the grass as we passed onwards through the

1 *

fields; but the sun rose in a clear atmosphere, and the day mellowed, as it advanced, into one of those delightful days of early spring, which give so pleasing an earnest of whatever is mild and genial in the better half of the year   All the workmen rested at midday, and I went to enjoy my half-hour alone on a mossy knoll in the neighboring wood, which commands through the trees a wide prospect of the bay and the opposite shore.   There was not a wrinkle on the water, nor a cloud in the sky, and the branches were as moveless in the calm as if they had been traced on canvas.   From a wooded promontory that stretched half way across the frith, there ascended a thin column of smoke.   It rose straight as the line of a plummet for more than a thousand yards, and then, on reaching a thinner stratum of air, spread out equally on every side, like the foliage of a stately tree.   Ben Wevis rose to the west, white with the yet unwasted snows of winter, and as sharply defined in the clear atmosphere, as if all its sunny slopes and blue retiring hollows had been chiselled in marble.   A line of snow ran along the opposite hills, all above was white, and all below was purple.   They reminded me of the pretty French story, in which an old artist is described as tasking the ingenuity of his future son-in-law, by giving him, as a subject for his pencil, a flower-piece composed of only white flowers, of which the one half were to bear their proper color, the other half a deep purple hue, and yet all be perfectly natural; and how the young man resolved the riddle, and gained his mistress, by introducing a transparent purple vase into the picture, and making the light pass through it on the flowers that were drooping over the edge. I returned to the quarry, convinced that a very exquisite pleasure may be a very cheap one, and that the busiest employments may afford leisure enough to enjoy it.

The gunpowder had loosened a large mass in one of the inferior strata, and our first employment, on resuming our labors, was to raise it from its bed. I assisted the other workmen in placing it on edge, and was much struck by the appearance of the platform on which it had rested. The entire surface was ridged and furrowed like a bank of sand that had been left by the tide an hour before. I could trace every bend and curvature, every cross hollow and counter ridge of the corresponding phenomena; for the resemblance was no half resemblance — it was the thing itself; and I had observed it a hundred and a hundred times, when sailing my little schooner in the shallows left by the ebb. But what had become of the waves that had thus fretted the solid rock, or of what element had they been composed? I felt as completely at fault as Robinson Crusoe did on his discovering the print of the man's foot on the sand. The evening furnished me with still further cause of wonder. We raised another block in a different part of the quarry, and found that the area of a circular depression in the stratum below was broken and flawed in every direction, as if it had been the bottom of a pool recently dried up, which had shrunk and split in the hardening. Several large stones came rolling down from the diluvium in the course of the afternoon. They were of different qualities from the Sandstone below, and from one another; and, what was more wonderful still, they were all rounded and water-worn, as if they had been tossed about in the sea, or the bed of a river, for hundreds of years. There could not, surely, be a more conclusive proof that the bank which had enclosed them so long could not have been created on the rock on which it rested. No workman ever manufactures a half-worn article, and the stones were all half-worn! And if not the bank, why then the sandstone underneath? I was lost in conjecture, and found I had food enough for thought that evening, without once thinking of the unhappiness of a life of labor.

The immense masses of diluvium which we had to clear away rendered the working of the quarry laborious and expensive, and all the party quitted it in a few days, to make trial of another that seemed to promise better. The one we left is situated, as I have said, on the southern shore of an inland bay — the Bay of Cromarty; the one to which we removed has been opened in a lofty wall of cliffs that overhangs the northern shore of the Moray Frith. I soon found I was to be no loser by the change. Not the united labors of a thousand men for more than a thousand years could have furnished a better section of the geology of the district than this range of cliffs. It may be regarded as a sort of chance dissection on the earth's crust. We see in one place the primary rock, with its veins of granite and quartz, its dizzy precipices of gneiss, and its huge masses of hornblende; we find the secondary rock in another, with its beds of sandstone and shale, its spars, its clays, and its nodular limestones. We discover the still little known but highly interesting fossils of the Old Red Sandstone in one deposition, we find the beautifully preserved shells and lignites of the Lias in another. There are the remains of two several creations at once before us. The shore, too, is heaped with rolled fragments of almost every variety of rock, — basalts, ironstones, hypersthenes, porphyries, bituminous shales, and micaceous schists. In short, the young geologist, had he all Europe before him, could hardly choose for himself a better field. I had, however, no one to tell me so at the time, for geology had not yet travelled so far north; and so, without guide or vocabulary, I had to grope my way as I best might, and find out all its wonders for myself. But so slow was the process, and so much was I a seeker in the dark, that the facts contained in these few sentences were the patient gatherings of years.

In the course of the first day's employment, I picked up a nodular mass of blue limestone, and laid it open by a stroke of the hammer. Wonderful to relate, it contained inside a beautifully finished piece of sculpture — one of the volutes apparently of an Ionic capital; and not the far-famed walnut of the fairy tale, had I broken the shell and found the little dog lying within, could have surprised me more. Was there another such curiosity in the whole world? I broke open a few other nodules of similar appearance, — for they lay pretty thickly on the shore, — and found that there might. In one of these there were what seemed to be the scales of fishes, and the impressions of a few minute bivalves, prettily striated; in the centre of another there was actually a piece of decayed wood. Of all Nature's riddles these seemed to me to be at once the most interesting, and the most difficult to expound. I treasured them carefully up, and was told by one of the workmen to whom I showed them, that there was a part of the shore about two miles farther to the west, where curiously shaped stones, somewhat like the heads of boarding-pikes, were occasionally picked up; and that in his father's days the country people called them thunderbolts, and deemed them of sovereign efficacy in curing bewitched cattle. Our employer, on quitting the quarry for the building on which we were to be engaged, gave all the workmen a half-holiday. I employed it in visiting the place where the thunderbolts had fallen so thickly, and found it a richer scene of wonder than I could have fancied in even my dreams.

What first attracted my notice was a detached group of low lying skerries, wholly different in form and color from the sandstone cliffs above, or the primary rocks a little farther to the west. I found them composed of thin strata of limestone, alternating with thicker beds of a black slaty substance, which, as I ascertained in the course of the evening, burns with a powerful flame, and emits a strong bituminous odor The layers into which the beds readily separate are hardly an eighth part of an inch in thickness, and yet on every layer there are the impressions of thousands and tens of thousands of the various fossils peculiar to the Lias. We may turn over these wonderful leaves one after one, like the leaves of a herbarium, and find the pictorial records of a former creation in every page. Scallops, and gryphites, and ammonites, of almost every variety peculiar to the formation, and at least some eight or ten varieties of belemnite ; twigs of wood, leaves of plants, cones of an extinct species of pine, bits of charcoal, and the scales of fishes ; and, as if to render their pictorial appearance more striking, though the leaves of this interesting volume are of a deep black, most of the impressions are of a chalky whiteness. I was lost in admiration and astonishment, and found my very imagination paralyzed by an assemblage of wonders, that seemed to outrival, in the fantastic and the extravagant, even its wildest conceptions I passed on from ledge to ledge, like the traveller of the tale through the city of statues, and at length found one of the supposed aerolites I had come in quest of, firmly imbedded in a mass of shale. But I had skill enough to determine that it was other than what it had been deemed. A very near relative, who had been a sailor in his time on almost every ocean, and had visited almost every quarter of the globe, had brought home one of these meteoric stones with him from the coast of Java. It was of a cylindrical shape and vitreous texture, and it seemed to have parted in the middle when in a half-molten state, and to have united again, somewhat awry, ere it had cooled enough to have lost the adhesive quality. But there was nothing organic in its structure, whereas the stone I had now found was organized very curiously indeed. It was of a conical form and filamentary texture, the filaments radiating in straight lines from the centre to the circumference. Finely-marked veins like white threads ran transversely through these in its upper half to the point, while the space below was occupied by an internal cone, formed of plates that lay parallel to the base, and which, like watch-glasses, were concave on the under side, and convex on the upper. I learned in time to call this stone a belemnite, and became acquainted with enough of its history to know that it once formed part of a variety of cuttle-fish, long since extinct.

My first year of labor came to a close, and I found that the amount of my happiness had not been less than in the last of my boyhood. My knowledge, too, had increased in more than the ratio of former seasons; and as I had acquired the skill of at least the common mechanic, I had fitted myself for independence. The additional experience of twenty years has not shown me that there is any necessary connection between a life of toil and a life of wretchedness; and when I have found good men anticipating a better and a happier time than either the present or the past, the conviction that in every period of the world's history the great bulk of mankind must pass their days in labor, has not in the least inclined me to scepticism.

My curiosity, once fully awakened, remained awake, and my opportunities of gratifying it have been tolerably ample. I have been an explorer of caves and ravines — a loiterer along sea-shores — a climber among rocks — a laborer in quarries. My profession was a wandering one. I remember passing direct, on one occasion, from the wild western coast of Ross-shire, where the Old Red Sandstone leans at a high angle against the prevailing Quartz Rock of the district, to where, on the southern skirts of Mid-Lothian, the Mountain Limestone rises amid the coal. I have resided one season on a raised beach of the Moray Frith. I have spent the season immediately following amid the ancient granites and contorted schists of the central Highlands. In the north I have laid open by thousands the shells and lignites of the Oolite; in the south I have disinterred from their matrices of stone or of shale the huge reeds and tree ferns of the Carboniferous period. I have been taught by experience, too, how necessary an acquaintance with geology of both extremes of the kingdom is to the right understanding of the formations of either. In the north, there occurs a vast gap in the scale. The Lias leans unconformably against the Old Red Sandstone, there is no Mountain Limestone, no Coal Measures, none of the New Red Marls or Sandstones, Under or Upper. There are at least three entire systems omitted. But the upper portion of the scale is well nigh complete. In one locality we may pass from the Lower to the Upper Lias, in another from the Inferior to the Great Oolite, and onward to the Oxford Clay and the Coral Rag. We may explore, in a third locality, beds identical in their organisms with the Wealden of Sussex. In a fourth we find the flints and fossils of the Chalk. The lower part of the scale is also well nigh complete. The Old Red Sandstone is amply developed in Moray, Caithness, and Ross; and the Grauwacke, in its more ancient unfossiliferous type, rather extensively in Banffshire. But to acquaint one's self with the three missing formations, — to complete one's knowledge of the entire scale by filling up the hiatus, — it is necessary to remove to the south. The geology of the Lothians is the geology of at least two thirds of the gap, and perhaps a little more ; — the geology of Arran wants, it is supposed, only the Upper New Red Sandstone to fill it entirely.

One important truth I would fain press on the attention of my lowlier readers. There are few professions, however humble, that do not present their peculiar advantages of observation ; there are none, I repeat, in which the exercise of the faculties does not lead to enjoyment. I advise the stonemason, for instance, to acquaint himself with Geology. Much of his time must be spent amid the rocks and quarries of widely separated localities. The bridge or harbor is no sooner completed in one district, than he has to remove to where the gentleman's seat, or farm-steading is to be erected in another; and so, in the course of a few years, he may pass over the whole geological scale, even when restricted to Scotland, from the Grauwacke of the Lammermuirs, to the Wealden of Moray, or the Chalk-flints of Banffshire and Aberdeen ; and this, too, with opportunities of observation, at every stage, which can be shared with him by only the gentleman of fortune, who devotes his whole time to the study. Nay, in some respects, his advantages are superior to those of the amateur himself. The latter must often pronounce a formation unfossiliferous when, after the examination of at most a few days, he discovers in it nothing organic ; and it will be found that half the mistakes of geologists have arisen from conclusions thus hastily formed. But the working-man, whose employments have to be carried on in the same formation for months, perhaps years, together, enjoys better opportunities for arriving at just decisions. There are, besides, a thousand varieties of accident which lead to discovery — floods, storms, landslips, tides of unusual height, ebbs of extraordinary fall · and the man who plies his labor at all sea-

2

sons in the open air has by much the best chance of profiting by these. There are formations which yield their organisms slowly to the discoverer, and the proofs which establish their place in the geological scale more tardily still. I was acquainted with the Old Red Sandstone of Ross and Cromarty for nearly ten years ere I had ascertained that it is richly fossiliferous — a discovery which, in exploring this formation in those localities, some of our first geologists had failed to anticipate. I was acquainted with it for nearly ten years more ere I could assign to its fossils their exact place in the scale.

In the following chapters I shall confine my observations chiefly to this system and its organisms. To none of the others, perhaps, excepting the Lias of the north of Scotland, have I devoted an equal degree of attention ; nor is there a formation among them which, up to the present time, has remained so much a *terra incognita* to the geologist. The space on both sides has been carefully explored to its upper and lower boundary ; the space between has been suffered to remain well nigh a chasm. Should my facts regarding it — facts constituting the slow gatherings of years — serve as stepping-stones laid across, until such time as geologists of greater skill, and more extended research, shall have bridged over the gap, I shall have completed half my design. Should the working-man be encouraged by my modicum of success to improve his opportunities of observation, I shall have accomplished the whole of it. It cannot be too extensively known, that nature is vast and knowledge limited ; and that no individual, however humble in place or acquirement, need despair of adding to the general fund.

CHAPTER II.

The Old Red Sandstone — Till very lately its Existence as a distinct Formation disputed — Still little known. — Its great Importance in the Geological Scale — Illustration. — The North of Scotland girdled by an immense Belt of Old Red Sandstone. — Line of the Girdle along the Coast — Marks of vast Denudation. — Its Extent partially indicated by Hills on the Western Coast of Ross-shire. — The System of Great Depth in the North of Scotland. — Difficulties in the way of estimating the Thickness of Deposits. — Peculiar Formation of Hill — Illustrated by Ben Nevis. — Caution to the Geological Critic. — Lower Old Red Sandstone immensely developed in Caithness. — Sketch of the Geology of that County. — Its strange Group of Fossils — Their present place of Sepulture. — Their ancient Habitat. — Agassiz. — Amazing Progress of Fossil Ichthyology during the last few Years. — Its Nomenclature. — Learned Names repel unlearned Readers. — Not a great deal in them.

" The Old Red Sandstone," says a Scottish geologist, in a digest of some recent geological discoveries, which appeared a short time ago in an Edinburgh newspaper, " has been hitherto considered as remarkably barren of fossils " The remark is expressive of a pretty general opinion among geologists of even the present time, and I quote it on this account. Only a few years have gone by since men of no low standing in the science disputed the very existence of this formation — system rather, for it contains at least three distinct formations ; and but for the influence of one accomplished geologist, the celebrated author of the *Silurian System*, it would have been probably degraded from its place in the scale altogether. " You must inevitably give up the Old Red Sandstone," said an ingenious foreigner to Mr Murchison, when on a visit to England about four years ago, and whose celebrity among his own countrymen rested chiefly on his researches in the more ancient formations, — " you must inevitably give up the Old Red Sandstone : it is a mere local deposit, a doubtful accumulation huddled up in a corner, and has no type or representative abroad." " I would willingly give it up if nature would," was the reply ; " but it assuredly exists, and I cannot " In a recently published tabular exhibition of the geological scale by a continental geologist, I could not distinguish this system at all. There are some of our British geologists, too, who still regard it as a sort of debatable tract, entitled to no independent status. They find, in what they deem its upper beds, the fossils of the Coal Measures, and the lower graduating apparently into the Silurian System ; and regard the whole as a sort of common, which should be divided as proprietors used to divide commons in Scotland half a century ago, by giving a portion to each of the bordering territories. Even the better informed geologists, who assign to it its proper place as an independent formation, furnished with its own organisms, contrive to say all they know regarding it in a very few paragraphs. Lyell, in the first edition of his admirable elementary work, published only two years ago, devotes more than thirty pages to his description of the Coal Measures, and but two and a half to his notice of the Old Red Sandstone. *

---

* As the succinct notice of this distinguished geologist may serve as a sort of pocket map to the reader in indicating the position of the system, its three great deposits, and its extent, I take the liberty of transferring it entire.

" OLD RED SANDSTONE.

" It was stated that the Carboniferous formation was surmounted by one called the ' New Red Sandstone,' and underlaid by another called the Old Red, which last was formerly merged in the Carboniferous System but is now found to be distinguishable by its fossils. The

It will be found, however, that this hitherto neglected system yields in importance to none of the others, whether we take into account its amazing depth, the great extent to which it is developed both at home and abroad, the interesting links which it furnishes in the zoological scale, or the vast period of time which it represents. There are localities in which the depth of the Old Red Sandstone fully equals the elevation of Mount Ætna over the level of the sea, and in which it contains three distinct groups of organic remains,

---

Old Red Sandstone is of enormous thickness in Herefordshire, Worcestershire, Shropshire, and South Wales, where it is seen to crop out beneath the Coal Measures, and to repose on the Silurian Rocks   In that region, its thickness has been estimated by Mr. Murchison at no less than ten thousand feet.   It consists there of —

" 1st. A quartzose conglomerate, passing downwards into chocolate-red and green sandstone and marl

" 2d   Cornstone and marl, (red and green argillaceous spotted marls, with irregular courses of impure concretionary limestone, provincially called Cornstone, mottled red and green ; remains of fishes)

" 3d   Tilestone, (finely laminated hard reddish or green micaceous or quartzose sandstones, which split into tiles , remains of mollusca and fishes)

" I have already observed that fossils are rare in marls and sandstones in which the red oxide of iron prevails.   In the Cornstone, however, of the counties above mentioned, fishes of the genera Cephalaspis and Onchus have been discovered.   In the Tilestone, also, Ichthyodorulites of the genus Onchus have been obtained, and a species of Dipterus, with mollusca of the genera Avicula, Arca, Cucullæa, Terebratula, Lingula, Turbo, Trochus, Turritella, Bellerophon, Orthoceras, and others.

" By consulting geological maps, the reader will perceive that, from Wales to the north of Scotland, the Old Red Sandstone appears in patches, and often in large tracts.   Many fishes have been found in it at Caithness, and various organic remains in the northern part of

2 *

the one rising in beautiful progression over the other. Let
the reader imagine a digest of English history, complete
from the times of the invasion of Julius Cæsar to the reign
of that Harold who was slain at Hastings, and from the times
of Edward III down to the present day, but bearing no
record of the Williams, the Henrys, the Edwards, the John,
Stephen, and Richard, that reigned during the omitted period,
or of the striking and important events by which their several reigns were distinguished. A chronicle thus mutilated
and incomplete would be no unapt representation of a geological history of the earth in which the period of the Upper
Silurian would be connected with that of the Mountain Limestone, or of the limestone of Burdie House, and the period
of the Old Red Sandstone omitted

The eastern and western coasts of Scotland, which lie to

Fifeshire, where it crops out from beneath the Coal formation, and
spreads into the adjoining northern half of Forfarshire ; forming, together with trap, the Sidlaw Hills and valley of Strathmore. A
large belt of this formation skirts the northern borders of the Grampians, from the seacoast at Stonehaven and the Frith of Tay to the
opposite western coast of the Frith of Clyde. In Forfarshire, where,
as in Herefordshire, it is many thousand feet thick, it may be divided
into three principal masses — 1st. Red and mottled marls, cornstone,
and sandstone , 2d. Conglomerate, often of vast thickness ; 3d Tilestones, and paving-stone, highly micaceous, and containing a slight
admixture of carbonate of lime   In the uppermost of these divisions,
but chiefly in the lowest, the remains of fish have been found, of the
genus named by M Agassiz Cephalaspis, or buckler-headed, from
the extraordinary shield which covers the head, and which has often
been mistaken for that of a trilobite of the division Asaphus. A
gigantic species of fish, of the genus Holoptychius, has also been
found by Dr Fleming in the Old Red Sandstone of Fifeshire." —
Lyell's *Elements*, ‡ p. 452-4. (See Note A.)

the north of the Friths of Forth and Clyde, together with the southern flank of the Grampians and the northern coast of Sutherland and Caithness, appear to have been girdled at some early period by immense continuous beds of Old Red Sandstone. At a still earlier time, the girdle seems to have formed an entire mantle, which covered the enclosed tract from side to side. The interior is composed of what, after the elder geologists, I shall term primary rocks — porphyries, granites, gneisses, and micaceous schists; and this central nucleus, as it now exists, seems set in a sandstone frame. The southern bar of the frame is still entire: it stretches along the Grampians from Stonehaven to the Frith of Clyde. The northern bar is also well nigh entire · it runs unbroken along the whole northern coast of Caithness, and studs, in three several localities, the northern coast of Sutherland, leaving breaches of no very considerable extent between. On the east, there are considerable gaps, as along the shores of Aberdeenshire.* The sandstone, however, appears at Gamrie, in the county of Banff, in a line parallel to the coast, and, after another interruption, follows the coast of the Moray Frith far into the interior of the great Caledonian valley, and then running northward along the shores of Cromarty, Ross, and Sutherland, joins, after another brief interruption, the northern bar at Caithness. The western bar has also its

---

* The progress of discovery has shown, since this passage was written, that these gaps are not quite so considerable as I had supposed. The following paragraph, which appeared in July, 1843, in an Aberdeen paper, bears directly on the point, and is worthy of being preserved. —

"ARTESIAN WELL.

"The greatest of these interesting works yet existing in Aberdeen has just been successfully completed at the tape-works of Messrs.

breaches towards the south; but it stretches, almost without interruption, for about a hundred miles, from the near neighborhood of Cape Wrath to the southern extremity of Applecross; and though greatly disturbed and overflown by the traps of the inner Hebrides, it can be traced by occasional patches on towards the southern bar. It appears on the northern shore of Loch Alsh, on the eastern shore of Loch Eichart, on the southern shore of Loch Eil, on the coast and islands near Oban, and on the east coast of Arran. Detached hills and island-like patches of the same formation occur in several parts of the interior, far within the frame or

---

Milne, Low, and Co, Woolmanhill. The bore is 8 inches in diameter, and 250 feet 9 inches deep. It required nearly eleven months' working to complete the excavation

"In its progress, the following strata were cut through in succession : —

6 feet		vegetable mould
18	"	gray or bluish clay.
20	"	sand and shingle, enclosing rolled stones of various sizes.
6	"	light blue clay
3	"	rough sand and shingle.
115	"	Old Red Sandstone conglomerate, composed of red clay, quartz, mica and rolled stones
74	"	alternating strata of compact, fine-grained Red Sandstone, varying in thickness from 1 to 7 feet, and clay, varying from 6 inches to 12 feet thick
8	"	9 inches, mica-slate formation, the first two feet of which were chiefly a hard, brown quartzose substance, containing iron, manganese, and carbonate of lime.

250 feet, 9 inches.

"The temperature of the water at the bottom of the well, when completed, was found to be within a fraction of 50° Fahrenheit, and the average temperature of the locality, deduced from twenty-three years' observation, by the late George Innes, F. R. S, is 47° 1: hence, nearly 3 degrees of increase appear as the effects of central heat. The supply of water obtained is excellent in quality, and suf-

girdle. It caps some of the higher summits in Sutherlandshire; it forms an oasis of sandstone among the primary
districts of Strathspey, it rises on the northern shores of
Loch Ness in an immense mass of conglomerate, based on
a small-grained, red granite, to a height of about three thousand feet over the level; and on the north-western coast of
Ross-shire it forms three immense insulated hills, of at
least no lower altitude, that rest unconformably on a base of
gneiss

There appear every where in connection with these patches
and eminences, and with the surrounding girdle, marks of
vast denudation. I have often stood fronting the three Ross-

---

ficient in quantity for all the purposes of the works. Such an opportunity of investigating the geology of the locality can but rarely
occur; and, in the present instance, the proprietor and managers
afforded every facility to scientific inquirers for conducting examina-
tions. To make the bearings of the case clear and simple, the following is quoted from Mr. Miller's work on the Old Red Sandstone
[The writer here quotes the above passage, and then proceeds.] Mr.
Miller will be glad to learn, that though the convulsions of nature
have shattered the 'frame' along the shores of Aberdeenshire, yet
the fragments are not lost, as will be seen from the section above
described, they are here reposing *in situ* under the accumulated
debris of uncounted ages — chiefly the 'boulder clay,' and sedimentary deposits of the Dee and Don, during a period when they mingled
their waters in the basin in which Aberdeen now stands. The primary rocks — the settings — our granites, of matchless beauty —
stand out in bold relief a mile or two westward from the seacoast
Within this year or two, the 'Old Red' has been discovered at De-
vanha, Union Grove, Huntly Street, Glenburnie, Balgownie, and
various other localities to the northward. Hence it may reasonably
be inferred, that our fragment of the 'frame' envelops the primary
rocks under our city, and along the coast for a considerable distance
between the Dee and the Buchaness." — *Aberdeen Constitutional.*

shire hills * at sunset in the finer summer evenings, when the
clear light threw the shadows of their gigantic, cone-like
forms far over the lower tract, and lighted up the lines of
their horizontal strata, till they showed like courses of masonry in a pyramid.   They seem at such times as if colored
by the geologist, to distinguish them from the surrounding
tract, and from the base on which they rest as on a common
pedestal.   The prevailing gneiss of the district reflects a
cold, bluish hue, here and there speckled with white, where
the weathered and lichened crags of intermingled quartz
rock jut out on the hill-sides from among the heath.   The
three huge pyramids, on the contrary, from the deep red of
the stone, seem flaming in purple.   There spreads all around
a wild and desolate landscape of broken and shattered hills,
separated by deep and gloomy ravines, that seem the rents
and fissures of a planet in ruins, and that speak distinctly of
a period of convulsion, when upheaving fires from the abyss,
and ocean currents above, had contended in sublime antag-
onism, the one slowly elevating the entire tract, the other
grinding it down and sweeping it away.   I entertain little
doubt that, when this loftier portion of Scotland, including
the entire Highlands, first presented its broad back over the
waves, the upper surface consisted exclusively, from the one
extremity to the other — from Benlomond to the Maidenpaps
of Caithness — of a continuous tract of Old Red Sandstone;
though, ere the land finally emerged, the ocean currents of
ages had swept it away, all except in the lower and last-
raised borders, and in the detached localities, where it still
remains, as in the pyramidal hills of western Ross-shire, to
show the amazing depth to which it had once overlaid the

---

* Suil Veinn, Coul Beg, and Coul More.

inferior rocks. The Old Red Sandstone of Morvheim, in
Caithness, overlooks all the primary hills of the district, from
an elevation of three thousand five hundred feet.

The depth of the system, on both the eastern and western
coasts of Scotland, is amazingly great — how great, I shall not
venture to say. There are no calculations more doubtful than
those of the geologist. The hill just instanced (Morvheim) is
apparently composed from top to bottom of what in Scotland
forms the lowest member of the system — a coarse conglomerate ; and yet I have nowhere observed this inferior member, when I succeeded in finding a section of it directly vertical, more than a hundred yards in thickness — less than
one tenth the height of the hill. It would be well nigh as
unsafe to infer that the three thousand five hundred feet of
altitude formed the real thickness of the conglomerate, as to
infer that the thickness of the lead which covers the dome
of St. Paul's is equal to the height of the dome. It is always
perilous to estimate the depth of a deposit by the height of a
hill that seems externally composed of it. unless, indeed, like
the pyramidal hills of Ross-shire, it be unequivocally a hill
dug out by denudation, as the sculptor digs his eminences
out of the mass. In most of our hills, the upheaving agency
has been actively at work, and the space within is occupied
by an immense nucleus of inferior rock, around which the
upper formation is wrapped like a caul, just as the vegetable
mould or the diluvium wraps up this superior covering in
turn. One of our best known Scottish mountains — the gigantic Ben Nevis — furnishes an admirable illustration of
this latter construction of hill. It is composed of three zones
or rings of rock, the one rising over and out of the other,
like the cases of an opera-glass drawn out. The lower zone
is composed of gneiss and mica-slate, the middle zone of

granite, the terminating zone of porphyry. The elevating power appears to have acted in the centre, as in the well-known case of Jorullo, in the neighborhood of the city of Mexico, where a level tract four square miles in extent rose, about the middle of the last century, into a high dome of more than double the height of Arthur's Seat.* In the formation of our Scottish mountain, the gneiss and mica-slate of the district seem to have been upheaved, during the first period

---

* It is rarely that the geologist catches a hill in the act of forming, and hence the interest of this well-attested instance. From the period of the discovery of America to the middle of the last century, the plains of Jorullo had undergone no change of surface, and the seat of the present hill was covered by plantations of indigo and sugar-cane, when, in June, 1759, hollow sounds were heard, and a succession of earthquakes continued for sixty days, to the great consternation of the inhabitants. After the cessation of these, and in a period of tranquillity, on the 28th and 29th of September, a horrible subterranean noise was again heard, and a tract four square miles in extent rose up in the shape of a dome or bladder, to the height of sixteen hundred and seventy feet above the original level of the plain   The affrighted Indians fled to the mountains ; and from thence looking down on the phenomenon, saw flames issuing from the earth for miles around the newly-elevated hill, and the softened surface rising and falling like that of an agitated sea, and opening into numerous rents and fissures   Two brooks which had watered the plantations precipitated themselves into the burning chasms. The scene of this singular event was visited by Humboldt about the beginning of the present century. At that period, the volcanic agencies had become comparatively quiescent, the hill, however, retained its original altitude, a number of smaller hills had sprung up around it; and the traveller found the waters of the engulfed rivulets escaping at a high temperature from caverns charged with sulphureous vapors and carbonic acid gas. There were inhabitants of the country living at the time who were more than twenty years older than the hill of Jorullo, and who had witnessed its rise

of Plutonic action in the locality, into a rounded hill of moderate altitude, but of huge base. The upheaving power continued to operate — the gneiss and mica-slate gave way a-top — and out of this lower dome there arose a higher dome of granite, which, in an after and terminating period of the internal activity, gave way in turn to yet a third and last dome of porphyry Now, had the elevating forces ceased to operate just ere the gneiss and mica-slate had given way, we would have known nothing of the interior nucleus of granite — had they ceased just ere the granite had given way, we would have known nothing of the yet deeper nucleus of porphyry ; and yet the granite and the porphyry would as suredly have been there. Nor could any application of the measuring rule to the side of the hill have ascertained the thickness of its outer covering — the gneiss and the mica schist. The geologists of the school of Werner used to illustrate what we may term the anatomy of the earth, as seen through the spectacles of their system, by an onion and its coats . they represented the globe as a central nucleus. encircled by concentric coverings, each covering constituting a geological formation. The onion, through the introduction of a better school, has become obsolete as an illustration ; but to restore it again, though for another purpose, we have merely to cut it through the middle, and turn downwards the planes formed by the knife It then represents, with its coats, hills such as we describe — hills such as Ben Nevis, ere the granite had perforated the gneiss, or the porphyry broken through the granite.

If it be thus unsafe, however, to calculate on the depth of deposits by the altitude of hills, it is quite as unsafe for the geologist, who has studied a formation in one district, to set himself to criticise the calculations of a brother geologist by whom it has been studied in a different and widely-separated

3

district. A deposit in one locality may be found to possess
many times the thickness of the same deposit in another.
There are exposed, beside the Northern and Southern Sutors
of Cromarty, two nearly vertical sections of the coarse conglomerate bed, which forms, as I have said, in the north of
Scotland, the base of the Old Red System, and which rises
to so great an elevation in the mountain of Morvheim. The
sections are little more than a mile apart; and yet, while
the thickness of this bed in the one does not exceed one hundred feet, that of the same bed in the other somewhat exceeds
two hundred feet. More striking still — under the Northern
Sutor, the entire Geology of Caithness, with all its vast beds,
and all its numerous fossils, from the granitic rock of the Ord
hill, the southern boundary of the county, to the uppermost
sandstones of Dunnet-head, its extreme northern corner, is
exhibited in a vertical section not more than three hundred
yards in extent. And yet so enormous is the depth of the
deposit in Caithness, that it has been deemed by a very superior geologist to represent three entire formations — the Old
Red System, by its unfossiliferous, arenaceous, and conglomerate beds; the Carboniferous System, by its dark-colored
middle schists, abounding in bitumen and ichthyolites; and
the New Red Sandstone, by the mottled marls and mouldering sandstones that overlie the whole * A slight sketch of
the Geology of Caithness may not be deemed uninteresting
This county includes, in the state of greatest development

---

* Dr. Hibbert, whose researches among the limestones of Burdie
House have been of such importance to Geology, was of this opinion
I find it also expressed in the admirable geological appendix affixed
by the Messrs. Anderson to their *Guide to the Highlands and Islands of
Scotland*. "No beds of real coal," say these gentlemen, "have been
discovered in Caithness; and it would thus appear that the middle

any where yet known, that fossiliferous portion of the Old
Red Sandstone which I purpose first to describe, and which
will yet come to be generally regarded as an independent
formation, as unequivocally characterized by its organic
remains as the formations either above or below it.

The county of Sutherland stretches across the island from
the German to the Atlantic Ocean, and presents, throughout
its entire extent, — except where a narrow strip of the Oolitic
formation runs along its eastern coast, and a broken belt of
Old Red Sandstone tips its capes and promontories on the
west, — a broken and tumultuous sea of primary hills.
Scarce any of our other Scottish counties are so exclusively
Highland, nor are there any of them in which the precipices
are more abrupt, the valleys more deep, the rivers more
rapid, or the mountains piled into more fantastic groups and
masses.   The traveller passes into Caithness, and finds himself surrounded by scenery of an aspect so entirely dissimilar,
that no examination of the rocks is necessary to convince him
of a geological difference of structure.   An elevated and uneven plain spreads around and before him, league beyond
league, in tame and unvaried uniformity, — its many hollows
darkened by morasses, over which the intervening eminences
rise in the form rather of low moory swellings, than of hills,
— its coasts walled round by cliffs of gigantic altitude, that
elevate the district at one huge stride from the level of the
sea, and skirted by vast stacks and columns of rock, that

---

schistose system of the county, containing the fossil fish, is in geological character and position intermediate between the Old and New
Red Sandstone formations, but not identical with the Carboniferous
Limestone, or the true Coal Measures, although probably occupying
the place of one or other of them "— p. 198

stand out like the advanced pickets of the land amid the
ceaseless turmoil of the breakers. The district, as shown on
the map, presents nearly a triangular form — the Pentland
Frith and the German Ocean describing two of its sides,
while the base is formed by the line of boundary which separates it from the county of Sutherland.

Now, in a geological point of view, this angle may be regarded as a vast pyramid, rising perpendicularly from the
basis furnished by the primary rocks of the latter county, and
presenting newer beds and strata as we ascend, until we
reach the apex. The line from south to north in the angle —
from Morvheim to Dunnet-head — corresponds to the line of
ascent from the top to the bottom of the pyramid The first
bed, reckoning from the base upwards, — the ground tier of
the masonry, if I may so speak, — is the great conglomerate.
It runs along the line of boundary from sea to sea, — from
the Ord of Caithness on the east, to Portskerry on the north ;
and rises, as it approaches the primary hills of Sutherland,
into a lofty mountain chain of bold and serrated outline, which
attains its greatest elevation in the hill of Morvheim This
great conglomerate bed, the base of the system, is represented
in the Cromarty section, under the Northern Sutor, by a bed
two hundred and fifteen feet in thickness. The second tier
of masonry in the pyramid, and which also runs in a nearly
parallel line from sea to sea, is composed mostly of a coarse
red and yellowish sandstone, with here and there beds of pebbles enclosed, and here and there deposits of green earth and
red marl. It has its representative in the Cromarty section,
in a bed of red and yellow arenaceous stone, one hundred
and fourteen feet six inches in thickness. These two inferior
beds possess but one character, — they are composed of the
same materials, with merely this difference, that the rocks

which have been broken into pebbles for the construction of the one, have been ground into sand for the composition of the other. Directly over them, the middle portion of the pyramid is occupied by an enormous deposit of dark-colored bituminous schist, slightly micaceous, calcareous, or semi-calcareous, — here and there interlaced with veins of carbonate of lime, - - here and there compact and highly siliceous, — and bearing in many places a mineralogical character difficult to be distinguished from that at one time deemed peculiar to the harder grauwacke schists. The Caithness flagstones, so extensively employed in paving the footways of our larger towns, are furnished by this immense middle tier or belt, and represent its general appearance From its lowest to its highest beds it is charged with fossil fish and obscure vegetable impressions, and we find it represented in the Cromarty section by alternating bands of sandstones, stratified clays, and bituminous and nodular limestones, which form altogether a bed three hundred and fifty-five feet in thickness ; nor does this bed lack its organisms. animal and vegetable, generically identical with those of Caithness The apex of the pyramid is formed of red mouldering sandstones and mottled marls, which exhibit their uppermost strata high over the eddies of the Pentland Firth, in the huge precipices of Dunnet-head, and which are partially represented in the Cromarty section by an unfossiliferous sandstone bed of unascertained thickness ; but which can be traced for about eighty feet from the upper limestones and stratified clays of the middle member, until lost in overlying beds of sand and shingle.

I am particular, at the risk, I am afraid, of being tedious, in thus describing the Geology of this northern county, and of the Cromarty section, which represents and elucidates it. They illustrate more than the formations of two insulated

3 *

districts: they represent also a vast period of time in the
history of the globe.   The pyramid, with its three huge bars,
its foundations of granitic rock, its base of red conglomerate,
its central band of dark-colored schist, and its lighter tinted
apex of sandstone, is inscribed from bottom to top, like an
Egyptian obelisk, with a historical record.   The upper and
lower sections treat of tempests and currents — the middle is
" written within and without " with wonderful narratives of
animal life ; and yet the whole, taken together, comprises but
an earlier portion of that chronicle of existences and events
furnished by the Old Red Sandstone.   It is, however, with
this earlier portion that my acquaintance is most minute.

My first statement regarding it must be much the reverse
of the borrowed one with which this chapter begins.   *The
fossils are remarkably numerous, and in a state of high preservation.*   I have a hundred solid proofs by which to establish the truth of the assertion, within less than a yard of me.
Half my closet walls are covered with the peculiar fossils of
the Lower Old Red Sandstone, and certainly a stranger
assemblage of forms have rarely been grouped together ; —
creatures whose very type is lost, fantastic and uncouth, and
which puzzle the naturalist to assign them even their class ;
— boat-like animals, furnished with oars and a rudder ; — fish
plated over, like the tortoise, above and below, with a strong
armor of bone, and furnished with but one solitary rudder-
like fin ; other fish less equivocal in their form, but with the
membranes of their fins thickly covered with scales ; — creatures bristling over with thorns ; others glistening in an enamelled coat, as if beautifully japanned — the tail, in every instance among the less equivocal shapes, formed not equally,
as in existing fish, on each side the central vertebral column,
but chiefly on the lower side — the column sending out its

diminished vertebræ to the extreme termination of the fin. All the forms testify of a remote antiquity — of a period whose " fashions have passed away." The figures on a Chinese vase or an Egyptian obelisk are scarce more unlike what now exists in nature, than the fossils of the Lower Old Red Sandstone.

Geology, of all the sciences, addresses itself most powerfully to the imagination, and hence one main cause of the interest which it excites. Ere setting ourselves minutely to examine the peculiarities of these creatures, it would be perhaps well that the reader should attempt realizing the *place* of their existence, and relatively the *time* — not of course with regard to dates and eras, for the geologist has none to reckon by, but with respect to formations. They were the denizens of the same portion of the globe which we ourselves inhabit, regarded not as a tract of country, but as a piece of ocean crossed by the same geographical lines of latitude and longitude Their present place of sepulture in some localities, had there been no denudation, would have been raised high over the tops of our loftiest hills — at least a hundred feet over the conglomerates which form the summit of Morvheim, and more than a thousand feet over the snow-capped Ben Wyvis. Geology has still greater wonders I have seen belemnites of the Oolite — comparatively a modern formation — which had been dug out of the sides of the Himalaya mountains, seventeen thousand feet over the level of the sea. But let us strive to carry our minds back, not to the place of sepulture of these creatures, high in the rocks, — though that I shall afterwards attempt minutely to describe, — but to the place in which they lived, long ere the sauroid fishes of Burdie House had begun to exist, or the corallines of the mountain limestone had spread out their multitudinous arms in a sea gradually shallowing, and out of which the land had already partially emerged.

A continuous ocean spreads over the space now occupied by the British islands : in the tract covered by the green fields and brown moors of our own country, the bottom, for a hundred yards downwards, is composed of the debris of rolled pebbles and coarse sand intermingled, long since consolidated into the lower member of the Old Red Sandstone ; the upper surface is composed of banks of sand, mud, and clay ; and the sea, swarming with animal life, flows over all. My present object is to describe the inhabitants of that sea.

Of these, the greater part yet discovered have been named by Agassiz, the highest authority as an ichthyologist in Europe or the world, and in whom the scarcely more celebrated Cuvier recognized a naturalist in every respect worthy to succeed him   The comparative amount of the labors of these two great men in fossil ichthyology, and the amazing acceleration which has taken place within the last few years in the progress of geological science, are illustrated together, and that very strikingly, by the following interesting fact — a fact derived directly from Agassiz himself, and which must be new to the great bulk of my readers.   When Cuvier closed his researches in this department, he had named and described, for the guidance of the geologist, ninety-two distinct species of fossil fish ; nor was it then known that the entire geological scale, from the Upper Tertiary to the Grauwacke inclusive, contained more.   Agassiz commenced his labors ; and, in a period of time little exceeding fourteen years, he has raised the number of species from ninety-two to sixteen hundred.   And this number, great as it is, is receiving accessions almost every day.   In his late visit to Scotland, he found eleven new species, and one new genus, in the collection of

Lady Cumming of Altyre, all from the upper beds of that lower member of the Old Red Sandstone represented by the dark-colored schists and inferior sandstones of Caithness. He found forty-two new species more in a single collection in Ireland, furnished by the Mountain Limestone of Armagh.

Some of my humbler readers may possibly be repelled by his names ; they are, like all names in science, unfamiliar in their respect to mere English readers, just because they are names not for England alone, but for England and the world. I am assured, however, that they are all composed of very good Greek, and picturesquely descriptive of some peculiarity in the fossils they designate. One of his ichthyolites, with a thorn or spine in each fin, bears the name of *Acanthodes*, or thorn-like ; another with a similar mechanism of spines attached to the upper part of the body, and in which the pectoral or hand-fins are involved, has been designated the *Cheiracanthus*, or thorn-hand ; a third covered with curiously-fretted scales, has been named the *Glyptolepis*, or carved-scale ; and a fourth, roughened over with berry-like tubercles, that rise from strong osseous plates, is known as the *Coccosteus*, or berry-on-bone. And such has been his principle of nomenclature. The name is a condensed description. But though all his names mean something, they cannot mean a great deal ; and as learned words repel unlearned readers, I shall just take the liberty of reminding mine of the humbler class, that there is no legitimate connection between Geology and the dead languages. The existences of the Old Red Sandstone had lived for ages, and had been dead for myriads of ages, ere there was Greek enough in the world to furnish them with names. There is no working-man, if he be a per-

son of intelligence and information, however unlearned, in
the vulgar acceptation of the phrase, who may not derive as
much pleasure and enlargement of idea from the study of
Geology, and acquaint himself as minutely with its truths, as
if possessed of all the learning of Bentley.

CHAPTER III.

MR. LYELL's brilliant and popular work, *The Principles of Geology*, must have introduced to the knowledge of most of my readers the strange theories of Lamarck. The ingenious foreigner, on the strength of a few striking facts, which prove that, to a certain extent, the instincts of species may be improved and heightened, and their forms changed from a lower to a higher degree of adaptation to their circumstances, has concluded that there is a natural progress from the in-ferior orders of being towards the superior; and that the off-spring of creatures low in the scale in the present time, may hold a much higher place in it, and belong to different and nobler species, a few thousand years hence. The descend-ants of the *ourang-outang*, for instance, may be employed in some future age in writing treatises on Geology, in which they shall have to describe the remains of the *quadrumana* as belonging to an extinct order. Lamarck himself, when bearing home in triumph with him the skeleton of some huge

(35)

salamander or crocodile of the Lias, might indulge, consist-
ently with his theory, in the pleasing belief that he had possessed himself of the bones of his grandfather — a grandfather removed, of course, to a remote degree of consan-
guinity, by the intervention of a few hundred thousand
great-greats. Never yet was there a fancy so wild and extravagant but there have been men bold enough to dignify it
with the name of philosophy, and ingenious enough to find
reasons for the propriety of the name

The setting-dog is *taught* to set ; he squats down and points
at the game ; but the habit is an acquired one — a mere trick
of education. What, however, is merely acquired habit in
the progenitor, is found to pass into instinct in the descend-
ant · the puppy of the setting-dog squats down and sets
untaught — the educational trick of the parent is mysteriously transmuted into an original principle in the offspring. The
adaptation which takes place in the forms and constitution of
plants and animals, when placed in circumstances different
from their ordinary ones, is equally striking. The woody
plant of a warmer climate, when transplanted into a colder,
frequently exchanges its ligneous stem for a herbaceous one,
as if in anticipation of the killing frosts of winter ; and,
dying to the ground at the close of autumn, shoots up again
in spring. The dog, transported from a temperate into a
frigid region, exchanges his covering of hair for a covering
of wool ; when brought back again to his former habitat, the
wool is displaced by the original hair And hence, and from
similar instances, the derivation of an argument, good so far
as it goes, for changes in adaptation to altered circumstances of the organization of plants and animals, and for
the improvability of instinct. But it is easy driving a principle too far. The elasticity of a common bow, and the

strength of an ordinary arm, are fully adequate to the transmission of an arrow from one point of space to another point
a hundred yards removed; but he would be a philosopher
worth looking at, who would assert that they were equally
adequate for the transmission of the same arrow from points
removed, not by a hundred yards, but by a hundred miles.
And such, but still more glaring, has been the error of Lamarck. He has argued on this principle of improvement
and adaptation — which, carry it as far as we rationally may,
still leaves the vegetable a vegetable, and the dog a dog —
that, in the vast course of ages, inferior have risen into superior natures, and lower into higher races; that molluscs and
zoophytes have passed into fish and reptiles, and fish and
reptiles into birds and quadrupeds; that unformed, gelatinous
bodies, with an organization scarcely traceable, have been
metamorphosed into oaks and cedars; and that monkeys and
apes have been transformed into human creatures, capable of
understanding and admiring the theories of Lamarck. Assuredly there is no lack of faith among infidels; their
" vaulting " credulity o'erleaps revelation, and " falls on the
other side." One of the first geological works I ever read
was a philosophical romance, entitled *Telliamed*, by a M.
Maillet, an ingenious Frenchman of the days of Louis XV.
This Maillet was by much too great a philosopher to credit
the scriptural account of Noah's flood; and yet he could believe, like Lamarck, that the whole family of birds had existed
at one time as fishes, which, on being thrown ashore by the
waves, had got feathers by accident; and that men themselves
are but the descendants of a tribe of sea-monsters, who, tiring
of their proper element, crawled up the beach one sunny
morning, and, taking a fancy to the land, forgot to return.*

---

* Few men could describe better than Maillet. His extravagances

4

"How easy," says this fanciful writer, "is it to conceive
the change of a winged fish, flying at times through the water,
at times through the air, into a bird flying always through
the air!" It is a law of nature, that the chain of being,

---

are as amusing as those of a fairy tale, and quite as extreme. Take
the following extract as an instance : —

"Winged or flying fish, stimulated by the desire of prey, or the fear
of death, or pushed near the shore by the billows, have fallen among
reeds or herbage, whence it was not possible for them to resume their
flight to the sea, by means of which they had contracted their first
facility of flying. Then their fins, being no longer bathed in the sea-
water, were split, and became warped by their dryness. While they
found, among the reeds and herbage among which they fell, any ali-
ments to support them, the vessels of their fins, being separated, were
lengthened and clothed with beards, or, to speak more justly, the membranes, which before kept them adherent to each other, were metamorphosed The beard formed of these warped membranes was
lengthened. The skin of these animals was insensibly covered with
a down of the same color with the skin, and this down gradually increased The little wings they had under their belly, and which,
like their wings, helped them to walk in the sea, became feet, and
served them to walk on land. There were also other small changes
in their figure. The beak and neck of some were lengthened, and
those of others shortened. The conformity, however, of the first
figure subsists in the whole, and it will be always easy to know it.
Examine all the species of fowls, large and small, even those of the
Indies, those which are tufted or not, those whose feathers are
reversed, such as we see at Damietta — that is to say, whose plu-
mage runs from the tail to the head — and you will find species
of fish quite similar, scaly or without scales. All species of parrots,
whose plumages are so different, the rarest and the most singu-
lar-marked birds, are, conformable to fact, painted like them with
black, brown, gray, yellow, green, red, violet color, and those of gold
and azure ; and all this precisely in the same parts where the plumages of those birds are diversified in so curious a manner." —
Telliamed, p. 224, ed. 1750

from the lowest to the highest form of life, should be, in some degree, a continuous chain; that the various classes of existence should shade into one another, so that it often proves a matter of no little difficulty to point out the exact line of demarcation where one class or family ends, and another class or family begins. The naturalist passes from the vegetable to the animal tribes, scarcely aware, amid the perplexing forms of intermediate existence, at what point he quits the precincts of the one to enter on those of the other. All the animal families have, in like manner, their connecting links; and it is chiefly out of these that writers such as Lamarck and Maillet construct their system. They confound gradation with progress. Geoffrey Hudson was a very short man, and Goliath of Gath a very tall one, and the gradations of the human stature lie between. But gradation is not progress; and though we find full-grown men of five feet, five feet six inches, six feet, and six feet and a half, the fact gives us no earnest whatever that the race is rising in stature, and that at some future period the average height of the human family will be somewhat between ten and eleven feet. And equally unsolid is the argument, that from a principle of gradation in races would deduce a principle of progress in races. The tall man of six feet need entertain quite as little hope of rising into eleven feet as the short man of five; nor has the fish that occasionally flies any better chance of passing into a bird than the fish that only swims.

Geology abounds with creatures of the intermediate class: there are none of its links more numerous than its connecting links; and hence its interest, as a field of speculation, to the assertors of the transmutation of races. But there is a fatal incompleteness in the evidence, that destroys its character as such. It supplies in abundance those links of generic connection, which, as it were, marry together dissimilar races; but it furnishes no genealogical link to show that the existences of one race derive their lineage from the existences of another. The scene shifts, as we pass from formation to formation; we are introduced in each to a new *dramatis personæ;* and there exist no such proofs of their being at once different and yet the same, as those produced in the *Winter's Tale,* to show that the grown shepherdess of the one scene is identical with the exposed infant of the scene that went before. Nay, the reverse is well nigh as strikingly the case, as if the grown shepherdess had been introduced into the earlier scenes of the drama, and the child into its concluding scenes.

The argument is a very simple one. Of all the vertebrata, fishes rank lowest, and in geological history appear first. We find their remains in the Upper and Lower Silurians, in the Lower, Middle, and Upper Old Red Sandstone, in the Mountain Limestone, and in the Coal Measures; and in the latter formation the first reptiles appear.* Fishes seem to have been the master existences of two great systems, mayhap of three, ere the age of reptiles began. Now fishes differ very much among themselves · some rank nearly as low as worms, some nearly as high as reptiles; and if fish could have risen into reptiles, and reptiles into mammalia, we would necessarily expect to find lower orders of fish passing into higher, and taking precedence of the higher in their appearance in point of time, just as in the *Winter's Tale* we see the infant preceding the adult. If such be not the case — if fish made their first appearance, not in their least perfect, but in their most perfect state — not in their nearest approximation to the worm, but in their nearest approximation to the reptile — there is no room for progression, and the argument

* See Note B.

falls. Now it is a geological fact, that it is fish of the higher
orders that appear first on the stage, and that they are found
to occupy exactly the same level during the vast period represented by five succeeding formations. There is no progression. If fish rose into reptiles, it must have been by
sudden transformation — it must have been as if a man who
had stood still for half a lifetime should bestir himself all at
once, and take seven leagues at a stride. There is no getting rid of miracle in the case — there is no alternative between creation and metamorphosis. The infidel substitutes
progression for Deity; Geology robs him of his god.

But no man who enters the geological field in quest of the
wonderful, need pass in pursuit of his object from the true to
the fictitious. Does the reader remember how in Milton's
sublime figure, the body of Truth is represented as hewn in
pieces, and her limbs scattered over distant regions, and how
her friends and disciples have to go wandering all over the
world in quest of them? There is surely something very
wonderful in the fact, that, in uniting the links of the chain
of creation into an unbroken whole, we have in like manner
to seek for them all along the scale of the geologist; — some
we discover among the tribes first annihilated — some among
the tribes that perished at a later period — some among the
existences of the passing time We find the present incomplete without the past — the recent without the extinct. There
are marvellous analogies which pervade the scheme of Provi-
dence, and unite, as it were, its lower with its higher parts.
The perfection of the works of Deity is a perfection entire
in its components; and yet these are not contemporaneous,
but successive : it is a perfection which includes the dead as
well as the living, and bears relation, in its completeness, not
to time, but to eternity.

4 *

We find the organisms of the Old Red Sandstone supply-
ing an important link, or, rather, series of links, in the ichthyological scale, which are wanting in the present creation, and
the absence of which evidently occasions a wide gap between
the two grand divisions or series of fishes — the bony and
the cartilaginous. Of this, however, more anon. Of all the
organisms of the system, one of the most extraordinary, and
the one in which Lamarck would have most delighted, is the
Pterichthys, or winged fish, an ichthyolite which the writer
had the pleasure of introducing to the acquaintance of geologists nearly three years ago, but which he first laid open to
the light about seven years earlier. Had Lamarck been the
discoverer, he would unquestionably have held that he had
caught a fish almost in the act of wishing itself into a bird.
There are wings which want only feathers, a body which
seems to have been as well adapted for passing through the
air as the water, and a tail by which to steer. And yet there
are none of the fossils of the Old Red Sandstone which less
resemble any thing that now exists than its *Pterichthys*. I
fain wish I could communicate to the reader the feeling with
which I contemplated my first-found specimen. It opened
with a single blow of the hammer; and there, on a ground
of light-colored limestone, lay the effigy of a creature fashioned apparently out of jet, with a body covered with plates,
two powerful looking arms, articulated at the shoulders, a
head as entirely lost in the trunk as that of the ray or the
sun-fish, and a long, angular tail. My first-formed idea regarding it was, that I had discovered a connecting link
between the tortoise and the fish — the body much resembles
that of a small turtle, and why, I asked, if one formation
gives us sauroid fishes, may not another give us chelonian
ones? or if in the Lias we find the body of the lizard

mounted on the paddles of the whale, why not find in the Old Red Sandstone the body of the tortoise mounted in a somewhat similar manner? The idea originated in error; but as it was an error which not many naturalists could have corrected at the time, it may be deemed an excusable one, more especially by such of my readers as may have seen well-preserved specimens of the creature, or who examine the subjoined prints. (Nos. I. and II.) I submitted some of my specimens to Mr. Murchison, at a time when that gentleman was engaged among the fossils of the Silurian System, and employed on his great work, which has so largely serves to extend geological knowledge regarding those earlier periods in which animal life first began. He was much interested in the discovery : it furnished the geologist with additional data by which to regulate and construct his calculations, and added a new and very singular link to the chain of existence in its relation to human knowledge Deferring to Agassiz, as the highest authority, he yet anticipated the decision of that naturalist regarding it, in almost every particular. I had inquired, under the influence of my first impression, whether it might not be considered as a sort of intermediate existence between the fish and the chelonian. He stated, in reply, that he could not deem it referrible to any family of reptiles; that, if not a fish, it approached more closely to the crustacea than to any other class ; and that he had little doubt Agassiz would pronounce it to be an ichthyolite of that ancient order to which the *Cephalaspis* belongs, and which seems to have formed a connecting link between crustacea and fishes * The specimens submitted to

---

* The aborigines of South America deemed it wonderful that the Europeans who first visited them should, without previous concert,

Mr Murchison were forwarded to Agassiz. They were much
more imperfect than some which I have since disinterred ;
and to restore the entire animal from them would require
powers such as those possessed by Cuvier in the past age, and
by the naturalist of Neufchatel in the present. Broken as
they were, however, Agassiz at once decided from them that
the creature must have been a fish.

I have placed one of the specimens before me. Imagine
the figure of a man rudely drawn in black on a gray ground,
the head cut off at the shoulders, the arms spread at full, as
in the attitude of swimming, the body rather long than otherwise, and narrowing from the chest downwards, one of the
legs cut away at the hip-joint, and the other, as if to preserve
the balance, placed directly under the centre of the figure,

---

agree in reading after the same manner the same scrap of manuscript,
and in deriving the same piece of information from it. The writer
experienced on this occasion a somewhat similar feeling. His specimens seemed written in a character cramp enough to suggest
those doubts regarding original meaning which lead to various readings ; but the geologist and the naturalist agreed in perusing them
after exactly the same fashion — the one in London, the other in
Neufchatel. Such instances give confidence in the findings of science   The decision of Mr. Murchison I subjoin in his own words —
his numbers refer to various specimens of *Pterichthys* " As to your
fossils 1, 2, 3, we know nothing of them here, (London,) except that
they remind me of the occipital fragments of some of the Caithness
fishes.   I do not conceive they can be referrible to any reptile ;
for, if not fishes, they more closely approach to crustaceans than to
any other class.   I conceive, however, that Agassiz will pronounce
them to be fishes, which, together with the curious genus *Cephalaspis*
of the Old Red Sandstone, form the connecting links between crustaceans and fishes.   Your specimens remind one in several respects of
the *Cephalaspis*."

PLATE I.

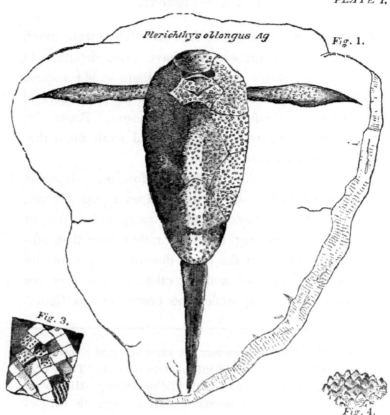

Pterichthys oblongus Ag

Fig. 1.

Fig. 3.

Fig. 4.

P Milleri

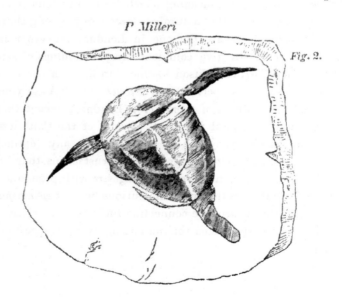

Fig. 2.

which it seems to support. Such, at a first glance, is the appearance of the fossil. The body was of very considerable depth, perhaps little less deep proportionally from back to breast than the body of the tortoise ; the under part was flat ; the upper rose towards the centre into a roof-like ridge ; and both under and upper were covered with a strong armor of bony plates, which, resembling more the plates of the tortoise than those of the crustacean, received their accessions of growth at the edges or sutures. The plates on the under side are divided by two lines of suture, which run, the one longitudinally through the centre of the body, the other transversely, also through the centre ; and they would cut one another at right angles, were there not a lozenge-shaped plate inserted at the point where they would otherwise meet. There are thus five plates on the lower or belly part of the animal. They are all thickly tubercled outside with wart-like prominences, (see Plate I , fig. 4 ;) the inner present appearances indicative of a bony structure. The plates on the upper side are more numerous and more difficult to describe, just as it would be difficult to describe the forms of the various stones which compose the ribbed and pointed roof of a Gothic cathedral, the arched ridge or hump of the back requiring, in a somewhat similar way, a peculiar form and arrangement of plates. The apex of the ridge is covered by a strong hexagonal plate, fitted upon it like a cap or helmet, and which nearly corresponds in place to the flat central plate of the under side. There runs around it a border of variously formed plates, that diminish in size and increase in number towards the head, and which are separated, like the pieces of a dissected map, by deep sutures. They all present the tubercled surface. The eyes are placed in front, on a prominence considerably lower than the roof-like ridge of the back; the mouth seems to have opened, as in many fishes, in the edge of the creature's snout, where a line running along the back would bisect a line running along the belly; but this part is less perfectly shown by my specimens than any other. The two arms, or paddles, are placed so far forward as to give the body a disproportionate and decapitated appearance. From the shoulder to the elbow, if I may employ the terms, there is a swelling, muscular appearance, as in the human arm; the part below is flattened, so as to resemble the blade of an oar, and terminates in a strong, sharp point. The tail—the one leg on which, as exhibited in one of my specimens, the creature seems to stand—is of considerable length, more than equal to a third of the entire figure, and of an angular form, the base representing the part attached to the body, and the apex its termination. It was covered with small tubercled, rhomboidal plates, like scales, (see Plate I., fig. 3,) and where the internal structure is shown, there are appearances of a vertebral column, with rib-like processes standing out at a sharp angle. The ichthyolite, in my larger specimens, does not much exceed seven inches in length; and I despatched one to Agassiz, rather more than two years ago, whose extreme length did not exceed an inch. Such is a brief, and, I am afraid, imperfect sketch of a creature whose very type seems no longer to exist. ·But for the purposes of the geologist, the descriptions of the graver far exceed those of the pen, and the accompanying prints will serve to supply all that may be found wanting in the text. Fig. 1, in Plate I., and fig. 2, in Plate II., are both restorations—the first of the upper, and the second of the under, part of the creature. It may, however, encourage the confidence of the naturalist, who for the first time looks upon forms so strange, to be informed that Plate I., with its

PLATE II.

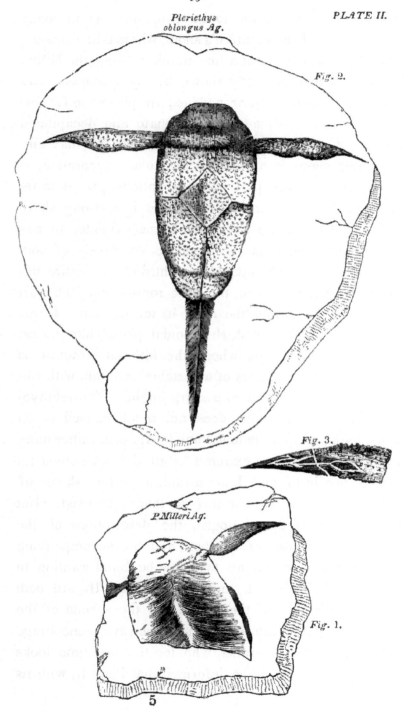

Pleriethys oblongus Ag.

Fig. 2.

Fig. 3.

P. Milleri Ag.

Fig. 1.

5

two figures, was submitted to Agassiz during his recent brief stay in Edinburgh, and that he as readily recognized in it the species of the two kinds which it exhibits, as he had previously recognized the species of the originals in the limestone.

Agassiz, in the course of his late visit to Scotland, found six species of the *Pterichthys* * — three of these, and the wings of a fourth, in the collection of the writer. The differences by which they are distinguished may be marked by even an unpractised eye, especially in the form of the bodies and wings. Some are of a fuller, some of a more elongated, form ; in some the body resembles a heraldic shield, of nearly the ordinary shape and proportions ; in others the shield stretches into a form not very unlike that of a Norway skiff, from the midships forward. In some of the varieties, too, the wings are long and comparatively slender ; in others shorter, and of greater breadth : in some there is an inflection resembling the bend of an elbow ; in others there is a continuous swelling from the termination to the shoulder, where a sudden narrowing takes place immediately over the articulation. I had inferred somewhat too hurriedly, though perhaps naturally enough, that these wings, or arms, with their strong sharp points and oar-like blades, had been at once paddles and spears — instruments of motion and weapons of defence ; and hence the mistake of connecting the creature with the Chelonia. I am informed by Agassiz, however, that they were weapons of defence only, which, like the occipital spines of the river bull-head, were erected in moments of danger or

---

* Agassiz now reckons ten distinct species of *Pterichthys* — *P. arenatus, P. cancriformis, P. cornutus, P. major, P. Milleri. P. latus, P. oblongus, P. productus, P. testudinarius,* and *P. hydrophilus,* of these, nine species belong to the Lower, and one — the *Pterichthys hydrophilus* — to the Upper Old Red Sandstone.

alarm, and at other times lay close by the creature's side; and that the sole instrument of motion was the tail, which. when covered by its coat of scales, was proportionally of a somewhat larger size than the tail shown in the print, which. as in the specimens from whence it was taken, exhibits but the obscure and uncertain lineaments of the skeleton. The river bull-head, when attacked by an enemy, or immediately as it feels the hook in its jaws, erects its two spines at nearly right angles with the plates of the head, as if to render itself as difficult of being swallowed as possible. The attitude is one of danger and alarm; and it is a curious fact, to which I shall afterwards have occasion to advert, that in this attitude nine tenths of the *Pterichthyes* of the Lower Old Red Sandstone are to be found. We read in the stone a singularly preserved story of the strong instinctive love of life, and of the mingled fear and anger implanted for its preservation — " The champions in distorted postures threat." It presents us, too, with a wonderful record of violent death falling at once, not on a few individuals, but on whole tribes.

Next to the *Pterichthys* of the Lower Old Red I shall place its contemporary the *Coccosteus* of Agassiz, a fish which, in some respects, must have somewhat resembled it. Both were covered with an armor of thickly tubercled bony plates, and both furnished with a vertebrated tail. The plates of the one. when found lying detached in the rock, can scarcely be distinguished from those of the other · there are the same marks, as in the plates of the tortoise, of accessions of growth at the edges — the same cancellated bony structure within, the same kind of tubercles without. The forms of the creatures themselves, however, were essentially different. I have compared the figure of the *Pterichthys*, as shown in some of my better specimens, to that of a man with the head cut off at the

PLATE III.

Coccosteus Cuspidatus Ag.

Fig. 1.

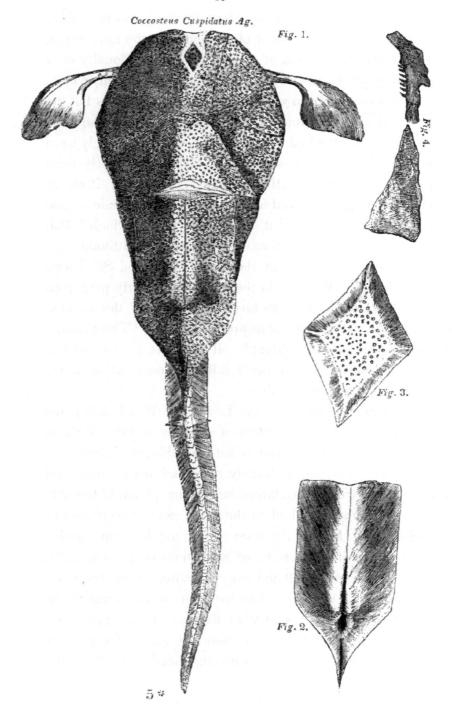

Fig. 4.

Fig. 3.

Fig. 2.

THE OLD RED SANDSTONE.

shoulders, one of the legs also wanting, and the arms spread
to the full. The figure of the *Coccosteus* I would compare
to a boy's kite. (See Plate III., fig. 1.) There is a rounded
head, a triangular body, a long tail attached to the apex of
the triangle, and arms thin and rounded where they attach to
the body, and spreading out towards their termination like
the ancient one-sided shovel which we see sculptured on old
tombstones, or the rudder of an ancient galley.* The
manner in which the plates are arranged on the head is
peculiarly beautiful; but I am afraid I cannot adequately
describe them. A ring of plates, like the ring-stones of an
arch, runs along what may be called the hoop of the kite;
the form of the keystone-plate is perfect; the shapes of the
others are elegantly varied, as if for ornament; and what
would be otherwise the opening of the arch, is filled up with
one large plate, of an outline singularly elegant. A single
plate, still larger than any of the others, covers the greater
part of the creature's triangular body, to the shape of which
it nearly conforms. It rises saddle-wise towards the centre:
on the ridge there is a longitudinal groove ending in a perforation, a little over the apex, (Plate III., fig. 2;) two small lateral plates on either side fill up the base of the angle; and
the long tail, with its numerous vertebral joints, terminates the
figure.

Does the reader possess a copy of Lyell's lately published
elementary work, edition 1838? If so, let him first turn up
the description of the Upper Silurian rocks, from Murchison,
which occurs in page 459, and mark the form of the trilobite
Asaphus caudatus, a fossil of the Wenlock formation. (See

---

* I have since ascertained that these seeming arms or paddles were
simply plates of a peculiar form. (See Plate IX.)

Sil. Syst., Plate VII.)   The upper part, or head, forms a cres·
cent ; the body rises out of the concave with a sweep somewhat resembling that of a Gothic arch ; the outline of the
whole approximates to that of an egg, the smaller end terminating in a sharp point.   Let him remark, further, that this
creature was a *crustaceous* animal, of the crab or lobster
class, and then turn up the brief description of the Old Red
Sandstone in the same volume, page 454, and mark the form
of the *Cephalaspis*, or buckler-head — a *fish* of a formation
immediately over that in which the remains of the trilobite
most abound.   He will find that the fish and the crustacean
are wonderfully alike.   The fish is more elongated, but both
possess the crescent-shaped head, and both the angular and
apparently jointed body.*   They illustrate admirably how
two distinct orders may meet.   They exhibit the points, if I
may so speak, at which the plated fish is linked to the shelled
crustacean.   Now, the *Coccosteus* is a stage further on ; it is
more unequivocally a fish.   It is a *Cephalaspis* with an articulated tail attached to the angular body, and the horns of the
crescent-shaped head cut off.

Some of the specimens which exhibit this creature are

---

* Really jointed in the case of the trilobite ; only apparently so in
that of the *Cephalaspis*.   The body of the trilobite, like that of the
lobster, was barred by transverse, oblong, overlapping plates, and between every two plates there was a joint ; the body of the *Cephalaspis*,
in like manner, was barred by transverse, oblong, overlapping scales,
between which there existed no such joints.   It is interesting to observe how nature, in thus bringing two such different classes as fishes
and crustacea together, gives to the higher animal a sort of pictorial
resemblance to the lower, in parts where the construction could not
be identical without interfering with the grand distinctions of the
classes.

exceedingly curious. In one, a coprolite still rests in the abdomen ; and a common botanist's microscope shows it thickly speckled over with minute scales, the indigestible exuviæ of fish on which the animal had preyed. In the abdomen of another we find a few minute pebbles — just as pebbles are occasionally found in the stomach of the cod — which had been swallowed by the creature attached to its food. Is there nothing wonderful in the fact, that men should be learning at this time of day how the fishes of the Old Red Sandstone lived, and that there were some of them rapacious enough not to be over nice in their eating ?

The under part of the creature is still very imperfectly known : it had its central lozenge-shaped plate, like that on the under side of the *Pterichthys*, but of greater elegance, (see Plate III., fig. 3,) round which the other plates were ranged. " What an appropriate ornament, if set in gold ! " said Dr. Buckland, on seeing a very beautiful specimen of this central lozenge in the interesting collection of Professor Traill of Edinburgh, — " What an appropriate ornament for a lady geologist ! " There are two marked peculiarities in the jaws of the *Coccosteus*, as shown in most of the specimens, illustrative of the lower part of the creature, which I have yet seen. The teeth, instead of being fixed in sockets, like those of quadrupeds and reptiles, or merely placed on the bone, like those of fish of the common varieties, seem to have been cut out of the solid, like the teeth of a saw or the teeth in the mandibles of the beetle, or in the nippers of the lobster, (Plate III., fig. 4 ;) and there appears to have been something strangely anomalous in the position of the jaws — something too anomalous, perhaps, to be regarded as proven by the evidence of the specimens yet found, but which may be mentioned with the view of directing attention to it

" Do not be deterred," said Agassiz, in the course of one of the interviews in which he obligingly indulged the writer of these chapters, who had mentioned to him that one of his opinions, just confirmed by the naturalist, had seemed so extraordinary that he had been almost afraid to communicate it, — " Do not be deterred, if you have examined minutely, by any dread of being deemed extravagant. The possibilities of existence run so deeply into the extravagant, that there is scarcely any conception too extraordinary for nature to realize." In all the more complete specimens which I have yet seen, *the position of the jaws is vertical, not horizontal ;* and yet the creature, as shown by the tail, belonged unquestionably to the vertebrata. Now, though the mouths of the crustaceous animals, such as the crab and lobster, open vertically, and a similar arrangement obtains among the insect tribes, it has been remarked by naturalists, as an invariable condition of that higher order of animals distinguished by vertebral columns, that their mouths open horizontally. What I would remark as very extraordinary in the *Coccosteus* — not, however, in the way of directly asserting the fact, but merely by way of soliciting inquiry regarding it — is, that it seems to unite to a vertebral column a vertical mouth, thus forming a connecting link between two orders of existences, by conjoining what is at once their most characteristic and most dissimilar traits.*

* These statements regarding the character of the teeth and the position of the jaws of the *Coccosteus* have been challenged by very high authorities I retain them, however, in this edition in their original form, as first made nearly six years ago. In at least two of my specimens of *Coccosteus* the teeth and jaw form unequivocally but one bone — a result, it is not improbable, of some after anchylosing process, but

I am acquainted with four species of *Coccosteus* — *C. deci-piens*, *C. cuspidatus*, *C. oblongus*, and a variety not yet named; and many more species may yet be discovered.* Of all the existences of the formation, this curious fish seems to have been one of the most abundant. In a few square yards of rock I have laid open portions of the remains of a dozen different individuals belonging to two of the four species, the *C. decipiens* and *C. cuspidatus*, in the course of a single evening None of the other kinds have yet been found at Cromarty These two differed from each other in the proportions which their general bulk bore to their length — slightly, too, in the arrangement of their occipital plates. The *Coccosteus latus*, as the name implies, must have been by much a massier fish than the other; and we find the arch-like form of the plates which covered its head more complete : the plate representing the keystone rests on the saddle-shaped plate in the centre, and the plates representing the spring stones of the arch exhibit a broader base. The accompanying print (Plate III) repre-ents the *Coccosteus cuspidatus*. The average length of the creature, including the tail, as shown in most of the Cromarty specimens, somewhat exceeded a foot. A few detached plates from Orkney, in the collection of Dr. Traill, must have belonged to an individual of fully twice that length.†

---

* A fifth species has been named *C. maximus*.   † See Note C.

---

which still solicits inquiry as not yet definitely accounted for. The matter of fact in the case is certainly one which should be determined, not analogically, but on its own proper evidence, as furnished by good specimens. As for the remark regarding the probable position of the creature's jaws, it was ventured on at first, as the reader may perceive, with much hesitation, and must now be regarded as more doubtful than ever. Its repetition here, however, will, I trust, be regarded as simply indicative of a wish on the part of the writer, that the question be kept open just a little longer, and that further examination be made. There is certainly something very peculiar about the mouth of the *Coccosteus* not yet understood, and singularly formed plates, connected with it, which have not been introduced into any restora-

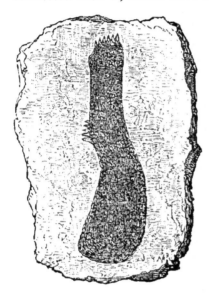

tion, and the use of which in the economy of the animal seem wholly unknown. [1850.—I have at length found a very perfect specimen of the nether jaw of *Coccosteus*, and am prepared to show that it was of a character altogether unique. It had its two groups of from six to eight teeth, (exactly where, in the human subject, the molars are placed,) that seem to have acted on corresponding groups in the intermaxillaries, and two other groups of from three to five teeth placed at right angles with these, direct in the symphysis, and that seem to have acted on each other. But though these unique teeth of the symphysis formed a vertical line of mouth, it joined on at right angles to a transverse line of the ordinary type, as the upright stroke of the letter T joins on to the horizontal line a-top.] Fourth edition.

CHAPTER IV.

Has the reader ever heard of the "griesly fisch" and the
"laithlic flood," described by that minstrel Bishop of Dunkeld
"who gave rude Scotland Virgil's page?" Both fish and
flood are the extravagances of a poet's dream. The flood
came rolling through a wilderness of bogs and quagmires,
under banks "dark as rocks the whilk the sey upcast." A
skeleton forest stretched around, doddered and leafless; and
through the "unblomit" and "barrant" trees

> "The quhissling wind blew mony bitter blast;"

the whitened branches "clashed and clattered;" the "vile
water rinnand o'erheid," and "routing as thonder," made "hid-
eous trubil;" and to augment the uproar, the "griesly fisch,"
like the fish of eastern story, raised their heads amid the foam,
and shrieked and yelled as they passed. "The grim monsters
fordeafit the hering with their schouts;" — they were both
fish and elves, and strangely noisy in the latter capacity; and
the longer the poet listened, the more frightened he became.

6   (55)

The description concludes, like a terrific dream, with his wanderings through the labyrinths of the dead forest, where all was dry and sapless above, and mud and marsh below, and with his exclamations of grief and terror at finding himself hopelessly lost in a scene of prodigies and evil spirits. And such was one of the wilder fancies in which a youthful Scottish poet of the days of Flodden indulged, ere taste had arisen to restrain and regulate invention.

Shall I venture to say, that the ichthyolites of the Old Red Sandstone have sometimes reminded me of the " fisch of the laithlic flood ? " They were hardly less curious. We find them surrounded, like these, by a wilderness of dead vegetation, and of rocks upcast from the sea ; and there are the footprints of storm and tempest around and under them. True, they must have been less noisy. Like the " gricsly fisch," however, they exhibit a strange union of opposite natures. One of their families — that of the *Cephalaspis* — seems almost to constitute a connecting link, says Agassiz, between fishes and crustaceans. They had, also, their families of sauroid, or reptile fishes — and their still more numerous families that unite the cartilaginous fishes to the osseous. And to these last the explorer of the Lower Old Red Sandstone finds himself mainly restricted. The links of the system are all connecting links, separated by untold ages from that which they connect ; so that, in searching for their representatives amid the existences of the present time, we find but the gaps which they should have occupied. And it is essentially necessary from this circumstance, in acquainting one's self with their peculiarities, to examine, if I may so express myself, the sides of these gaps, — the existing links at both ends to which the broken links should have pieced, — in short, all those more striking peculiarities of the exist-

ing disparted families which we find united in the intermediate families that no longer exist. Without some such
preparation, the inquirer would inevitably share the fate of
the poetical dreamer of Dunkeld, by losing his way in a laby-
rinth. In passing, therefore, with this object from the extinct to the recent, I venture to solicit, for a few paragraphs,
the attention of the reader.

Fishes, the fourth great class in point of rank in the animal kingdom, and, in extent of territory, decidedly the first,
are divided, as they exist in the present creation, into two distinct series — the osseous and the cartilaginous. The osseous
embraces that vast assemblage which naturalists describe as
" fishes properly so called," and whose skeletons, like those
of mammalia, birds, and reptiles, are composed chiefly of a
calcareous earth pervading an organic base. Hence the durability of their remains. In the cartilaginous series, on the
contrary, the skeleton contains scarce any of this earth   it is
a framework of indurated animal matter, elastic, semi-trans-
parent, yielding easily to the knife, and, like all mere animal
substances, inevitably subject to decay. I have seen the
huge cartilaginous skeleton of a shark lost in a mass of putrefaction in less than a fortnight. I have found the minutest
bones of the osseous ichthyolites of the Lias entire after the
lapse of unnumbered centuries.

The two series do not seem to precede or follow one
another in any such natural sequence as that in which the
great classes of the animal kingdom are arranged. The
mammifer takes precedence of the bird, the bird of the reptile, the reptile of the fish ; there is progression in the scale
— the arrangement of the classes is consecutive, not parallel. But in this great division there is no such progression ;
the osseous fish takes no precedence of the cartilaginous fish,

or the cartilaginous, as a series, of the osseous. The arrangement is parallel, not consecutive; but the parallelism, if I may so express myself, seems to be that of a longer with a shorter line; — the cartilaginous fishes, though much less numerous in their orders and families than the other, stretch farther along the scale in opposite directions, at once rising higher and sinking lower than the osseous fishes. The cartilaginous order of the sturgeons, — a roe-depositing tribe, devoid alike of affection for their young, or of those attachments which give the wild beasts of the forest partners in their dens, — may be regarded as fully abreast of by much the greater part of the osseous fishes, in both their instincts and their organization. The family of the sharks, on the other hand, and some of the rays, rise higher, as if to connect the class of fish with the class immediately above it — that of reptiles. Many of them are viviparous, like the mammalia — attached, it is said, to their young, and fully equal even to birds in the strength of their connubial attachments. The male, in some instances, has been known to pine away and die when deprived of his female companion.* But then, on the other hand, the cartilaginous fishes, in some of their tribes, sink as low beneath the osseous as they rise above them in others. The suckers, for instance, a cartilaginous family, are the most imperfect of all vertebral animals, some of them want even

---

* Some of the osseous fishes are also viviparous — the "viviparous blenny," for instance. The evidence from which the supposed affection of the higher fishes for their offspring has been inferred, is, I am afraid, of a somewhat equivocal character. The love of the sow for her litter hovers, at times, between that of the parent and that of the epicure, nor have we proof enough, in the present state of ichthyological knowledge, to conclude to which side the parental love of the fish inclines. The connubial affections of some of the higher

the sense of sight; they seem mere worms, furnished with fins and gills, and were so classed by Linnæus; but though now ascertained to be in reality fishes, they must be regarded as the lowest link in the scale — as connecting the class with the class *Vermes*, just as the superior cartilaginous fishes may be regarded as connecting it with the class *Reptilia*.

Between the osseous and the cartilaginous fishes there exist some very striking dissimilarities. The skull of the osseous fish is divided into a greater number of distinct bones, and possesses more movable parts, than the skulls of mammiferous animals: the skull of the cartilaginous fish, on the contrary, consists of but a single piece, without joint or suture. There is another marked distinction. The bony fish, if it approaches in form to that general type which we recognize amid all the varieties of the class as proper to fishes, and to which, in all their families, nature is continually inclining, will be found to have a tail branching out, as in the perch and herring, from the bone in which the vertebral column terminates; whereas the cartilaginous fish, if it also approach the general type, will be found to have a tail formed, as in the sturgeon and dog-fish, on both sides of the hinder portion of the spine, but developed much more largely on the under than on the upper side. In some instances, it is wanting on the upper side altogether. It may be as impossible to assign reasons for such relations as for those

---

families seem better established. Of a pair of gigantic rays (*Cephaloptera gioma*) taken in the Mediterranean, and described by Risso, the female was captured by some fishermen; and the male continued constantly about the boat, as if bewailing the fate of his companion, and was then found floating dead. — See Wilson's article ICHTHYOLOGY, *Encyc. Brit*, seventh edition.

6 *

which exist between the digestive organs and the hoofs of the ruminant animals; but it is of importance that they should be noted.*   It may be remarked, further, that the great bulk of fishes whose skeletons consist of cartilage have yet an ability of secreting the calcareous earth which composes bone, and that they are furnished with bony coverings, either partial or entire.   Their bones lie outside.   The thorn-back derives its name from the multitudinous hooks and spikes of bone that bristle over its body; the head, back, and operculum of the sturgeon are covered with bony plates; the thorns and prickles of the shark are composed of the same material.   The framework within is a framework of mere animal matter; but it was no lack of the osseous ingredient that led to the arrangement — an arrangement which we can alone refer to the will of that all-potent Creator, who can transpose his materials at pleasure, without interfering with the perfection of his work.   It is a curious enough circumstance, that some of the osseous fishes, as if entirely to reverse the condition of the cartilaginous ones, are partially covered with

---

* Dr. Buckland, in his *Bridgewater Treatise*, assigns satisfactory reasons for this construction of tail in sharks and sturgeons.   Of the fishes of these two orders, he states, "the former perform the office of scavengers, to clear the water of impurities, and have no teeth, but feed, by means of a soft, leather-like mouth, capable of protrusion and contraction, on putrid vegetables and animal substances at the bottom; and hence they have constantly to keep their bodies in an inclined position.   The sharks employ their tail in another peculiar manner — to turn their body, in order to bring their mouth, which is placed downwards beneath the head, into contact with their prey.   We find an important provision in every animal, to give a position of ease and activity to the head during the operation of feeding." — *Bridgewater Treatise*, p. 279, vol. i., first ed.

plates of cartilage. They are bone within, and cartilage without, just as others are bone without and cartilage within.

But how apply all this to the Geology of the Old Red Sandstone ? Very directly. The ichthyolites of this ancient formation hold, as has been said, an intermediate place, un-occupied among present existences, between the two series, and in some respects resemble the osseous, and in some the cartilaginous tribes The fact reminds one of Dr. Johnson's shrewd objection to the theory embraced by Soame Jenyns in his *Free Inquiry*, and which was the theory also of Pope and Bolingbroke. The metaphysician held, with the poet and his friend, that there exists a vast and finely graduated chain of being from Infinity to nonentity — from God to nothing; and that to strike out a single link would be to mar the perfection of the whole.* The moralist demonstrated, on the contrary, that this chain, in the very nature of things, must be incomplete at both ends — that between that which

---

* " See, through this air, this ocean, and this earth,
    All matter quick, and bursting into birth ,
    Above, how high progressive life may go !
    Around, how wide ! how deep extend below !
    Vast chain of being ! which from God began —
    Nature's ethereal, human angel, man,
    Beast, bird, fish, insect — what no eye can see,
    No glass can reach; from Infinite to thee —
    From thee to nothing. On superior powers
    Were we to press, inferior might on ours ;
    Or in the full creation leave a void,
    Where, one step broken, the great scale's destroyed :
    From Nature's chain, whatever link you strike,
    Tenth, or ten thousandth, breaks the chain alike."
                               Essay on Man.

does, and that which does not exist, there must be an infinite
difference — that the chain, therefore, cannot lay hold on
nothing He showed, further, that between the greatest of
finite existences and the adorable Infinite there must exist
another illimitable void — that the boundless and the bounded
are as widely separated in their natures and qualities as the
existent and the non-existent — that the chain, in short, cannot lay hold on Deity.   He asserted, however, that not only
is it thus incomplete at both ends, but that we must regard it
as well nigh as incomplete in many of its intermediate links
as at its terminal ones ; that it is already a broken chain,
seeing that between its various classes of existence myriads
of intermediate existences might be introduced, by graduating more minutely what must necessarily be capable of infinite gradation ; and that, to base an infidel theory on the
supposed completeness of what is demonstrably incomplete,
and on the impossibility of a gap existing in what is already
filled with gaps, is just to base one absurdity on another.*

---

* The following are the well-stated reasonings of Dr Johnson, a
writer who never did injustice to an argument for want of words to
express it in · —

"The scale of existence from Infinity to nothing cannot possibly
have being. The highest being not infinite must be at an infinite distance from Infinity.   Cheyne, who, with the desire inherent in math-
ematicians to reduce every thing to mathematical images, considers
all existence as a *cone*, allows that the basis is at an infinite distance
from the body, and in this distance between finite and infinite there
will be room forever for an infinite series of indefinable existence

"Between the lowest positive existence and nothing, whenever
we suppose positive existence to cease, is another chasm infinitely
deep, where there is room again for endless orders of subordinate nature, continued forever and ever, and yet infinitely superior to non-
existence.

Now, we find the Geology of what may be termed the second age of vertebrated existence (for the Lower Old Red Sandstone was such) coming curiously in to confirm the reasonings of Johnson. It shows us the greater part of the fish of an entire creation thus insinuated between two of the links of our own.

It is now several years since I was first led to suspect that the condition of the ichthyolites of the Old Red Sandstone was intermediate. I have alluded to the comparative indestructibility of the osseous skeleton, and the extreme liability to decay characteristic of the cartilaginous one. Of a skeleton in part osseous and in part cartilaginous, we must, of course, expect, when it occurs in a fossil state, to find the indestructible portions only. And when, in every instance, we find the fossil skeletons of a formation complete in some of their parts, and incomplete in others — the entire portions in-

---

"To these meditations humanity is unequal. But yet we may ask, not of our Maker, but of each other, since on the one side creation, whenever it stops, must stop infinitely below infinity, and on the other infinitely above nothing, what necessity there is that it should proceed so far either way — that being so high or so low should ever have existed We may ask, but I believe no created wisdom can give an adequate answer.

"Nor is this all In the scale, wherever it begins or ends, are infinite vacuities. At whatever distance we suppose the next order of beings to be above man, there is room for an intermediate order of beings between them ; and if for one order, then for infinite orders, since every thing that admits of more or less, and consequently all the parts of that which admits them, may be infinitely divided , so that, as far as we can judge, there may be room in the vacuity between any two steps of the scale, or between any two points of the cone of being, for infinite exertion of infinite power." — *Review of "A Free Inquiry"*

variably agreeing, and the wanting portions invariably agreeing also — it seems but natural to conclude that an original
difference must have obtained, and that the existing parts,
which we can at once recognize as bone, must have been
united to parts now wanting, which were composed of cartilage. The naturalist never doubts that the shark's teeth,
which he finds detached on the shore, or buried in some ancient formation, were united originally to cartilaginous jaws.
Now, in breaking open all the ichthyolites of the Lower Old
Red Sandstone, with the exception of those of the two families already described, we find that some of the parts are invariably wanting, however excellent the state of preservation
maintained by the rest. I have seen every scale preserved
and in its place — one set of both the larger and smaller
bones occupying their original position — jaws thickly set
with teeth still undetached from the head — the massy bones
of the skull still unseparated — the larger shoulder-bone, on
which the operculum rests, lying in its proper bed — the operculum itself entire — and all the external rays which support the fins, though frequently fine as hairs, spreading out
distinct as the fibres in the wing of the dragon-fly, or the
woody nerves in an oak-leaf. In no case, however, have I
succeeded in finding a single joint of the vertebral column,
or the trace of a single internal ray. No part of the internal
skeleton survives, nor does its disappearance seem to have had
any connection with the greater mass of putrescent matter
which must have surrounded it, seeing that the external rays
of the fins show quite as entire when turned over upon the
body, as sometimes occurs, as when spread out from it in
profile. Besides, in the ichthyolites of the chalk, no parts
of the skeleton are better preserved than the internal parts —
the vertebral joints, and the internal rays. The reader must

have observed, in the cases of a museum of Natural History, preparations of fish of two several kinds — preparations of the skeleton, in which only the osseous parts are exhibited, and preparations of the external form, in which the whole body is shown in profile, with the fins spread to the full, and at least half the bones of the head covered by the skin but in which the vertebral column and internal rays are wanting. Now, in the fossils of the chalk, with those of the other later formations, down to the New Red Sandstone, we find that the skeleton style of preparation obtains; whereas, in at least three fourths of the ichthyolites of the Lower Old Red, we find only what we may term the external style. I had marked, besides, another circumstance in the ichthyolites, which seemed, like a nice point of circumstantial evidence, to give testimony in the same line. The tails of all the ichthyolites, whose vertebral columns and internal rays are wanting, are unequally lobed, like those of the dog-fish and sturgeon, (both cartilaginous fishes,) and the body runs on to nearly the termination of the surrounding rays. The one-sided condition of tail exists, says Cuvier, in no recent osseous fish known to naturalists, except in the bony pike — a sauroid fish of the warmer rivers of America. With deference, however, to so high an authority, it is questionable whether the tail of the bony pike should not rather be described as a tail set on somewhat awry, than as a one-sided tail.

All these peculiarities I could but note as they turned up before me, and express, in pointing them out to a few friends, a sort of vague, because hopeless, desire, that good fortune might throw me in the way of the one man of all the world best qualified to explain the principle on which they occurred, and to decide whether fishes may be at once bony and cartilaginous. But that meeting was a contingency rather to be wished than hoped for — a circumstance within the bounds of the possible, but beyond those of the probable. Could the working-man of the north of Scotland have so much as dreamed that he was yet to enjoy an opportunity of comparing his observations with those of the naturalist of Neufchatel, and of having his inferences tested and confirmed ?

The opportunity did occur. The working-man did meet with Agassiz ; and many a query had he to put to him ; and never, surely, was inquirer more courteously entreated, or his doubts more satisfactorily resolved. The reply to almost my first question solved the enigma of nearly ten years' standing And finely characteristic was that reply of the frankness and candor of a great mind, that can afford to make it no secret, that, in its onward advances on knowledge, it may know to-day what it did not know yesterday, and that it is content to " gain by degrees upon the darkness." " Had you asked me the question a fortnight ago," said Agassiz, " I could not have replied to it. Since then, however, I have examined an ichthyolite of the Old Red Sandstone in which the vertebral joints are fortunately impressed on the stone, though the joints themselves have disappeared, and which, exactly resembling the vertebræ of the shark, must have been cartilaginous." In a subsequent conversation, the writer was gratified by finding most of his other facts and inferences authenticated and confirmed by those of the naturalist. I shall attempt introducing to the reader the peculiarities, general and specific, of the ichthyolites to which these facts and observations mainly referred, by describing such of the families as are most abundant in the formation, and the points in which they either resemble or differ from the existing fish of our seas.

Of these ancient families, the *Osteolepis*, or bony-scale,

PLATE IV

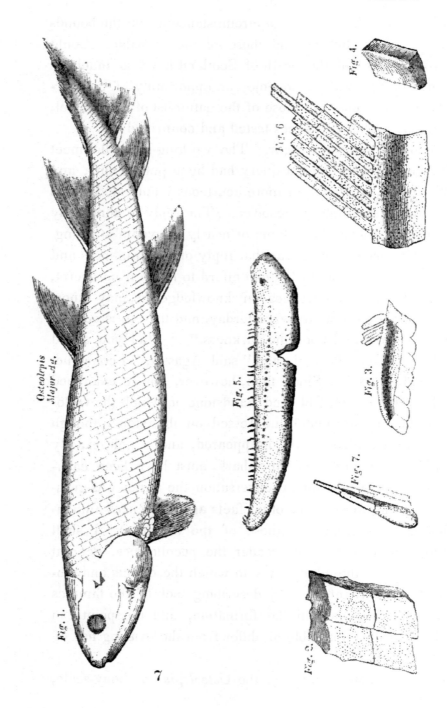

Fig. 4.

Fig. 6.

Osteolepis
Major .dy.

Fig. 5.

Fig. 3.

Fig. 7.

Fig. 1.

Fig. 2.

(see Plate IV., fig. 1,) may be regarded as illustrative of the general type. It was one of the first discovered of the Caithness fishes, and received its name in the days of Cuvier, from the osseous character of its scales, ere it was ascertained that it had numerous contemporaries, and that to all and each of these the same description applied. The scales of the fishes of the Lower Old Red Sandstone, like the plates and detached prickles of the purely cartilaginous fishes, were composed of a bony, not of a horny, substance, and were all coated externally with enamel. The circumstance is one of interest.

Agassiz, in his system of classification, has divided fishes into four orders, according to the form of their scales ; and his principle of division, though apparently arbitrary and trivial, is yet found to separate the class into great natural families, distinguished from one another by other and very striking peculiarities. One kind of scale, for instance, the placoid or broad-plated scale, is found to characterize all the cartilaginous fishes of Cuvier except the sturgeon ; — it is the characteristic of an otherwise well-marked series, whose families are furnished with skeletons composed of mere animal matter, and whose gills open to the water by spiracles. The fish of another order are covered by ctenoid or comb-shaped scales, the posterior margin of each scale being toothed somewhat like the edge of a saw or comb ; and the order, thus distinguished, is found wonderfully to agree with an order formed previously on another principle of classification, the Acanthopterygii, or thorny-finned order of Cuvier, excluding only the smooth-scaled families of this previously formed division, and including, in addition to it, the flat fish. A third order, the Cycloidean, is marked by simple marginated scales, like those of the cod, haddock, whiting, herring, salmon, &c. ; and this order is found to embrace chiefly the

Malacopterygii, or soft-finned order of Cuvier — an order to which all these well-known fish, with an immense multitude of others, belong. Thus the results of the principle of classification adopted by Agassiz wonderfully agree with the results of the less simple principles adopted by Cuvier and the other masters in this department of Natural History. Now, it is peculiar to yet a fourth order, the Ganoidean, or shining-scaled order, that by much the greater number of the genera which it comprises exist only in the fossil state. At least five sixths of the whole were ascertained to be extinct several years ago, at a time when the knowledge of fossil Ichthyology was much more limited than at present : the proportions are now found to be immensely greater on the side of the dead. And this order seems to have included all the semi-osseous, semi-cartilaginous ichthyolites of the Lower Old Red Sand-stone : the enamelled scale is the characteristic, according to Agassiz's principle of classification, of the existences that filled the gap so often alluded to as existing in the present creation. All their scales glitter with enamel : they bore to this order the relation that the cartilaginous fish bear to the Placoidean order, the thorny-finned fish to the Ctenoidean order, and the soft-finned fish to the Cycloidean order. It also included, with the semi-cartilaginous, the sauroid fish — those master existences and tyrants of the earlier vertebrata ; and both classes find their representatives among the comparatively few ganoid fishes of the present creation ; the one in the sturgeon family, which of all existing families approaches nearest in other respects to the extinct semi-cartilaginous fishes ; the other in the sauroid genus *Lepidosteus*, to which the bony pike belongs. The head, back, and sides of the sturgeon are defended, as has been already remarked, by longitudinal rows of hard osseous bosses — the bony pike is armed with enamelled osseous scales, of a stony hardness. It seems a somewhat curious circumstance, that fishes so unlike each other in their internal framework should thus resemble one another in their bony coverings, and in some slight degree in their structure of tail. One of the characteristics of sauroid fishes is the extreme compactness and hardness of their skeleton *

It requires skill such as that possessed by Agassiz, to determine that the uncouth *Coccosteus*, or the equally uncouth *Pterichthys*, of the Old Red Sandstone, with their long articulated tails and tortoise-like plates, were *bona fide* fishes; but there is no possibility of mistaking the *Osteolepis:* it is obvious to the least practised eye that it must have been a fish, and a handsome one Even a cursory examination, however, shows very striking peculiarities, which are found, on further examination, to characterize not this family alone, but at least one half the contemporary families besides. We are accustomed to see vertebrated animals with the bone uncovered in one part only, — that part the teeth, — and with the rest of the skeleton wrapped up in flesh and skin. Among the reptiles, we find a few exceptions;

---

* "The sauroid or lizard-like fishes," says Dr. Buckland, " combine in the structure, both of the bones and some of the soft parts, characters which are common to the class of reptiles. The bones of the skull are united by closer sutures than those of common fishes. The vertebræ articulate with the spinous processes of sutures, like the vertebræ of saurians; the ribs also articulate with the extremities of the spinous process. The caudal vertebræ have distinct chevron bones, and the general condition of the skeleton is stronger and more solid than in other fishes : the air bladder also is bifid and cellular, approaching to the character of lungs, and in the throat there is a glottis, as in sirens and salamanders, and many saurians." — Note to *Bridgewater Treatise*, p. 274, first edit.

but a creature with a skull as naked as its teeth, — the bone
being merely covered, as in these, by a hard, shining enamel,
— and with toes also of bare enamelled bone, would be
deemed an anomaly in creation. And yet such was the condition of the *Osteolepis*, and many of its contemporaries. The
enamelled teeth were placed in jaws which presented outside
a surface as naked and as finely enamelled as their own.
(See Plate IV, fig. 5.) The entire head was covered with
enamelled osseous plates, furnished inside like other bones, as
shown by their cellular construction, with their nourishing
bloodvessels, and perhaps their oil, and which rested apparently on the cartilaginous box, which must have enclosed the
brain, and connected it with the vertebral column. I cannot
better illustrate the peculiar condition of the fins of this
ichthyolite than by the webbed foot of a water-fowl. The
web or membrane in all the aquatic birds with which we are
acquainted not only connects, but also covers the toes. The
web or membrane in the fins of existing fishes accomplishes
a similar purpose; it both connects and covers the supporting
bones or rays. Imagine, however, a webbed foot in which
the toes — connected, but not covered — present, as in skeletons, an upper and under surface of naked bone: and a
very correct idea may be formed, from such a foot, of the
condition of fin which obtained among at least one half the
ichthyolites of the Lower Old Red Sandstone. The supporting bones or rays seem to have been connected laterally
by the membrane; but on both sides they presented bony
and finely enamelled surfaces. (See Plate IV., fig 6) In
this singular class of fish, all was bone without, and all was
cartilage within; and the bone in every instance, whether in
the form of jaws or of plates, of scales or of rays, presented
an external surface of enamel.

The fins are quite a study. I have alluded to the connecting membrane. In existing fish this membrane is the principal agent in propelling the creature; it strikes against the water, as the membrane of the bat's wing strikes against the air; and the internal skeleton serves but to support and stiffen it for this purpose. But in the fin of the *Osteolepis*, as in those of many of its contemporaries, we find the condition reversed. The rays were so numerous, and lay so thickly, side by side, like feathers in the wing of a bird, that they presented to the water a surface of bone, and the continuous membrane only served to support and bind them together. In the fins of existing fish we find a sort of bat-wing construction; in those of the *Osteolepis* a sort of bird-wing construction. The rays, to give flexibility to the organ which they compose, were all jointed, as in the soft-finned fish — as in the herring, salmon, and cod, for example; and we find in all the fins the anterior ray rising from the body in the form of an angular scale: it is a strong, bony scale in one of its joints, and a bony ray in the rest. The characteristic is a curious one.

It is again necessary, in pursuing our description, to refer for illustration to the purely cartilaginous fishes. In at least all the higher orders of these, furnished with movable jaws, such as the sturgeon, the ray, and the shark, the mouth is placed far below the snout. The dog-fish and thorn-back are familiar instances. Further, the mouth in bony fishes is movable on both the upper and under side, like the beak of the parrot; in the higher cartilaginous fishes it is movable, as in quadrupeds, on the under side only. In all their orders, too, except in that of the sturgeon, the gills open to the water by detached spiracles, or breathing-holes; but in the sturgeon, as in the osseous fishes, there is a continuous linear opening, shielded by an operculum, or gill-cover. In the *Osteolepis* the mouth opened below the snout, but not so far below it as in the purely cartilaginous fishes — not farther below it than in many of the osseous ones — than in the genus Aspro, for instance, or than in the genus Polynemus, or in even the haddock or cod. It was thickly furnished with slender and sharply-pointed teeth. I have hitherto been unable fully to determine whether, like the mouths of the osseous fishes, it was movable on both sides ; though, from the perfect form of what seems to be the intermaxillary bone, I cannot avoid thinking it was   The gills opened, as in the osseous fishes, in continuous lines, and were covered by large bony opercules — that on the enamelled side somewhat resemble round japanned shields. (See Note D.)

But while the head of the *Osteolepis*, with its appendages, thus resembled, in some points, the heads of the bony fishes, the tail, like those of most of its contemporaries, differed in no respect from the tails of cartilaginous ones, such as the sturgeon. The vertebral column seems to have run on to well nigh the extremity of the caudal fin, which we find developed chiefly on the under side. The tail was a one-sided tail. Take into account with these peculiarities — peculiarities such as the naked skull, jaws, and operculum, the naked and thickly-set rays, and the unequally lobed condition of tail — a body covered with scales, that glitter like sheets of mica, and assume, according to their position, the parallelogramical, rhomboidal, angular, or polygonal form — a lateral line raised, not depressed — a raised bar on the inner or bony side of the scales, which, like the doubled-up end of a tile, seems to have served the purpose of fastening them in their places — a general clustering of alternate fins towards the tail — and the *tout ensemble* must surely impart to the reader

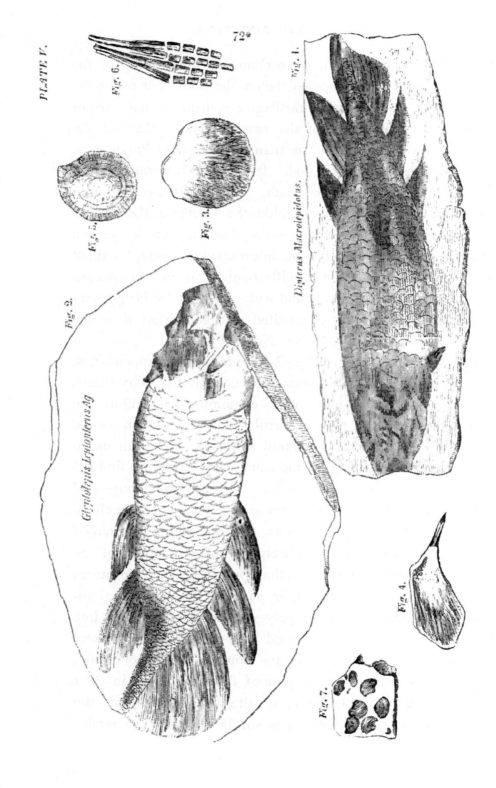

PLATE V.

72*

Fig. 6.

Fig. 1.

Dipterus Macrolepidotus.

Fig. 5.

Fig. 3.

Fig. 2.

Glyptolepis Leptopterus Ag

Fig. 4.

Fig. 7.

the idea of a very singular little fish. The ventral fins front the space which occurs between the two dorsals, and the anal fin the space which intervenes between the posterior dorsal fin and the tail. The length of the *Osteolepis*, in my larger specimens, somewhat exceeds a foot; in the smaller, it falls short of six inches. There exist at least three species of this ichthyolite, distinguished chiefly, in two of the instances, by the smaller and larger size of their scales, compared with the bulk of their bodies, and by punctulated markings on the enamel in the case of the third. This last, however, is no specific difference, but common to the entire genus, and to several other genera besides. The names are, *Osteolepis macrolepidotus*, *O. microlepidotus*, and *O. arenatus* *

Next to the *Osteolepis* we may place the *Dipterus*, or double-wing, of the Lower Old Red Sandstone, an ichthyolite first introduced to the knowledge of geologists by Mr. Murchison, who, with his friend, Mr. Sedgwick, figured and described it in a masterly paper on the older sedimentary formations of the north of Scotland, which appeared in the *Transactions of the Geological Society of London* for 1828. The name, derived from its two dorsals, would suit equally well, like that of the *Osteolepis*, many of its more recently discovered contemporaries. From the latter ichthyolite it differed chiefly in the position of its fins, which were opposite, not alternate; the double dorsals exactly fronting the anal and ventral fins. (See Plate V., fig. 1.) The *Diplopterus*, a nearly resembling ichthyolite of the same formation, also owes its name to the order and arrangement of its fins,

---

* To these have since been added *Osteolepis major*, *O. intermedius*, and *O nanus;* the two latter, however, Agassiz regards as doubtful.

which, like those of the *Dipterus*, were placed fronting each
other, and in pairs.   But the head, in proportion to the body,
was in greater size than in either the *Dipterus* or *Osteolepis*;
and the mouth, as indicated by the creature's length of jaw,
must have been of much greater width.   In their more striking characteristics, however, the three genera seem to have
nearly agreed.   In all alike, scales of bone glisten with enamel; their jaws, enamel without and bone within, bristle
thick with sharp-pointed teeth; closely-jointed plates, burnished like ancient helmets, cover their heads, and seem to
have formed a kind of outer table to skulls externally of bone
and internally of cartilage; their gill-covers consist each of
a single piece, like the gill-cover of the sturgeon; their tails
were formed chiefly on the lower side of their bodies; and
the rays of their fins, enamelled like their plates and their
scales, stand up over the connecting membrane, like the steel
or brass in that peculiar armor of the middle ages, whose
multitudinous pieces of metal were fastened together on a
groundwork of cloth or of leather.   All their scales, plates,
and rays present a similar style of ornament.   The shining
and polished enamel is mottled with thickly-set punctures, or,
rather, punctulated markings; so that a scale or plate, when
viewed through a microscope, reminds one of the cover of a
saddle.   Some of the ganoid scales of Burdie House present
surfaces similarly punctulated.*

---

* There exists, according to Agassiz, only a single species of *Dipterus* — *D. macrelepidotus*, whereas four species of *Diplopterus* have been
enumerated — *D. affinis*, *D. borealis*, *D. macrocephalus*, and *D. Agassizii*.
The existence of the last named, however, as a distinct species, is regarded as problematical by the distinguished naturalist whose name
has been affixed to it.

The *Glyptolepis*, or carved scale, may be regarded as the representative of a family of the Lower Old Red Sandstone, which, differing very materially from the genera described, had yet many traits in common with them, such as the bare, bony skull, the bony scales, the naked rays, and the unequally sided condition of tail. The fins, which were of considerable length in proportion to their breadth of base, and present in some of the specimens a pendulous-like appearance, cluster thick together towards the creature's lower extremities, leaving the upper portion bare. There are two dorsals placed as in the *Dipterus* and *Diplopterus* — the anterior directly opposite the ventral fin, the posterior directly opposite the anal. The tail is long and spreading ; — the rays, long and numerously articulated, are comparatively stout at their base, and slender as hairs where they terminate. The shoulder-bones are of huge dimensions, the teeth extremely minute. But the most characteristic parts of the creature are the scales. They are of great size, compared with the size of the animal. An individual not more than half a foot in length, the specimen figured, (see Plate V., fig. 2,) exhibits scales fully three eighth parts of an inch in diameter. In another more broken specimen there are scales a full inch across, and yet the length of the ichthyolite to which they belonged seems not to have much exceeded a foot and a half. Each scale consists of a double plate, an inner and an outer. The structure of the inner is not peculiar to the family or the formation : it is formed of a number of minute concentric circles, crossed by still minuter radiating lines — the one described, and the other proceeding from a common centre. (See Plate V., fig. 5) All scales that receive their accessions of growth equally at their edges exhibit, internally, a corresponding character. The outer plate presents an appearance less

8

common. It seems relieved into ridges that drop adown it like sculptured threads, some of them entire, some broken, some straight, some slightly waved, (see Plate V., fig. 3 ;) and hence the name of the ichthyolite. The plates of the head were ornamented in a similar style, but their threads are so broken as to present the appearance of dotted lines, the dots all standing out in bold relief. My collection contains three varieties of this family ; one of them disinterred from out the Cromarty beds about seven years ago, and the others only a little later, though partly from the inadequacy of a written description, through which I was led to confound the *Osteolepis* with the *Diplopterus*, and to regard the *Glyptolepis* as the *Osteolepis*, I was not aware until lately that the discovery was really such ; and under the latter name I described the creature in the *Witness* newspaper several weeks ere it had received the name which it now bears. It was first introduced to the notice of Agassiz, in Autumn last, by Lady Cumming of Altyre. The species, however, was a different one from any yet found at Cromarty.*

The *Cheirolepis*, or scaly pectoral, forms the representative of yet another family of the Lower Old Red Sandstone, and one which any eye, however unpractised, could at once distinguish from the families just described. Professor Traill of the University of Edinburgh, a gentleman whose researches in Natural History have materially extended the boundaries of knowledge, and whose frankness in communicating information is only equalled by his facility in acquiring it, was the first discoverer of this family, one variety of which, the *Cheirolepis Traillii*, bears his name. The figured speci-

---

* There are three species of Glyptolepis — *G. elegans*, *G. leptopterus*, and *G. microlepidotus*.

men (Plate VI., fig. 1) Agassiz has pronounced a new species, the discovery of the writer. In all the remains of this curious fish which I have hitherto seen, the union of the osseous with the cartilaginous, in the general framework of the creature, is strikingly apparent. The external skull, the great shoulder-bone, and the rays of the fins, are all unequivocally osseous ; the occipital and shoulder-bones, in particular, seem of great strength and massiveness, and are invariably preserved, however imperfect the specimen in other respects ; whereas, even in specimens the most complete, and which exhibit every scale and every ray, however minute, and show unchanged the entire outline of the animal, not a fragment of the internal skeleton appears. The *Cheirolepis* seems to have varied from fourteen to four inches in length. When seen in profile, the under line, as in the figured variety, seems thickly covered with fins, and the upper line well nigh naked. The large pectorals almost encroach on the ventral fins, and the ventrals on the anal fin ; whereas the back, for two thirds the entire length of the creature, presents a bare rectilinear ridge, and the single dorsal, which rises but a little way over the tail, immediately opposite the posterior portion of the anal fin, is comparatively of small size. The tail, which, in the general condition of being developed chiefly on the lower side, resembles the tails of all the creature's contemporaries, is elegantly lobed. The scales, in proportion to the bulk of the body which they cover, are not more than one twentieth the size of those of the *Osteolepis*. They are richly enamelled, and range diagonally from the shoulder to the belly in waving lines ; and so fretted is each individual scale by longitudinal grooves and ridges, that, on first bringing it under the glass, it seems a little bunch of glittering thorns, though, when more minutely examined, it is found to present somewhat the appearance of the outer side of the deep-sea cockle, with its strongly marked ribs and channels, the point in which the posterior point terminates representing the hinge   (See Plate VI., fig. 2.)   The bones of the head, enamelled like the scales, are carved into jagged inequalities, somewhat resembling those on the skin of the shark, but more irregular.   The sculpturings seem intended evidently for effect.   To produce harmony of appearance between the scaly coat and the enamelled occipital plates of bone, the surfaces of the latter are relieved, where they border on the shoulders, into what seem scales, just as the dead walls of a building are sometimes, for the sake of uniformity, wrought into blind windows.   The enamelled rays of the fins are finished, if I may so speak, after the same style.   They lie thick upon one another as the fibres of a quill, and like these, too, they are imbricated on the sides, so that the edge of each seems jagged into a row of prickles.   (See Plate VI., fig. 3)   The jaws of the *Cheirolepis* were armed with thickly-set sharp teeth, like those of its contemporaries, the *Osteolepis* and *Diplopterus.**

---

* There have been five species of Cheirolepis enumerated — *C. Cummingiæ, C. splendens, C. Traillii, C unilateralis,* and *C. Uragus.* The *Cheirolepis splendens* and *C. unilateralis* Agassiz regards as doubtful.

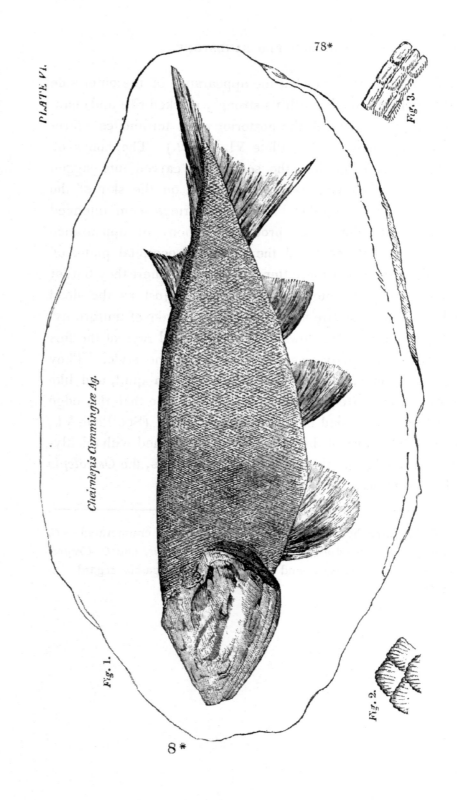

PLATE VI.

Cheirolepis Cummingiæ Ag.

Fig. 1.

Fig. 2.

Fig. 3.

78*

8*

CHAPTER V.

The Classifying Principle, and its Uses. — Three groups of Ichthyolites among the Organisms of the Lower Old Red Sandstone. — Peculiarities of the Third Group. — Its Varieties. — Description of the *Cheiracanthus*. — Of two unnamed Fossils of the same Order — Microscopic Beauty of these Ancient Fish. — Various Styles of Ornament which obtain among them. — The Molluscs of the Formation. — Remarkable chiefly for the Union of Modern with Ancient Forms which they exhibit — Its Vegetables. — Importance and Interest of the Record which it furnishes.

THERE rests in the neighborhood of Cromarty, on the upper stratum of one of the richest ichthyolite beds I have yet seen, a huge water-rolled boulder of granitic gneiss, which must have been a traveller, in some of the later periods of geological change, from a mountain range in the interior highlands of Ross-shire, more than sixty miles away It is an uncouth looking mass, several tons in weight, with a flat upper surface, like that of a table; and as a table, when engaged in collecting my specimens, I have often found occasion to employ it. I have covered it over, times without number, with fragments of fossil fish — with plates, and scales, and jaws, and fins, and, when the search proved successful, with entire ichthyolites. Why did I always arrange them, almost without thinking of the matter, into three groups? Why, even when the mind was otherwise employed, did the fragments of the *Coccosteus* and *Pterichthys* come to occupy one corner of the stone, and those of the various fish just described another corner, and the equally well-marked remains of a yet different division a third corner? The

(79)

process seemed almost mechanical, so little did it employ the attention, and so invariable were the results. The fossils of the surrounding bed always found their places on the huge stone in three groups, and at times there was yet a fourth group added — a group whose organisms belonged not to the animal, but the vegetable kingdom. What led to the arrangement, or in what did it originate ? In a principle inherent in the human mind — that principle of classification which we find pervading all science — which gives to each of the many cells of recollection its appropriate facts — and without which all knowledge would exist as a disorderly and shapeless mass, too huge for the memory to grasp, and too heterogeneous for the understanding to employ. I have described but two of the groups, and must now say a very little about the principle on which, justly or otherwise, I used to separate the third, and on the distinctive differences which rendered the separation so easy.

The recent bony fishes are divided, according to the Cuvierian system of classification, into two great orders, the soft-finned and the thorny-finned order — the *Malacopterygii* and the *Acanthopterygii*. In the former the rays of the fins are thin, flexible, articulated, branched : each ray somewhat resembles a jointed bamboo ; with this difference, however, that what seems a single ray at bottom, branches out into three or four rays a-top. In the latter, (the thorny-finned order,) — especially in their anterior dorsal, and perhaps anal fins, — the rays are stiff continuous spikes of bone, and each stands detached as a spear, without joint or branch. The perch may be instanced as a familiar illustration of this order — the gold-fish of the other. Now, between the fins of two sets — shall I venture to say orders ? — of the ichthyolites of the Lower Old Red Sandstone, an equally striking difference

obtains. The fin of the *Osteolepis*, with its surface of enamelled and minutely jointed bones, I have already described as
a sort of bird-wing fin. The naked rays, with their flattened surfaces, lay thick together as feathers in the wing of
a bird — so thick as to conceal the connecting membrane;
and fins of similar construction characterized the families
of the *Dipterus, Diplopterus, Glyptolepis, Cheirolepis, Holoptychius,* and, I doubt not, many other families of the same
period, which await the researches of future discoverers. But
the fins of another set of ichthyolites, their contemporaries,
may be described as bat-wing fins: they presented to the
water a broad expanse of membrane; and the solitary ray
which survives in each was not a jointed, but a continuous
spear-like ray. The fins of this set, or order, are thorny-fins,
like those of the *Acanthopterygii;* the anterior edge of each,
with the exception of, perhaps, the caudal fin, which differs in
construction from the others, is composed of a strong, bony
spike. Such, with some tacit reference, perhaps, to the similar Cuvierian principle of classification, were the distinctive
differences, on the strength of which I used to arrange two
of my groups of fossils on the granitic boulder; and the
influence of the same principle, almost instinctively exerted,
— for, in writing the previous pages, I scarce thought of its
existence, — has, I find, given to each group its own chapter.

Of the membranous-finned and thorny-rayed order of ichthyolites, the *Cheiracanthus,* or thorny-hand, (*i. e.* pectoral,)
may be regarded as an adequate representative. (See Plate
VII, fig. 1) The *Cheiracanthus* must have been an eminently
handsome little fish — slim, tapering, and described in all its
outlines, whether of the body or the fins, by gracefully waved
lines. It is, however, a rare matter to find it presenting its
original profile in the stone; — none of the other ichthyolites

are so frequently distorted as the *Cheiracanthus.* It seems to
have been more a cartilaginous and less an osseous fish than
most of its contemporaries However perfect the specimen,
no part of the internal skeleton is ever found, not even when
scales as minute as the point of a pin are preserved, and
every spine stands up in its original place. And hence, perhaps, a greater degree of flexibility, and consequent distor-
tion. The body was covered with small angular scales,
brightly enamelled, and delicately fretted into parallel ridges,
that run longitudinally along the upper half of the scale, and
leave the posterior portion of it a smooth, glittering surface. (See Plate VII., fig. 2.) They diminish in size towards the head, which, from the faint stain left on the stone,
seems to have been composed of cartilage exclusively, and
either covered with skin, or with scales of extreme minuteness. The lower edge of the operculum bears a tagged
fringe, like that of a curtain. The tail, a fin of considerable
power, had the unequal sided character common to the formation; and the slender and numerous rays on both sides
are separated by so many articulations as to present the appearance of parallelogramical scales. The other fins are
comparatively of small size. There is a single dorsal placed
about two thirds the entire length of the creature adown the
back; and exactly opposite its posterior edge is the anterior
edge of the anal fin. The ventral fins are placed high upon
the belly, somewhat like those of the perch; the pectorals
only a little higher. But it is rather in the construction of
the fins, than their position, that the peculiarities of the
Cheiracanthus are most marked. The anterior edge of each,
as in the pectorals of the existing genera *Cestracion* and
Chimæra, is formed of a strong, large spine. In the *Chimæra
borealis,* a cartilaginous fish of the Northern Ocean, the

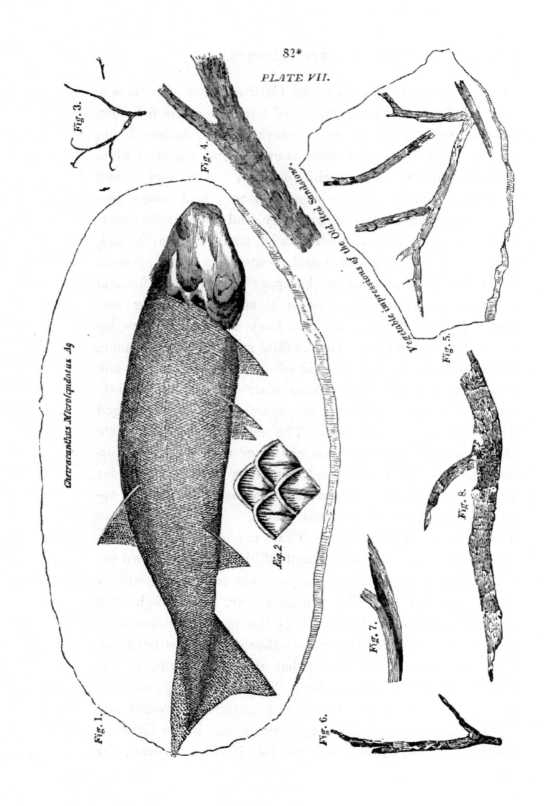

82*

PLATE VII.

Cheiracanthus Microlepidotus Ag

Fig. 1.

Fig. 2.

Fig. 3.

Fig. 4.

Vegetable impressions of the Old Red Sandstone.

Fig. 5.

Fig. 6.

Fig. 7.

Fig. 8.

spine seems placed in front of the weaker rays, just, if I may be allowed the comparison, as, in a line of mountaineers engaged in crossing a swollen torrent, the strongest man in the party is placed on the upper side of the line, to break off the force of the current from the rest   In the *Cheiracanthus*, however, each fin seems to consist of but a single spine, with an angular membrane fixed to it by one of its sides, and attached to the creature's body on the other.   Its fins are masts and sails — the spine representing the mast, and the membrane the sail ; and it is a curious characteristic of the order, that the membrane, like the body, of the ichthyolite, is thickly covered with minute scales.   The mouth seems to have opened a very little under the snout, as in the haddock ; and there are no indications of its having been furnished with teeth.*

An ichthyolite first discovered by the writer about three years ago, and introduced by him to the notice of Agassiz during his recent visit to Edinburgh, but still unfurnished with a name,† is a still more striking representative of this order than even the *Cheiracanthus*.   It must have been proportionally thick and short, like some of the tropical fishes, though rather handsome than otherwise.   (See Plate VIII , fig. 1.) The scales, minute, but considerably larger than those of the *Cheiracanthus*, are of a rhomboidal form, and so regularly striated — the striæ converging to a point at the posterior termination of each scale — that, when examined with a glass, the body appears as if covered with scallops.   (See Plate

---

* There have been three species of *Cheiracanthus* determined — *C. microlepidotus, C. minor,* and *C. Murchisoni.*

† Now determined to be a species of *Diplacanthus — D. longispinus.*

VIII., fig. 3.)   It seems a piece of exquisite shell-work, such
as we sometimes see on the walls of a grotto.   There are
two dorsals — the posterior, immediately over the tail, and
directly opposite the anal fin ; the anterior, somewhat higher
up than the ventrals ; and all the fins are of great size.   The
anterior edge of each is formed of a strong spine, round as
the handle of a halbert, and diminishing gradually and sym-
metrically to a sharp point.   Though formed externally of
solid bone, it seems to have been composed internally of cartilage, like the bones of some of the osseous fishes — those
of the halibut, for instance ; and the place of the cartilage is
generally occupied in the stone by carbonate of lime.   The
membrane which formed the body of the fin was covered,
like that of the *Cheiracanthus*, with minute scales, of the
same scallop-like pattern with the rest, but of not more than
one sixth the size of those which cover the creature's sides
and back.   Imagine two lug-sails stiffly extended between
the deck of a brigantine and her two masts, the latter
raking as far aft as to form an angle of sixty degrees with
the horizon, and some idea may be formed of the dorsals
of this singular fish.   They were lug-sails, formed not to be
acted upon by the air, but to act upon the water.   None of
my specimens show the head ; but, judging from analogies
furnished by the other families of the group, I entertain little
doubt that it will be found to be covered, not by bony plates,
but by minute scales, diminishing, as they approach the snout,
into mere points.   In none of the specimens does any part
of the internal skeleton survive.

My collection contains the remains of yet another fish of
this group, which was unfurnished with a name only a few
months ago, but which I first discovered about five years
since.   (See Plate VIII., fig. 2)   It is now designated the

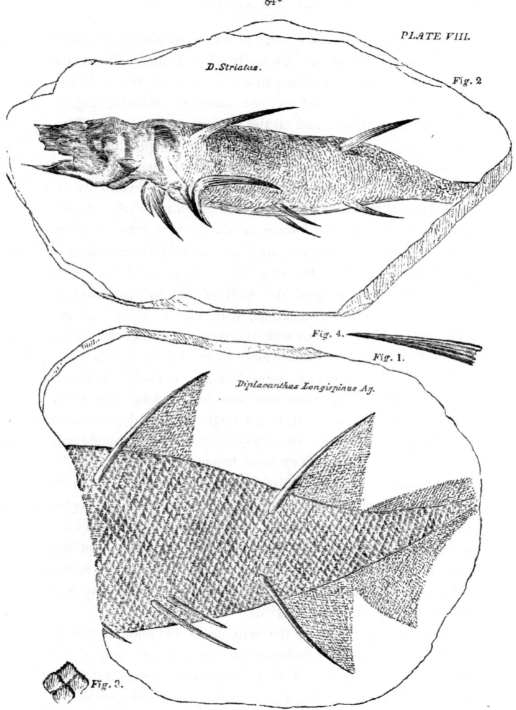

PLATE VIII.

D. Striatus.

Fig. 2

Fig. 4.

Fig. 1.

Diplacanthus Longispinus Ag.

Fig. 3.

Diplacanthus; and, though the smallest ichthyolite of the formation yet known, it is by no means the least curious. The length from head to tail, in some of my specimens, does not exceed three inches; the largest fall a little short of five. The scales, which are of such extreme minuteness that their peculiarities can be detected by only a powerful glass, resemble those of the *Cheiracanthus;* but the ridges are more waved, and seem, instead of running in nearly parallel lines, to converge towards the apex. There are two dorsals, the one rising immediately from the shoulder, a little below the nape, the other directly opposite the anal fin. The ventrals are placed near the middle of the belly. There is a curious mechanism of shoulder-bone involved with a lateral spine and with the pectorals. The creature, unlike the *Cheiracanthus,* seems to have been furnished with jaws of bone · there are fragments of bone upon the head, tubercled apparently on the outer surface; and minute cylinders of carbonate of lime running along all the larger bones, where we find them accidentally laid open, show that they were formed on internal bases of cartilage. But the best marked characteristic of the creature is furnished by the spines of its fins, which are of singular beauty. Each spine resembles a bundle of rods, or, rather, like a Gothic column, the sculptured semblance of a bundle of rods, which finely diminish towards a point, sharp and tapering as that of a rush. (See Plate VIII , fig. 4.) * The rest of the fin presents the appearance of a mere scaly membrane, and no part of the internal skeleton appears. Perhaps this last circumstance, common to all the ichthyolites of the formation, if we except the families of the *Coccosteus*

---

* Agassiz reckons four species of *Diplacanthus* — *D. crassispinus, D. longispinus, D. striatulus,* and *D. striatus.*

and *Pterichthys*, may throw some light on the apparently membranous condition of fin peculiar to the families of this order. What appears in the fossil a mere scaly membrane attached to a single spine of bone, may have had in the living animal a cartilaginous framework, like the fins of the dog-fish and thorn-back, that are amply furnished with rays of cartilage — though, of course, all such rays must have disappeared in the stone, like the rest of the internal skeleton. Unquestionably, the caudal fin of the two last described fossils must have been strengthened by some such internal framework; for, as they differ from the other fins, in being unprovided with osseous spines, they would have formed, without an internal skeleton, mere pendulous attachments, altogether unfitted to serve the purposes of instruments of motion. There may be found in the bony spines of all this order direct proof that, had there been an internal skeleton of bone, it would have survived. The spines run deep into the body, as a ship's masts run deep into her hulk; and we can see them standing up among the scales to their termination, in such bold relief, that, from a sort of pictorial illusion, they seem as if fixed to the creature's sides, and foreshortened, instead of rising in profile from its back or belly. (See Plate VIII., fig. 1) The observer will of course remember, that, in the living animal, the view of the spine must have terminated with the line of the profile, just as the view of a vessel's mast terminates with the deck, though the mast itself penetrates to the interior keel   Now, it must be deemed equally obvious, that, had the vertebral column been of bone, not of cartilage, instead of exhibiting no trace, even the faintest, of having ever existed, it would have stood out in as high relief as the internal buts or stocks of the spines   And such are the general characteristics of a few of the ichthyolites of this lower formation of the Old Red Sandstone — a few of the more striking forms, sculptured, if I may so speak, on the middle compartment of the Caithness pyramid. It would be easy rendering the list more complete at even the present stage, when the field is still so new that almost every laborer in it can exhibit genera and species unknown to his brother laborers. The remains of a species of *Holoptychius* have been discovered low in the formation, at Orkney, by Dr. Traill; similar remains have been found in it at Gamrie. In its upper beds the specimens seem so different from those in the lower, that, in extensive collections made from the inferior strata of one locality, Agassiz has been unable to identify a single specimen with the specimens of collections made from the superior strata of another, though the genera are the same. Meanwhile there are heads and hands at work on the subject, Geology has become a Briareus; and I have little doubt that, in five years hence, this third portion of the Old Red Sandstone will be found to contain as many distinct varieties of fossil fish as the whole geological scale was known to contain fifteen years ago.*

There is something very admirable in the consistency of style which obtains among the ichthyolites of this formation. In no single fish of either group do we find two styles of ornament — in scarce any two fishes do we find exactly the same style. I pass fine buildings almost every day. In some

---

* This prediction has been already more than accomplished. At the death of Cuvier, in 1832, there were but ninety-two species of fossil fish known to the geologist; Agassiz now enumerates one hundred and five species that belong to the Old Red Sandstone alone, and if we include doubtful species, on which he has not authoritatively decided — some of which, however, were included in the list of Cuvier — one hundred and fifty-one

there is a discordant jumbling — an Egyptian Sphinx, for instance, placed over a Doric portico . in all there prevails a
vast amount of timid imitation. The one repeats the other,
either in general outline or in the subordinate parts. But the
case is otherwise among the ichthyolites of the Old Red
Sandstone; nor does it lessen the wonder, that their nicer
ornaments should yield their beauty only to the microscope.
There is unity of character in every scale, plate, and fin —
unity such as all men of taste have learned to admire in
those three Grecian orders from which the ingenuity of Rome
was content to borrow, when it professed to invent — in the
masculine Doric, the chaste and graceful Ionic, the exquisitely elegant Corinthian; and yet the unassisted eye fails to discover the finer evidences of this unity : it would seem as if
the adorable Architect had wrought it out in secret with reference to the Divine idea alone. The artist who sculptured
the cherry-stone consigned it to a cabinet, and placed a microscope beside it; the microscopic beauty of these ancient
fish was consigned to the twilight depths of a primeval ocean
There is a feeling which at times grows upon the painter and
the statuary, as if the perception and love of the beautiful
had been sublimed into a kind of moral sense. Art comes
to be pursued for its own sake; the exquisite conception in
the mind, or the elegant and elaborate model, becomes all in
all to the worker, and the dread of criticism or the appetite
of praise almost nothing. And thus, through the influence
of a power somewhat akin to conscience, but whose province
is not the just and the good, but the fair, the refined, the exquisite, have works prosecuted in solitude, and never intended
for the world, been found fraught with loveliness. Sir
Thomas Lawrence, when finishing, with the most consum-
mate care, a picture intended for a semi-barbarous, foreign

court, was asked why he took so much pains with a piece destined, perhaps, never to come under the eye of a connoisseur.
" I cannot help it," he replied ; " I do the best I can, unable,
through a tyrant feeling, that will not brook offence, to do
any thing less." It would be perhaps over bold to attribute
any such overmastering feeling to the Creator ; yet certain it
is, that among his creatures well nigh all approximations
towards perfection, in the province in which it expatiates,
owe their origin to it, and that Deity in all his works is his
own rule.

The *Osteolepis* was cased, I have said, from head to tail, in
complete armor. The head had its plaited mail, the body its
scaly mail, the fins their mail of parallel and jointed bars ;
the entire suit glittered with enamel ; and every plate, bar,
and scale was dotted with microscopic points. Every ray
had its double or treble punctulated row, every scale or plate
its punctulated group ; the markings lie as thickly in proportion to the fields they cover, as the circular perforations in a
lace veil ; and the effect, viewed through the glass, is one of
lightness and beauty. In the *Cheirolepis* an entirely different
style obtains. The enamelled scales and plates glitter with
minute ridges, that show like thorns in a December morning
varnished with ice. Every ray of the fins presents its serrated
edge, every occipital plate and bone its sculptured prominences, every scale its bunch of prickle-like ridges. A more
rustic style characterized the *Glyptolepis*. The enamel of
the scales and plates is less bright ; the sculpturings are executed on a larger scale, and more rudely finished. The
relieved ridges, waved enough to give them a pendulous
appearance, drop adown the head and body. The rays of
the fins, of great length, present also a pendulous appearance. The bones and scales seem disproportionately large.

There is a general rudeness in the finish of the creature, if I may so speak, that reminds one of the tattooings of a savage or the corresponding style of art in which he ornaments the handle of his stone-hatchet or his war-club. In the *Cheiracanthus*, on the contrary, there is much of a minute and cabinet-like elegance. The silvery smoothness of the fins, dotted with scarcely visible scales, harmonized with a similar appearance of head ; a style of sculpture resembling the parallel etchings of the line-engraver fretted the scales ; the fins were small, and the contour elegant. I have already described the appearance of the unnamed fossils — the seeming shell-work that covered the sides of the one — its mast-like spines and sail-like fins ; and the Gothic-like peculiarities that characterized the other — its rodded, obelisk-like spines, and the external framework of bone that stretched along its pectorals.

Till very lately, it was held that the Old Red Sandstone of Scotland contained no mollusca. It seemed difficult, however, to imagine a sea abounding in fish, and yet devoid of shells. In all my explorations, therefore, I had an eye to the discovery of the latter, and on two several occasions I disinterred what I supposed might have formed portions of a cardium or terebratula. On applying the glass, however, the punctulated character of the surface showed that the supposed shells were but parts of the concave helmet-like plate that covered the snout of the *Osteolepis*. In the ichthyolite beds of Cromarty and Ross, of Moray, Banff, Perth, Forfar, Fife, and Berwickshire, not a single shell has yet been found ; but there have been discovered of late, in the upper beds of the Lower Old Red Sandstone in Orkney, the remains of a small, delicate bivalve, not yet described or figured but which very much resembles a *Venus*. (See Plate V., fig 7.) In the Tilestones of England, so carefully described by Mr Murchison in his *Silurian System*, shells are very abundant ; and the fact may now be regarded as established, that the Tilestones of Eng-land belong to a deposit contemporaneous with the ichthyolite beds of Caithness and Cromarty. They occupy the same place low in the base of the Old Red ; and there is at least one ichthyolite common to both,* and which does not occur in the superior strata of the system in either country — the *Dipterus maerolepidotus.* · The evidence that the fish and shells lived in the same period, and represent, therefore, the same formation, may be summed up in a single sentence. We learn from the Geology of Caithness that this species of *Dipterus* was unquestionably contemporary with all the other ichthyolites described ; — we learn from the Geology of Here-fordshire that the shells were as unquestionably contemporary with it. † These — the shells — are of a singularly mixed character, regarded as a group, uniting, says Mr. Murchison, forms at one time deemed characteristic of the more modern formations, — of the latter secondary, and even tertiary periods, — with forms the most ancient, and which characterize the molluscous remains of the transition rocks. Turbinated shells and bivalves of well nigh the recent type may be found lying side by side with chambered Orthoceratites and Tere-bratula. ‡

The vegetable remains of the formation are numerous, but obscure, consisting mostly of carbonaceous markings,

---

* *Silurian System*, part ii. p. 599.

† In Russia, too, as shown by the recent discoveries of Murchison, the Old Red fishes of Caithness, and the Old Red shells of Devon-shire, may be found lying embedded in the same strata.

‡ *Silurian System*, part i. p. 183.

such as might be formed by comminuted sea-weed. ' (See Plate VII.) Some of the impressions fork into branches at acute angles, (see figs. 4, 5, and 6 ;) some affect a waved outline, (see figs. 7 and 8,) most of them, however, are straight and undivided. They lie in some places so thickly in layers as to give the stone in which they occur a slaty character. One of my specimens shows minute markings, somewhat resembling the bird-like eyes of the Stigmaria Ficoides of the Coal Measures; — the branches of another terminate in minute hooks, that remind one of the hooks of the young tendrils of the pea when they first begin to turn. (See fig. 3.) In yet another there are marks of the ligneous fibre ; when examined by the glass, it resembles a bundle of horse-hairs lying stretched in parallel lines ; and in this specimen alone have I found aught approaching to proof of a terrestrial origin. The deposition seems to have taken place far from land ; and this lignite, if in reality such, had probably drifted far ere it at length became weightier than the supporting fluid, and sank * It is by no means rare to find fragments

---

* The organism here referred to has been since slit by the lapidary, and the sections carefully examined. It proves to be unequivocally a true wood of the coniferous class. The following is the decision regarding it of Mr William Nicol, of Edinburgh, confessedly one of our highest living authorities in that division of fossil botany which takes cognizance of the internal structure of lignites, and decides from their anatomy their race and family : —

Edinburgh, 19th July, 1845

DEAR SIR · — I have examined the structure of the fossil wood which you found in the Old Red Sandstone at Cromarty, and have no hesitation in stating, that the reticulated texture of the transverse sections, though somewhat compressed, clearly indicates a coniferous origin, but as there is not the slightest trace of a disk to be seen in the longitudinal sections parallel to the medullary rays, it is impossible to say whether it belongs to the Pine or Araucarian division   I am, &c ,

WILLIAM NICOL.

of wood that have been borne out to sea by the gulf stream
from the shores of Mexico or the West Indian Islands, stranded on the rocky coasts of Orkney and Shetland.*

The dissimilarity which obtains between the fossils of the
contemporary formations of this system in England and Scotland, is instructive. The group in the one consists mainly of
molluscous animals ; in the other, almost entirely of ichthyolites, and what seems to have been algæ. Other localities
may present us with yet different groups of the same period
— with the productions of its coasts, its lakes, and its rivers.
At present, we are but beginning to know just a little of its
littoral shells, and of the fish of its profounder depths. These
last are surely curious subjects of inquiry. We cannot catechise
our stony ichthyolites, as the necromantic lady of the *Arabian
Nights* did the colored fish of the lake, which had once been
a city, when she touched their dead bodies with her wand, and
they straightway raised their heads and replied to her queries
We would have many a question to ask them if we could —
questions never to be solved. But even the contemplation of
their remains is a powerful stimulant to thought The wonders of Geology exercise every faculty of the mind — reason,
memory, imagination ; and though we cannot put our fossils to the question, it is something to be so aroused as to
be made to put questions to one's self. I have referred to
the consistency of style which obtained among these ancient
fishes — the unity of character which marked every scale,
plate, and fin of every various family, and which distinguished it from the rest ; and who can doubt that the same
shades of variety existed in their habits and their instincts ?
We speak of the infinity of Deity — of his inexhaustible variety of mind ; but we speak of it until the idea becomes a
piece of mere commonplace in our mouths. It is well to be

10   * See Note E.

brought to feel, if not to conceive of it — to be made to know
that we ourselves are barren-minded, and that in Him "all
fulness dwelleth." Succeeding creations, each with its
myriads of existences, do not exhaust Him. He never repeats Himself. The curtain drops, at his command, over
one scene of existence full of wisdom and beauty; it rises
again, and all is glorious, wise, and beautiful as before, and
all is new. Who can sum up the amount of wisdom whose
record He has written in the rocks — wisdom exhibited in
the succeeding creations of earth, ere man was, but which
was exhibited surely not in vain? May we not say with
Milton, —

> Think not, though men were none,
> That heaven could want spectators, God want praise,
> Millions of spiritual creatures walked the earth,
> And these with ceaseless praise his works beheld ?

It is well to return on the record, and to read in its une
quivocal characters the lessons which it was intended to
teach. Infidelity has often misinterpreted its meaning, but
not the less on that account has it been inscribed for purposes
alike wise and benevolent. Is it nothing to be taught, with a
demonstrative evidence which the metaphysician cannot supply, that races are not eternal — that every family had its
beginning, and that whole creations have come to an end?

CHAPTER VI.

The Lines of the Geographer rarely right Lines. — These last, however, always worth looking at when they occur — Striking Instance in the Line of the Great Caledonian Valley. — Indicative of the Direction in which the Volcanic Agencies have operated. — Sections of the Old Red Sandstone furnished by the Granitic Eminences of the Line. — Illustration. — Lias of the Moray Frith. — Surmisings regarding its Original Extent — These lead to an Exploratory Ramble. — Narrative. — Phenomena exhibited in the course of half an hour's Walk — The little Bay — Its Strata and their Organisms.

THE natural boundaries of the geographer are rarely described by right lines. Whenever these occur, however, the geologist may look for something remarkable. There is one very striking example furnished by the north of Scotland. The reader, in consulting a map of the kingdom, will find that the edge of a ruler, laid athwart the country in a direction from south-west to north-east, touches the whole northern side of the great Caledonian Valley, with its long, straight line of lakes; and onwards, beyond the valley's termination at both ends, the whole northern side of Loch Eil and Loch Linnhe, and the whole of the abrupt and precipitous northern shores of the Moray Frith, to the extreme point of Tarbat Ness — a right line of considerably more than a hundred miles. Nor does the geography of the globe furnish a line better defined by natural marks. There is both rampart and fosse. On the one hand we have the rectilinear lochs and lakes, with an average profundity of depth more than equal to that of the German Ocean, and, added to these, the rectilinear lines of frith; on the other hand, with but few inter-

(95)

ruptions, there is an inclined wall of rock, which rises at a steep angle in the interior to nearly two thousand feet over the level of the Great Canal, and overhangs the sea towards its northern termination, in precipices of more than a hundred yards.*

The direction of this rampart and fosse — this Roman wall of Scottish geological history — seems to have been that in which the volcanic agencies chiefly operated in upheaving the entire island from the abyss. The line survives as a sort of foot-track, hollowed by the frequent tread of earthquakes, to mark the course in which they journeyed. Like one of the great lines in a trigonometrical survey, it enables us, too, to describe the lesser lines, and to determine their average bearing. *The volcanic agencies must have extended athwart the country from south-west to north-east* Mark in a map of the island — all the better if it be a geological one — the line in which most of our mountain ranges stretch across from the German Ocean to the Atlantic, — the line, too, in which our friths, lochs, and bays, on both the eastern and western coasts, and especially those of the latter, run into the interior. Mark, also, the line of the geological formations, where least broken by insulated groups of hills — the line, for instance, of the Old Red Sandstone belt, which flanks the southern base of the Grampians — the nearly parallel line of our Scottish Coal-field, in its course from sea to sea — the line* of the Grauwacke, which forms so large a portion of the south of Scotland — the line of the English Coalfield, of the Lias, of the Oolite, of the Chalk — and how in

---

* The valley of the Jordan, from the village of Laish to the southern extremity of the Dead Sea, furnishes another very remarkable instance of a geographical right line.

this process of diagonal lining, if I may so speak, the south-eastern portion of England comes to be cut off from the secondary formations altogether, and, but for the denudation of the valley of the Weald, would have exhibited only tertiary depositions. In all these lines, whether of mountains, lakes, friths, or formations, there is an approximation to parallelism with the line of the great Caledonian valley — proofs that the upheaving agency from beneath must have acted in this direction from some unknown cause, during all the immensely extended term of its operations, and along the entire length of the island. It is a fact not unworthy of remark, that the profound depths of Loch Ness undulated in strange sympathy with the reeling towers and clashing walls of Lisbon, during the great earthquake of 1755; and that the impulse, true to its ancient direction, sent the waves in huge furrows to the north-east and the south-west.

The north-eastern portion of this rectilinear wall or chain runs, for about thirty miles, through an Old Red Sandstone district. The materials which compose it are as unlike those of the plain out of which it arises, as the materials of a stone dike, running half-way into a field, are unlike the vegetable mould which forms the field's surface. The ridge itself is of a granitic texture — a true gneiss. At its base we find only conglomerates, sandstones, shales, and stratified clays, and these lying against it in very high angles. Hence the geological interest of this lower portion of the wall As has been shrewdly remarked by Mr. Murchison,* in one of his earlier papers, the gneiss seems to have been forced through the sandstone from beneath, in a solid, not a fluid form; and as the ridge a-top is a narrow one, and the sides

---

* See *Transactions of the London Geological Society* for 1828 p. 354.

10 *

remarkably abrupt — an excellent wedge, both in consistency
and form — instead of having acted on the surrounding aep-
ositions, as most of the south country traps have done that
have merely issued from a vent, and overlaid the upper
strata, it has torn up the entire formation from the very bottom.   Imagine a large wedge forced from below through a
sheet of thick ice on a river or pond.   First the ice rises in
an angle, that becomes sharper and higher as the wedge
rises ; then it cracks and opens, presenting its upturned edges
on both sides, and through comes the wedge   And this is a
very different process, be it observed, from what takes place
when the ice merely cracks, and the water issues through
the crack.   In the one case there is a rent, and water diffused over the surface ; in the other, there is the projecting
wedge, flanked by the upturned edges of the ice ; and these
edges, of course, serve as indices to decide regarding the
ice's thickness, and the various layers of which it is composed.   Now, such are the phenomena exhibited by the
wedge-like granitic ridge.   The Lower Old Red Sandstone,
tilted up against it on both sides, at an angle of about
eighty, exhibits in some parts a section of well nigh two
thousand feet, stretching from the lower conglomerate to
the soft, unfossiliferous sandstone, which forms in Ross and
Cromarty the upper beds of the formation.   There is a
mighty advantage to the geologist in this arrangement
When books are packed up in a deep box or chest, we have
to raise the upper tier ere we can see the tier below, and this
second tier ere we can arrive at a third, and so on to the bottom.   But when well arranged on the shelves of a library,
we have merely to run the eye along their lettered backs,
and we can thus form an acquaintance with them at a glance,
which in the other case would have cost us a good deal of

trouble. Now, in the neighborhood of this granitic wedge, or wall, the strata are arranged, not like books in a box, — such was their original position, — but like books on the shelves of a library. They have been unpacked and arranged by the uptilting agent, and the knowledge of them, which could only have been attained in their first circumstances by perforating them with a shaft of immense depth, may now be acquired simply by passing over their edges. A morning's saunter gives us what would have cost, but for the upheaving granite, the labor of a hundred miners for five years.

By far the greater portion of the life of the writer was spent within less than half an hour's walk of one of these upturned edges I have described the granitic rock, with reference to the disturbance it has occasioned as a wedge forced from below, and with reference to its rectilinear position in the sandstone district which it traverses, as a stone wall running half-way into a field It may communicate a still correcter and livelier idea to think of it as a row of wedges, such as one sometimes sees in a quarry when the workmen are engaged in cutting out from the mass some immense block, intended to form a stately column or huge architrave. The eminences, like the wedges, are separated, in some places the sandstone lies between — in others there occur huge chasms filled by the sea The Friths of Cromarty and Beauly, for instance, and the Bay of Munlochy, open into the interior between these wedge-like eminences ; — the well-known Sutors of Cromarty represent two of the wedges ; and it was the section furnished by the Southern Sutor that lay so immediately in the writer's neighborhood. The line of the Cromarty Frith forms an angle of about thirty-five degrees with that of the granitic line of wedge-like hills which it bisects ; and hence the peculiar shape of that tongue of land which forms the lower portion of the Black Isle, and which, washed by the Moray Frith on the one side, and by the Frith of Cromarty on the other, has its apex occupied by the Southern Sutor. Imagine a lofty promontory somewhat resembling a huge spear thrust horizontally into the sea — a ponderous mass of granitic gneiss, of about a mile in length, forming the head, and a rectilinear line of the Old Red Sandstone, more than ten miles in length, forming the shaft ; and such is the appearance which this tongue of land presents, when viewed from its north-western boundary, the Cromarty Frith. When viewed from the Moray Frith, — its south-western boundary, — we see the same granitic spear-head, but find the line of the shaft knobbed by the other granitic eminences of the chain.

Now on this tongue of land I first broke ground as a geologist. The quarry described in my introductory chapter, as that in which my notice was first attracted by the ripple markings, opens on the Cromarty Frith side of this huge spearshaft ; the quarry to which I removed immediately after, and beside which I found the fossils of the Lias, opens on its Moray Frith side. The uptilted section of sandstone occurs on both sides, where the shaft joins to the granitic spear-head, but the Lias I found on the Moray Frith side alone. It studs the coast in detached patches, sorely worn by the incessant lashings of the Frith ; and each patch bears an evident relation, in the place it occupies, to a corresponding knob or wedge in the granitic line. The Northern Sutor, as has been just said, is one of these knobs or wedges. It has its accompanying patch of Lias upheaved at its base, and lying unconformably, not only to its granitic strata, but also to its subordinate sandstones. The Southern Sutor, another of these knobs, has also its accompanying patch of Lias, which, though lying beyond the fall of the tide, strews the beach, after every storm from the east, with its shales and its fossils. The hill of Eathie is yet another knob of the series, and it, too, has its Lias patch The granitic wedges have not only uptilted the sandstone, but they have also upheaved the superincumbent Lias, which, but for their agency, would have remained buried under the waters of the Frith, and its ever accumulating banks of sand and gravel. I had remarked at an early period the correspondence of the granitic knobs with the Lias patches, and striven to realize the original place and position of the latter ere the disturbing agent had upcast them to the light. What, I have asked, was the extent of this comparatively modern formation in this part of the world, ere the line of wedges were forced through from below ? A wedge struck through the ice of a pond towards the centre breaks its continuity, and we find the ice on both sides the wedge ; whereas, when struck through at the pond edge, it merely raises the ice from the bank, and we find it, in consequence, on but one side the wedge. Whether, have I often inquired, were the granitic wedges of this line forced through the Lias at one of its edges, or at a comparatively central point? and about ten years ago I set myself to ascertain whether I could not solve the question. The Southern Sutor is a wedge open to examination on both its sides ; — the Moray Frith washes it upon one side, the Cromarty Frith on the other. Was the Lias to be found on both its sides ? If so, the wedge must have been forced *through* the formation, not merely *beside* it. It occurs, as I have said, on the Moray Frith side of the wedge ; and I resolved, on carefully exploring the Frith of Cromarty, to try whether it did not occur on that side too.

With this object I set out on an exploratory excursion, on a

delightful morning of August, 1830. The tide was falling,
it had already reached the line of half ebb; and from the
Southern Sutor to the low, long promontory on which the
town of Cromarty is built, there extended a broad belt of
mingled sand-banks and pools, accumulations of boulders, and
shingle, and large tracts darkened with algæ. I passed direct
by a grassy pathway to the Sutor, the granitic spear-head of
a late illustration, — and turned, when I reached the curved
and contorted gneiss, to trace through the broad belt left by
the retiring waters, and in a line parallel to what I have
described as the shaft of the huge spear, the beds and strata
of the Old Red Sandstone in their ascending succession. I
first crossed the conglomerate base of the system, here
little more than a hundred feet in thickness The ceaseless dash of the waves, which smooth most other rocks,
has a contrary effect on this bed, except in a few localities,
where its arenaceous cement of base is much indurated.
Under both the Northern and Southern Sutors the softer
cement yields to the incessant action, while the harder pebbles stand out in bold relief; so that, wherever it presents a
mural front to the breakers, we are reminded, by its appearance, of the artificial rockwork of the architect. It roughens
as the rocks around it polish. Quitting the conglomerate, I
next passed over a thick bed of coarse red and yellow sandstone, with here and there a few pebbles sticking from its
surface, and here and there a stratum of finer-grained fissile
sandstone inserted between the rougher strata. I then crossed
over a strata of an impure grayish limestone, and a slaty
clay, abounding, as I long afterwards ascertained, in ichthyolites and vegetable remains. There are minute veins in the
limestone (apparently cracks filled up) of a jet black bituminous substance, resembling anthracite; the stratified clay

is mottled by layers of semi-aluminous, semi-calcareous nodules, arranged like layers of flint in the upper Chalk. These nodules, when cut up and polished, present very agreeable combinations of color; there is generally an outer ring of reddish brown, an inner ring of pale yellow, and a central patch of red, and the whole is prettily veined with dark-colored carbonate of lime.* Passing onwards and upwards in the line of the strata, I next crossed over a series of alternate beds of coarse sandstone and stratified clay, and then lost sight of the rock altogether, in a wide waste of shingle and boulder-stones, resting on a dark blue argillaceous diluvium, sometimes employed in that part of the country, from its tenacious and impermeable character, for lining ponds and dams, and as mortar for the foundations of low-lying houses, exposed in wet weather to the sudden rise of water. The numerous boulders of this tract have their story to tell, and it is a curious one. The Southern Sutor, with its multitudinous fragments of gneiss, torn from its sides by the sea, or loosened by the action of frosts and storms, and rolled down its precipices, is only a few hundred yards away;—its base, where these lie thickest, has been swept by tempests, chiefly from the east, for thousands and thousands of years; and the direct effect of these tempests, regarded as transporting agents, would have been to strew this stony tract with those detached fragments. The same billow that sends its long roll from the German Ocean to sweep the base of the Sutor, and to leap up against its precipices to the height of eighty and a hundred feet, breaks in foam, only a minute after, over this stony tract;

---

* A concretionary limestone of the Old Red system in England, variegated with purple and green, was at one time wrought as a marble. — *Silurian System*, Part I. p. 176.

which has, in consequence, its sprinkling of fragments of gneiss, transported by an agency so obvious. But for every one such fragment which it bears, we find at least ten boulders that have been borne for forty and fifty miles in the opposite direction from the interior of the country — a direction in which no transporting agency now exists. The tempests of thousands of years have conveyed for but a few hundred yards not more than a tithe of the materials of this tract; nine tenths of the whole have been conveyed by an older agency over spaces of forty and fifty miles. How immensely more powerful, then, or how immensely protracted in its operation, must that older agency have been!

I passed onwards, and reached a little bay, or, rather, angular indentation of the coast, in the neighborhood of the town. It was laid bare by the tide, this morning, far beyond its outer opening; and the huge, table-like boulder, which occupies nearly its centre, and to which, in a former chapter, I have had occasion to refer, held but a middle place between the still darkened flood-line that ran high along the beach, and the brown line of ebb that bristled far below with forests of the rough-stemmed tangle. This little bay, or inflection of the coast, serves as a sort of natural wear in detaining floating drift-weed, and is often found piled, after violent storms from the east, with accumulations, many yards in extent, and several feet in depth, of kelp and tangle, mixed with zoophytes and mollusca, and the remains of fish killed among the shallows by the tempest. Early in the last century, a large body of herrings, pursued by whales and porpoises, were stranded in it, to the amount of several hundred barrels; and it is said that salt and cask failed the packers when but comparatively a small portion of the shoal were cured, and that by much the greatest part of them were car-

ried away by the neighboring farmers for manure. Ever
since the formation of the present coast-line, this natural wear
has been arresting, tide after tide, its heaps of organic matter,
but the circumstances favorable to their preservation have
been wanting : they ferment and decay when driven high on
the beach ; and the next spring-tide, accompanied by a gale
from the west, sweeps every vestige of them away ; and so,
after the lapse of many centuries, we find no other organisms
among the rounded pebbles that form the beach of this little
bay, than merely a few broken shells, and occasionally a
mouldering fish-bone.   Thus very barren formations may
belong to periods singularly rich in organic existences. When
what is now the little bay was the bottom of a profound
ocean, and far from any shore, the circumstances for the
preservation of its organisms must have been much more
favorable.   In no locality in the Old Red Sandstone with
which I am acquainted have such beautifully preserved fossils been found.   But I anticipate

In the middle of the little bay, and throughout the greater
part of its area, I found the rock exposed — a circumstance
which I had marked many years before, when a mere boy,
without afterwards recurring to it as one of interest   But I
had now learned to look at rocks with another eye ; and the
thought which first suggested itself to me regarding the rock
of the little bay was, that I had found the especial object of
my search — the Lias   The appearances are in some respects not dissimilar. The Lias of the north of Scotland is
represented in some localities by dark-colored, unctuous
clays, in others by grayish black sandstones, that look like
indurated mud, and in others by beds of black fissile shale,
alternating with bands of coarse, impure limestone, and
studded between the bands with limestone nodules of richer

11

quality and finer grain. The rock laid bare in the little bay
is a stratified clay, of a gray color tinged with olive, and occurring in beds separated by indurated bands of gray, micaceous sandstone. They also abound in calcareous nodules.
The dip of the strata, too, is very different from that of the
beds which lean against the gneiss of the Sutor. Instead of
an angle of eighty, it presents an angle of less than eight.
The rocks of the little bay must have lain beyond the disturbing, uptilting influence of the granitic wedge. So
thickly are the nodules spread over the surface of some of
the beds, that they reminded me of floats of broken ice on
the windward side of a lake after a few days' thaw, when
the edges of the fragments are smoothed and rounded, and
they press upon one another, so as to cover, except in the
angular interstices, the entire surface.

I set myself carefully to examine The first nodule I laid
open contained a bituminous looking mass, in which I could
trace a few pointed bones and a few minute scales. The
next abounded in rhomboidal and finely enamelled scales, of
much larger size and more distinct character. I wrought on
with the eagerness of a discoverer entering for the first time
in a *terra incognita* of wonders. Almost every fragment of
clay, every splinter of sandstone, every limestone nodule,
contained its organism — scales, spines, plates, bones, entire
fish ; but not one organism of the Lias could I find — no ammonites, no belemnites, no gryphites, no shells of any kind :
the vegetable impressions were entirely different ; and not a
single scale, plate, or ichthyodorulite could I identify with
those of the newer formation. I had got into a different
world, and among the remains of a different creation ; but
where was its proper place in the scale ? The beds of the
little bay are encircled by thick accumulations of diluvium

and debris, nor could I trace their relation to a single known rock. I was struck, as I well might, by the utter strangeness of the forms — the oar-like arms of the *Pterichthys* and its tortoise-like plates — the strange, buckler-looking head of the *Coccosteus*, which, I suppose, might possibly be the back of a small tortoise, though the tubercles reminded me rather of the skin of the shark — the polished scales and plates of the *Osteolepis* — the spined and scaled fins of the *Cheiracanthus* — above all, the one-sided tail of at least eight out of the ten or twelve varieties of fossil which the deposit contained. All together excited and astonished me. But some time elapsed ere I learned to distinguish the nicer generic differences of the various organisms of the formation. I found fragments of the *Pterichthys* on this morning; but I date its discovery, in relation to the mind of the discoverer, more than a twelvemonth later * I confounded the *Cheiracanthus*, too, with its single-spined, membranous dorsal, with *Diplacanthus* ichthyolite, furnished with two such dorsals; and the *Diplopterus* with the *Osteolepis* Still, however, I saw enough to

---

* I find, by some notes, which had escaped my notice when drawing up for the *Witness* newspaper the sketches now expanded into a volume, that in the year 1834 I furnished the collection of a geological friend, the Rev. John Swanson, minister of the parish of Small Isles, in the Outer Hebrides, with a well-marked specimen of the *Pterichthys Milleri*. The circumstance pleasingly reminds me of the first of all my early acquaintance, who learned to deem the time not idly squandered that was spent in exploring the wonders of bygone creations Does the minister of Small Isles still remember the boy who led him in quest of petrifactions — himself a little boy at the time — to a deep, solitary cave on the Moray Frith, where they lingered amidst stalactites and mosses till the wild sea had surrounded them unmarked, barring all chance of retreat, and the dark night came on ?

exhilarate and interest : I wrought on till the advancing tide
came splashing over the nodules, and a powerful August sun
had risen towards the middle sky ; and were I to sum up all
my happier hours, the hour would not be forgotten in which
I sat down on a rounded boulder of granite, by the edge of
the sea, when the last bed was covered, and spread out on the
beach before me the spoils of the morning.

CHAPTER VII.

Further Discoveries of the Ichthyolite Beds. — Found in one Locality under a Bed of Peat. — Discovered in another beneath an ancient Burying-ground. — In a third underlying the Lias Formation. — In a fourth overtopped by a still older Sandstone Deposit — Difficulties in ascertaining the true Place of a newly-discovered Formation. — Caution against drawing too hasty Inferences from the mere circumstance of Neighborhood. — The Writer receives his first Assistance from without. — *Geological Appendix* of the Messrs Anderson, of Inverness. — Further Assistance from the Researches of Agassiz. — Suggestions — Dr John Malcolmson — His Extensive Discoveries in Moray. — He submits to Agassiz a Drawing of the *Pterichthys.* — Place of the Ichthyolites in the Scale at length determined — Two distinct Platforms of Being in the Formation to which they belong

I COMMENCED forming a small collection, and set myself carefully to examine the neighboring rocks for organisms of a similar character The eye becomes practised in such researches, and my labors were soon repaid. Directly above the little bay there is a cornfield, and beyond the field a wood of forest trees; and in this wood. in the bottom of a watercourse, scooped out of the rock through a bed of peat, I found the stratified clay charged with scales. A few hundred yards farther to the west there is a deep, wooded ravine cut through a thick bed of red diluvial clay. The top of the bank directly above is occupied by the ruins of an ancient chapel, and a group of moss-grown tombstones; and in the gorge of this ravine, underlying the little field of graves by about sixty feet, I discovered a still more ancient place of sepulture — that of the ichthyolites. I explored every bank, rock, and ravine on the northern or Cromarty Frith side of the tongue of land, with its terminal point of granitic gneiss, to which I have had such frequent occasion to refer, and then turned to explore the southern, or Moray Frith side, in the rectilinear line of the great valley. And here I was success-ful on a larger scale. A range of lofty sandstone cliffs, hol-lowed by the sea, extends for a distance of about two miles between two of the granitic knobs or wedges of the line — the Southern Sutor and the hill of Eathie. And along well nigh the entire length of this range of cliffs, I succeeded in tracing a continuous ichthyolite bed, abounding in remains, and lying far below the Lias, and unconformable to it. I pur-sued my researches, and in the sides of a romantic precipi-tous dell, through which the Burn of Eathie — a small, mossy stream — finds its way to the Moray Frith, I again discovered the fish-beds running deep into the interior of the country, with immense strata of a pale yellow sandstone resting over them, and strata of a chocolate red lying below   But their place in the geological scale was still to fix.

I had seen enough to convince me that they form a contin-uous convex stratum in the sandstone spear-shaft, covering it saddle-wise from side to side, dipping towards the Moray Frith on the south, and to the Cromarty Frith on the north — that, as in a *bona fide* spear-shaft, the annual ring or layer of growth of one season is overlaid by the annual rings of suc-ceeding seasons, and underlaid by those of preceding ones; so this huge semi-ring of fossiliferous clays and limestones had its underlying semi-ring of Red Sandstone, and its over-lying semi-rings of yellow, of red, and of gray sandstone. I knew, besides, that beneath there was a semi-ring of conglom-erate, the base of the system; and that, for more than two hundred yards upwards, ring followed ring in unbroken succession — now sandstone, now limestone, now stratified clay. But though intimately acquainted with these lower rocks for more than a hundred fathoms from their base upwards, and with the upper rocks on both sides the ichthyolitic bed for more than a hundred feet, there was an intervening hiatus, whose extent at this period I found it impossible to ascertain And hence my uncertainty regarding the place of the ichthyolites, seeing that whole formations might be represented by the occurring gap. On the Moray Frith side, where the sections are of huge extent, a doubtful repeat in the strata at one point of junction, and an abrupt fault at another, cuts off the upper series of beds to which the organisms belong, from the lower to which the great conglomerate belongs. On the Cromarty Frith side the sections are mere detached patches, obscured at every point by diluvium and soil; and, in conceiving of the whole as a continuous line, with the Lias a-top and the granite group at the bottom, I was ever reminded of those coast-lines of the ancient geographers, where a few uncertain dots, a few deeper markings, and here and there a blank space or two, showed the blended results of conjecture and discovery — whether they give a *Terra Incognita Australia* to the one hemisphere, or a North-Western passage to the other. The ichthyolites in a section so doubtful might be regarded as belonging to either the Old or the New Red Sandstone — to the Coal Measures, or to the Mountain Limestone. All was uncertainty.

One remark in the passing it may teach the young geologist to be cautious in his inferences, and illustrate, besides, those gaps which occur in the geological scale I had now discovered the ichthyolite beds in five different localities; in one of these — the first discovered — there is no overlying stratum; it seems as if the bed formed the top of the forma-

tion : in all the others the overlying stratum is different, and
belongs to distant and widely separated ages.   We cut in one
locality through a peat moss — part of the ruins, perhaps, of
one of those forests which covered, about the commencement
of the Christian era, well nigh the entire surface of the island,
and sheltered the naked inhabitants from the legions of Agric-
ola.   We find, as we dig, huge trunks of oak and elm, cones
of the Scotch fir, handfuls of hazel-nuts, and bones and horns
of the roe and the red deer.   The writer, when a boy, found
among the peat the horn of a gigantic elk.   And, forming
the bottom of this recent deposit, and *lying conformably to it*,
we find the ichthyolite beds, with their antique organisms.
The remains of oak and elm leaves, and of the spikes and
cones of the pine, lie within half a foot of the remains of
the *Coccosteus* and *Diplopterus*.   We dig in another locality
through an ancient burying-ground ; we pass through a superior stratum of skulls and coffins, and an inferior stratum,
barren in organic remains, and then arrive at the stratified
clays, with their ichthyolites.   In a third locality we find
these in junction with the Lias, and underlying its lignites,
ammonites, and belemnites, just as we see them underlying, in
the other two, the human bones and the peat moss.   And in
yet a fourth locality we see them overlaid by immense arenaceous   beds, that belong evidently, as their mineralogical
character testifies, to either the Old or the New Red Sandstone.   The convulsions and revolutions of the geological world,
like those of the political, are sad confounders of place and
station, and bring into close fellowship the high and the low ;
nor is it safe in either world, — such have been the effects of
the disturbing agencies, — to judge of ancient relations by
existing neighborhoods, or of original situations by present
places of occupancy.   " Misery," says Shakspeare, " makes

strange bedfellows " The changes and convulsions of the
geological world have made strange bedfellows too. I have
seen fossils of the Upper Lias and of the Lower Old Red Sandstone washed together by the same wave, out of what might
be taken, on a cursory survey, for the same bed, and then
mingled with recent shells, algæ, branches of trees, and fragments of wrecks on the same sea-beach.

Years passed, and in 1834 I received my first assistance
from without, through the kindness of the Messrs. Anderson,
of Inverness, who this year published their *Guide to the
Highlands and Islands of Scotland* — a work which has
never received half its due measure of praise. It contains,
in a condensed and very pleasing form, the accumulated
gleanings, for half a lifetime, of two very superior men,
skilled in science, and of highly cultivated taste and literary
ability ; whose remarks, from their intimate acquaintance
with every foot-breadth of country which they describe, invariably exhibit that freshness of actual observation, recorded
on the spot, which Gray regarded as " worth whole cart-loads
of recollection." But what chiefly interested me in their
work was its dissertative appendices — admirable digests of
the Natural History, Antiquities, and Geology of the country.
The appendix devoted to Geology, consisting of fifty closely
printed pages, — abridged in part from the highest geological
authorities, and in much greater part the result of original
observation, — contains, beyond comparison, the completest
description of the rocks, fossils, and formations of the Northern and Western Highlands, which has yet been given to the
public in a popular form. I perused it with intense interest,
and learned from it, for the first time, of the fossil fishes of
Caithness and Gamrie.

There was almost nothing known, at the period, of the

oryctology of the older rocks — little, indeed, of that of the
Old Red Sandstone, in its proper character as such ; and with
no such guiding clew as has since been furnished by Agassiz,
and the later researches of Mr. Murchison, the writer of the
appendix had recorded as his ultimate conclusion, that " the
middle schistoze system of Caithness, containing the fossil
fish, was intermediate in geological character and position
between the Old and New Red Sandstone formations " The
ichthyolites of Gamrie he described as resembling those of
Caithness ; and I at once recognized, in his minute descriptions of both, the fossil fish of Cromarty. The mineralogical
accompaniments, too, seemed nearly the same. In Caithness,
the animal remains are mixed up in some places with a black
bituminous matter like tar. I had but lately found among the
beds of the little bay a mass of soft adhesive bitumen, her-
metically sealed up in the limestone, which, when broken
open, reminded me, from the powerful odor it cast, and which
filled for several days the room in which I kept it, of the old
Gaulish mummy of which we find so minute account in the
Natural History of Goldsmith. The nodules which enclosed
the organisms at Gamrie were described as of a sub-crystalline,
radiating, fibrous structure. So much was this the case with
some of the nodules at Cromarty, that they had often reminded
me, when freshly broken, though composed of pure carbonate
of lime, of masses of asbestos. The scales and bones of
the Caithness ichthyolites were blended, it was stated, with
the fragments of a " supposed tortoise nearly allied to trionyx ;"
one of the ichthyolites, a *Dipterus*, was characterized by large
scales, a double dorsal, and a one-sided tail ; the entire lack
of shells and zoophytes was remarked, and the abundance of
obscure vegetable impressions. In short, had the accomplished writer of the appendix been briefly describing the beds

at Cromarty, instead of those of Caithness and Gamrie, he might have employed the same terms, and remarked the same circumstances — the striated nodules, the mineral tar, the vegetable impressions, the absence of shells and zoophytes, the large-scaled, and double-finned ichthyolites — the peculiarities of which applied equally to the *Dipterus* and *Diplopterus* — and the supposed tortoise, in which I once recognized the *Coccosteus*. It was much to know, that this doubtful formation — for as doubtful I still regarded it — was of such considerable extent, and occurred in localities so widely separated. I corresponded with the courteous author of the appendix, at that time General Secretary to the Northern Institution for the Promotion of Science and Literature, and Conservator of its Museum ; and, forwarding to him duplicates of some of my better specimens, had, as I had anticipated, the generic identity of the Cromarty ichthyolites with those of Caithness and Gamrie fully confirmed.

My narrative is, I am afraid, becoming tedious ; but it embodies somewhat more than the mere history of a sort of Robinson Crusoe in Geology, cut off for years from all intercourse with his kind. It contains, also, the history of a formation in its connection with science ; and the reader will, I trust, bear with me for a few pages more Seasons passed ; and I received new light from the researches of Agassiz, which, if it did not show me my way more clearly, rendered it at least more interesting, by associating with it one of those wonderful truths, stranger that fictions, which rise ever and anon from the profounder depths of science, and whose use, in their connection with the human intellect, seems to be to stimulate the faculties. I have often had occasion to refer to the one-sided condition of tail characteristic of the ichthyolites of the Old Red Sandstone. It characterizes, says Agassiz, the fish of all the more ancient formations. At one certain point in the descending scale Nature entirely alters her plan in the formation of the tail. All the ichthyolites above are fashioned after one particular type — all below after another and different type   The bibliographer can tell at what periods in the history of letters one character ceased to be employed and another came into use. Black letter, for instance, in our own country, was scarce ever resorted to for purposes of general literature after the reign of James VI. ; and in manuscript writing the Italian hand superseded the Saxon about the close of the seventeenth century.   Now, is it not truly wonderful to find an analogous change of character in that pictorial history of the past which Geology furnishes ?   From the first appearance of vertebrated existences to the middle beds of the New Red Sandstone, — a space including the Upper Ludlow rocks, the Old Red Sandstone in all its members, the Mountain Limestone, with the Limestone of Burdie House, the Coal Measures, the Lower New Red, and the Magnesian Limestone, — we find only the ancient or unequally lobed type of tail.   In all the formations above, including the Lias, the Oolite, Middle, Upper, and Lower, the Wealden, the Green-Sand, the Chalk, and the Tertiary, we find only the equally-lobed condition of tail.   And it is more than probable, that, with the tail, the character of the skeleton also changed ; that the more ancient type characterized, throughout, the semi-cartilaginous order of fishes, just as the more modern type characterizes the osseous fishes ; and that the upper line of the Magnesian Limestone marks the period at which the order became extinct.   Conjecture lacks footing in grappling with a revolution so extensive and so wonderful   Shall I venture to throw out a suggestion on the subject, in connection with another suggestion which has emanated from one of the first of living geologists? Fish, of all existing creatures, seem the most capable of sustaining high degrees of heat, and are to be found in some of the hot springs of Continental Europe, where it is supposed scarce any other animal could live. Now, all the fish of the ancient type are thickly covered by a defensive armor of bone, arranged in plates, bars, or scales, or all the three modes together, as in the *Osteolepis* and one half its contemporaries. The one-sided tail is united invariably to a strong cuirass. And it has been suggested by Dr. Buckland, that this strong cuirass may have formed a sort of defence against the injurious effects of a highly heated surrounding medium. The suggestion is, of course, based purely on hypothesis. It may be stated, in direct connection with it, however, that in the Lias — the first richly fossiliferous formation overlying that in which the change occurred — we find, for the first time in the geological system, decided indications of a change of seasons. The foot-prints of winter are left impressed amid the lignites of the Cromarty Lias. In a specimen now before me, the alternations of summer heat and winter cold are as distinctly marked in the annual rings as in the pines or larches of our present forests, whereas in the earlier lignites, contemporary with ichthyolites of the ancient type, either no annual rings appear, or the markings, if present, are both faint and unfrequent. *Just ere winter began to take its place among the seasons, the fish fitted for living in a highly heated medium disappeared :* they were created to inhabit a thermal ocean, and died away as it cooled down. Fish of a similar type may now inhabit the seas of Venus, or even of Jupiter, which, from its enormous bulk, though greatly more distant from the sun than our earth, may still powerfully retain the internal heat.

12

I still pursued my inquiries, and received a valuable auxiliary in a gentleman from India, Dr. John Malcolmson, of Madras — a member of the London Geological Society, and a man of high scientific attainments and great general knowledge. Above all, I found him to possess, in a remarkable degree, that spirit of research, almost amounting to a passion, which invariably marks the superior man. He had spent month after month under the burning sun of India, amid fever marshes and tiger jungles, acquainting himself with the unexplored geological field which, only a few years ago, that vast continent presented, and in collecting fossils hitherto unnamed and undescribed. He had pursued his inquiries, too, along the coasts of the Red Sea, and far upwards on the banks of the Nile ; and now, in returning for a time to his own country, he had brought with him the determination of knowing it thoroughly as a man of science and a geologist. I had the pleasure of first introducing him to the ichthyolites of the Lower Old Red Sandstone, by bringing him to my first-discovered bed, and laying open, by a blow of the hammer, a beautiful *Osteolepis*. He was much interested in the fossils of my little collection, and at once decided that the formation which contained them could be no representative of the Coal Measures. After ranging over the various beds on both sides the rectilinear ridge, and acquainting himself thoroughly with their organisms, he set out to explore the Lower Old Red Sandstones of Moray and Banff, hitherto deemed peculiarly barren, but whose character too much resembled that of the rocks which he had now ascertained to be so abundant in fossils, not to be held worthy of further examination. He explored the banks of the Spey, and found the ichthyolite beds extensively developed at Dipple, in the middle of an Old Red Sandstone district. He pursued his researches, and traced the formation in ravines and the beds of rivers, from the village of Buckie to near the field of Culloden ; he found it exposed in the banks of the Nairn, in the ravines above Cawdor Castle, on the eastern side of the hill of Rait, at Clune, Lethenbar, and in the vale of Rothes — and in every instance low in the Old Red Sandstone. The formation hitherto deemed so barren in remains proved one of the richest of them all, if not in tribes and families, at least in individual fossils ; and the reader may form some idea of the extent in which it has already been proved fossiliferous, when he remembers that the tract includes as its extremes Orkney, Gamrie, and the north-eastern gorge of the great Caledonian Valley. The ichthyolites were discovered in the latter locality in the quarry of Inches, three miles beyond Inverness, by Mr. George Anderson, the gentleman to whose geological attainments, as one of the authors of the *Guide Book*, I have lately had occasion to refer.

I had now corresponded for several years with a little circle of geological friends, and had described in my letters, and in some instances had attempted to figure in them, my newly-found fossils. A letter which I wrote early in 1838 to Dr. Malcolmson, then at Paris, and which contained a rude drawing of the *Pterichthys*, was submitted to Agassiz, and the curiosity of the naturalist was excited. He examined the figure, rather, however, with interest than surprise, and read the accompanying description, not in the least inclined to scepticism by the singularity of its details. He had looked on too many wonders of a similar cast to believe that he had exhausted them, or to evince any astonishment that Geology should be found to contain one wonder more. Some months after, I sent a restored drawing of the same fossil to the Elgin Scientific Society. I must state, however, that the restoration was by no means complete The paddle-like arms were placed further below the shoulders than in any actual species; and I had transferred, by mistake, to the creature's upper side, some of the plates of the *Coccosteus.* Still the type was unequivocally that of the *Pterichthys.* The secretary of the Society, Mr Patrick Duff, an excellent geologist, to whose labors, in an upper formation of the Old Red Sandstone, I shall have afterwards occasion to refer, questioned, as he well might, some of the details of the figure, and we corresponded for several weeks regarding it, somewhat in the style of Jonathan Oldbuck and his antiquarian friend, who succeeded in settling the meaning of two whole words, in an antique inscription, in little more than two years. Most of the other members looked upon the entire drawing, so strange did the appearance seem, as embodying a fiction of the same class with those embodied in the pictured griffins and unicorns of mythologic Zoology; and, in amusing themselves with it, they bestowed on its betailed and bepaddled figure, as if in anticipation of Agassiz, the name of the draughtsman. Not many months after, however, a *bona fide Pterichthys* turned up in one of the newly discovered beds of Nairnshire, and the Association ceased to joke, and began to wonder. I merely mention the circumstance in connection with a right challenged, at the late meeting of the British Association at Glasgow, by a gentleman of Elgin, to be regarded as the original discoverer of the *Pterichthys.* I am, of course, far from supposing that the discovery was not actually made, but regret that it should have been kept so close a secret at a time when it might have stood the other discoverer of the creature in such stead.

The exact place of the ichthyolites in the system was still to fix. I was spending a day, early in the winter of 1839,

among the nearly vertical strata that lean against the Northern Sutor. The section there presented is washed by the
tide for nearly three hundred yards from where it rests on
the granitic gneiss; and each succeeding stratum in the
ascending order may be as clearly traced as the alternate
white and black squares in a marble pavement. First there
is a bed of conglomerate two hundred and fifteen feet in
thickness, "identical in structure," say Professor Sedgwick
and Mr. Murchison, "with the older red conglomerates of
Cumberland and the Island of Arran,* and which cannot be
distinguished from those conglomerates which lean against
the southern flank of the Grampians, and on which Dunnot-
tar Castle is built. Immediately above the conglomerate
there is a hundred and fourteen feet more of coarse sandstone strata, of a reddish yellow hue, with occasionally a few
pebbles enclosed, and then twenty-seven feet additional of
limestone and stratified clay. There are no breaks, no
faults, no thinning out of strata — all the beds lie parallel,
showing regular deposition. I had passed over the section
twenty times before, and had carefully examined the limestone and the clay, but in vain. On this occasion, however,
I was more fortunate. I struck off a fragment. It contained
a vegetable impression of the same character with those of
the ichthyolite beds; and after an hour's diligent search, I
had turned out from the heart of the stratum plates and scales
enough to fill a shelf in a museum — the helmet-like snout

---

* Different in one respect from the conglomerates of Arran. It
abounds in rolled fragments of granite, whereas in those of Arran
there occur no pebbles of this rock. Arran has now its granite in
abundance; the northern locality has none, though, when the conglomerates of the Lower Old Red Sandstone were in the course of
forming, the case was exactly the reverse.

of an *Osteolepis*, the thorn-like spine of a *Cheiracanthus*, and
a *Coccosteus* well nigh entire. I had at length, after a search
of nearly ten years, found the true place of the ichthyolite
bed. The reader may smile, but I hope the smile will be a
good-natured one ; a simple pleasure may be not the less sincere on account of its simplicity , and " little things are great
to little men." I passed over and over the strata, and found
there could be no mistake The place of the fossil fish in
the scale is little more than a hundred feet above the top, and
not much more than a hundred yards above the base of the
great conglomerate ; and there lie over it in this section about
five hundred feet of soft, arenaceous stone, with here and
there alternating bands of limestone and beds of clay studded
with nodules — all belonging to the inferior Old Red Sandstone.

The enormous depth of the Old Red Sandstone of Eng
land has been divided by Mr Murchison into three members,
or formations — the division adopted in his *Elements* by Mr.
Lyell, as quoted in an early chapter. These are, the lowest,
or Tilestone formation, the middle, or Cornstone formation,
and the uppermost, or Quartzose conglomerate formation.
The terms are derived from mineralogical characters, and in
adequate as designations, therefore, like that of the Old Red
Sandstone itself, which, in many of its deposits, is not sandstone, and is not *red*. But they serve to express great natural
divisions. Now the Tilestone member of England represents, as I have already stated, this Lower Old Red Sandstone formation of Scotland ; but its extent of vertical development, compared with that of the other two members of
the system, is strikingly different in the two countries. The
Tilestones compose the least of the three divisions in England ; their representative in Scotland forms by much the

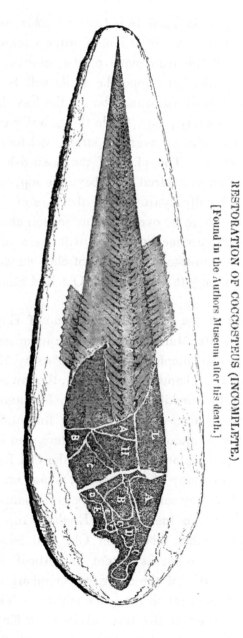

PLATE IX.

RESTORATION OF COCCOSTEUS (INCOMPLETE.)

[Found in the Author's Museum after his death.]

greatest of the three ; and there seems to be zoological as well as lithological evidence that its formation must have occupied no brief period. *The same genera occur in its upper as in its lower beds, but the species appear to be different.* I shall briefly state the evidence of this very curious fact.

The seat of Sir William Gordon Cumming, of Altyre, is in the neighborhood of one of the Morayshire deposits discovered by Mr. Malcolmson ; and for the greater part of the last two years Lady Gordon Cumming has been engaged in making a collection of its peculiar fossils, which already fills an entire apartment. The object of her Ladyship was the illustration of the Geology of the district, and all she sought in it on her own behalf was congenial employment for a singularly elegant and comprehensive mind. But her labors have rendered her a benefactor to science. Her collection was visited, shortly after the late meeting of the British Association in Glasgow, by Agassiz and Dr. Buckland ; and great was the surprise and delight of the philosophers to find that the whole was new to Geology. All the species, amounting to eleven, and at least one of the genera, that of the *Glyptolepis*, were different from any Agassiz had ever seen or described before. The deposit so successfully explored by her Ladyship occurs high in the lower formation. Agassiz, shortly after, in comparing the collection of Dr. Traill (a collection formed at Orkney) with that of the writer, (a collection made at Cromarty,) was struck by the specific identity of the specimens. In the instances in which the genera agreed, he found that the species agreed also, though the ichthyolites of both differed specifically from the ichthyolites of Caithness, which occur chiefly in the upper beds of the formation, and from those also of Lady Cumming of Altyre, which occur, as I have said, at the top. And in examining into the cause, it was found that the two collections, though furnished by localities more than a hundred miles apart, were yet derived, if I may so express myself, from the same low platform, both alike representing the fossiliferous base of the system, and both removed but by a single stage from the great unfossiliferous conglomerate below. Thus there seem to be what may be termed two stories of being in this lower formation — stories in which the groups, though generically identical, are specifically dissimilar.*

---

* Since this period, however, several species identical with those of Cromarty have been found in the Morayshire deposits.

CHAPTER VIII.

Upper Formations of the Old Red Sandstone — Room enough for each and to spare. — Middle, or Cornstone Formation. — The *Cephalaspis* its most characteristic Organism — Description. — The Den of Balruddery richer in the Fossils of this middle Formation than any other Locality yet discovered. — Various Contemporaries of the *Cephalaspis*. — Vegetable Impressions. — Gigantic Crustacean. — *Seraphim.* — Ichthyodorulites. — Sketch of the Geology of Forfarshire. — Its older Deposits of the Cornstone Formation. — The Quarries of Carmylie — Their Vegetable and Animal Remains — The Upper Formation. — Wide Extent of the Fauna and Flora of the earlier Formations. — Probable Cause.

HITHERTO I have dwelt almost exclusively on the fossils of the Lower Old Red Sandstone, and the history of their discovery: I shall now ascend to the organisms of its higher platforms. The system in Scotland, as in the sister kingdom, has its middle and upper groups, and these are in no degree less curious than the inferior group already described, nor do they more resemble the existences of the present time. Does the reader remember the illustration of the pyramid employed in an early chapter — its three parallel bars, and the strange hieroglyphics of the middle bar? Let him now imagine another pyramid, inscribed with the remaining and later history of the system. We read, as before, from the base upwards, but find the broken and half-defaced characters of the second erection descending into the very soil, as in those obelisks of Egypt round which the sands of the desert have been accumulating for ages. Hence a hiatus in our history for future excavators to fill; and it contains many such blanks, every unfossiliferous bar in either pyramid represent-

(125)

ing a gap in the record. Three distinct formations the group undoubtedly contains — perhaps more; nor will the fact appear strange to the reader who remembers how numerous the formations are that lie over and under it, and that its vast depth of ten thousand feet equals that of the whole secondary system from top to bottom. Eight such formations as the Oolite, or ten such formations as the Chalk, could rest, the one over the other, in the space occupied by a group so enormous. To the evidence of its three distant formations, which is of a very simple character, I shall advert as I go along.

The central or Cornstone division of the system in England is characterized throughout its vast depth by a peculiar family of ichthyolites, which occur in none of the other divisions. I have already had occasion to refer to the *Cephalaspis.* Four species of this fish have been discovered in the Cornstones of Hereford, Salop, Worcester, Monmouth, and Brecon;* "and as they are always found," says Mr. Murchison, "in the same division of the Old Red System, they have become valuable auxiliaries in enabling the geologist to identify its subdivisions through England and Wales, and also to institute direct comparisons between the different strata of the Old Red Sandstone of England and Scotland."† The *Cephalaspis* is one of the most curious ichthyolites of the system. (See Plate XIII., fig. 1.) Has the reader ever seen a saddler's cutting knife? — a tool with a crescent-shaped blade, and the handle fixed transversely in the centre of its concave side. In general outline the *Cephalaspis* resembled this tool — the crescent-shaped blade representing the head the transverse handle the body. We have but to give the

---

* *Cephalaspis Lewisii, C. Lloydii, C. Lyellii,* and *C. rostratus*
† See Note E 2.

handle an angular, instead of a rounded shape, and to press together the pointed horns of the crescent, till they incline towards each other, and the convex, or sharpened edge, is elongated into a semi-ellipse, cut in the line of its shortest diameter, in order to produce the complete form of the *Cephalaspis*. The head, compared with the body, was of great size — comprising fully one third the creature's entire length. In the centre, and placed closely together, as in many of the flat fish, were the eyes. Some of the specimens show two dorsals, and an anal and caudal fin. The thin and angular body presents a jointed appearance, somewhat like that of a lobster or trilobite. Like the bodies of most of the ichthyolites of the system, it was covered with variously formed scales of bone ; the creature's head was cased in strong plates of the same material, the whole upper side lying under one huge buckler — and hence the name *Cephalaspis*, or buckler-head. In proportion to its strength and size, it seems to have been amply furnished with weapons of defence. Such was the strength and massiveness of its covering, that its remains are found comparatively entire in arenaceous rocks impregnated with iron, in which few other fossils could have survived. Its various species, as they occur in the Welsh and English Cornstones, says Mr. Murchison, seem " not to have been suddenly killed and entombed, but to have been long exposed to submarine agencies, such as the attacks of animals, currents, concretionary action," &c. ; and yet, " though much dismembered, the geologist has little difficulty in recognizing even the smallest portions of them " Nor does it seem to have been quite unfurnished with offensive weapons. The sword-fish, with its strong and pointed spear, has been known to perforate the oaken ribs of the firmest built vessels ; and poised and directed by its lesser fins, and impelled by its

13

powerful tail, it may be regarded either as an arrow or javelin flung with tremendous force, or as a knight speeding to the encounter with his lance in rest. Now there are missiles employed in Eastern warfare, which, instead of being pointed like the arrow or javelin, are edged somewhat like the crooked falchion or saddler's cutting-knife, and which are capable of being cast with such force, that they have been known to sever a horse's leg through the bone; and if the sword-fish may be properly compared to an arrow or javelin, the combative powers of the *Cephalaspis* may be illustrated, it is probable, by a weapon of this kind — the head all around its elliptical margin presenting a sharp edge, like that of a cutting-knife, or falchion. Its impetus, however, must have been comparatively small, for its organs of motion were so: it was a bolt carefully fashioned, but a bolt cast from a feeble bow. But if weak in the assault, it must have been formidable when assailed. " The pointed horns of the crescent," said Agassiz to the writer, " seem to have served a similar purpose with the spear-like wings of the *Pterichthys*," — the sole difference consisting in the circumstance, that the spears of the one could be elevated or depressed at pleasure, whereas those of the other were ever fixed in the warlike attitude. And such was the *Cephalaspis* of the Cornstones — not only the most characteristic, but in England and Wales almost the sole organism of the formation. (See Note F.)

Now of this curious ichthyolite we find no trace among the fossils of the Lower Old Red Sandstone. It occurs neither in Orkney nor Cromarty, Caithness nor Gamrie, Nairnshire nor the inferior ichthyolite beds of Moray. Neither in England nor in Scotland is it to be found in the Tilestone formation, or its equivalent It is common, however, in the Old Red Sandstone of Forfarshire; and it occurs at Balruddery

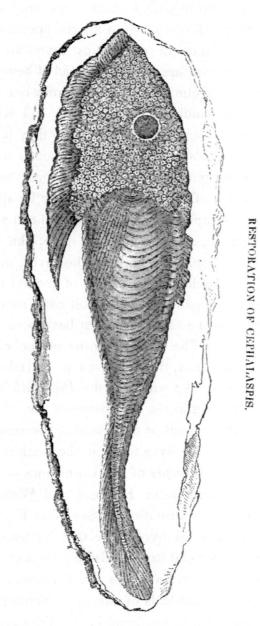

PLATE X.

RESTORATION OF CEPHALASPIS.

in the Gray Sandstones which form on both sides the Tay, where the Tilestone formation seems wanting, the apparent base of the system It is exclusively a medal of the middle empire. (See Note G)

In the last-mentioned locality, in a beautifully wooded dell, known as the Den of Balruddery, the *Cephalaspis* is found associated with an entire group of other fossils, the recent discovery of Mr. Webster, the proprietor, who, with a zeal through which geological knowledge promises to be materially extended, and at an expense of much labor, has made a collection of all the organisms of the Den yet discovered. These the writer had the pleasure of examining in the company of Mr. Murchison and Dr Buckland · he was afterwards present when they were examined by Agassiz, and not a single organism of the group could be identified on either occasion, by any member of the party, with those of the lower or upper formations. Even the genera are dissimilar. The fossils of the Lias scarce differ more from those of the Coal Measures, than the fossils of the Middle Old Red Sandstone from the fossils of the formations that rest over and under them. Each formation has its distinct group — a fact so important to the geologist, that he may feel an interest in its further verification through the decision of yet another high authority. The superior Old Red Sandstones of Scotland were first ascertained to be fossiliferous by Professor Fleming, of King's College, Aberdeen,* confessedly one of the first

---

* The Upper Old Red Sandstones of Moray were ascertained to be fossiliferous at nearly the same time by Mr. Martin, of the Anderson Institution, Elgin. There is a mouldering conglomerate precipice termed the *Scat-Craig*, about four miles to the south of the town, more abundant in remains than perhaps any of the other deposits of

naturalists of the age, and who, to his minute acquaintance with existing forms of being, adds an acquaintance scarcely less minute with those forms of primeval life that no longer exist He it was who first discovered, in the Upper Old Red Sandstones of Fifeshire, the large scales and plates of that strikingly characteristic ichthyolite of the higher formation, now known as the *Holoptychius* — of which more anon ; and, unquestionably, no one acquainted with his writings, or the character of his mind, can doubt that he examined carefully.

---

the formation yet discovered, and in this precipice Mr Martin first commenced his labors in the Red Sandstone of the district, and found it a mine of wonders. It is a place of singular interest — a rock of sepulchres ; and its teeth, scales, and single bones occur in a state of great entireness, though, ere the deposit was formed, the various ichthyolites whose remains it contains seem to have been broken up, and their fragments scattered. Accumulations of larger and smaller pebbles alternate in the strata ; and the bulkier bones and teeth are found invariably among the bulkier pebbles, thus showing that they were operated upon by the same laws of motion which operated on the inorganic contents of the deposit. At a considerably later period the fossils of the upper group were detected in the precipitous and romantic banks of the Findhorn, by Dr Malcolmson, of Madras, when prosecuting his discoveries of the organisms of the lower formation. He found them, also, though in less abundance, in a splendid section exhibited in the Burn of Lethen, a rivulet of Moray, and yet again in the neighborhood of Altyre. The Rev Mr. Gordon, of Birnie, and Mr. Robertson, of Inverugie, have been also discoverers in the district. To the geological labors of Mr. Patrick Duff, of Elgin, in the same field, I have already had occasion incidentally to refer The patient inquiries of this gentleman have been prosecuted for years in all the formations of the province, from the Weald of Linksfield, with its peculiar lacustrine remains — lignites, minute fresh-water shells, and the teeth, spines, and vertebræ of fish and saurians — down to the base of the Old Red Sandstone, with its *Coccostei, Dipteri,* and *Pterichthyes.*

Now, a few years since, I had the pleasure of introducing
Professor Fleming to the Organisms of the Lower Old Red
Sandstone, as they occur in the neighborhood of Cromarty ;
and, notwithstanding his extensive acquaintance with the
upper fossils of the system, he found himself, among the
lower, in an entirely new field.   His knowledge of the one
group served but to show him how very different it was from
the other.   With the organisms of the lower he minutely
acquainted himself ; he collected specimens from Gamrie,

His acquaintance with the organisms of the *Scat-Craig* is at once more
extensive and minute than that of, perhaps, any other geologist ; and
his collection of them very valuable, representing, as it does, a formation of much interest, still little known.   Mr. Duff is at present engaged on a volume descriptive of the Geology of the province of
Moray, a district extensively explored of late years, and abundant in
its distinct groups of organisms, but of which general readers have
still much to learn ; and from no one could they learn more regarding
it than from Mr Duff.   It is still only a few months since the Upper
Old Red Sandstones of the southern districts of Scotland were found
to be fossiliferous, and the writer is chiefly indebted for his acquaintance with their organisms to a tradesman of Berwickshire, Mr. William Stevenson, of Dunse, who, on perusing some of the geological
articles which appeared in the *Witness* newspaper during the course
of the last autumn, sent him a parcel of fossils disinterred from out the
deep belt of Red Sandstone which leans to the south in that locality,
against the grauwacke of the Lammermuirs.   Mr. Stevenson had
recently discovered them, he stated, near Preston-haugh, about two
miles north of Dunse, in a fine section of alternating Sandstone and
conglomerate strata that lie unconformably on the grauwacke.   They
consist of scales and occipital plates of the *Holoptychius*, with the remains of a bulky, but very imperfectly preserved ichthyodorulite,
and the coarse, arenaceous matrices which surround them seem identical with the red gritty Sandstones of the Findhorn and the *Scat-
Craig.*

Caithness, and Cromarty, and studied their peculiarities; and yet, on being introduced last year to the discoveries of Mr. Webster at Balruddery, he found his acquaintance with both the upper and lower groups stand him in but the same stead that his first acquired knowledge of the upper group had stood him a few years before. He agreed with Agassiz in pronouncing the group at Balruddery essentially a new group. Add to this evidence the well weighed testimony of Mr. Murchison regarding the three formations which the Old Red Sandstone contains in England, where the entire system is found continuous, the Cornstone overlying the Tilestone, and the Quartzose conglomerate the Cornstone; take into account the fact that, there, each formation has its characteristic fossil, identical with some characteristic fossil of the corresponding formation of Scotland — that the Tilestones of the one, and the lower group of the other, have their *Dipterus* in common — that the Cornstones of the one, and the middle group of the other, have their *Cephalaspis* in common — that the Quartzose conglomerate of the one, and the upper group of the other, have their *Holoptychius* in common; and then say whether the proofs of distinct succeeding formations can be more surely established. If, however, the reader still entertain a doubt, let him consult the singularly instructive section of the entire system, from the Carboniferous Limestone to the Upper Silurian, given by Mr. Murchison, in his *Silurian System*, (Part II., Plate XXXI, fig 1,) and he will find the doubt vanish. But to return to the fossils of the Cornstone group.

The characteristic fossil of this deposit, the *Cephalaspis*, occurs in considerable abundance in Forfarshire, and in a much more entire state than in the Cornstones of England and Wales. The rocks to which it belongs are also devel-

oped, though more sparingly, in the northern extremity of
Fife, in a line parallel to the southern shores of the Tay.
But of all the localities yet known, the Den of Balruddery is
that in which the peculiar organisms of the formation may be
studied with best effect. The oryctology of the Cornstones of
England seems restricted to four species of the *Cephalaspis*.
In Fife, all the organisms of the formation yet discovered are
exclusively vegetable — darkened impressions of stems like
those of the inferior ichthyolite beds, confusedly mixed with
what seem slender and pointed leaflets drawn in black, and
numerous circular forms, which have been deemed the remains of the seed-vessels of some unknown sub-aerial plant.
" These last occur," says Professor Fleming, the original discoverer, " in the form of circular flat patches, not equalling
an inch in diameter, and composed of numerous smaller con-
tiguous circular pieces ; " the *tout ensemble* resembling " what
might be expected to result from a compressed berry, such as
the bramble or the rasp." In Forfarshire, the remains of the
Cephalaspis are found associated with impressions of a different character, though equally obscure — impressions of polished surfaces carved into seeming scales ; but in Balruddery
alone are the vegetable impressions of the one locality, and
the scaly impressions of the other, together with the characteristic ichthyolites of England and Forfarshire, found associated with numerous fossils besides, many of them obscure,
but all of them of interest, and all of them new to Geology

One of the strangest organisms of the formation is a fossil
lobster, of such huge proportions, that one of the average
sized lobsters, common in our markets, might stretch its entire length across the continuous tail-flap in which the creature terminated.* And it is a marked characteristic of the
fossil, that the terminal flap should be continuous ; in all the

* See Note H.

existing varieties with which I am acquainted, it is divided into angular sections. The claws nearly resembled those of the common lobster; their outline is similar; there is the same hawk-bill curvature outside, and the inner sides of the pincers are armed with similar teeth-like tubercles. The immense shield which covered the upper part of the creature's body is more angular than in the existing varieties, and resembles, both in form and size, one of those lozenge-shaped shields worn by knights of the middle ages on gala days, rather for ornament than use, and on which the herald still inscribes the armorial bearing of ladies who bear title in their own right. As shown in some of the larger specimens, the length of this gigantic crustacean must have exceeded four feet. Its shelly armor was delicately fretted with the forms of circular or elliptical scales. On all the many plates of which it was composed we see these described by gracefully waved lines, and rising apparently from under one another, row beyond row. They were, however, as much the mere semblance of scales as those relieved by the sculptor on the corslet of a warrior's effigy on a Gothic tomb — mere sculpturings on the surface of the shell. This peculiarity may be regarded as throwing light on the hitherto doubtful impressions of the sandstone of Forfarshire — impressions, as has been said, of smooth surfaces carved into seeming scales. They occur as impressions merely, the sandstone retaining no more of the original substance of the organism than the impressed wax does of the substance of the seal; and the workmen in the quarries in which they occur, finding form without body, and struck by the resemblance which the delicately waved scales bear to the sculptured markings on the wings of cherubs — of all subjects of the chisel the most common — fancifully termed them *Seraphim*. They have turned out, as was anticipated,

to be the detached plates of some such crustacean as the lobster of Balruddery. (See Note H 2)

The ability displayed by Cuvier in restoring, from a few
broken fragments of bone, the skeleton of the entire animal
to which the fragments had belonged, astonished the world
He had learned to interpret signs as incomprehensible to
every one else as the mysterious handwriting on the wall had
been to the courtiers of Belshazzar. The condyle of a jaw
became in his hands a key to the character of the original
possessor ; and in a few mouldering vertebræ, or in the dilap-
idated bones of a fore-arm or a foot, he could read a curious
history of habits and instincts. In common with several gentlemen of Edinburgh, all men known to science, I was as
much struck with the skill displayed by Agassiz in piecing
together the fragments of the huge crustacean of Balruddery,
and in demonstrating its nature as such The numerous
specimens of Mr Webster were opened out before us. On
a previous morning I had examined them, as I have said, in
the company of Mr. Murchison and Dr. Buckland ; they had
been seen also by Lord Greenock, Dr. Traill, and Mr. Charles
M'Laren ; and then fragments of new and undescribed fishes
had been at once recognized with reference to at least their
class. But the collection contained organisms of a different
kind, which seemed inexplicable to all — forms of various
design, but so regularly mathematical in their outlines that
they might be all described by a ruler and a pair of compasses, and yet the whole were covered by seeming scales.
There were the fragments of scaly rhombs, of scaly cres-
cents, of scaly circles, with scaly parallelograms attached to
them, and of several other regular compound figures besides.
Mr. Murchison, familiar with the older fossils, remarked the
close resemblance of the seeming scales to those of the *Ser-*

aphim of Forfarshire, but deferred the whole to the judgment
of Agassiz ; no one else hazarded a conjecture. Agassiz
glanced over the collection. One specimen especially caught
his attention — an elegantly symmetrical one. It seemed a
combination of the parallelogram and the crescent · there
were pointed horns at each end ; but the convex and concave
lines of the opposite sides passed into almost parallel right
lines towards the centre. His eye brightened as he contemplated it. " I will tell you," he said, turning to the company
— "I will tell you what these are — the remains of a huge
lobster " He arranged the specimens in the group before
him with as much apparent ease as I have seen a young girl
arranging the pieces of ivory or mother-of-pearl in an Indian
puzzle. A few broken pieces completed the lozenge-shaped
shield ; two detached specimens, placed on its opposite sides,
furnished the claws ; two or three semi-rings, with serrated
edges, composed the jointed body ; the compound figure,
which but a minute before had so strongly attracted his attention, furnished the terminal flap ; and there lay the huge lobster before us, palpable to all. There is homage due to
supereminent genius, which nature spontaneously pays when
there are no low feelings of envy or jealousy to interfere
with her operations ; and the reader may well believe that it
was willingly rendered on this occasion to the genius of
Agassiz.

The terminal flap of this gigantic crustacean was, as I
have said, continuous. The creature, however, seems to
have had contemporaries of the same family, whose construction in the divisions of the flap resembled more the lobsters
of the present day ; and the reader may see in the subjoined
print the representation of a very characteristic fragment of
an animal of this commoner type, from the Middle Sandstones

PLATE XI.

136*

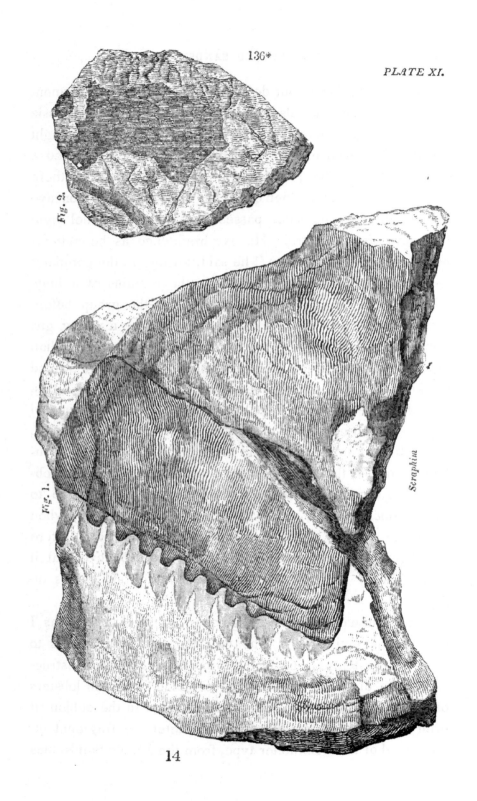

Fig. 2.

Fig. 1.

Seraphin

14

of Forfarshire. (See Plate XI., fig. 1.) It is a terminal flap*— one of several divisions — curiously fretted by scale-like markings, and bearing on its lower edge a fringe, cut into angular points, somewhat in the style of the Vandyke edgings of a ruff or the lacings of a dead-dress. It may be remarked, in passing, that our commoner lobsters bear, on the corresponding edge, fringes of strong, reddish-colored hair. The form altogether, from its wing-like appearance, its feathery markings, and its angular points, will suggest to the reader the origin of the name given it by the Forfarshire workmen. With another such flap spreading out in the contrary direction, and a periwigged head between them, we would have one of the sandstone cherubs of our country churchyards complete.

There occur among the other organisms of Balruddery numerous ichthyodorulites — fin-spines, such as those to which I have called the attention of the reader in describing the thorny-finned fish of the lower formation.† But the ichthyodorulites of Balruddery differ essentially from those of Caithness, Moray, and Cromarty. These last are described on both sides, in every instance, by either straight, or slightly curved lines; whereas one of the describing lines in a Balruddery variety is broken by projecting prickles, that resemble sharp, hooked teeth set in a jaw, or, rather, the entire ichthyodorulite resembles the sprig of a wild rose-bush, bearing its peculiar aquiline shaped thorns on one of its sides. Buckland, in his *Bridgewater Treatise*, and Lyell, in his *Elements*, refer to this peculiarity of structure in ichthyodorulites of the latter formations. The hooks are invariably ranged on the concave or posterior edge of the spine, and were employed, it is supposed, in elevating the fin. Another ichthyodorulite of the formation resembles, in the Gothic

* See Note H 2.   * See Note G 2.

cast of its roddings, those of the *Diplacanthus* of the Lower Old Red Sandstone described in pages 84 and 85 of the present volume, and figured in Plate VIII., fig. 2, except that it was proportionally stouter, and traversed at its base by lines running counter to the striæ that furrow it longitudinally. Of the other organisms of Balruddery I cannot pretend to speak with any degree of certainty. Some of them seem to have belonged to the *Radiata;* some are of so doubtful a character that it can scarce be determined whether they took their place among the forms of the vegetable or animal kingdoms. One organism in particular, which was at first deemed the jointed stem of some plant resembling a calamite of the Coal Measures, was found by Agassiz to be the slender limb of a crustacean. A minute description of this interesting deposit, with illustrative prints, would be of importance to science. it would serve to fill a gap in the scale. The geological pathway, which leads upwards to the present time from those ancient formations in which organic existence first began, has been the work of well nigh as many hands as some of our longer railroads : each contractor has taken his part; very extended parts have fallen to the share of some, and admirably have they executed them ; but the pathway is not yet complete, and the completion of a highly curious portion of it awaits the further labors of Mr. Webster, of Balruddery.

A considerable portion of the rocks of this middle formation in Scotland are of a bluish-gray color in Balruddery, they resemble the mudstones of the Silurian System , they form at Carmylie the fissile, bluish-gray pavement, so well known in commerce as the pavement of Arbroath ; they occur as a hard, micaceous building-stone in some parts of Fifeshire; in others they exist as beds of friable, stratified

clay, that dissolve into unctuous masses where washed by
the sea. In England, the formation consists, throughout its
entire depth, of beds of red and green marl, with alternating
beds of the nodular limestones, to which it owes its name,
and with here and there an interposing band of indurated
sandstone.

The Cornstone formation is more extensively developed in
Forfarshire than in any other district in Scotland; and from
this circumstance the result of the writer's observations regarding it, during the course of a recent visit, may be of
some little interest to the reader. About two thirds the entire area of this county is composed of Old Red Sandstone.
It forms a portion of that great belt of the system which, extending across the island from the German Ocean to the Frith
of Clyde, represents the southern bar of the huge sandstone
frame in which the Highlands of Scotland is set. The Grampians run along its inner edge — composing part of the primary nucleus which the frame encloses: the Sidlaw Hills
run through its centre in a line nearly parallel to these, and
separated from them by Strathmore, the great valley of An-
gus. The valley and the hills thus form, if I may so express
myself, the mouldings of the frame — mouldings somewhat
resembling the semi-recta of the architect. There is first,
reckoning from the mountains downwards, an immense concave curve — the valley; then an immense convex one — the
hills; and then a half curve bounded by the sea. The illustration may further serve to show the present condition of the
formation: it is a frame much worn by denudation, and —
just as in a *bona fide* frame — it is the higher mouldings that
have suffered most. Layer after layer has been worn down
on the ridges, exactly as on a raised moulding we may see
the gold leaf, the red pigment, and the whiting, all ground

14 *

down to the wood; while in the hollow moulding beside it, on
the contrary, the gilt is still fresh and entire. We find in the
hollows the superior layers of the frame still overlying the
inferior ones, and on the heights the inferior ones laid bare.
To descend in the system, therefore, we have to climb a hill
— to rise in it, we have to descend into a valley. We find
the lowest beds of the system any where yet discovered in
the county on the moory heights of Carmylie; its newer deposits may be found on the sea-shore, beside the limeworks
of Hedderwick, and in the central hollows of Strathmore.

The most ancient beds in the county yet known belong, as
unequivocally shown by their fossils, to but the middle formation of the system. They have been quarried for many
years in the parish of Carmylie; and the quarries, as may
be supposed, are very extensive, stretching along a moory
hill-side for considerably more than a mile, and furnishing
employment to from sixty to a hundred workmen. The eye
is first caught, in approaching them, as we surmount a long,
flat ridge, which shuts them out from the view of the distant
sea, by what seems a line of miniature windmills, the sails
flaring with red lead, and revolving with the lightest breeze
at more than double the rate of the sails of ordinary mills.
These are employed — a lesson probably borrowed from the
Dutch — in draining the quarries, and throw up a very considerable body of water. The line of the excavations resembles a huge drain, with nearly perpendicular sides — a consequence of the regular and well-determined character of the
joints with which the strata are bisected. The stone itself is
a gray, close-grained fissile sandstone, of unequal hardness,
and so very tough and coherent — qualities which it seems
to owe in part to the vast abundance of mica which it contains — that it is quite possible to strike a small hammer

through some of the larger flags, without shattering the edges of the perforation. Hence its value for various purposes which common sandstone is too brittle and incoherent to serve. It is extensively used in the neighborhood as a roofing slate; it is employed, too, in the making of water cisterns, grooved and jointed as if wrought out of wood, and for the tops of lobby and billiard tables. I have even seen snuff-boxes fashioned out of it, as a sort of mechanical feat by the workmen, — a purpose, however, which it seems to serve only indifferently well, — and single slabs of it cut into tolerably neat window frames for cottages. It is most extensively used, however, merely as a paving-stone for lobbies and lower floors, and the footways of streets. When first deposited, and when the creatures whose organic remains it still preserves careered over its numerous platforms, it seems to have existed as a fine, muddy sand, formed apparently of disintegrated grauwacke rocks, analogous in their mineral character to the similarly colored grauwacke of the Lammermuirs, or of primary slates ground down by attrition into mud, and mixed up with the pulverized fragments of schistose gneiss and mica schist.

I was first struck, on descending among the workmen, by the comparative abundance of the vegetable remains. In some parts of the quarries almost every layer of the strata is covered by carbonaceous markings — irregularly grooved stems, branching out into boughs at acute angles, and that at the first glance seem the miniature semblances of the trunks of gnarled oaks and elms, blackened in a morass, and still retaining the rough bark, chapped into furrows : oblong, leaf-like impressions, too, and impressions of more slender form, that resemble the narrow, parallel edged leaves of the sea-grass weed. I observed, in particular, one large bunch of

r'band-like leaflets converging into a short stem, so that the
whole resembled a scourge of cords; and I would fain have
detached it from the rock, but it lay on a mouldering film of
clay, and broke up with my first attempt to remove it. A
stalk of sea-grass weed plucked up by the roots, and compressed in a herbarium, would present a somewhat similar
appearance. Among the impressions there occur irregularly
shaped patches, reticulated into the semblance of polygonal
meshes. They remind one of pieces of ill-woven lace; for
the meshes are unequal in size, and the polygons irregular
(See Plate XI., fig. 2.) When first laid open, every mesh is
filled with a carbonaceous speck; and from their supposed
resemblance to the eggs of the frog, the workmen term them
puddock spawn. They are supposed by Mr. Lyell to form
the remains of the eggs of some gasteropodous mollusc of the
period. I saw one flagstone, in particular, so covered with
these reticulated patches, and so abundant, besides, in vegetable impressions of both the irregularly furrowed and grass-
weed-looking class, that I could compare it to only the bottom
of a ditch beside a hedge, matted with withered grass,
strewed with blackened twigs of the hawthorn, and mottled
with detached masses of the eggs of the frog.* All the larger
vegetables are resolved into as pure a coal as the plants of
the Coal Measures themselves — the kind of data, doubtless,
on which unfortunate coal speculators have often earned dis-
appointment at large expense. None of the vegetables
themselves, however, in the least resemble those of the carboniferous period.

The animal remains, though less numerous, are more
interesting. They are identical with those of the Den of
Balruddery. I saw, in the possession of the superintendent of the quarries, a well-preserved head of the *Cephalas-*

* See Note I, Plate XII.

PLATE XII.

PARKA DECIPIENS.

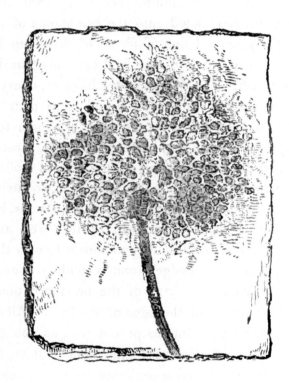

The above engraving is from a specimen in the private collection of
Lord Kinnaird, at Rossie Priory.

pis Lyelhi. The crescent-shaped horns were wanting, and the outline a little obscure; but the eyes were better marked than in almost any other specimen I have yet seen, and the circular star-like tubercles which roughen the large occipital buckler, to which the creature owes its name, were tolerably well defined. I was shown the head of another individual of the same species in the centre of a large slab, and nothing could be more entire than the outline. The osseous plate still retained the original brownish-white hue of the bone, and its radiated porous texture; and the sharp crescent-shaped horns were as sharply defined as during the lifetime of the strangely organized creature which they had defended. In both specimens the thin angular body was wanting. Like almost all the other fish of the Old Red Sandstone, the bony skeleton of the *Cephalaspis* was external — as much so as the shell of the crab or lobster : it presented at all points an armor of bone, as complete as if it had been carved by the ivory-turner out of a solid block; while the internal skeleton, which in every instance has disappeared, seems to have been composed of cartilage. I have compared its general appearance to a saddler's cutting-knife ; — I should, perhaps, have said a saddler's cutting-knife divested of the wooden handle — the broad, bony head representing the blade, and the thin angular body the iron stem usually fixed in the wood. No existence of the present creation at all resembles the *Cephalaspis*. Were we introduced to the living creatures which now inhabit the oceans and rivers of Mars and Venus, we could find nothing among them more strange in appearance, or more unlike our living acquaintances of the friths and streams than the *Cephalaspides* of Carmylie. (See Note F.)

I observed, besides, in the quarry, remains of the huge

crustacean of Balruddery. The plates of the *Cephalaspis*
retain the color of the original bone, the plates of the crustacean, on the contrary, are of a deep red tint, which contrasts
strongly with the cold gray of the stone. They remind one,
both in shape and hue, of pieces of ancient iron armor, fretted
into semi-elliptical scales, and red with rust. I saw with one
of the workmen what seemed to have been the continuous
tail-flap of an individual of very considerable size. It seemed
curiously puckered where it had joined to the body, much in
the manner that a gown or Highlander's kilt is puckered
where it joins to the waistband ; and the outline of the whole
plate was marked by what I may venture to term architectural
elegance. The mathematician could have described it with
his ruler and compasses. The superintendent pointed out to
me another plate in a slab dressed for a piece of common
pavement. It was a regularly formed parallelogram, and had
obviously composed one of the jointed plates which had covered the creature's body. I could not so easily assign its
place to yet a third plate in the possession of the Rev. Mr.
Wilson, of Carmylie. It is colored, like the others, and like
them, too, fretted into minute scales, but the form is exactly
that of a heart — not such a heart as the anatomist would
draw, but such a heart, rather, as we see at times on valen-
tines of the humbler order, or on the ace of hearts in a pack
of cards. Possibly enough it may have been the breastplate
of this antique crustacean of the Cornstones The spawn of
our common blue lobster is composed of spherical black
grains, of nearly the size of mustard-seed. It struck me as
not very improbable that the reticulated markings of the flagstones of Carmylie may have been produced by the minute
eggs of this fossil crustacean, covered up by some hastily
deposited layer of mingled mud and sand, and forced into the

polygonal form by pressing against each other, and by the weight from above. (See Note I)

The gray fissile bed in which these organisms occur was perforated to its base on two several occasions, and in different parts of the quarries — in one instance, merely to ascertain its depth ; in the other, in the course of excavating a tunnel. In the one case it was found to rest on a bed of trap, which seemed to have insinuated itself among the strata with as little disturbance, and which lay nearly as conformably to them as the greenstone bed of Salisbury Crags does to the alternating sandstones and clays which both underlie and overtop it. In the other instance the excavators arrived at a red, aluminous sandstone, veined by a purplish-colored oxide of iron. The upper strata of the quarry are overlaid by a thick bed of grayish-red conglomerate.

Leaving behind us the quarries of Carmylie, we descend the hill-side, and rise in the system as we lower our level and advance upon the sea. For a very considerable distance we find the rock covered up by a deep-red diluvial clay, largely charged with water-worn boulders, chiefly of the older primary rocks, and of the sandstone underneath. The soil on the higher grounds is moory and barren — a consequence, in great part, of a hard, ferruginous pan, which interposes like a paved floor between the diluvium and the upper mould, and which prevents the roots of the vegetation from striking downwards into the tenacious subsoil. From its impervious character, too, it has the effect of rendering the surface a bog for one half the year, and an arid, sun-baked waste for the other. It seems not improbable that the heaths which must have grown and decayed on these heights for many ages, may have been main agents in the formation of this pavement of barrenness. Of all plants, they are said to contain most iron

15

According to Fourcroy, a full twelfth part of the weight of
oak, when dried, is owing to the presence of this almost universally diffused metal ; and the proportion in our common
heaths is still larger.   It seems easy to conceive how that, as
generation after generation withered on these heights, and
were slowly resolved into a little mossy dust, the minute metallic particles which they had contained would be carried
downwards by the rains through the lighter stratum of soil,
till, reaching the impermeable platform of tenacious clay beneath, they would gradually accumulate there, and at length
bind its upper layer, as is the nature of ferruginous oxide,
into a continuous stony crust.   Bog iron, and the clay ironstone, so abundant in the Coal Measures, and so extensively
employed in our iron-works, seem to have owed their accumulation in layers and nodules to a somewhat similar process,
through the agency of vegetation.   But I digress.

The rock appears in the course of the Elliot, a few hundred yards above the pastoral village of Arbirlot.   We find
it uptilted on a mass of claystone amygdaloid, that has here
raised its broad back to the surface amid the middle shales
and sandstones of the system.   The stream runs over the
intruded mass ; and where the latter terminates, and the
sandstones lean against it, the waters leap from the harder to
the softer rock, immediately beside the quiet parish burying-
ground, in a cascade of some eight or ten feet.   From this
point, for a full mile downwards, we find an almost continuous
section of the sandstone — stratum leaning against stratum
— in an angle of about thirty.   The portion of the system
thus exhibited must amount to many hundred yards in vertical
extent ; but as I could discover no data by which to determine regarding the space which may intervene between its
lowest stratum and the still lower beds of Carmylie, I could

form no guess respecting the thickness of the whole. In a bed of shale, about a quarter of a mile below the village, I detected several of the vegetable impressions of Carmylie, especially those of the grass-weed looking class, and an imperfectly preserved organism resembling the parallelogramical scale of a *Cephalaspis*. The same plants and animals seem to have existed on this high platform as on the Carmylie platform far beneath.

A little farther down the course of the stream, and in the immediate neighborhood of the old weather-worn tower of the Ouchterlonies, there occurs what seems a break in the strata. The newer sandstones seem to rest unconformably on the older sandstones which they overlie. The evening on which I explored the course of the Elliot was drizzly and unpleasant, and the stream swollen by a day of continuous rain, and so I could not examine so minutely as in other circumstances I would have done, or as was necessary to establish the fact. In since turning over the *Elements* of Lyell, however, I find, in his section of Forfarshire, that a newer deposit of nearly horizontal strata of sandstone and conglomerate lies unconformably, in the neighborhood of the sea, on the older sandstones of the district; and the appearances observed near the old tower mark, it is probable, one of the points of junction — a point of junction also, if I may be so bold as venture the suggestion, of the formation of the *Holoptychius nobilissimus* with the formation of the *Cephalaspis* — of the quartzose conglomerate with the Cornstones. In my hurried survey, however, I could find none of the scales or plates of the newer ichthyolite in this upper deposit, though the numerous spherical markings of white, with their centrical points of darker color, show that at one time the organisms of these upper beds must have been very abundant.

We pass to the upper formation of the system. Over the belt of mingled gray and red there occurs in the pyramid a second deep belt of red conglomerate and variegated sandstone, with a band of lime a-top, and over the band a thick belt of yellow sandstone, with which the system terminates * Thus the second pyramid consists mineralogically, like the first, of three great divisions, or bands; its two upper belts belonging, like the three belts of the other, to but one formation — the formation known in England as the Quartzose Conglomerate. It is largely developed in Scotland. We find it spread over extensive areas in Moray, Fife, Roxburgh, and Berwick shires. In England, it is comparatively barren in fossils; the only animal organic remains yet detected in it being a single scale of the *Holoptychius* found by Mr. Murchison, and though it contains vegetable organisms in more abundance, so imperfectly are they preserved, that little else can be ascertained regarding them than that they were land

---

* There still exists some uncertainty regarding the order in which the upper beds occur. Mr Duff, of Elgin, places the limestone band above the yellow sandstone; Messrs. Sedgwick and Murchison assign it an intermediate position between the red and yellow. The respective places of the gray and red sandstones are also disputed, and by very high authorities, Dr. Fleming holding that the gray sandstones overlie the red, (see *Cheek's Edinburgh Journal* for February, 1831,) and Mr. Lyell, that the red sandstones overlie the gray, (see *Elements of Geology*, first edit., pp. 99–100.) The order adopted above consorts best with the results of the writer's observations, which have, however, been restricted chiefly to the north country He assigns to the limestone band the middle place assigned to it by Messrs. Sedgwick and Murchison, and to the gray sandstone the inferior position assigned to it by Mr. Lyell; aware, however, that the latter deposit has not only a coping, but also a basement, of red sandstone — the basement forming the upper member of the lower formation.

plants, but not identical with the plants of the Coal Measures.* In Scotland, the formation is richly fossiliferous, and the remains belong chiefly to the animal kingdom. It is richly fossiliferous, too, in Russia, where it was discovered by Mr. Murchison, during the summer of last year, spread over areas many thousand square miles in extent. And there, as in Scotland, the *Holoptychius* seems its most characteristic fossil.

The fact seems especially worthy of remark. The organisms of some of the newer formations differ entirely, in widely separated localities, from their contemporary organisms, just as, in the existing state of things, the plants and animals of Great Britain differ from the plants and animals of Lapland or of Sierra Leone A geologist who has acquainted himself with the belemnites, baculites, turrilites, and sea-urchins of the Cretaceous group in England and the north of France, would discover that he had got into an entirely new field among the hippurites, sphærulites, and nummulites of the same formations, in Greece, Italy, and Spain ; nor, in passing the tertiary deposits, would he find less striking dissimilarities between the gigantic, mail-clad megatherium and huge mastodon of the Ohio and the La Plate, and the monsters, their contemporaries, the hairy mammoth of Siberia, and the hippopotamus and rhinoceros of England and the Continent. In the more ancient geological periods, ere the seasons began, the case is essentially different : the contemporary formations, when widely separated, are often very unlike in mineralogical character, but in their fossil contents they are almost always identical. In these earlier ages, the atmospheric temperature seems to have depended more on the internal heat of the earth, only partially cooled down from its original state, than on the earth's configuration or the influence of the sun Hence a widely spread equality of

15 *   * See Note K.

climate — a greenhouse equalization of heat, if I may so speak ; and hence. too, it would seem, a widely spread Fauna and Flora. The greenhouses of Scotland and Sweden produce the same plants with the greenhouses of Spain and Italy ; and when the world was one vast greenhouse, heated from below, the same families of plants, and the same tribes of animals, seem to have ranged over spaces immensely more extended than those geographical circles in which, in the present time, the same plants are found indigenous, and the same animals native. The fossil remains of the true Coal Measures are the same to the westward of the Alleghany Mountains as in New Holland, India, Southern Africa, the neighborhood of Newcastle, and the vicinity of Edinburgh. And I entertain little doubt that, on a similar principle, the still more ancient organisms of the Old Red Sandstone will be found to bear the same character all over the world.

CHAPTER IX.

Fossils of the Upper Old Red Sandstone much more imperfectly preserved than those of the Lower. — The Causes obvious — Difference between the two Groups, which first strikes the Observer, a
Difference in Size. — The *Holoptychius* a characteristic Ichthyolite
of the Formation. — Description of its huge Scales. — Of its Occipital Bones, Fins, Teeth, and General Appearance. — Contemporaries of the *Holoptychius.* — Sponge-like Bodies — Plates resembling those of the Sturgeon. — Teeth of various Forms, but all
evidently the Teeth of Fishes — Limestone Band, and its probable
Origin. — Fossils of the Yellow Sandstone. — The *Pterichthys* of
Dura Den — Member of a Family peculiarly characteristic of the
System — No intervening Formation between the Old Red Sandstone and the Coal Measures. — The *Holoptychius* contemporary for
a time with the *Megalichthys.* — The Columns of Tubal Cain

THE different degrees of entireness in which the geologist
finds his organic remains, depend much less on their age than
on the nature of the rock in which they occur; and as the
arenaceous matrices of the Upper and Middle Old Red Sandstones have been less favorable to the preservation of their
peculiar fossils than the calcareous and aluminous matrices
of the Lower, we frequently find the older organisms of the
system fresh and unbroken, and the more modern existing as
mere fragments.   A fish thrown into a heap of salt would be
found entire after the lapse of many years; a fish thrown
into a heap of sand would disappear in a mass of putrefaction in a few weeks; and only the less destructible parts,
such as the teeth, the harder bones, and perhaps a few of the
scales, would survive.   Now, limestone, if I may so speak,
is the preserving salt of the geological world; and the con-

(151)

servative qualities of the shales and stratified clays of the
Lower Old Red Sandstone are not much inferior to those of
lime itself; while, in the Upper Old Red, we have merely
beds of consolidated sand, and these, in most instances, rendered less conservative of organic remains than even the
common sand of our shores, by a mixture of the red oxide of
iron.   The older fossils, therefore, like the mummies of
Egypt, can be described well nigh as minutely as the existences of the present creation; the newer, like the comparatively modern remains of our churchyards, exist, except in a
few rare cases, as mere fragments, and demand powers such
as those of a Cuvier or an Agassiz to restore them to their
original combinations.   But cases, though few and rare, do
occur in which, through some favorable accident connected with the death or sepulture of some individual existence of the period, its remains have been preserved almost
entire ; and one such specimen serves to throw light on whole
heaps of the broken remains of its contemporaries.   The
single elephant, preserved in an iceberg beside the Arctic
Ocean, illustrated the peculiarities of the numerous extinct
family to which it belonged, whose bones and huge tusks
whiten the wastes of Siberia.   The human body found in an
Irish bog, with the ancient sandals of the country still attached to its feet by thongs, and clothed in a garment of
coarse hair, gave evidence that bore generally on the degree of
civilization attained by the inhabitants of an entire district in
a remote age.   In all such instances, the character and appearance of the individual bear on those of the tribe.   In at-
tempting to describe the organisms of the Lower Old Red
Sandstone, where the fossils lie as thickly in some localities as
herrings on our coasts in the fishing season, I felt as if I had
whole tribes before me.   In describing the fossils of the

Upper Old Red Sandstone, I shall have to draw mostly from single specimens. But the evidence may be equally sound so far as it goes.

The difference between the superior and inferior groups of the system which first strikes an observer, is a difference in the size of the fossils of which these groups are composed. The characteristic organisms of the Upper Old Red Sandstone are of much greater bulk than those of the Lower, which seem to have been characterized by a mediocrity of size throughout the entire extent of the formation. The largest ichthyolites of the group do not seem to have much exceeded two feet or two feet and a half in length; its smaller average from an inch to three inches. A jaw in the possession of Dr. Traill —that of an Orkney species of *Platygnathus*, and by much the largest in his collection — does not exceed in bulk the jaw of a full-grown coal-fish or cod; his largest *Coccosteus* must have been a considerably smaller fish than an ordinary-sized turbot; the largest ichthyolite found by the writer was a *Diplopterus*, of, however, smaller dimensions than the ichthyolite to which the jaw in the possession of Dr. Traill must have belonged; the remains of another *Diplopterus* from Gamrie, the most massy yet discovered in that locality, seem to have composed the upper parts of an individual about two feet and a half in length. The fish, in short, of the lower ocean of the Old Red Sandstone — and I can speak of it throughout an area which comprises Orkney and Inverness, Cromarty, and Gamrie, and which must have included about ten thousand square miles — ranged in size between the stickleback and the cod; whereas some of the fish of its upper ocean were covered by scales as large as oyster-shells, and armed with teeth that rivalled in bulk those of the croco-dile. They must have been fish on an immensely larger

scale than those with which the system began.   There have
been scales of the *Holoptychius* found in Clashbennie which
measure three inches in length by two and a half in breadth,
and a full eighth part of an inch in thickness.   There occur
occipital plates of fishes in the same formation in Moray, a
full foot in length by half a foot in breadth.   The fragment
of a tooth still attached to a piece of the jaw, found in the
sandstone cliffs that overhang the Findhorn, measures an inch
in diameter at the base.   A second tooth of the same formation, of a still larger size, disinterred by Mr Patrick Duff
from out the conglomerates of the *Scat-Craig*, near Elgin,
and now in his possession, measures two inches in length by
rather more than an inch in diameter.   (See Plate XIII , fig 4)
There occasionally turn up in the sandstones of Perthshire
ichthyodorulites that in bulk and appearance resemble the
teeth of a harrow rounded at the edges by a few months' wear,
and which must have been attached to fins not inferior in
general bulk to the dorsal fin of an ordinary-sized porpoise.
In short, the remains of a Patagonian burying-ground would
scarcely contrast more strongly with the remains of that bat-
tle-field described by Addison, in which the pygmies were annihilated by the cranes, than the organisms of the upper
formation of the Old Red Sandstone contrast with those of
the lower.*

Of this upper formation the most characteristic and most
abundant ichthyolite, as has been already said, is the *Holop-*

* I have permitted this paragraph to remain as originally written,
though the comparatively recent discovery of a gigantic *Holoptychius* (?)
in the Lower Old Red Sandstone of Thurso, by Mr Robert Dick of
that place, (see introductory note,) bears shrewdly against its general
line of statement.   But it will at least, serve to show how large an

Cephalaspis Lyellii. Agass.

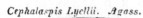

Fig. 1.

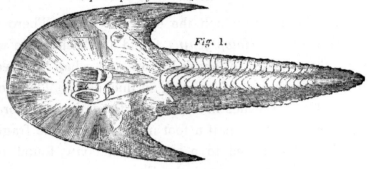

Holoptychius Nobilissimas. Agass.

Fig. 2.

Fig. 3.

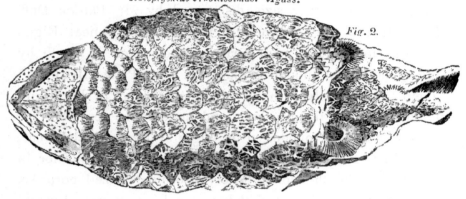

Fig. 4.

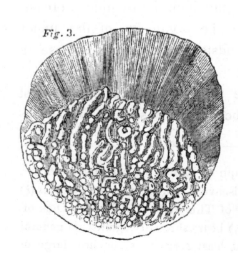
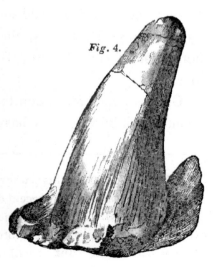

tychius. The large scales and plates, and the huge teeth, belong to this genus. It was first introduced to the notice of geologists in a paper read before the Wernerian Society in May, 1830, by Professor Fleming, and published by him in the February of the following year, in *Cheek's Edinburgh Journal.* Only detached scales and the fragment of a tooth had as yet been found, and these he minutely described as such, without venturing to hazard a conjecture regarding the character or family of the animal to which they had belonged. They were submitted some years after to Agassiz, by whom they were referred, though not without considerable hesitation, to the genus *Gyrolepis;* and the doubts of both naturalists serve to show how very uncertain a guide mere analogy proves to even men of the first order, when brought to bear on organisms of so strange a type as the ichthyolites of the Old Red Sandstone. At this stage, however, an almost entire specimen of the creature was discovered in the sandstones of Clashbennie, by the Rev. James Noble, of St. Madoes, a gentleman who, by devoting his leisure hours to Geology, has extended the knowledge of this upper formation, and whose name has been attached by Agassiz to its characteristic fossil, now designated the *Holoptychius nobilissimus.* His specimen at once decided that the creature had been no *Gyrolepis,* but the representative of a new genus not less strangely organized, and quite as unlike the existences of the present times as any existence of all the past. So marked are the

---

amount of negative evidence may be dissipated by a single positive fact, and to inculcate on the geologist the necessity of cautious induction. An individual *Holoptychius* of Thurso must have been at least thrice the size of the *Holoptychius* of the Upper Old Red formation, as exhibited in the specimen of Mr Noble, of St Madoes.

16

pecularities of the *Holoptychius,* that they strike the commonest observer.

The scales are very characteristic.   They are massy elliptical plates, scarcely less bulky in proportion to their extent of surface than our smaller copper coin, composed internally of bone, and externally of enamel, and presenting on the one side a porous structure, and on the other, when well preserved, a bright, glossy surface.   The upper, or glossy side, is the more characteristic of the two.   I have placed one of them before me.   Imagine an elliptical ivory counter, an inch and a half in length by an inch in breadth, and nearly an eighth part of an inch in thickness, the larger diameter forming a line which, if extended, would pass longitudinally from head to tail through the animal which the scale covered. On the upper or anterior margin of this elliptical counter, imagine a smooth selvedge or border three eighth parts of an inch in breadth.   Beneath this border there is an inner border of detached tubercles, and beneath the tubercles large undulating furrows, which stretch longitudinally towards the lower end of the ellipsis.   Some of these waved furrows run unbroken and separate to the bottom, some merge into their neighboring furrows at acute angles, some branch out and again unite, like streams which enclose islands, and some break into chains of detached tubercles   (See Plate XIII, fig 3.) No two scales exactly resemble one another in the minuter pecularities of their sculpture, if I may so speak, just as no two pieces of lake or sea may be roughened after exactly the same pattern during a gale; and yet in general appearance they are all wonderfully alike.   Their *style* of sculpture is the same — a style which has sometimes reminded me of the Runic knots of our ancient north country obelisks   Such was the scale of the creature *   The head, which was small,

* See Note L.

PLATE XIV.

FIGURE OF HOLOPTYCHIUS.

compared with the size of the body, was covered with bony
plates, roughened after a pattern somewhat different from
that of the scales, being tubercled rather than ridged; but
the tubercles present a confluent appearance, just as chains
of hills may be described as confluent, the base of one hill
running into the base of another. The operculum seems to
have been covered by one entire plate — a peculiarity observable, as has been remarked, among some of the ichthyolites of the Lower Old Red Sandstone, such as the *Diplopterus*, *Dipterus*, and *Osteolepis*. And it, too, has its fields of
tubercles, and its smooth marginal selvedge, or border, on
which the lower edges of the upper occipital plates seem to
have rested, just as, in the roof of a slated building, part of
the lower tier of slates is overtopped and covered by the tier
above. The scales towards the tail suddenly diminish at
the ventral fins to about one fourth the size of those on the
upper part of the body, the fins themselves are covered at
their bases, which seem to have been thick and fleshy like
the base of the pectoral fin in the cod or haddock, with scales
still more minute ; and from the scaly base the rays diverge
like the radii of a circle, and terminate in a semicircular outline. The ventrals are placed nearer the tail, says Agassiz,
than in any other ganoid fish. (See Plate XIII, fig. 2.)

But no such description can communicate an adequate conception to the reader of the strikingly picturesque appearance
of the *Holoptychius*, as shown in Mr. Noble's splendid specimen. There is a general massiveness about the separate
portions of the creature, that imparts ideas of the gigantic.
independently of its bulk as a whole ; just as a building of
moderate size, when composed of very ponderous stones, has
a more imposing effect than much larger buildings in which
the stones are smaller. The body measures a foot across, by

16 *

two feet and a half in length, exclusive of the tail, which is
wanting; but the armor in which it is cased might have
served a crocodile or alligator of five times the size. It lies
on its back, on a mass of red sandstone; and the scales and
plates still retain their bony color, slightly tinged with red,
like the skeleton of some animal that had lain for years in a
bed of ferruginous marl or clay   The outline of the occipital portion of the specimen forms a low Gothic arch, of an
intermediate style between the round Saxon and the pointed
Norman.   This arch is filled by two angular, pane-like plates,
separated by a vertical line, that represents, if I may use the
figure, the dividing astragal of the window; and the under
jaw, with its two sweeping arcs, or branches, constitutes the
frame.   All of the head which appears is that under portion
of it which extends from the upper part of the belly to the
snout.   The belly itself is thickly covered by huge carved
scales, that, from their massiveness and regular arrangement,
remind one of the flags of an ancient stone roof.   The carv-
ing varies, as they descend towards the tail, being more in
the ridged style below, and more in the tubercled style above.
So fairly does the creature lie on its back, that the ventral
fins have fallen equally, one on each side, and, from their
semicircular form, remind one of the two pouch holes in a
lady's apron, with their laced flaps.   The entire outline of
the fossil is that of an elongated ellipsis, or rather spindle, a
little drawn out towards the caudal extremity.   The places
of all the fins are not indicated, but, as shown by other specimens, they seem to have been crowded together towards the
lower extremity, like those of the *Glyptolepis*, an ichthyolite
which, in more than one respect, the *Holoptychius* must have
resembled, and which, from this peculiarity, presents a brush-
like appearance — the head and shoulders representing the

handle, and the large and thickly clustered fins the spreading bristles.*

Some of the occipital bones of the *Holoptychius* are very curious and very puzzling. There are pieces rounded at one of the ends, somewhat in the manner of the neck joints of our better known quadrupeds, and which have been mistaken for vertebræ, but which present evidently, at the apparent joint, the enamel peculiar to the outer surface of all the plates and scales of the creature, and which belonged, it is probable, to the snout. There are saddle-shaped bones, too, which have been regarded as the central occipital plates of a new species of *Coccosteus*, but whose style of confluent tubercle belongs evidently to the *Holoptychius*. The jaws are exceedingly curious. They are composed of as solid bone as we usually find in the jaws of mammalia; and the outer surface, which is covered in animals of commoner structure with portions of the facial integuments, we find polished and japanned, and fretted into tubercles. The jaws of the creature, like those of the *Osteolepis* of the lower formation, were naked jaws; it is, indeed, more than probable that all its real bones were so, and that the internal skeleton was cartilaginous. A row of thickly-set, pointed teeth ran along the japanned edges of the mouth — what, in fish of the ordinary construction, would be the lips; and inside this row there was a second and widely-set row of at least twenty times the bulk of the other, and which stood up over and beyond it, like spires in a city over the rows of lower buildings in front. A nearly similar disposition of teeth seems also to have characterized the

* There are now six species of *Holoptychius* enumerated — *H. Andersoni, H. Flemingii, H. giganteus, H. Murchisoni, H. nobilissimus, and H. Omaliusii.*

Holoptychius of the Coal Measures, but the contrast in size
was somewhat less marked. One of the most singularly
formed bones of the formation will be found, I doubt not,
when perfect specimens of the upper part of the creature
shall be procured, to have belonged to the *Holoptychius*. It
is a huge ichthyodorulite, formed, box-like, of four nearly
rectangular planes, terminating in a point, and ornamented
on two of the sides by what, in a work of art, the reader
would at once term a species of Chinese fretwork. Along
the centre there runs a line of lozenges, slightly truncated
where they unite, just as, in plants that exhibit the cellular
texture, the lozenge-shaped cells may be said to be truncated.
At the sides of the central line, there run lines of half lozenges, which occupy the space to the edges. Each lozenge
is marked by lines parallel to the lines which describe it,
somewhat in the manner of the plates of the tortoise. The
centre of each is thickly tubercled ; and what seems to have
been the anterior plane of the ichthyodorulite is thickly tubercled also, both in the style of the occipital plates and jaws of
the *Holoptychius*. This curious bone, which seems to have
been either hollow inside, or, what is more probable, filled
with cartilage, measures, in some of the larger specimens,
an inch and a half across at the base on its broader planes,
and rather more than half an inch on its two narrower
ones.*

Geologists have still a great deal to learn regarding the
contemporaries of the *Holoptychius nobilissimus*. The
lower portion of that upper formation to which it more

---

* This bone has been since assigned by Agassiz to a new genus, of
which no other fragments have yet been found, but which has been
named provisionally *Placothorax paradoxus*.

especially belongs — the portion represented in our second pyramid by the conglomerate and sandstone bar — though unfavorable to the preservation of animal remains, represents assuredly no barren period. It has been found to contain bodies apparently organic, that vary in shape like the sponges of our existing seas, which in general appearance they somewhat resemble, but whose class, and even kingdom, are yet to fix.*   It contains, besides, in considerable abundance,

---

* These organisms, if in reality such, are at once very curious and very puzzling. They occur in some localities in great abundance. A piece of Clashbennie flagstone, somewhat more than two feet in length, by fifteen inches in breadth, kindly sent me for examination by the Rev. Mr. Noble, of St. Madoes, bears no fewer than twelve of them on its upper surface, and presents the appearance of a piece of rude sculpture, not very unlike those we sometimes see in country churchyards, on the tombstones of the times of the Revolution. All the twelve vary in appearance. Some of them are of a pear shape — some are irregularly oval — some resemble short cuts of the bole of a tree — some are spread out like ancient manuscripts, partially unrolled — one of the number seems a huge, though not over neatly formed acorn, an apprentice mason's first attempt — the others are of a shape so irregular as to set comparison and description at defiance. They almost all agree, however, when cut transversely, in presenting flat, elliptical arcs as their sectional lines — in having an upper surface comparatively smooth, and an under surface nearly parallel to it, thickly corrugated — and in being all coated with a greasy, shining clay, of a deeper red than the surrounding stone. I was perhaps rather more confident of their organic character after I had examined a few merely detached specimens, than now that I have seen a dozen of them together   It seems at least a circumstance to awaken doubt, that though they occur in various positions on the slab — some extending across it, some lying diagonally, some running lengthwise — the corrugations of their under surfaces should run lengthwise in all — furrowing them in every possible angle, and giving evidence, not appar-

though in a state of very imperfect preservation, scales that differ from those of the *Holoptychius*, and from one another. One of these, figured and described by Professor Fleming in *Cheek's Edinburgh Journal*, bearing on its upper surface a mark like a St. Andrew's cross, surrounded by tubercled dottings, and closely resembling in external appearance some of the scales of the common sturgeon, " may be referred with some probability," says the Professor, " to an extinct species of the genus *Accipenser.** The deposit, too, abounds

---

ently to the influences of an organic law, internal to each, but of the operation of some external cause, acting on the whole in one direction.

* May I crave the attention of the reader to a brief statement of fact? I have said that Professor Fleming, when he minutely described the scales of the *Holoptychius*, hazarded no conjecture regarding the generic character of the creature to which they had belonged; he merely introduced them to the notice of the public as the scales of some " vertebrated animal, probably those of a fish " I now state that he described the scales of a contemporary ichthyolite as bearing, in external appearance, a " close resemblance to some of the scales of the common sturgeon " It has been asserted, that it was the scales of the *Holoptychius* which he thus described, " referring them to an extinct species of the genus *Accipenser*," and the assertion has been extensively credited, and by some of our highest geological authorities. Agassiz himself, evidently in the belief that the professor had fallen into a palpable error, deems it necessary to prove that the *Holoptychius* could have borne " no relation to the *Accipenser* or sturgeon." Mr. Murchison, in his *Silurian System*, refers also to the supposed mistake. The person with whom the misunderstanding seems to have originated is the Rev. Dr. Anderson, of Newburgh. About a twelvemonth after the discovery of Professor Fleming in the sandstones of Drumdryan, a similar discovery was made in the sandstones of Clashbennie by a geologist of Perth, who, on submitting his new found scales to Dr. Anderson, concluded, with the Doctor, that they

in teeth, various enough in their forms to indicate a corresponding variety of families and genera among the ichthyolites to which they belonged. Some are nearly straight, like those of the *Holoptychius* of the Coal Measures ; some are bent, like the beak of a hawk or eagle, into a hook-form ; some incline first in one direction, and then in the opposite one,

---

could be no other than *oyster shells*, though eventually, on becoming acquainted with the decision of Professor Fleming regarding them, both gentlemen were content to alter their opinion, and to regard them as scales. The Professor, in his paper on the Old Red Sandstone in *Cheek's Journal*, referred incidentally to the *oyster shells* of Clashbennie — a somewhat delicate subject of allusion ; and in Dr. Anderson's paper on the same formation, which appeared about seven years after, in the *New Journal* of Professor Jameson, the geological world was told, for the first time, that Professor Fleming had described a scale of Clashbennie *similar to those of Drumdryan*, (*i. e.*, those of the *Holoptychius*,) as bearing a "close resemblance to some of the scales on the common sturgeon," and as probably referable to some "extinct species of the genus *Accipenser*." Now, Professor Fleming, instead of stating that the scales were at all similar, had stated very pointedly that they were entirely different ; and not only had he *described* them as different, but he had also *figured* them as different, and had placed the figures side by side, that the difference might be the better seen. To the paper of the Professor, which contained this statement, and to which these figures were attached, Dr. Anderson referred, as "read before the Wernerian Society ;" — he quoted from it in the Professor's words — he drew some of the more important facts of his own paper from it — in his late Essay on the Geology of Fife he has availed himself of it still more largely, though with no acknowledgment ; it has constituted, in short, by far the most valuable of all his discoveries in connection with the Old Red Sandstone, and apparently the most minutely examined ; and yet, so completely did he fail to detect Professor Fleming's carefully drawn distinction between the scales of the *Holoptychius* and those of its contemporary that when Agassiz, misled apparently by the Doctor's own

like nails that have been drawn out of a board by the car-
penter at two several wrenches, and bent in opposite angles
at each wrench ; some are bulky and squat, some long and
slender ; and in almost all the varieties, whether curved or
straight, squat or slim, the base is elegantly striated like the
flutings of the column.   In the splendid specimen found in

---

statement, had set himself to show that the scaly giant of the formation could have been no sturgeon, the Doctor had the passage in
which the naturalist established the fact transferred into a Fife newspaper, with, of course, the laudable intention of preventing the Fife
public from falling into the *absurd mistake* of Professor Fleming.
There seems to be something rather inexplicable in all this ; but there
can be little doubt Dr. Anderson could satisfactorily explain the
whole matter without once referring to the *oyster shells* of Clashbennie.
It is improbable that he could have wished or intended to injure the
reputation of a gentleman to whose freely-imparted instructions he is
indebted for much the greater portion of his geological skill — whose
remarks, written and spoken, he has so extensively appropriated in
his several papers and essays — and whose character is known far beyond the limits of his country, for untiring research, philosophic dis-
crimination, and all the qualities which constitute a naturalist of the
highest order.   Dr. Johnston, of Berwick, in his *History of British
Zoophytes*, (a work of an eminently scientific character,) justly "as-
cribes to the labois and writings" of Professor Fleming "no small
share in diffusing that taste for Natural History which is now abroad"
And as an interesting corroboration of the fact, I may state, that Dr.
Malcolmson, of Madras, lately found an elegant Italian translation of
Fleming's Philosophy of Zoology, high in repute among the elite of
Rome.   Lest it should be supposed I do Dr. Anderson injustice in
these remarks, I subjoin the grounds of them in the following extracts
from professor Fleming's paper in *Cheek's Journal*, and from the paper
in *Jameson's New Edinburgh Journal*, in which the Doctor purports to
give a digest of the former, without once referring, however, to the
periodical in which it is to be found · —
"In the summer of 1827," says Dr Fleming, " I obtained from

the sandstones of the Findhorn, the tooth is still attached to a portion of the jaw, and shows, from the nature of the attachment, that the creature to which it belonged must have been a true fish, not a reptile. The same peculiarity is observable in two other very fine specimens in the collection of Mr. Patrick Duff, of Elgin. Both in saurians and in toothed

---

Drumdryan quarry, to the south of Cupar, situate in the higher strata of yellow sandstone, certain organisms, which I readily referred to the scales of vertebrated animals, probably those of a fish. The largest (see Plate II, fig. 1, '*figure of a scale of the Holoptychius*') was one inch and one tenth in length, about one inch and two tenths in breadth, and not exceeding the fiftieth of an inch in thickness The part which, when in its natural position, had been imbedded in the cuticle, is comparatively smooth, exhibiting, however, in a very distinct manner, the semicircularly parallel layers of growth with obsolete diverging striæ, giving to the surface, when under a lens, a reticulated aspect The part naturally exposed is marked with longitudinal, waved, rounded, anastomosing ridges, which are smooth and glossy. The whole of the inside of the scale is smooth, though exhibiting with tolerable distinctness the layers of growth. The form and structure of the object indicated plainly enough that it had been a scale, a conclusion confirmed by the detection of the phosphate of lime in its composition. At this period I inserted a short notice of the occurrence of these scales in our provincial newspaper, the *Fife Herald*, for the purpose of attracting the attention of the workmen and others in the neighborhood, in order to secure the preservation of any other specimens which might occur.

"Nearly a year after these scales had been discovered, not only in the upper, but even in some of the lower beds of the Yellow Sandstone, I was informed that *oyster shells* had been found in a quarry in the Old Red Sandstone at Clashbennie, near Errol, in Perthshire, and that specimens were in the possession of a gentleman in Perth. Interested in the intelligence, I lost no time in visiting Perth, and was gratified to find that the supposed oyster shells were, in fact, similar to those which I had ascertained to occur in a higher part of the series.

17

cetaceæ, such as the porpoise, the teeth are inserted in sockets. In the ichthyolites of this formation, so far as these are illustrated by its better specimens, the teeth, as in existing fish, are merely placed flat upon the jaw, or in shallow pits, which seem almost to indicate that the contrivance of sockets might be afterwards resorted to. Immediately over the sandstone

---

The scales were, however, of a larger size, some of them exceeding three inches in length, and one eighth of an inch in thickness. Upon my visit to the quarry, I found the scales, as in the Yellow Sandstone, most abundant in those parts of the rock which exhibited a brecciated aspect. Many patches a foot in length, full of scales, have occurred, but as yet no entire impression of a fish has been obtained

"Another scale, DIFFERING FROM THOSE ALREADY NOTICED, (see Plate II., fig. 3, '*figure of an oblong tubercled plate traversed diagonally by lines, which, bisecting one another a little above the centre, resembles a St. Andrew's cross, and marked on the edges by faintly radiating lines,*') is about an inch and a quarter in length, and an inch in breadth. In external appearance it bears a very close resemblance to some of the scales on the common sturgeon, and may, with some probability, be referred to an extinct species of the genus *Accipenser*." — (*Cheek's Edinburgh Journal,* Feb 1831, p. 85)

"Dr. Fleming, in 1830," says Dr. Anderson, "read before the Wernerian Society a notice 'on the occurrence of scales of vertebrated animals in the Old Red Sandstone of Fifeshire.' These organisms, as described by him, occurred in the Yellow Sandstone of Drumdryan and the Gray Sandstone of Parkhill. From the former locality scales of a fish were obtained. . . . . The same paper (Professor Fleming's) contains a notice of SIMILAR SCALES in the Old Red Sandstone of Clashbennie, near Errol, in Perthshire, ONE OF WHICH is described as bearing 'a very close resemblance to some of the scales on the common sturgeon, and may with some probability be referred to an extinct species of the genus *Accipenser* '" — (*Professor Jameson's Edin. New Phil. Journal,* Oct. 1837, p 138.)

and conglomerate belt in which these organisms occur, there rests, as has been said, a band of limestone, and over the limestone a thick bed of yellow sandstone, in which the system terminates, and which is overlaid in turn by the lower beds of the carboniferous group

The limestone band is unfossiliferous, and resembling, in mineralogical character, the Cornstones of England and Wales, it has been described as the Cornstone of Scotland; but the fact merely furnishes one illustration of many, of the inadequacy of a mineralogical nomenclature for the purposes of the geologist   In the neighborhood of Cromarty the lower formation abounds in beds of nodular limestone, identical in appearance with the Cornstone; — in England similar beds occur so abundantly in the middle formation, that it derives its name from them; — in Fife they occur in the upper formation exclusively.   Thus the formation of the *Coccosteus* and *Dipterus* is a cornstone formation in the first locality; that of the *Cephalaspis* and the gigantic lobster in the second; that of the *Holoptychius nobilissimus* in the third.   We have but to vary our field of observation to find all the formations of the system *Cornstone formations* in turn.   The limestone band of the upper member presents exactly similar appearances in Moray as in Fife.   It is in both of a yellowish green or gray color, and a concretionary structure, consisting of softer and harder portions, that yield so unequally to the weather, as to exhibit in exposed cliffs and boulders a brecciated aspect, as if it had been a mechanical, not a chemical deposit; though its origin must unquestionably have been chemical.   It contains minute crystals of galena, and abounds in masses of a cherty, siliceous substance that strikes fire with steel, and which, from the manner in which they are incorporated with the rock, show that they must have been

formed along with it. From this circumstance, and from the
general resemblance it bears to the deposits of the thermal
waters of volcanic districts which precipitate siliceous mixed
with calcareous matter, it has been suggested, and by no mean
authority, that it must have derived its origin from hot springs.
The bed is several yards in thickness; and as it appears both
in Moray and in Fife, in localities at least a hundred and
twenty miles apart, it must have been formed, if formed at
all, in this manner, at a period when the volcanic agencies
were in a state of activity at no great distance from the
surface.

The upper belt of yellow stone, the terminal layer of the
pyramid, is fossiliferous both in Moray and Fife — more
richly so in the latter county than even the conglomerate belt
that underlies it, and its organisms are better preserved. It
was in this upper layer, in Drumdryan quarry, to the south
of Cupar, that Professor Fleming found the first-discovered
scales of the *Holoptychius*. At Dura Den, in the same
neighborhood, a singularly rich deposit of animal remains
was laid open a few years ago, by some workmen, when employed in excavating a water-course for a mill. The organisms lay crowded together, a single slab containing no fewer
than thirty specimens, and all in a singularly perfect state of
preservation. The whole space excavated did not exceed forty
square yards in extent, and yet in these forty yards there
were found several genera of fishes new to Geology, and not
yet figured nor described — a conclusive proof in itself that
we have still very much to learn regarding the fossils of the
Old Red Sandstone. By much the greater portion of the
remains disinterred on this occasion were preserved by a lady
in the neighborhood, and the news of the discovery spreading over the district, the Rev. Dr. Anderson, of Newburgh,

was fortunately led to discover them anew in her possession.
The most abundant organism of the group was a variety of
Pterichthys — the sixth species of this very curious genus now
discovered in the Old Red Sandstones of Scotland ; and as the
Doctor had been lucky enough to find out for himself, some
years before, that the scales of the *Holoptychius* were oyster
shells, he now ascertained, with quite as little assistance from
without, that the *Pterichthys* must have been surely a huge
beetle As a beetle, therefore, he figured and described it in
the pages of a Glasgow topographical publication — *Fife Illustrated.* True, the characteristic elytra were wanting,
and some six or seven tubercle plates substituted in their
room ; nor could the artist, with all his skill, supply the creature with more than two legs ; but ingenuity did much for it,
notwithstanding ; and by lengthening the snout, insect-like,
into a point — by projecting an eye, insect-like, on what had
mysteriously grown into a head — by rounding the body, insect-like, until it exactly resembled that of the large " twilight
shard " — by exaggerating the tubercles seen in profile on the
paddles until they stretched out, insect-like, into bristles —
and by carefully sinking the tail, which was not insect-like, and
for which no possible use could be discovered at the time —
the Doctor succeeded in making the *Pterichthys* of Dura Den
a very respectable beetle indeed. In a later publication, an
Essay on the Geology of Fifeshire, which appeared in September last in the *Quarterly Journal of Agriculture*, he states,
after referring to his former description, that among the higher
geological authorities some were disposed to regard the creature as an extinct crustaceous animal, and some as belonging
to a tribe closely allied to the *Chelonia.* Agassiz, as the
writer of these chapters ventured some months ago to pre-
dict, has since pronounced it a fish — a *Pterichthys* specifica'ly

17 *

different from the five varieties of this ichthyolite which occur
in the lower formation of the system, but generically the
same. I very lately enjoyed the pleasure of examining the
bona fide ichthyolite itself — one of the specimens of Dura
Den, and apparently one of the more entire — in the collection of Professor Fleming   Its character as a *Pterichthys* I
found very obvious ; but neither the Professor nor myself
was ingenious enough to discover in it any trace of the beetle
of Dr. Anderson *

Is it not interesting to find this very curious genus in both
the lowest and highest fossiliferous beds of the system, and
constituting, like the *Trilobite* genus of the Silurian group,
its most characteristic organism ?† The *Trilobite* has a wide
geological range, extending from the upper Cambrian rocks
to the upper Coal Measures   But though the range of the
genus is wide, that of every individual species of which it
consists is very limited.   The *Trilobites* of the upper Coal
Measures differ from those of the Mountain Limestone ;

---

* This interesting ichthyolite has since been regarded by Agassiz
as the representative of a distinct genus, to which he gives the name
Pamphractus.   As exhibited in his restoration, however, it seems to
differ little, if at all, (if I may venture the suggestion,) from a *Pterichthys* viewed on the upper side.   In Agassiz's beautiful restoration
of *Pterichthys,* and his accompanying prints of the fossils illustrative
of that genus, it is, with but one doubtful exception, the under side
of the animal that is presented , and hence a striking difference apparent between his representations of the two genera, which would
scarce obtain had the upper, not the under side of *Pterichthys* been
exhibited.   In verification of this remark, let the reader who has access to the *Monographic Poissons Fossiles* compare the restoration of
Pamphractus (Old Red, Tab. VI , fig. 2) with the upper side of *Pterichthys,* as figured in this volume, Plate I , fig. 1, making, of course,
the due allowance for a difference of species.

† See Note M.

these again, with but one exception, from the *Trilobites* of
the upper Silurian strata ; these yet again from the *Trilobites*
of the underlying middle beds ; and these from the *Trilobites*
that occur in the base of the system.   Like the coins and
medals of the antiquary, each represents its own limited
period , and the whole taken together yield a consecutive
record.   But while we find them merely scattered over the
later formations in which they occur, and that very sparingly,
in the Silurian System we find them congregated in such
vast crowds, that their remains enter largely into the composition of many of the rocks which compose it   The *Trilobite*
is the distinguishing organism of the group, marrying, if I
may so express myself, its upper and lower beds ; and what
the *Trilobite* is to the Silurian formations, the *Pterichthys*
seems to be to the formations of the Old Red Sandstone ;
with this difference, that, so far as is yet known, it is restricted
to this system alone, occurring in neither the Silurian System
below, nor in the Coal Measures above

I am but imperfectly acquainted with the localities in
which the upper beds of the Old Red Sandstone unde lie
the lower beds of the Coal Measures, or where any grada on
of character appears.   The upper yellow sandstone bel is
extensively developed in Moray, but it contains no trace of
carbonaceous matter in even its higher strata, and no ot er
remains than those of the *Holoptychius* and its contemporaries   The system in the north of Scotland differs as muc
from the carboniferous group in its upper as in its lower
rocks ; and a similar difference has been remarked in Fife
where the groups appear in contact a few miles to the west
of St Andrew's.   In England, in repeated instances, the
junction, as shown by Mr. Murchison, in singularly instructive
sections, is well marked, the carboniferous limestones resting

conformably on the Upper Old Red Sandstone. No other
system interposed between them.

There is a Rabbinical tradition that the sons of Tubal-
Cain, taught by a prophet of the coming deluge, and unwil-
ling that their father's arts should be lost in it to posterity,
erected two obelisks of brass, on which they inscribed a
record of his discoveries, and that thus the learning of the
family survived the cataclysm. The flood subsided, and the
obelisks, sculptured from pinnacle to base, were found fast
fixed in the rock. Now, the twin pyramids of the Old Red
Sandstone, with their party-colored bars, and their thickly
crowded inscriptions, belong to a period immensely more
remote than that of the columns of the antediluvians, and
they bear a more certain record. I have, perhaps, dwelt too
long on their various compartments ; but the Artist by whom
they have been erected, and who has preserved in them so
wonderful a chronicle of his earlier works, has willed surely
that they should be read, and I have perused but a small portion of the whole   Years must pass ere the entire record
can be deciphered ; but, of all its curiously inscribed sentences, the result will prove the same — they will all be found
to testify of the Infinite Mind.

CHAPTER X.

Speculations in the Old Red Sandstone, and their Character. — George, first Earl of Cromarty. — His Sagacity as a Naturalist at fault in one Instance. — Sets himself to dig for Coal in the Lower Old Red Sandstone. — Discovers a fine Artesian Well. — Value of Geological Knowledge in an economic View. — Scarce a Secondary Formation in the Kingdom in which Coal has not been sought for. — Mineral Springs of the Lower Old Red Sandstone. — Strathpeffer. — Its Peculiarities whence derived — Chalybeate Springs of Easter Ross and the Black Isle. — Petrifying Springs. — Building-Stone and Lime of the Old Red Sandstone. — Its various Soils.

THERE has been much money lost, and a good deal won, in speculations connected with the Old Red Sandstone. The speculations in which money has been won have consorted, if I may so speak, with the character of the system, and those in which money has been lost have not. Instead, however, of producing a formal chapter on the economic uses to which its various deposits have been applied, or the unfortunate undertakings which an acquaintance with its geology would have prevented, I shall throw together, as they occur to me, a few simple facts illustrative of both.

George, first Earl of Cromarty, seems, like his namesake and contemporary, the too celebrated Sir George M'Kenzie, of Roseavoch, to have been a man of an eminently active and inquiring mind. He found leisure, in the course of a very busy life, to write several historical dissertations of great research, and a very elaborate *Synopsis Apocalyptica*. He is the author, too, of an exceedingly curious letter on the "Second Sight," addressed to the philosophic Boyle, which con-

(173)

tains a large amount of amusing and extraordinary fact; and
his description of the formation of a peat-moss in the central
Highlands of Ross-shire has been quoted by almost every
naturalist who, since the days of the sagacious nobleman,
has written on the formation of peat.   His life was extended
to extreme old age; and as his literary ardor remained un-
diminished till the last, some of his writings were produced
at a period when most other men are sunk in the incurious
indifferency and languor of old age.   And among these later
productions are his remarks on peat.   He relates that, when
a very young man, he had marked, in passing on a journey
through the central Highlands of Ross-shire, a wood of very
ancient trees, doddered and moss-grown, and evidently passing into a state of death through the last stages of decay.
He had been led by business into the same district many
years after, when in middle life, and found that the wood had
entirely disappeared, and that the heathy hollow which it had
covered was now occupied by a green, stagnant morass, unvaried in its tame and level extent by either bush or tree.
In his old age he again visited the locality, and saw the green
surface roughened with dingy-colored hollows, and several
Highlanders engaged in it in cutting peat in a stratum several
feet in depth.   What he had once seen an aged forest had
now become an extensive peat-moss.

Some time towards the close of the seventeenth century
he purchased the lands of Cromarty, where his turn for minute observation seems to have anticipated — little, however,
to his own profit — some of the later geological discoveries.
There is a deep, wooded ravine in the neighborhood of the
town, traversed by a small stream, which has laid bare, for
the space of about forty yards in the opening of the hollow,
the gray sandstone and stratified clays of the inferior fish

bed. The locality is rather poor in ichthyolites, though I have found in it, after minute search, a few scales of the *Osteolepis*, and on one occasion one of the better marked plates of the *Coccosteus;* but in the vegetable impressions peculiar to the formation it is very abundant. These are invariably carbonaceous, and are not unfrequently associated with minute patches of bitumen, which, in the harder specimens, present a coal-like appearance ; and the vegetable impressions and the bitumen seem to have misled the sagacious nobleman into the belief that coal might be found on his new property. He accordingly brought miners from the south, and set them to bore for coal in the gorge of the ravine. Though there was probably a register kept of the various strata through which they passed, it must have long since been lost ; but from my acquaintance with this portion of the formation, as shown in the neighboring sections, where it lies uptilted against the granitic gneiss of the Sutors, I think I could pretty nearly restore it. They would first have had to pass for about thirty feet through the stratified clays and shales of the ichthyolite bed, with here and there a thin band of gray sandstone, and here and there a stratum of lime ; they would next have had to penetrate through from eighty to a hundred feet of coarse red and yellow sandstone, the red greatly predominating. They would then have entered the great conglomerate, the lowest member of the formation ; and in time, if they continued to urge their fruitless labors, they would arrive at the primary rock, with its belts of granite, and its veins and huge masses of hornblende. In short, there might be some possibility of their penetrating to the central fire, but none whatever of their ever reaching a vein of coal. From a curious circumstance, however, they were prevented from ascertaining, by actual experience, the utter barrenness of the formation.

Directly in the gorge of the ravine, where we may see
the partially wooded banks receding as they ascend from
the base to the centre, and then bellying over from the
centre to the summit, there is a fine chalybeate spring, surmounted by a dome of hewn stone. It was discovered by
the miners when in quest of the mineral which they did
not and could not discover, and forms one of the finest specimens of a true Artesian well which I have anywhere seen.
They had bored to a considerable depth, when, on withdrawing the kind of auger used for the purpose, a bolt of water,
which occupied the whole diameter of the bore, came rushing
after, like the jet of a fountain, and the work was prosecuted
no further ; for, as steam-engines were not yet invented, no
pit could have been wrought with so large a stream issuing
into it ; and as the volume was evidently restricted by the size
of the bore, it was impossible to say how much greater a
stream the source might have supplied. The spring still continues to flow towards the sea, between its double row of
cresses, at the rate of about a hogshead per minute — a rate
considerably diminished, it is said, from its earlier volume, by
some obstruction in the bore. The waters are not strongly
tinctured — a consequence, perhaps, of their great abundance ;
but we may see every pebble and stock in their course envel-
oped by a ferruginous coagulum, resembling burnt sienna,
that has probably been disengaged from the dark red sandstone below, which is known to owe its color to the oxide of
iron. A Greek poet would probably have described the inci-
dent as the birth of the Naiad ; in the north, however, which,
in an earlier age, had also its Naiads, though, like the fish of
the Old Red Sandstone, they have long since become extinct
the recollection of it is merely preserved by tradition, as a cu
rious, though by no means poetical fact, and by the name of

the well, which is still known as the well of the *coal-heugh* —
the old Scotch name for a coal-pit. Calderwood tells us, in
his description of a violent tempest which burst out immediately as his persecutor, James VI., breathed his last, that in
Scotland the sea rose high upon the land, and that many
" *coal-heughs* were drowned."

There is no science whose value can be adequately estimated by economists and utilitarians of the lower order. Its
true quantities cannot be represented by arithmetical figures or
monetary tables ; for its effects on mind must be as surely
taken into account as its operations on matter, and what it has
accomplished for the human intellect as certainly as what it
has done for the comforts of society or the interests of commerce. Who can attach a marketable value to the discoveries of Newton ? I need hardly refer to the often-quoted
remark of Johnson ; the beauty of the language in which it is
couched has rendered patent to all the truth which it conveys.
" Whatever withdraws us from the power of the senses," says
the moralist — " whatever makes the past, the distant, or the
future, predominate over the present, advances us in the dig-
nity of thinking beings." And Geology, in a peculiar manner, supplies to the intellect an exercise of this ennobling
character. But it has, also, its cash value. The time and
money squandered in Great Britain alone in searching for
coal in districts where the well-informed geologist could have
at once pronounced the search hopeless, would much more
than cover the expense at which geological research has been
prosecuted throughout the world. There are few districts in
Britain occupied by the secondary deposits, in which, at one
time or another, the attempt has not been made. It has been
the occasion of enormous expenditure in the south of England among the newer formations, where the coal, if it at all

18

occurs, (for we occasionally meet with wide gaps in the scale,) must be buried at an unapproachable depth   It led in Scotland — in the northern county of Sutherland — to an unprofitable working for many years of a sulphureous lignite of the inferior Oolite, far above the true Coal Measures.   The attempt I have just been describing was made in a locality as far beneath them   There is the scene of another and more modern attempt in the same district, on the shores of the Moray Frith, in a detached patch of Lias, where a fossilized wood would no doubt be found in considerable abundance, but no continuous vein even of lignite.   And it is related by Dr. Anderson, of Newburgh, that a fruitless and expensive search after coal has lately been instituted in the Old Red Sandstone beds which traverse Strathearn and the Carse of Gowrie, in the belief that they belong not to the Old, but to the *New* Red Sandstone — a formation which has been successfully perforated in prosecuting a similar search in various parts of England.   All these instances — and there are hundreds such — show the economic importance of the study of fossils.   The Oolite has its veins of apparent coal on the coast of Yorkshire, and its still more amply developed veins — one of them nearly four feet in thickness — on the eastern coast of Sutherlandshire ; the Lias has its coniferous fossils in great abundance, some of them converted into a lignite which can scarce be distinguished from a true coal ; and the bituminous masses of the Lower Old Red, and its carbonaceous markings, appear identical, to an unpractised eye, with the impressions on the carboniferous sandstones, and the bituminous masses which they, too, are occasionally found to enclose. Nor does the mineralogical character of its middle beds differ in many cases from that of the lower members of the New Red Sandstone.   I have seen the older rock in the north

of Scotland as strongly saliferous as any of the newer sandstones, of well nigh as bright a brick-red tint, of as friable and
mouldering a texture, and variegated as thickly with its specks
and streaks of green and buff-color. But in all these instances
there are strongly characterized groups of fossils, which, like
the landmarks of the navigator, or the findings of his quad-
rant, establish the true place of the formations to which they
belong. Like the patches of leather, of scarlet, and of blue,
which mark the line attached to the deep-sea lead, they show
the various depths at which we arrive. The Earls of Sutherland set themselves to establish a coal-work among the
chambered univalves of the Oolite, and a vast abundance of
its peculiar bivalves. The coal-borers who perforated the
Lias near Cromarty passed every day to and from their work
over one of the richest deposits of animal remains in the
kingdom — a deposit full of the most characteristic fossils;
and drove their auger through a thousand belemnites and
ammonites of the upper and inferior Lias, and through gryphites and ichthyodorulites innumerable. The sandstones of
Strathearn and the Carse of Gowrie yield their plates and
scales of the *Holoptychius*, the most abundant fossil of the
Upper Old Red ; and the shale of the little dell in which the
first Earl of Cromarty set his miners to work, contains, as I
have said, plates of the *Coccosteus* and scales of the *Osteolepis* — fossils found only in the Lower Old Red. Nature, in
all these localities, furnished the index, but men lacked the
skill necessary to decipher it.* I may mention that, inde-

---

* There occurs in Mr. Murchison's *Silurian System* a singularly
amusing account of one of the most unfortunate of all coal-boring
enterprises, the unlucky projector, a Welsh farmer, having set himself to dig for coal in the lowest member of the system, at least six

pendently of their well-marked organisms, there is a simple
test through which the lignites of the newer formations may
be distinguished from the true coal of the carboniferous system.   Coal, though ground into an impalpable powder, retains its deep black color, and may be used as a black pigment; lignite, on the contrary, when fully levigated, assumes
a reddish, or, rather, umbry hue.

I have said that the waters of the well of the coal-heugh
are chalybeate — a probable consequence of their infiltration
through the iron oxides of the superior beds of the formation,
and their subsequent passage through the deep red strata of

---

formations beneath the only one at which the object of his search
could have been found.   Mr Murchison thus relates the story : —

"At Tin-y-coed I found a credulous farmer ruining himself in excavating a horizontal gallery in search of coal, an ignorant miner
being his engineer.   The case may serve as a striking example of the
coal-boring mania in districts which cannot by possibility contain that
mineral; and a few words concerning it may, therefore, prove a sal-
utary warning to those who speculate for coal in the Silurian Rocks.
The farmhouse of Tin-y-coed is situated on the sloping sides of a hill
of trap, which throw off, upon its north-western flank, thin beds of
black grauwacke shale, dipping to the west-north-west at a high angle.   The color of the shale, and of the water that flowed down its
sides, the pyritous veins, and other vulgar symptoms of coal-bearing
strata, had long convinced the farmer that he possessed a large hid-
den mass of coal, and, unfortunately, a small fragment of real anthracite was discovered, which burnt like the best coal.   Miners were
sent for, and operations commenced.   To sink a shaft was imprac-
ticable, both from the want of means, and the large volume of water.
A slightly inclined gallery was therefore commenced, the mouth of
which was opened at the bottom of the hill, on the side of the little
brook which waters the dell.   I have already stated that, in many
cases, where the intrusive trap throws off the shale, the latter preserves its natural and unaltered condition to within a certain distance

the inferior bed. There could be very curious chapters written on mineral springs, in their connection with the formations
through which they pass. Smollett's masterpiece, honest old
Matthew Bramble, became thoroughly disgusted with the Bath
waters on discovering that they filtered through an ancient
burying-ground belonging to the Abbey, and that much of
their peculiar taste and odor might probably be owing to the
" rotten bones and mouldering carcasses" through which
they were strained. Some of the springs of the Old Red
Sandstone have also the churchyard taste, but the bones and
carcasses through which they strain are much older than
those of the Abbey burying-ground at Bath The bitumen

---

of the trap; and so it was at Tin-y-coed, for the level proceeded for
155 feet with little or no obstacle. Mounds of soft black shale attest-
ed the rapid progress of the adventurers, when suddenly they came
to a 'change of metal.' They were now approaching the nucleus of
the little ridge, and the rock they encountered was, as the men informed me, ' as hard as iron,' viz., of lydianized schist, precisely analogous to that which is exposed naturally in ravines where all the
phenomena are laid bare. The deluded people, however, endeavored
to penetrate the hardened mass, but the vast expense of blasting it
put a stop to the undertaking, not, however, without a thorough conviction on the part of the farmer, that, could he but have got through
that hard stuff, he would most surely have been well recompensed,
for it was just thereabouts that they began to find 'small veins of
coal.' It has been before shown, that portions of anthracite are not
unfrequent in the altered shale, where it is in contact with the intrusive rock. And the occurrence of the smallest portion of anthracite
is always sufficient to lead the Radnorshire farmer to suppose that
he is very near 'El Dorado.' Amid all their failures, I never met
with an individual who was really disheartened, a frequent exclama-
tion being, 'O, if our squires were only men of spirit, we should
have as fine coal as any in the world!' " — (Silurian System, Part I.,
p. 328)

18*

of the strongly impregnated rocks and clay-beds of this for
mation, like the bitumen of the still more strongly impregnated limestones and shales of the Lias, seems to have had
rather an animal than vegetable origin. The shales of the
Eathie Lias burn like turf soaked in oil, and yet they hardly
contain one per cent. of vegetable matter. In a single cubic
inch, however, I have counted about eighty molluscous
organisms, mostly ammonites, and minute striated scallops;
and the mass, when struck with the hammer, still yields the
heavy odor of animal matter in a state of decay. The lower
fish-beds of the Old Red are, in some localities, scarcely less
bituminous. The fossil scales and plates, which they enclose
burn at the candle; they contain small cavities filled with a
strongly scented, semi-fluid bitumen, as adhesive as tar, and
as inflammable; and for many square miles together the bed
is composed almost exclusively of a dark-colored, semi-calcareous, semi-aluminous schist, scarcely less fetid, from the
great quantity of this substance which it contains, than the
swine-stones of England. Its vegetable remains bear but a
small proportion to its animal organisms; and from huge accumulations of these last decomposing amid the mud of a
still sea, little disturbed by tempests or currents, and then suddenly interred by some widely spread catastrophe, to ferment
and consolidate under vast beds of sand and conglomerate
the bitumen * seems to have been elaborated   These bituminous schists, largely charged with sulphuret of iron, run
far into the interior, along the flanks of the gigantic Ben We-

---

* "In the slaty schists of Seefeld, in the Tyrol," say Messrs Sedgwick and Murchison, "there is such an abundance of a similar bitumen, that it is largely extracted for medicinal purposes." — (Geol.
Trans. for 1829, p 131)

vis, and through the exquisitely pastoral valley of Strathpeffer. The higher hills which rise over the valley are formed
mostly of the great conglomerate — Knockferril, with its vit-
rified fort — the wooded and precipitous ridge over Brahan
— and the middle eminences of the gigantic mountain on the
north , but the bottom and the lower slopes of the valley are
occupied by the bituminous and sulphureous schists of the
fish-bed, and in these, largely impregnated with the peculiar
ingredients of the formation, the famous medicinal springs of
the Strath have their rise They contain, as shown by chemical analysis, the sulphates of soda, of lime, of magnesia,
common salt, and, above all, sulphuretted hydrogen gas —
elements which masses of sea-mud, charged with animal
matter, would yield as readily to the chemist as the medicinal
springs of Strathpeffer Is it not a curious reflection, that
the commercial greatness of Britain, in the present day, should
be closely connected with the towering and thickly spread
forests of arboraceous ferns and gigantic reeds — vegetables
of strange form and uncouth names — which flourished and
decayed on its surface, age after age, during the vastly extended term of the carboniferous period, ere the mountains
were yet upheaved, and when there was as yet no man to till
the ground ? Is it not a reflection equally curious, that the
invalids of the present summer should be drinking health,
amid the recesses of Strathpeffer, from the still more ancient
mineral and animal debris of the lower ocean of the Old Red
Sandstone, strangely elaborated for vast but unreckoned periods in the bowels of the earth ? The fact may remind us of
one of the specifics of a now obsolete school of medicine,
which flourished in this country about two centuries ago, and
which included in its *materia medica* portions of the human
frame. Among these was the flesh of Egyptian mummies,

impregnated with the embalming drugs — the dried muscles
and sinews of human creatures who had walked in the streets
of Thebes or of Luxor three thousand years ago.

The commoner mineral springs of the formation, as might
be anticipated, from the very general diffusion of the oxide
to which it owes its color, are chalybeate.   There are districts in Easter-Ross and the Black Isle in which the traveller
scarcely sees a runnel by the way-side that is not half choked
up by its fox-colored coagulum of oxide.   Two of the most
strongly impregnated chalybeates with which I am acquainted
gush out of a sandstone bed, a few yards apart, among the
woods of Tarbat House, on the northern shore of the Frith
of Cromarty.   They splash among the pebbles with a half-
gurgling, half-tinkling sound, in a solitary but not unpleasing
recess, darkened by alders and willows ; and their waters,
after uniting in the same runnel, form a little, melancholy
looking *lochan*, matted over with weeds, and edged with flags
and rushes, and which swarms in early summer with the
young of the frog in its tadpole state, and in the after months
with the black water-beetle and the newt.   The circumstance
is a somewhat curious one, as the presence of iron as an oxide has been held so unfavorable to both animal and vegetable life, that the supposed poverty of the Old Red Sandstone
in fossil remains has been attributed to its almost universal
diffusion at the period the deposition was taking place.   Were
the system as poor as has been alleged, however, it might be
questioned, on the strength of a fact such as this, whether
the iron militated so much against the living existences of
the formation, as against the preservation of their remains
when dead.

Some of the springs which issue from the ichthyolite beds
along the shores of the Moray Frith are largely charged, not

with iron, like the well of the coal-heugh, or the springs of
Tarbat House, nor yet with hydrogen and soda, like the spa
of Strathpeffer, but with carbonate of lime. When employed
for domestic purposes, they choke up, in a few years, with a
stony deposition, the spouts of tea-kettles. On a similar
principle, they plug up their older channels, and then burst
out in new ones; nor is it uncommon to find among the cliffs
little hollow recesses, long since divested of their waters by
this process, that are still thickly surrounded by coral-like in-
crustations of moss and lichens, grass and nettle-stalks, and
roofed with marble-like stalactites. I am acquainted with at
least one of these springs of very considerable volume, and ded-
icated of old to an obscure Roman Catholic saint, whose name
it still bears, (St. Bennet,) which presents phenomena not unworthy the attention of the young geologist. It comes gush-
ing from out the ichthyolite bed, where the latter extends, in
the neighborhood of Cromarty, along the shores of the Moray
Frith: and after depositing in a stagnant morass an accumulation of a grayish-colored and partially consolidated traver-
tin, escapes by two openings to the shore, where it is absorbed
among the sand and gravel. A storm about three years ago
swept the beach several feet beneath its ordinary level, and
two little moles of conglomerate and sandstone, the work of
the spring, were found to occupy the two openings. Each
had its fossils — comminuted sea-shells, and stalks of hardened
moss; and in one of the moles I found imbedded a few of
the vertebral joints of a sheep. It was a recent formation
on a small scale, bound together by a calcareous cement furnished by the fish-beds of the inferior Old Red Sandstone,
and composed of sand and pebbles, mostly from the granitic
gneiss of the neighboring hill, and organisms, vegetable and
animal, from both the land and the sea.

The Old Red Sandstone of Scotland has been extensively employed for the purposes of the architect, and its limestones occasionally applied to those of the agriculturist. As might be anticipated in reference to a deposit so widely spread, the quality of both its sandstones and its lime is found to vary exceedingly in even the same beds when examined in different localities. Its inferior conglomerate, for instance, in the neighborhood of Cromarty, weathers so rapidly, that a fence built of stones furnished by it little more than half a century ago, has mouldered in some places into a mere grass-covered mound. The same bed in the neighborhood of Inverness is composed of a stone nearly as hard and quite as durable as granite, and which has been employed in paving the streets of the place — a purpose which it serves as well as any of the igneous or primary rocks could have done. At Redcastle, on the northern shore of the Frith of Beauly, the same conglomerate assumes an intermediate character, and forms, though coarse, an excellent building stone, which, in some of the older ruins of the district, presents the marks of the tool as sharply indented as when under the hands of the workman. Some of the sandstone beds of the system are strongly saliferous; and these, however coherent they may appear, never resist the weather until first divested of their salt. The main ichthyolite bed on the northern shore of the Moray Frith is overlaid by a thick deposit of a finely-tinted yellow sandstone of this character, which, unlike most sandstones of a mouldering quality, resists the frosts and storms of winter, and wastes only when the weather becomes warm and dry. A few days of sunshine affect it more than whole months of high winds and showers. The heat crystallizes at the surface the salt which it contains; the crystals, acting as wedges, throw off minute particles of the stone; and thus, mechani-

cally at least, the degrading process is the same as that to
which sandstones of a different but equally inferior quality
are exposed during severe frosts. In the course of years,
however, this sandstone, when employed in building, loses its
salt; crust after crust is formed on the surface, and either
forced off by the crystals underneath, or washed away by the
rains; and then the stone ceases to waste, and gathers on its
weathered inequalities a protecting mantle of lichens.* The
most valuable quarries in the Old Red System of Scotland yet
discovered, are the flagstone quarries of Caithness and Carmylie. The former have been opened in the middle schists
of the lower, or Tilestone formation of the system ; the latter,
as I have had occasion to remark oftener than once, in the
Cornstone, or middle formation. The quarries of both Carmylie and Caithness employ hundreds of workmen, and their
flagstones form an article of commerce. The best building-
stone of the north of Scotland — best both for beauty and
durability — is a pure Quartzose Sandstone furnished by the
upper beds of the system. These are extensively quarried
in Moray, near the village of Burghead, and exported to all
parts of the kingdom. The famous obelisk of Forres, so

* When left to time the process is a tedious one, and, ere its accomplishment, the beauty of the masonry is always in some degree destroyed. The following passage, from a popular work, points out a
mode by which it might possibly be anticipated, and the waste of surface prevented : — " A hall of which the walls were constantly damp
though every means were employed to keep them dry, was about to
be pulled down, when M Schmithall recommended, as a last resource,
that the walls should be washed with sulphuric acid, (vitriol.) It
was done, and the deliquescent salts being decomposed by acid, the
walls dried, and the hall was afterwards free from dampness." — (Rec-
reations in Science.)

interesting to the antiquary — which has been described by
some writers as formed of a species of stone unknown in the
district, and which, according to a popular tradition, was
transported from the Continent — is evidently composed of
this Quartzose Sandstone, and must have been dug out of
one of the neighboring quarries. And so coherent is its texture, that the storms of, perhaps, ten centuries have failed
to obliterate its rude but impressive sculptures.

The limestones of both the upper and lower formations of
the system have been wrought in Moray with tolerable success. In both, however, they contain a considerable per
centage of siliceous and argillaceous earth. The system,
though occupying an intermediate place between two metal-
liferous deposits, — the giauwacke and the carboniferous
limestone, — has not been found to contain workable veins
any where in Britain. and in Scotland no metallic veins of any
kind, with the exception of here and there a few slender
threads of ironstone, and here and there a few detached crystals of galena. Its wealth consists exclusively in building
and paving stone, and in lime. Some of the richest tracts of
corn land in the kingdom rest on the Old Red Sandstone —
the agricultural valley of Strathmore, for instance, and the
fertile plains of Easter-Ross: Caithness has also its deep,
corn-bearing soils, and Moray has been well known for centuries as the granary of Scotland. But in all these localities
the fertility seems derived rather from an intervening subsoil
of tenacious diluvial clay, than from the rocks of the system.
Wherever the clay is wanting, the soil is barren. In the moor
of the Milbuy, — a tract about fifty square miles in extent, and
lying within an hour's walk of the Friths of Cromarty and
Beauly, — a thin covering of soil rests on the sandstones of the

lower formation. And so extreme is the barrenness of this moor, that notwithstanding the advantages of its semi-insular situation, it was suffered to lie as an unclaimed common until about twenty-five years ago, when it was parcelled out among the neighboring proprietors.

19

CHAPTER XI.

PHYSIOGNOMY is no idle or doubtful science in connection with Geology. The physiognomy of a country indicates, almost invariably, its geological character. There is scarce a rock among the more ancient groups that does not affect its peculiar form of hill and valley. Each has its style of landscape; and as the vegetation of a district depends often on the nature of the underlying deposits, not only are the main outlines regulated by the mineralogy of the formations which they define, but also in many cases the manner in which these outlines are filled up. The coloring of the landscape is well nigh as intimately connected with its Geology as the drawing. The traveller passes through a mountainous region of gneiss. The hills, which, though bulky, are shapeless, raise their huge backs so high over the brown, dreary moors, which, unvaried by precipice or ravine, stretch away for miles from their feet, that even amid the heats of midsummer the snow gleams in streaks and patches from their summits. And yet so vast is their extent of base, and their tops so truncated, that they seem but half-finished hills notwithstanding — hills interdicted somehow in the forming, and the work stopped ere the upper stories had been added.   He pursues his journey and enters a district of micaceous schist.   The hills are no longer truncated, or the moors unbroken ; the heavy ground-swell of the former landscape has become a tempestuous sea, agitated by powerful winds and conflicting tides   The picturesque and somewhat fantastic outline is composed of high, sharp peaks, bold, craggy domes, steep, broken acclivities, and deeply serrated ridges , and the higher hills seem as if set round with a framework of props and buttresses, that stretch out on every side like the roots of an ancient oak.   He passes on, and the landscape varies ; the surrounding hills, though lofty, pyramidal, and abrupt, are less rugged than before ;   and the ravines, though still deep and narrow, are walled by ridges no longer serrated and angular, but comparatively rectilinear and smooth.   But the vegetation is even more scanty than formerly ; the steeper slopes are covered with streams of debris, on which scarce a moss or lichen finds root ; and the conoidal hills, bare of soil from their summits half way down, seem so many naked skeletons, that speak of the decay and death of nature   All is solitude and sterility   The territory is one of Quartz rock.   Still the traveller passes on : the mountains sink into low swellings ; long rectilinear ridges run out towards the distant sea, and terminate in bluff, precipitous headlands.   The valleys, soft and pastoral, widen into plains, or incline in long-drawn slopes of gentlest declivity.   The streams, hitherto so headlong and broken, linger beside their banks, and then widen into firths and estuaries.   The deep soil is covered by a thick mantle of vegetation — by forest trees of largest growth, and rich fields of corn ; and the solitude of the mountains has given place to a busy population. He has left behind him the primary regions, and entered on one of the secondary districts.

And these less rugged formations have also their respective styles — marred and obliterated often by the Plutonic agency, which imparts to them in some instances its own character, and in some an intermediate one, but in general distinctly marked, and easily recognized. The Chalk presents its long inland lines of apparent coast, that send out their rounded headlands, cape beyond cape, into the wooded or coin-covered plains below. Here and there, there juts up at the base of the escarpement a white, obelisk-like stack; here and there, there opens into the interior a narrow, grassy bay, in which noble beeches have cast anchor. There are valleys without streams; and the landscape a-top is a scene of arid and uneven downs, that seem to rise and fall like the sea after a storm. We pass on to the Oolite . the slopes are more gentle, the lines of rising ground less continuous, and less coast-like; the valleys have their rivulets, and the undulating surface is covered by a richer vegetation We enter on a district of New Red Sandstone. Deep, narrow ravines intersect elevated platforms. There are lines of low precipices, so perpendicular and so red, that they seem as if walled over with new brick; and here and there, amid the speckled and mouldering sandstones, that gather no covering of lichen, there stands up a huge, altar-like mass of lime, mossy and gray, as if it represented a remoter antiquity than the rocks around it. The Coal Measures present often the appearance of vast lakes frozen over during a high wind, partially broken afterwards by a sudden thaw, and then frozen again. Their shores stand up around them in the form of ridges and mountain chains of the older rocks; and their surfaces are grooved into flat valleys and long lines of elevation Take, as an instance, the scenery about Edinburgh The Ochil Hills and the Grampians form the distant shores of the seeming lake or basin on the one s.de, the range of the Lammermuirs and the Pentland group on the other; the space between is ridged and furrowed in long lines, that run in nearly the same direction from north-east to south-west, as if, when the binding frost was first setting in, the wind had blown from off the northern or southern shore.

But whence these abrupt, precipitous hills that stud the landscape, and form, in the immediate neighborhood of the city, its more striking features? They belong — to return to the illustration of the twice-frozen lake — to the middle period of thaw, when the ice broke up; and, as they are composed chiefly of matter ejected from the abyss, might have characterized equally any of the other formations Their very striking forms, however, illustrate happily the operations of the great agencies on which, in the secondary and transition deposits, all the peculiarities of scenery depend. The molten matter from beneath seems to have been injected, in the first instance, through rents and fissures among the carboniferous shales and sandstones of the district, where it lay cooling in its subterranean matrices, in beds and dikes, like metal in the moulds of the founder; and the places which it occupied must have been indicated on the surface but by curves and swellings of the strata. The denuding power then came into operation in the form of tides and currents, and ground down the superincumbent rocks. The injected masses, now cooled and hardened, were laid bare; and the softer framework of the moulds in which they had been cast was washed from their summits and sides, except where long ridges remained attached to them in the lines of the current, as if to indicate the direction in which they had broken its force. Every larger stone in a water-course, after the torrent fed by a thunder shower has just subsided, shows on the

same principle, its trail of sand and shingle piled up behind
it. The outlines of the landscape were modified yet further
by the yielding character of the basement of sandstone or
shale on which the Plutonic beds so often rest. The base
ment crumbled away as the tides and waves broke against it.
The injected beds above, undermined in the process, and with
a vertical cleavage, induced by their columnar tendency, fell
down in masses that left a front perpendicular as a wall.
Each bed came thus to present its own upright line of precipice ; and hence — when they rise bed above bed, as often
occurs — the stair-like outline of hill to which the trap rocks
owe their name ; hence the outline of the Dalmahoy Crags,
for instance, and of the southern and western front of Salisbury Crags.

In all the sedimentary formations the peculiarities of scenery depend on three circumstances — on the Plutonic agencies, the denuding agencies, and the manner and proportions
in which the harder and softer beds of the deposits on which
these operated alternate with one another. There is an union
of the active and the passive in the formation of landscape ;
that which disturbs and grinds down, and that which, according to its texture and composition, affects, if I may so speak,
a peculiar style of being ground down and disturbed ; and it
is in the passive circumstances that the peculiarities chiefly
originate. Hence it is that the scenery of the Chalk differs
from the scenery of the Oolite, and both from that of the
Coal Measures. The Old Red Sandstone has also its peculiarities of prospect, which vary according to its formations,
and the amount and character of the disturbing and denuding
agencies to which these have been exposed Instead, however, of crowding its various, and, in some instances, dissimilar features into one landscape, I shall introduce to the reader

a few of its more striking and characteristic scenes, as exhibited in various localities, and by different deposits, beginning first with its conglomerate base.

The great antiquity of this deposit is unequivocally indicated by the manner in which we find it capping, far in the interior, in insulated beds and patches, some of our loftier hills, or, in some instances, wrapping them round, as with a caul, from base to summit. It mixes largely, in our northern districts, with the mountain scenery of the country, and imparts strength and boldness of outline to every landscape in which it occurs. Its island-like patches affect generally a bluff parabolic or conical outline; its loftier hills present rounded, dome-like summits, which sink to the plain on the one hand in steep, slightly concave lines, and on the other in lines decidedly convex, and a little less steep. The mountain of boldest outline in the line of the Caledonian Valley (Mealforvony) is composed externally of this rock. Except where covered by the diluvium, it seems little friendly to vegetation. Its higher summits are well nigh as bare as those of the primary rocks; and when a public road crosses its lower ridges, the traveller generally finds that there is no paving process necessary to procure a hardened surface, for his wheels rattle over the pebbles embedded in the rock. On the sea-coast, in several localities, the deposit presents striking peculiarities of outline. The bluff and rounded precipices stand out in vast masses, that affect the mural form, and present few of the minuter angularities of the primary rocks. Here and there a square buttress of huge proportions leans against the front of some low-browed crag, that seems little to need any such support, and casts a length of shadow athwart its face. There opens along the base of the rock a line of rounded, shallow caves, or what seem rather the open-

ings of caves not yet dug, and which testify of a period when
the sea stood about thirty feet higher on our coasts than at
present.   A multitude of stacks and tabular masses lie
grouped in front, perforated often by squat, heavy arches;
and stacks, caverns, buttresses, crags, and arches, are all
alike mottled over by the thickly-set and variously colored
pebbles.   There is a tract of scenery of this strangely
marked character in the neighborhood of Dunottar, and two
other similar tracts in the far north, where the hill of Nigg,
in Ross-shire, declines towards the Lias deposit in the Bay of
Shandwick, and where, in the vicinity of Inverness, a line
of bold, precipitous coast runs between the pyramidal wooded
eminence which occupies the south-eastern corner of Ross,
and the tower-like headlands that guard the entrance of the
Bay of Munlochy   In the latter tract, however, the conglomerate is much less cavernous than in the other two *

The sea-coast of St. Vigeans, in Forfarshire, has been
long celebrated for its romantic scenery and its caves; and
though it belongs rather to the conglomerate base of the upper formation than to the great conglomerate base of the
lower, it is marked, from the nature of the materials — materials common to both — by features indistinguishable from
those which characterize the sea-coasts of the older deposit.
Its wall of precipices averages from a hundred to a hundred
and eighty feet in height — no very great matter compared
with some of our northern lines, but the cliffs make up for
their want of altitude by their bold and picturesque combinations of form; and I scarce know where a long summer's
day could well be passed more agreeably than among their
wild and solitary recesses   The incessant lashings of the sea
have ground them down into shapes the most fantastic.   Huge
stacks, that stand up from amid the breakers, are here and

* See Note N.

there perforated by round, heavy-browed arches, and cast the morning shadows inland athwart the cavern-hollowed precipices behind The never-ceasing echoes reply, in long and gloomy caves, to the wild tones of the sea. Here a bluff promontory projects into the deep, green water, and the white foam, in times of tempest, dashes up a hundred feet against its face. There a narrow strip of vegetation, spangled with wild flowers, intervenes between the beach and the foot of the cliffs that sweep along the bottom of some semicircular bay ; but we see, from the rounded caves by which they are studded, and the polish which has blunted their lower angularities, that at some early period the breakers must have dashed for ages against their bases The *Gaylet Pot*, a place of interest, from its very striking appearance, to more than geologists, is connected with one of the deep-sea promontories We see an oblong hollow in the centre of a corn-field, that borders on the cliffs. It deepens as we approach it, and on reaching the edge we find ourselves standing on the verge of a precipice about a hundred and fifty feet in depth, and see the waves dashing along the bottom. On descending by a somewhat precarious path, we find that a long, tunnel-like cavern communicates with the sea, and mark, through the deep gloom of the passage, the sunlight playing beyond ; and now and then a white sail passing the opening, as if flitting across the field of a telescope. The *Gaylet Pot* seems originally to have been merely a deep, straight cave, hollowed in the line of a fault by the waves ; and it owes evidently its present appearance to the falling in of the roof for about a hundred yards, at its inner extremity.

We pass from the conglomerate to the middle and upper beds of the lower formation, and find scenery of a different character in the districts in which they prevail The aspect is

less bold and rugged, and affects often long horizontal lines,
that stretch away without rise or depression, amid the surrounding inequalities of the landscape for miles and leagues, and
that decline to either side, like roofs of what the architect
would term a low pitch.   The ridge of the Leys in the eastern opening of the Caledonian Valley, so rectilinear in its
outline, and so sloping in its sides, presents a good illustration
of this peculiarity.   The rectilinear ridge which runs from
the Southern Sutor of Cromarty far into the interior of the
country, and which has been compared in a former chapter
to the shaft of a spear, furnishes another illustration equally
apt.*   Where the sloping sides of these roof-like ridges
decline, as in the latter instance, towards an exposed sea-
coast, we find the slope terminating often in an abrupt line of
rock dug out by the waves   It is thus a roof set on walls,
and furnished with eaves   A ditch just finished by the laborer presents regularly sloping sides ; but the little stream that
comes running through gradually widens its bed by digging
furrows into the slopes, the undermined masses fall in and are
swept away, and, in the course of a few months, the sides are
no longer sloping, but abrupt.   And such, on a great scale,

---

* The valleys which separate these ridges form often spacious friths
and bays, the frequent occurrence of which in the Old Red Sandstone
constitutes, in some localities, one of the characteristics of the system.
Mark in a map of the north of Scotland, how closely friths and estuaries lie crowded together between the counties of Sutherland and Inverness.   In a line of coast little more than forty miles in extent,
there occur four arms of the sea — the Friths of Cromarty, Beauly,
and Dornoch, and the Bay of Munlochy   The Frith of Tay and the
Basin of Montrose are also semi-marine valleys of the Old Red Sandstone.   Two of the finest harbors in Britain, or the world, belong to it
— Milford Haven, in South Wales, and the Bay of Cromarty.

has been the process through which coast-lines that were originally paved slopes have become walls of precipices. The waves cut first through the outer strata ; and every stratum thus divided comes to present two faces — a perpendicular face in the newly-formed line of precipice, and another horizontal face lying parallel to it, along the shore. One half the severed stratum seems as if rising out of the sea, the other half as if descending from the hill : the geologist who walks along the beach finds the various beds presented in duplicate — a hill-bed on the one side, and a sea-bed on the other. There occurs a very interesting instance of this arrangement in the bold line of coast on the northern shore of the Moray Frith, so often alluded to in a previous chapter, as extending between the Southern Sutor and the Hill of Eathie ; and which forms the wall of a portion of the roof-like ridge last described. The sea first broke in a long line through strata of red and gray shale, next through a thick bed of pale-yellow stone, then through a continuous bed of stratified clays and nodular limestone, and, last of all, through a bed, thicker than any of the others, of indurated red sandstone. The line of cliffs formed in this way rises abruptly for about a hundred yards on the one hand ; the shore stretches out for more than double the same space on the other ; on both sides the beds exactly correspond ; and to ascend in the line of the strata from the foot of the cliffs, we have either to climb the hill, or to pass downwards at low ebb to the edge of the sea. The section is of interest, not only from the numerous organisms, animal and vegetable, which its ichthyolite beds contain, but from the illustration which it also furnishes of denudation to a vast extent from causes still in active operation. A line of precipices a hundred yards in height, and more than two miles in length, has been dug out of the slope by the slow wear of the waves, in the unreckoned course of that period during which the present sea was bounded in this locality by the existing line of coast. (See Frontispiece, sect. 3.)

I know not a more instructive walk for the young geologist than that furnished by the two miles of shore along which this section extends. Years of examination and inquiry would fail to exhaust it. It presents us, I have said, with the numerous organisms of the Lower Old Red Sandstone ; it presents us also, towards its western extremity, with the still more numerous organisms of the Lower and Upper Lias ; nor are the inflections and faults which its strata exhibit less instructive than its fossils or its vast denuded hollow. I have climbed along its wall of cliffs during the height of a tempestuous winter tide, when waves of huge volume, that had begun to gather strength under the night of the Northern Ocean, were bursting and foaming below ; and as the harder pebbles, uplifted by the surge, rolled by thousands and tens of thousands along the rocky bottom, and the work of denudation went on, I have thought of the remote past, when the same agents had first begun to grind down the upper strata, whose broken edges now projected high over my head on the one hand, and lay buried far under the waves at my feet on the other. Almost all mountain chains present their abrupter escarpements to the sea, though separated from it in many instances by hundreds of miles — a consequence, it is probable, of a similar course of denudation, ere they had attained their present altitude, or the plains at their feet had been elevated over the level of the ocean. Had a rise of a hundred feet taken place in this northern district in the days of Cæsar, the whole upper part of the Moray Frith would have been laid dry, and it would now have seemed as inexplicable that this roof-like ridge should present so rugged a line of wall to the distant sea, as that the Western Ghauts of India should invariably turn their steepest declivities to the basin of the Indian Ocean, or that, from the Arctic Circle to the southern extremity of Patagonia, the huge mountain-chain of America should elevate its dizzy precipices in the line of the Pacific.

Let us take another view of this section. It stretches between two of the granitic knobs or wedges to which I have had such frequent occasion to refer — the Southern Sutor of Cromarty, and the Hill of Eathie ; and the edges of the strata somewhat remind one of the edges of a bundle of deals laid flatways on two stones, and bent towards the middle by their own weight. But their more brittle character is shown by the manner in which their ends are broken and uptilted against the granitic knobs on which they seem to rest ; and towards the western knob the whole bundle has been broken across from below, and the opening occasioned by the fracture forms a deep, savage ravine, skirted by precipices, that runs far into the interior, and exhibits the lower portion of the system to well nigh its base. Will the reader spend a very few minutes in exploring the solitary recesses of this rocky trench — it matters not whether as a scene-hunter or a geologist ? We pass onwards along the beach through the middle line of the denuded hollow. The natural rampart that rises on the right ascends towards the uplands in steep slopes, lined horizontally by sheep-walks, and fretted by mossy knolls, and churchyard like ridges — or juts out into abrupt and weathered crags, crusted with lichens and festooned with ivy — or recedes into bosky hollows, roughened by the sloe-thorn, the wild-rose, and the juniper ; on the left the wide extent of the Moray Frith stretches out to the dim horizon, with its vein-like currents, and its undulating lines of coast ; while before us we

see, far in the distance, the blue vista of the Great Valley,
with its double wall of jagged and serrated hills, and directly
in the opening, the gray, diminished spires of Inverness. We
reach a brown mossy stream, of just volume enough to sweep
away the pebbles and shells that have been strewed in its
course by the last tide; and see, on turning a sudden angle,
the precipices cleft to their base by the ravine that has yielded
its waters a passage from the interior

We enter along the bed of the stream. A line of mural
precipices rises on either hand — here advancing in ponderous
overhanging buttresses, there receding into deep, damp recesses, tapestried with ivy, and darkened with birch and hazel.
A powerful spring, charged with lime, comes pouring by a
hundred different threads over the rounded brow of a beetling
crag, and the decaying vegetation around it is hardening into
stone.   The cliffs vary their outline at every step, as if assuming in succession all the various combinations of form that
constitute the wild and the picturesque; and the pale hues of
the stone seem, when brightened by the sun, the very tints a
painter would choose to heighten the effect of his shades, or to
contrast most delicately with the luxuriant profusion of bushes
and flowers that wave over the higher shelves and crannies.
A colony of swallows have built from time immemorial under
the overhanging strata of one of the loftier precipices; the fox
and badger harbor in the clefts of the steeper and more inaccessible banks. As we proceed, the dell becomes wilder
and more deeply wooded, the stream frets and toils at our
feet — here leaping over an opposing ridge — there struggling
in a pool — yonder escaping to the light from under some
broken fragment of cliff.   There is a richer profusion of
flowers, a thicker mantling of ivy and honeysuckle; and after
passing a semicircular inflection of the bank, that waves

from base to summit with birch, hazel, and hawthorn, we find the passage shut up by a perpendicular wall of rock about thirty feet in height, over which the stream precipitates itself, in a slender column of foam, into a dark, mossy basin. The long arms of an intermingled clump of birches and hazels stretch half way across, tripling with their shade the apparent depth of the pool, and heightening in an equal ratio the white flicker of the cascade, and the effect of the bright patches of foam which, flung from the rock, incessantly revolve on the eddy.

Mark now the geology of the ravine. For about half way from where it opens to the shore, to where the path is obstructed by the deep mossy pool and the cascade, its precipitous sides consist of three bars or stories. There is first, reckoning from the stream upwards, a broad bar of pale red; then a broad bar of pale lead color; last and highest, a broad bar of pale yellow; and above all, there rises a steep green slope, that continues its ascent till it gains the top of the ridge. The middle, lead-colored bar is an ichthyolite bed, a place of sepulture among the rocks, where the dead lie by myriads The yellow bar above is a thick bed of saliferous sandstone. We may see the projections on which the sun has beat most powerfully covered with a white crust of salt; and it may be deemed worthy of remark, in connection with the circumstance, that its shelves and crannies are richer in vegetation than those of the other bars. The pale red bar below is composed of a coarser and harder sandstone, which forms an upper moiety of the arenaceous portion of the great conglomerate. Now mark, further, that on reaching a midway point between the beach and the cascade, this triple-barred line of precipices abruptly terminates, and a line of precipices of coarse conglomerate as abruptly begins. I occasionally pass a continuous wall, built at two different periods and composed of two different kinds of materials the one half of it is formed of white sandstone, the other half of a dark-colored basalt; and the place where the sandstone ends and the basalt begins is marked by a vertical line, on the one side of which all is dark colored, while all is of a light color on the other. Equally marked and abrupt is the vertical line which separates the triple-barred from the conglomerate cliffs of the ravine of Eathie. The ravine itself may be described as a fault in the strata; but here is a fault, lying at right angles with it, on a much larger scale: the great conglomerate on which the triple bars rest has been cast up at least two hundred feet, and placed side by side with them. And yet the surface above bears no trace of the catastrophe. Denuding agencies of even greater power than those which have hollowed out the cliffs of the neighboring coast, or whose operations have been prolonged through periods of even more extended duration, have ground down the projected line of the upheaved mass to the level of the undisturbed masses beside it. Now, mark further, as we ascend the ravine, that the grand cause of the disturbance appears to illustrate, as it were, and that very happily, the manner in which the fault was originally produced. The precipice, over which the stream leaps at one bound into the mossy hollow, is composed of granitic gneiss, and seems evidently to have intruded itself, with much disturbance, among the surrounding conglomerate and sandstones A few hundred yards higher up the dell, there is another much loftier precipice of gneiss, round which we find the traces of still greater disturbance; and, higher still, yet a third abrupt precipice of the same rock. The gneiss rose, trap-like, in steps, and carried up the sandstone before it in detached squares. Each step has its answering fault immediately over it; and the fault where the triple bars and the conglomerate meet is merely a fault whose step of granitic gneiss stopped short ere it reached the surface. But the accompanying section (see Frontispiece, sect. 4) will better illustrate the geology of this interesting ravine, than it can be illustrated by any written description. I may remark, ere taking leave of it, however, that its conglomerates exhibit a singularly large amount of false stratification at an acute angle with the planes of the real strata, and that a bed of mouldering sandstone near the base of the system may be described, from its fissile character, as a tilestone.*

---

* There is a natural connection, it is said, between wild scenes and wild legends, and some of the traditions connected with this romantic and solitary dell illustrate the remark. Till a comparatively late period, it was known at many a winter fireside as a favorite haunt of the fairies — the most poetical of all our old tribes of spectres, and at one time one of the most popular. I have conversed with an old woman, who, when a very little girl, had seen myriads of them dancing, as the sun was setting, on the further edge of the dell, and with a still older man, who had the temerity to offer one of them a pinch of snuff at the foot of the cascade. Nearly a mile from where the ravine opens to the sea, it assumes a gentler and more pastoral character, the sides, no longer precipitous, descend towards the stream in green, sloping banks; and a beaten path, which runs between Cromarty and Rosemarkie, winds down the one side and ascends the other. More than sixty years ago, one Donald Calder, a Cromarty shopkeeper, was journeying by this path shortly after nightfall. The moon, at full, had just risen, but there was a silvery mist sleeping on the lower grounds, that obscured her light; and the dell, in all its extent, was so overcharged by the vapor, that it seemed an immense, overflooded river winding through the landscape. Donald had reached its farther edge, and could hear the rush of the stream from the deep obscurity of the abyss below, when there rose from the opposite side a strain of the most delightful music he had ever heard.

20 *

I know comparatively little of the scenery of the middle, or Cornstone formation. Its features in England are bold and striking; in Scotland, of a tamer and more various character. The Den of Balruddery is a sweet, wooded dell, marked by no characteristic peculiarities. Many of the seeming peculiarities of the formation in Forfarshire, as in Fife, may be traced to the disturbing trap. The appearance exhibited is that of uneven plains, that rise and fall in long, undulating ridges —an appearance which any other member of the system might have presented. We find the upper formation associated with scenery of great, though often wild

---

He staid and listened. The words of a song, of such simple beauty that they seemed without effort to stamp themselves on his memory, came wafted in the music, and the chorus, in which a thousand tiny voices seemed to join, was a familiar address to himself — "Hey, Donald Calder, ho, Donald Calder." "There are nane of my Navity acquaintance," thought Donald, "who sing like that. Wha can it be?" He descended into the cloud; but in passing the little stream the music ceased, and on reaching the spot on which the singer had seemed stationed, he saw only a bare bank sinking into a solitary moor, unvaried by either bush or hollow in which the musician might have lain concealed. He had hardly time, however, to estimate the marvels of the case, when the music again struck up, but on the opposite side of the dell, and apparently from the very knoll on which he had so recently listened to it. The conviction that it could not be other than supernatural overpowered him, and he hurried homewards under the influence of a terror so extreme, that, unfortunately for our knowledge of fairy literature, it had the effect of obliterating from his memory every part of the song except the chorus. The sun rose as he reached Cromarty, and he found that, instead of having lingered at the edge of the dell for only a few minutes — and the time had seemed no longer — he had spent beside it the greater part of the night.

The fairies have deserted the Burn of Eathie, but we have proof,

beauty ; and nowhere is this more strikingly the case than in the province of Moray, where it leans against the granitic gneiss of the uplands, and slopes towards the sea in long plains of various fertility, deep and rich, as in the neighborhood of Elgin, or singularly bleak and unproductive, as in the far-famed " heath near Forres." Let us select the scene where

---

quite as conclusive as the nature of the case admits, that when they ceased to be seen there it would have been vain to have looked for them any where else. There is a cluster of turf-built cottages grouped on the southern side of the ravine ; a few scattered knolls, and a long, partially wooded hollow, that seems a sort of covered way leading to the recesses of the dell, interpose between them and the nearer edge, and the hill rises behind. On a Sabbath morning, nearly sixty years ago, the inmates of this little hamlet had all gone to church, all except a herd-boy and a little girl, his sister, who were lounging beside one of the cottages ; when, just as the shadow of the garden dial had fallen on the line of noon, they saw a long cavalcade ascending out of the ravine through the wooded hollow. It winded among the knolls and bushes , and, turning round the northern gable of the cottage beside which the sole spectators of the scene were stationed, began to ascend the eminence towards the south. The horses were shaggy, diminutive things, speckled dun and gray , the riders, stunted, misgrown, ugly creatures, attired in antique jerkins of plaid, long gray cloaks, and little red caps, from under which their wild, uncombed locks shot out over their cheeks and foreheads. The boy and his sister stood gazing in utter dismay and astonishment, as rider after rider, each one more uncouth and dwarfish than the one that had preceded it, passed the cottage and disappeared among the brushwood, which at that period covered the hill, until at length the entire rout, except the last rider, who lingered a few yards behind the others, had gone by. " What are ye, little mannie ? and where are ye going?" inquired the boy, his curiosity getting the better of his fears and his prudence. "Not of the race of Adam," said the creature, turning for a moment in his saddle , " the People of Peace shall never more be seen in Scotland "

the Findhorn, after hurrying over ridge and shallow, amid
combinations of rock and wood, wildly picturesque as any
the kingdom affords, enters on the lower country, with a
course less headlong, through a vast trench scooped in the
pale red sandstone of the upper formation. For miles above
the junction of the newer and older rocks the river has been
toiling in a narrow and uneven channel, between two upright
walls of hard gray gneiss, thickly traversed, in every com-
plexity of pattern, by veins of a light red, large grained
granite. The gneiss abruptly terminates, but not so the wall
of precipices. A lofty front of gneiss is joined to a lofty
front of sandstone, like the front walls of two adjoining
houses; and the broken and uptilted strata of the softer stone
show that the older and harder rocks must have invaded it
from below. A little farther down the stream, the strata assume what seems, in a short extent of frontage, a horizontal
position, like courses of ashlar in a building, but which, when
viewed in the range, is found to incline at a low angle towards
the distant sea. Here, as in many other localities, the young
geologist must guard against the conclusion, that the rock is
necessarily low in the geological scale which he finds resting
against the gneiss. The gneiss, occupying a very different
place from that on which it was originally formed, has been
thrust into close neighborhood with widely separated formations. The great conglomerate base of the system rests over
it in Orkney, Caithness, Ross, Cromarty, and Inverness; and
there is no trace of what should be the intervening grauwacke. The upper formation of the system leans upon it
here. We find the Lower Lias uptilted against it at the Hill
of Eathie — the great Oolite on the eastern coast of Sutherland; and as the flints and chalk fossils of Banff and Aberdeen are found lying immediately over it in these counties,

it is probable that the denuded members of the Cretaceous group once rested upon it there. The fact that a deposit should be found lying in contact with the gneiss, furnishes no argument for the great antiquity or the fundamental character of that deposit; and it were well that the geologist who sets himself to estimate the depth of the Old Red Sandstone, or the succession of its various formations, should keep the circumstance in view. That may be in reality but a small and upper portion of the system which he finds bounded by the gneiss on its under side, and by the diluvium on its upper.

We stand on a wooded eminence, that sinks perpendicularly into the river on the left, in a mural precipice, and descends with a billowy swell into the broad, fertile plain in front, as if the uplands were breaking in one vast wave upon the low country. There is a patch of meadow on the opposite side of the stream, shaded by a group of ancient trees, gnarled and mossy, and with half their topmost branches dead and white as the bones of a skeleton. We look down upon them from an elevation so commanding, that their uppermost twigs seem on well nigh the same level with their interlaced and twisted roots, washed bare on the bank edge by the winter floods. A colony of herons has built from time immemorial among the branches. There are trees so laden with nests that the boughs bend earthwards on every side, like the boughs of orchard trees in autumn : and the bleached and feathered masses which they bear — the cradles of succeeding generations — glitter gray through the foliage in continuous groups, as if each tree bore on its single head all the wigs of the Court of Session. The solitude is busy with the occupations and enjoyments of instinct. The birds, tall and stately, stand by troops in the shallows, or wade warily, as the fish glance by, to the edge of the current, or rising, with the slow flap of wing and sharp creak peculiar to the tribe, drop suddenly into their nests. The great forest of Darnaway stretches beyond, feathering a thousand knolls, that reflect a colder and grayer tint as they recede, and lessen, and present on the horizon a billowy line of blue. The river brawls along under pale red cliffs, wooded a-top. It is through a vast burial-yard that it has cut its way — a field of the dead so ancient, that the sepulchres of Thebes and Luxor are but of the present day in comparison — resting-places for the recently departed, whose funerals are but just over. These mouldering strata are charged with remains, scattered and detached as those of a churchyard, but not less entire in their parts — occipital bones, jaws, teeth, spines, scales — the dust and rubbish of a departed creation. The cliffs sink as the plain flattens, and green, sloping banks of diluvium take their place; but they again rise in the middle distance into an abrupt and lofty promontory, that, stretching like an immense rib athwart the level country, projects far into the stream, and gives an angular inflection to its course. There ascends from the apex a thin, blue column of smoke — that of a lime-kiln. That ridge and promontory are composed of the thick limestone band, which, in Moray as in Fife, separates the pale red from the pale yellow beds of the Upper Old Red Sandstone; and the flattened tracts on both sides show how much better it has resisted the denuding agencies than either the yellow strata that rests over it, or the pale red strata which it overlies.

CHAPTER XL.

" THERE are only two different aspects," says Dr Thomas Brown, " in which matter can be viewed   We may consider it simply as it exists in space, or as it exists in time.   As it exists in space we inquire into its composition, or, in other words, endeavor to discover what are the elementary bodies that coexist in the space which it occupies ; as it exists in time, we inquire into its susceptibilities or its powers, or, in other words, endeavor to trace all the various changes which have already passed over it, or of which it may yet become the subject."

Hitherto I have very much restricted myself to the consideration of the Old Red Sandstone as it exists in *space* — to the consideration of it as we now find it.   I shall now attempt presenting it to the reader as it existed in *time* — during the succeeding periods of its formation, and when its existences lived and moved as the denizens of primeval oceans.   It is one thing to describe the appearance of a forsaken and des-

(211)

ert country, with its wide wastes of unprofitable sand, its broken citadels and temples, its solitary battle-plains, and its gloomy streets of caverned and lonely sepulchres ; and quite another to record its history during its days of smiling fields, populous cities, busy trade, and monarchical splendor. We pass from the dead to the living — from the cemetery, with its high piles of mummies and its vast heaps of bones, to the ancient city, full of life and animation in all its streets and dwellings.

Two great geological periods have already come to their close ; and the floor of a widely-spread ocean, to which we can affix no limits, and of whose shores or their inhabitants nothing is yet known, is occupied to the depth of many thousand feet by the remains of bygone existences. Of late, the geologist has learned from Murchison to distinguish the rocks of these two periods — the lower as those of the Cambrian, the upper as those of the Silurian group. The lower — representative of the first glimmering twilight of being — of a dawn so feeble that it may seem doubtful whether in reality the gloom had lightened — must still be regarded as a period of uncertainty. Its ripple-marked sandstones, and its half coherent accumulations of dark-colored strata, which decompose into mud, show that every one of its many plains must have formed in succession an upper surface of the bottom of the sea; but it remains for future discoverers to determine regarding the shapes of life that burrowed in its ooze, or careered through the incumbent waters. In one locality it would seem as if a few worms had crawled to the surface, and left their involved and tortuous folds doubtfully impressed on the stone. Some of them resemble miniature cables, carelessly coiled ; others, furnished with what seem numerous legs, remind us of the existing Nereidina of our sandy shoies — those red-blooded, many-legged worms, resembling elongated centipedes, that wriggle with such activity among the mingled mud and water, as we turn over the stones under which they had sheltered. Were creatures such as these the lords of this lower ocean ? Did they enter first on the stage, in that great drama of being in which poets and philosophers, monarchs and mighty conquerors, were afterwards to mingle as actors ? Does the reader remember that story in the *Arabian Nights,* in which the battle of the magicians is described ? At an early stage of the combat a little worm cieeps over the pavement ; at its close two terrible dragons contend in an atmosphere of fire But even the worms of the Cambrian System can scarce be regaided as established. The evidence respecting their place and their nature must still be held as involved in some such degree of doubt as attaches to the researches of the antiquary. when engaged in tracing what their iemains much resemble — the involved sculpturings of some Runic obelisk, weathered by the stoims of a thousand winters There is less of doubt, however, regarding the existences of the upper group of rocks — the Silurian

The depth of this group, as estimated by Mr. Murchison, is equal to double the height of our highest Scottish mountains ; and four distinct platforms of being range in it, the one over the other, like stories in a building. Life abounded on all these platforms, and in shapes the most wonderful. The peculiar encrinites of the group rose in miniature forests, and spread forth their sentient petals by millions and tens of millions amid the waters ; vast ridges of corals peopled by their innumerable builders, — numbeis without number, — rose high amid the shallows ; the chambered shells had become abundant — the simpler testacea still more so ; extinct forms of the graptolite, or sea-pen, existed by myriads ;

21

and the formation had a class of creatures in advance of the
many-legged annelids of the other   It had its numerous family
of trilobites, — crustaceans nearly as high in the scale as the
common crab, — creatures with crescent-shaped heads, and
jointed bodies, and wonderfully constructed eyes, which, like the
eyes of the bee and the butterfly, had the cornea cut into facets
resembling those of a multiplying glass. Is the reader acquainted with the form of the common *Chiton* of our shores
— the little boat-shaped shell-fish, that adheres to stones and
rocks like the limpet, but which differs from every variety of
limpet, in bearing as its covering a jointed, not a continuous shell?
Suppose a chiton with two of its terminal joints cut away, and a
single plate of much the same shape and size, but with two eyes
near the centre, substituted instead, and the animal, in form at
least, would be no longer a chiton, but a trilobite   There are
appearances, too, which lead to the inference that the habits
of the two families, though representing different orders of
being, may not have been very unlike   The chiton attaches
itself to the rock by a muscular sucker or foot, which, extending ventrally along its entire length, resembles that of the
slug or the snail, and enables it to crawl like them, but still
more slowly, by a succession of adhesions. The locomotive
powers of the trilobite seem to have been little superior to
those of the chiton. If furnished with legs at all, it must
have been with soft rudimentary membranaceous legs, little
fitted for walking with ; and it seems quite as probable, from
the peculiarly shaped under margin of its shell, formed, like
that of the chiton, for adhering to flat surfaces, that, like the
slug and the snail, it was unfurnished with legs of any kind,
and crept on the abdomen   The vast conglomerations of
trilobites for which the Silurian rocks are remarkable, are
regarded as further evidence of a sedentary condition   Like

Ostreæ, *Chitones*, and other sedentary animals, they seemed to have adhered together in vast clusters, trilobite over trilobite, in the hollows of submarine precipices, or on the flat, muddy bottom below. And such were the master existences of three of the four Silurian platforms, and of the greater part of the fourth, if, indeed, we may not regard the chambered molluscs, their contemporaries, — creatures with their arms clustered round their heads, and with a nervous system composed of a mere knotted cord, — as equally high in the scale. We rise to the topmost layers of the system, — to an upper gallery of its highest platform, — and find nature mightily in advance.

Another and superior order of existences had sprung into being at the fiat of the Creator — creatures with the brain lodged in the head, and the spinal cord enclosed in a vertebrated column. In the period of the Upper Silurian, fish properly so called, and of very perfect organization, had become denizens of the watery element, and had taken precedence of the crustacean, as, at a period long previous, the crustacean had taken precedence of the annelid. In what form do these, the most ancient beings of their class, appear? As cartilaginous fishes of the higher order. Some of them were furnished with bony palates, and squat, firmly-based teeth, well adapted for crushing the stone-cased zoophytes and shells of the period, fragments of which occur in their fœcal remains; some with teeth that, like those of the fossil sharks of the later formations, resemble lines of miniature pyramids, larger and smaller alternating; some with teeth sharp, thin, and so deeply serrated that every individual tooth resembles a row of poniards set upright against the walls of an armory; and these last, says Agassiz, furnished with weapons so murderous, must have been the pirates of the period. Some had their fins guarded with long

spines, hooked like the beak of an eagle ; some with spines
of straighter and more slender form, and ribbed and furrowed
longitudinally like columns ; some were shielded by an armor
of bony points ; and some thickly covered with glistening
scales. If many ages must have passed ere fishes appeared,
there was assuredly no time required to elevate their lower
into their higher families. Judging, too, from this ancient
deposit, they seem to have been introduced, not by individuals and pairs, but by whole myriads

> " Forthwith the sounds and seas, each creek and bay,
>   With fry innumerable swarmed , and shoals
>   Of fish, that with their fins and shining scales
>   Glide under the green wave in plumps and sculls,
>   Banked the mid sea."   .

The fish-bed of the Upper Ludlow Rock abounds more in
osseous remains than an ancient burying-ground   The stratum,
over wide areas, seems an almost continuous layer of matted
bones, jaws, teeth, spines, scales, palatal plates, and shagreen-
like prickles, all massed together, and converted into a substance of so deep and shining a jet color, that the bed, when
" first discovered, conveyed the impression," says Mr Murch
ison, " that it enclosed a triturated heap of black beetles."
And such are the remains of what seem to have been the first
existing vertebrata. Thus, ere our history begins, the existences of two great systems, the Cambrian and the Silurian,
had passed into extinction, with the exception of what seem a
few connecting links, exclusively molluscs, that are found in
England to pass from the higher beds of the Ludlow rocks
into the Lower or Tilestone beds of the Old Red Sandstone.*

---

* "Upwards of eight hundred extinct species of animals have been
described as belonging to the earliest, or Protozoic and Silurian period,

The exuviæ of at least four platforms of being lay entombed furlong below furlong, amid the gray, mouldering mudstones, the harder arenaceous beds, the consolidated clays, and the concretionary limestones, that underlay the ancient ocean of the Lower Old Red. The earth had already become a vast sepulchre, to a depth beneath the bed of the sea equal to at least twice the height of Ben Nevis over its surface.

The first scene in the *Tempest* opens amid the confusion and turmoil of the hurricane — amid thunders and lightnings, the roar of the wind, the shouts of the seamen, the rattling of cordage, and the wild dash of the billows. The history of the period represented by the Old Red Sandstone seems, in what now forms the northern half of Scotland, to have opened in a similar manner. The finely-laminated lower Tilestones of England were deposited evidently in a calm sea. During the contemporary period in our own country, the vast space which now includes Orkney and Lochness, Dingwall, and Gamrie, and many a thousand square mile besides, was the scene of a shallow ocean, perplexed by powerful currents, and agitated by waves. A vast stratum of water-rolled pebbles, varying in depth from a hundred feet to a hundred yards, remains in a thousand different localities, to testify of the disturbing agencies of this time of commotion. The hardest masses which the stratum encloses, — porphyries of vitreous fracture that cut glass as readily as flint, and masses of quartz that strike fire quite as profusely from steel, — are yet polished and ground down into bullet-like forms, not an angu-

---

and of these only about one hundred are found also in the overlying Devonian series; while but fifteen are common to the whole Palæozoic period, and not one extends beyond it."— (*M. de Verneuil and Count D'Archiac*, quoted by Mr. D. T. Ansted. 1844.)

21 *

lar fragment appearing in some parts of the mass for yards together. The debris of our harder rocks rolled for centuries in the beds of our more impetuous rivers, or tossed for ages along our more exposed and precipitous sea-shores could not present less equivocally the marks of violent and prolonged attrition than the pebbles of this bed. And yet it is surely difficult to conceive how the bottom of any sea should have been so violently and so equally agitated for so greatly extended a space as that which intervenes between Mealforvony in Inverness-shire and Pomona in Orkney in one direction, and between Applecross and Trouphead in another — and for a period so prolonged, that the entire area should have come to be covered with a stratum of rolled pebbles of almost every variety of ancient rock, fifteen stories' height in thickness. The very variety of its contents shows that the period must have been prolonged. A sudden flood sweeps away with it the accumulated debris of a range of mountains ; but to blend together, in equal mixture, the debris of many such ranges, as well as to grind down their roughnesses and angularities, and fill up the interstices with the sand and gravel produced in the process, must be a work of time. I have examined with much interest, in various localities, the fragments of ancient rock inclosed in this formation. Many of them are no longer to be found *in situ*, and the group is essentially different from that presented by the more modern gravels. On the shores of the Frith of Cromarty, for instance, by far the most abundant pebbles are of a blue schistose gneiss : fragments of gray granite and white quartz are also common ; and the sea-shore at half ebb presents at a short distance the appearance of a long belt of bluish gray, from the color of the prevailing stones which compose it. The prevailing color of the conglomerate of the district, on the contrary, is a deep red. It contains pebbles of small-grained, red granite, red quartz rock, red feldspar, red porphyry, an impure red jasper, red hornstone, and a red granitic gneiss, identical with the well-marked gneiss of the neighboring Sutors. This last is the only rock now found in the district, of which fragments occur in the conglomerate. It must have been exposed at the time to the action of the waves, though afterwards buried deep under succeeding formations, until again thrust to the surface by some great internal convulsion, of a date comparatively recent.*

The period of this shallow and stormy ocean passed. The bottom, composed of the identical conglomerate which now forms the summit of some of our loftiest mountains, sank throughout its wide area to a depth so profound as to be little affected by tides or tempests. During this second period there took place a vast deposit of coarse sandstone strata, with here and there a few thin beds of rolled pebbles. The general subsidence of the bottom still continued, and, after a

---

* The vast beds of unconsolidated gravel with which one of the later geological revolutions has half filled some of our northern valleys, and covered the slopes of the adjacent hills, present, in a few localities, appearances somewhat analogous to those exhibited by this ancient formation. There are uncemented accumulations of water-rolled pebbles, in the neighborhood of Inverness, from ninety to a hundred feet in thickness. But this stratum, unlike the more ancient one, wanted continuity. It must have been accumulated, too, under the operation of more partial, though immensely more powerful agencies. There is a mediocrity of size in the enclosed fragments of the old conglomerate, which gives evidence of a mediocrity of power in the transporting agent. In the upper gravels, on the contrary, one of the agents could convey from vast distances blocks of stone eighty and a hundred tons in weight. A new cause of tremendous energy had come into operation in the geological world.

deposit of full ninety feet had overlain the conglomerate, the depth became still more profound than at first. A fine, semi-calcareous, semi-aluminous deposition took place in waters perfectly undisturbed. And here we first find proof that this ancient ocean literally swarmed with life — that its bottom was covered with miniature forests of algæ, and its waters darkened by immense shoals of fish.

In middle autumn, at the close of the herring season, when the fish have just spawned, and the congregated masses are breaking up on shallow and skerry, and dispersing by myriads over the deeper seas, they rise at times to the surface by a movement so simultaneous, that for miles and miles around the skiff of the fisherman nothing may be seen but the bright glitter of scales, as if the entire face of the deep were a blue robe spangled with silver. I have watched them at sunrise at such seasons on the middle of the Moray Frith, when, far as the eye could reach, the surface has been ruffled by the splash of fins, as if a light breeze swept over it, and the red light has flashed in gleams of an instant on the millions and tens of millions that were leaping around me, a handbreadth into the air, thick as hail-stones in a thunder-shower. The amazing amount of life which the scene included, has imparted to it an indescribable interest. On most occasions the inhabitants of ocean are seen but by scores and hundreds; for in looking down into their green twilight haunts, we find the view bounded by a few yards, or at most a few fathoms; and we can but calculate on the unseen myriads of the surrounding expanse by the seen few that occupy the narrow space visible. Here, however, it was not the few, but the myriads, that were seen — the innumerable and inconceivable whole — all palpable to the sight as a flock on a hill-side; or, at least, if all was not palpable, it was only because sense

has its limits in the lighter as well as in the denser medium —
that the multitudinous distracts it, and the distant eludes it,
and the far horizon bounds it. If the scene spoke not of infinity in the sense in which Deity comprehends it, it spoke
of it in at least the only sense in which man can compre-
hend it.

Now, we are much in the habit of thinking of such amazing multiplicity of being — when we think of it at all — with
reference to but the later times of the world's history. We
think of the remote past as a time of comparative solitude.
We forget that the now uninhabited desert was once a populous city. Is the reader prepared to realize, in connection
with the Lower Old Red Sandstone — the second period of
vertebrated existence — scenes as amazingly fertile in life as
the scene just described — oceans as thoroughly occupied
with being as our friths and estuaries when the herrings con-
gregate most abundantly on our coasts? There are evidences too sure to be disputed that such must have been the
case. I have seen the ichthyolite beds, where washed bare
in the line of the strata, as thickly covered with oblong, spin-
dle-shaped nodules as I have ever seen a fishing bank covered with herrings; and have ascertained that every individual nodule had its nucleus of animal matter — that it was
a stone coffin in miniature, holding enclosed its organic mass
of bitumen or bone — its winged, or enamelled, or thorn-
covered ichthyolite.

At this period of our history, some terrible catastrophe involved in sudden destruction the fish of an area at least a
hundred miles from boundary to boundary, perhaps much
more. The same platform in Orkney as at Cromarty is
strewed thick with remains, which exhibit unequivocally the
marks of violent death. The figures are contorted, contract-

ed, curved; he tail in many instances is bent round to the head; the spines stick out; the fins are spread to the full, as in fish that die in convulsions. The *Pterichthys* shows its arms extended at their stiffest angle, as if prepared for an enemy. The attitudes of all the ichthyolites on this platform are attitudes of fear, anger, and pain. The remains, too, appear to have suffered nothing from the after attacks of predaceous fishes; none such seem to have survived. The record is one of destruction at once widely spread and total, so far as it extended. There are proofs that, whatever may have been the cause of the catastrophe, it must have taken place in a sea unusually still. The scales, when scattered by some slight undulation, are scattered to the distance of only a few inches, and still exhibit their enamel entire, and their peculiar fineness of edge. The spines, even when separated, retain their original needle-like sharpness of point. Rays, well nigh as slender as horse-hairs, are enclosed unbroken in the mass. Whole ichthyolites occur, in which not only all the parts survive, but even the expression which the stiff and threatening attitude conveyed when the last struggle was over. Destruction must have come in the calm, and it must have been of a kind by which the calm was nothing disturbed. In what could it have originated? By what quiet but potent agency of destruction were the innumerable existences of an area perhaps ten thousand square miles in extent annihilated at once, and yet the medium in which they had lived left undisturbed by its operations? Conjecture lacks footing in grappling with the enigma, and expatiates in uncertainty over all the known phenomena of death. Diseases of mysterious origin break out at times in the animal kingdom, and well nigh exterminate the tribes on which they fall. The present generation has seen a hundred millions of the human family swept away by a disease unknown to our fathers. Virgil describes the fatal murrain that once depopulated the Alps, not more as a poet than as a historian. The shell-fish of the rivers of North America died in such vast abundance during a year of the present century, that the animals, washed out of their shells, lay rotting in masses beside the banks, infecting the very air. About the close of the last century, the haddock well nigh disappeared, for several seasons together, from the eastern coasts of Scotland; and it is related by Creech, that a Scotch shipmaster of the period sailed for several leagues on the coast of Norway, about the time the scarcity began, through a floating shoal of dead haddocks.* But the ravages of no such disease, however

---

* I have heard elderly fishermen of the Moray Frith state, in connection with what they used to term "the haddock dearth" of this period, that, for several weeks ere the fish entirely disappeared, they acquired an extremely disagreeable taste, as if they had been boiled in tobacco juice, and became unfit for the table. For the three following years they were extremely rare on the coast, and several years more elapsed ere they were caught in the usual abundance. The fact related by Creech, a very curious one, I subjoin in his own words; it occurs in his third *Letter to Sir John Sinclair.* "On Friday, the 4th December, 1789, the ship *Brothers,* Captain Stewart, arrived at Leith from Archangel, who reported that, on the coast of Lapland and Norway, he sailed many leagues through immense quantities of dead haddocks floating on the sea. He spoke several English ships, who reported the same fact. It is certain that haddocks, which was the fish in the greatest abundance in the Edinburgh market, have scarcely been seen there these three years. In February, 1790, three haddocks were brought to market, which, from their scarcity, sold for 7s 6d."

The dead haddocks seen by the Leith shipmaster were floating by thousands, and most of their congeners among what fishermen term "the white fish," such as cod, ling, and whiting, also float when

extensive, could well account for some of the phenomena of this platform of death. It is rarely that disease falls equally on many different tribes at once, and never does it fall with instantaneous suddenness; whereas in the ruin of this platform from ten to twelve distinct genera seem to have been equally involved; and so suddenly did it perform its work, that its victims were fixed in their first attitude of terror and surprise. I have observed, too, that groups of adjoining nodules are charged frequently with fragments of the

---

dead; whereas the bodies of fish whose bowels and air-bladders are comparatively small and tender, lie at the bottom. The herring fisherman, if the fish die in his nets, finds it no easy matter to buoy them up; and if the shoal entangled be a large one, he fails at times, from the great weight, in recovering them at all, losing both nets and herrings. Now, if a corresponding difference obtained among fish of the extinct period — if some rose to the surface when they died, while others remained at the bottom — we must, of course, expect to find their remains in very different degrees of preservation — to find only scattered fragments of the floaters, while of the others many may occur comparatively entire. Even should they have died on the same beds, too, we may discover their remains separated by hundreds of miles. The haddocks that disappeared from the coast of Britain were found floating in shoals on the coasts of Norway. The remains of an immense body of herrings, that weighed down, a few seasons since, the nets of a crew of fishermen, in a muddy hollow of the Moray Frith, and defied the utmost exertions of three crews united to weigh them from the bottom, are, I doubt not, in the muddy hollow still. On a principle thus obvious it may be deemed not improbable that the ichthyolites of the Lower Old Red Sandstone might have had numerous contemporaries, of which, unless in some instances the same accident which killed also entombed them, we can know nothing in their character as such, and whose broken fragments may yet be found in some other locality, where they may be regarded as characteristic of a different formation.

same variety of ichthyolite; and the circumstance seems fraught with evidence regarding both the original habits of the creatures, and the instantaneous suddenness of the destruction by which they were overtaken. They seem, like many of our existing fish, to have been gregarious, and to have perished together ere their crowds had time to break up and disperse.

Fish have been found floating dead in shoals beside submarine volcanoes — killed either by the heated water, or by mephitic gases. There are, however, no marks of volcanic activity in connection with the ichthyolite beds — no marks, at least, which belong to nearly the same age with the fossils. The disturbing granite of the neighboring eminences was not upheaved until after the times of the Oolite. But the volcano, if such was the destroying agent, might have been distant; nay, from some of the points in an area of such immense extent, it *must* have been distant. The beds abound, as has been said, in lime; and the thought has often struck me that calcined lime, cast out as ashes from some distant crater, and carried by the winds, might have been the cause of the widely-spread destruction to which their organisms testify. I have seen the fish of a small trouting stream, over which a bridge was in the course of building, destroyed in a single hour, for a full mile below the erection, by the few troughfuls of lime that fell into the water when the centring was removed.

22

CHAPTER XIII.

Successors of the exterminated Tribes — The Gap slowly filled. —
Proof that the Vegetation of a Formation may long survive its
Animal Tribes. — Probable Cause — Immensely extended Period
during which Fishes were the Master-existences of our Planet. —
Extreme Folly of an Infidel Objection illustrated by the Fact. —
Singular Analogy between the History of Fishes as Individuals
and as a Class — Chemistry of the Lower Formation. — Principles
on which the Fish-enclosing Nodules were probably formed. —
Chemical Effect of Animal Matter in discharging the Color from
Red Sandstone — Origin of the prevailing tint to which the System owes its Name — Successive Modes in which a Metal may exist — The Restorations of the Geologist void of Color. — Very different Appearance of the Ichthyolites of Cromarty and Moray.

THE period of death passed, and over the innumerable
dead there settled a soft, muddy sediment, that hid them from
the light, bestowing upon them such burial as a November
snow-storm bestows on the sere and blighted vegetation of
the previous summer and autumn. For an unknown space
of time, represented in the formation by a deposit about fifty
feet in thickness, the waters of the depopulated area seem to
have remained devoid of animal life. A few scales and
plates then begin to appear. The fish that had existed outside the chasm seem to have gradually gained upon it, as
their numbers increased, just as the European settlers of
America have been gaining on the backwoods, and making
themselves homes amid the burial-mounds of a race extinct
for centuries. For a lengthened period, however, these finny
settlers must have been comparatively few — mere squatters
in the waste. In the beds of stratified clay in which their

remains first occur, over what we may term the densely
crowded platform of violent death, the explorer may labor
for hours together without finding a single scale

It is worthy of remark, however, that this upper bed
abounds quite as much in the peculiar vegetable impressions
of the formation as the lower platform itself   An abundance
equally great occurs in some localities only a few inches over
the line of the exterminating catastrophe.   Thickets of exactly the same algæ, amid which the fish of the formation
had sheltered when living, grew luxuriantly over their graves
when dead   The agencies of destruction which annihilated
the animal life of so extended an area, spared its vegetation ;
just as the identical forests that had waved over the semi-
civilized aborigines of North America continued to wave over
the more savage red men, their successors, long after the
original race had been exterminated   The inference deduci-
ble from the fact, though sufficiently simple, seems in a geological point of view a not unimportant one   *The flora of a
system may long survive its fauna ; so that that may be but
one formation, regarded with reference to plants, which may
be two or more formations, regarded with reference to animals*   No instance of any such phenomenon occurs in the
later geological periods.   The changes in animal and vegetable life appear to have run parallel to each other from the
times of the tertiary formations down to those of the coal ;
but in the earlier deposits the case must have been different.
The animal organisms of the newer Silurian strata form essentially different groups from those of the Lower Old Red
Sandstone, and both differ from those of the Cornstone divisions ; and yet the greater portion of their vegetable remains
seem the same.   The stem-like impressions of the fucoid bed
of the Upper Ludlow Rocks cannot be distinguished from

those of the ichthyolite beds of Cromarty and Ross, nor these again from the impressions of the Arbroath pavement, or the Den of Balruddery. Nor is there much difficulty in conceiving how the vegetation of a formation should come to survive its animals. What is fraught with health to the existences of the vegetable kingdom, is in many instances a deadly poison to those of the animal. The grasses and water-lilies of the neighborhood of Naples flourish luxuriantly amid the carbonic acid gas which rests so densely over the pools and runnels out of which they spring, that the bird stoops to drink, and falls dead into the water. The lime that destroys the reptiles, fish, and insects of a thickly inhabited lake or stream, injures not a single flag or bulrush among the millions that line its edges. The two kingdoms exist under laws of life and death so essentially dissimilar, that it has become one of the common-places of poetry to indicate the blight and decline of the tribes of the one by the unwonted luxuriancy of the productions of the other. Otway tells us, in describing the horrors of the plague which almost depopulated London, that the " destroying angel stretched his arm " over the city,

> " Till in th' untrodden streets unwholesome grass
> Grew of great stalk, and color gross,
> A melancholic poisonous green "

The work of deposition went on; a bed of pale yellow saliferous sandstone settled, tier over tier, on a bed of stratified clay, and was itself overlaid by another bed of stratified clay in turn. And this upper bed had also its organisms. The remains of its sea-weed still spread out thick and dark amid the foldings of the strata, and occasionally its clusters of detached scales. But the circumstances were less favora-

ble to the preservation of entire ichthyolites than those under
which the organisms of the lower platform were wrapped up
in their stony coverings The matrix, which is more micaceous
than the other, seems to have been less conservative, and the
waters were probably less still The process went on. Age
succeeded age, and one stratum covered up another. Genera-
ations lived, died, and were entombed in the ever-growing
depositions. Succeeding generations pursued their instincts by
myriads, happy in existence, over the surface which covered
the broken and perishing remains of their predecessors, and
then died and were entombed in turn, leaving a higher platform, and a similar destiny to the generations that succeeded
Whole races became extinct, through what process of destruction who can tell ? Other races sprang into existence through
that adorable power which One only can conceive, and One
only can exert An inexhaustible variety of design expatiated
freely within the limits of the ancient type. The main conditions remained the same — the minor details were dissimilar.
Vast periods passed ; a class low in the scale still continued to
furnish the master existences of creation : and so immensely
extended was the term of its sovereignty, that a being of limited faculties, if such could have existed uncreated, and witnessed the whole, would have inferred that the power of the
Creator had reached its extreme boundary, when fishes had
been called into existence, and that our planet was destined
to be the dwelling-place of no nobler inhabitants. If there
be men dignified by the name of philosophers, who can hold
that the present state of being, with all its moral evil, and all
its physical suffering, is to be succeeded by no better and
happier state, just because " all things have continued as they
were " for some five or six thousand years, how much sounder
and more conclusive would the inference have been which

22 *

could have been based, as in the supposed case, on a period perhaps a hundred times more extended ?

There exist wonderful analogies in nature between the geological history of the vertebrated animals as an order, and the individual history of every mammifer — between the history, too, of fish as a class, and that of every single fish. "It has been found by Tiedemann," says Mr. Lyell, "that the brain of the fœtus in the higher class of vertebrated animals assumes in succession the various forms which belong to fishes, reptiles, and birds, before it acquires those additions and modifications which are peculiar to the mammiferous tribes." "In examining the brain of the mammalia," says M. Serres, "at an early stage of life, you perceive the cerebral hemispheres consolidated, as in fish, in two vesicles isolated one from the other; at a later period you see them affect the configuration of the cerebral hemispheres of reptiles; still later, again, they present you with the forms of those of birds; and finally, at the era of birth, the permanent forms which the adult mammalia present." And such seems to have been the history of the vertebrata as an order, as certainly as that of the individual mammifer. The fish preceded the reptile in the order of creation, just as the crustacean had preceded the fish, and the annelid the crustacean. Again, though the fact be somewhat more obscure, the reptile seems to have preceded the bird We find, however, unequivocal traces of the feathered tribes in well-marked foot-prints impressed on a sandstone in North America, at most not more modern than the Lias, but which is generally supposed to be of the same age with the New Red Sandstone of Germany and our own country In the Oolite — at least one, perhaps two formations later — the bones of the two species of mammiferous quadrupeds have been found, apparently of the marsu-

pial family ; and these, says Mr. Lyell, afford the only example yet known of terrestrial mammalia in rocks of a date anterior to the older tertiary formations. The reptile seems to
have preceded the bird, and the bird the mammiferous animal. Thus the fœtal history of the nervous system in the individual mammifer seems typical, in every stage of its progress, of the history of the grand division at the head of
which the mammifer stands. Agassiz, at the late meeting of
the British Association in Glasgow, mentioned an analogous
fact. After describing the one-sided tail of the more ancient
fish, especially the fish of the Old Red Sandstone, — the subjects of his illustration at the time, — he stated, as the result
of a recent discovery, that the young of the salmon in their
fœtal state exhibit the same unequally-sided condition of tail
which characterizes those existences of the earlier ages of
the world. The individual fish, just as it begins to exist, presents the identical appearances which were exhibited by the
order when the order began to exist. Is there nothing wonderful in analogies such as these — analogies that point through
the embryos of the present time to the womb of Nature, big
with its multitudinous forms of being ? Are they charged
with no such nice evidence as a Butler would delight to contemplate, regarding that unique *style* of Deity, if I may so express myself, which runs through all his works, whether we
consider him as God of Nature, or Author of Revelation ?
In this style of type and symbol did He reveal himself of
old to his chosen people ; in this style of allegory and para-
ble did He again address himself to them, when he sojourned
among them on earth.

The chemistry of the formation seems scarce inferior in
interest to its zoology ; but the chemist had still much to do
for Geology, and the processes are but imperfectly known.

There is no field in which more laurels await the philosophical chemist than the geological one. I have said that all the calcareous nodules of the ichthyolite beds seem to have had originally their nucleus of organic matter. In nine cases out of ten the organism can be distinctly traced ; and in the tenth there is almost always something to indicate where it lay — an elliptical patch of black, or an oblong spot, from which the prevailing color of the stone has been discharged, and a lighter hue substituted. Is the reader acquainted with Mr. Pepys's accidental experiment, as related by Mr Lyell, and recorded in the first volume of the *Geological Transactions* ? It affords an interesting proof that animal matter, in a state of putrefaction, proves a powerful agent in the decomposition of mineral substances held in solution, and of their consequent precipitation. An earthen pitcher, containing several quarts of sulphate of iron, had been suffered to remain undisturbed and unexamined in a corner of Mr. Pepys's laboratory for about a twelvemonth. Some luckless mice had meanwhile fallen into it, and been drowned ; and when it at length came to be examined, an oily scum, and a yellow, sulphureous powder, mixed with hairs, were seen floating on the top, and the bones of the mice discovered lying at the bottom ; and it was found, that over the decaying bodies the mineral components of the fluid had been separated and precipitated in a dark-colored sediment, consisting of grains of pyrites and of sulphur, of copperas in its green and crystalline form, and of black oxide of iron. The animal and mineral matters had mutually acted upon one another ; and the metallic sulphate, deprived of its oxygen in the process, had thus cast down its ingredients. It would seem that over the putrefying bodies of the fish of the Lower Old Red Sandstone the water had deposited in like manner, the lime with which it was

charged; and hence the calcareous nodules in which we find
their remains enclosed. The form of the nodule almost invariably agrees with that of the ichthyolite within; it is a
coffin in the ancient Egyptian style. Was the ichthyolite
twisted half round in the contorted attitude of violent death?
the nodule has also its twist Did it retain its natural pos-
ture? the nodule presents the corresponding spindle form.
Was it broken up, and the outline destroyed? the nodule is
flattened and shapeless. In almost every instance the form
of the organism seems to have regulated that of the stone.
We may trace, in many of these concretionary masses, the
operations of three distinct principles, all of which must have
been in activity at one and the same time. They are wrapped
concentrically each round its organism: they split readily
in the line of the enclosing stratum, and are marked by its
alternating rectilinear bars of lighter and darker color, and
they are radiated from the centre to the circumference.
Their concentric condition shows the chemical influences of
the decaying animal matter; their fissile character and parallel layers of color indicate the general deposition which
was taking place at the time; and their radiated structure
testifies to that law of crystalline attraction, through which,
by a wonderful masonry, the invisible but well-cut atoms
build up their cubes, their rhombs, their hexagons, and their
pyramids, and are at once the architects and the materials of
the structure which they rear.

Another and very different chemical effect of organic matter may be remarked in the darker colored arenaceous deposits of the formation, and occasionally in the stratified clays
and nodules of the ichthyolite bed. In a print-work, the
whole web is frequently thrown into the vat and dyed of one
color; but there afterwards comes a discharging process;

some chemical mixture is dropped on the fabric; the dye disappears wherever the mixture touches; and in leaves, and sprigs, and patches, according to the printer's pattern, the cloth assumes its original white. Now the colored deposits of the Old Red Sandstone have, in like manner, been subjected to a discharging process. The dye has disappeared in oblong or circular patches of various sizes, from the eighth of an inch to a foot in diameter; the original white has taken its place; and so thickly are these speckles grouped in some of the darker-tinted beds, that the surfaces, where washed by the sea, present the appearance of sheets of calico. The discharging agent was organic matter; the uncolored patches are no mere surface films, for, when cut at right angles, their depth is found to correspond with their breadth, the circle is a sphere, the ellipsis forms the section of an egg-shaped body, and in the centre of each we generally find traces of the organism in whose decay it originated. I have repeatedly found single scales, in the ichthyolite beds, surrounded by uncolored spheres about the size of musket bullets. It is well for the young geologist carefully to mark such appearances — to trace them through the various instances in which the organism may be recognized and identified, to those in which its last vestiges have disappeared. They are the hatchments of the geological world, and indicate that life once existed where all other record of it has perished.*

---

* Some of the clay-slates of the primary formations abound in these circular, uncolored patches, bearing in their centres, like the patches of the Old Red Sandstone, half obliterated nuclei of black. Were they, too, once fossiliferous? and do these blank erasures remain to testify to the fact? I find the organic origin of the patches in the

It is the part of the chemist to tell us by what peculiar action of the organic matter the dye was discharged in these
spots and patches. But how was the dye itself procured?
From what source was the immense amount of iron derived,
which gives to nearly five sixths of the Old Red Sandstone
the characteristic color to which it owes its name? An examination of its lowest member, the great conglomerate,
suggests a solution of the query. I have adverted to the large
proportion of red-colored pebbles which this member con-

Old Red Sandstone remarked by Professor Fleming as early as the
year 1830, and the remark reiterated by Dr. Anderson, of Newburgh,
in nearly the same words, but with no acknowledgment, ten years
later. The following is the minute and singularly faithful description
of the Professor : —

"On the surface of the strata in the lower beds, circular spots,
nearly a foot in diameter, may be readily perceived by their pale yellow colors, contrasted with the dark red of the surrounding rock.
These spots, however, are not, as may at first be supposed, mere su-
perficial films, but derive their circular form from a colored sphere to
which they belong. This sphere is not to be distinguished from the
rest of the bed by any difference in mechanical structure, but merely
by the absence of much of that oxide of iron with which the other
portion of the mass is charged. The circumference of this colored
sphere is usually well defined, and at its centre may always be ob
served matter of a darker color, in some cases disposed in concentric
layers, in others of calcareous and crystalline matter, the remains
probably of some vegetable or animal organism, the decomposition of
which exercised a limited influence on the coloring matter of the sur
rounding rock. In some cases I have observed these spheres slightly
compressed at opposite sides, in a direction parallel with the plane of
stratification — the result, without doubt, of the subsidence or contraction of the mass, after the central matter or nucleus had ceased
to exercise its influence." — (*Cheek's Edinburgh Journal*, Feb. 1831,
p. 82.)

tains, and, among the rest, to a red granitic gneiss, which must have been exposed over wide areas at the time of its deposition, and which, after the lapse of a period which extended from at least the times of the Lower Old Red to those of the Upper Oolite, was again thrust upwards to the surface, to form the rectilinear chain of precipitous eminences to which the hills of Cromarty and of Nigg belong. This rock is now almost the sole representative, in the north of Scotland, of the ancient rocks whence the materials of the Old Red Sandstone were derived. It abounds in hæmatic iron ore, diffused as a component of the stone throughout the entire mass, and which also occurs in it in ponderous insulated blocks of great richness, and in thin, thread-like veins. When ground down, it forms a deep red pigment, undistinguishable in tint from the prevailing color of the sandstone, and which leaves a stain so difficult to be effaced, that shepherds employ it in some parts of the Highlands for marking their sheep. Every rawer fragment of the rock bears its hæmatic tinge; and were the whole ground by some mechanical process into sand, and again consolidated, the produce of the experiment would be undoubtedly a deep red sandstone. In an upper member of the lower formation — that immediately over the ichthyolite beds — different materials seem to have been employed. A white, quartzy sand and a pale-colored clay form the chief ingredients; and though the ochry-tinted coloring matter be also iron, it is iron existing in a different condition, and in a more diluted form The oxide deposited by the chalybeate springs which pass through the lower members of the formation, would give to white sand a tinge exactly resembling the tint borne by this upper member.

The passage of metals from lower to higher formations,

and from one combination to another, constitutes surely a highly interesting subject of inquiry. The transmission of iron in a chemical form, through chalybeate springs, from deposits in which it had been diffused in a form merely mechanical, is of itself curious; but how much more so its passage and subsequent accumulation, as in bog-iron and the iron of the Coal Measures, through the agency of vegetation! How strange, if the steel axe of the woodman should have once formed part of an ancient forest! — if, after first existing as a solid mass in a primary rock, it should next have come to be diffused as a red pigment in a transition conglomerate — then as a brown oxide in a chalybeate spring — then as a yellowish ochre in a secondary sandstone — then as a component part in the stems and twigs of a thick forest of arboraceous plants — then again as an iron carbonate, slowly accumulating at the bottom of a morass of the Coal Measures — then as a layer of indurated bands and nodules of brown ore, underlying a seam of coal — and then, finally, that it should have been dug out, and smelted, and fashioned, and employed for the purpose of handicraft, and yet occupy, even at this stage, merely a middle place between the transmigrations which have passed, and the changes which are yet to come. Crystals of galena sometimes occur in the nodular limestones of the Old Red Sandstone; but I am afraid the chemist would find it difficult to fix their probable genealogy.

In at least one respect, every geological history must of necessity be unsatisfactory; and, ere I pass to the history of the two upper formations of the system, the reader must permit me to remind him of it. There have been individuals, it has been said, who, though they could see clearly the forms of objects wanted, through some strange organic defect, the

23

faculty of perceiving their distinguishing colors, however well marked these might be. The petals of the rose have appeared to them of the same sombre hue with its stalk; and they have regarded the ripe scarlet cherry as undistinguishable in tint from the green leaves under which it hung. The face of nature to such men must have for ever rested under a cloud; and a cloud of similar character hangs over the pictorial restorations of the geologist The history of this and the last chapter is a mere profile drawn in black, an outline without color — in short, such a chronicle of past ages as might be reconstructed, in the lack of other and ampler materials, from tombstones and charnel-houses I have had to draw the portrait from the skeleton. My specimens show the general form of the creatures I attempt to describe, and not a few of their more marked peculiarities; but many of the nicer elegancies are wanting; and the "complexion to which they have come" leaves no trace by which to discover the complexion they originally bore. And yet color is a mighty matter to the ichthyologist. The "fins and shining scales," "the waved coats, dropt with gold," the rainbow dyes of beauty of the watery tribes, are connected often with more than mere external character. It is a curious and interesting fact, that the hues of splendor in which they are bedecked are, in some instances, as intimately associated with their instincts — with their feelings, if I may so speak — as the blush which suffuses the human countenance is associated with the sense of shame, or its tint of ashy paleness or of sallow with emotions of rage, or feelings of a panic terror. Pain and triumph have each their index of color among the mute inhabitants of our seas and rivers. Poets themselves have bewailed the utter inadequacy of words to describe the varying tints and shades of beauty with which the agonies of death dye the scales of the dolphin, and how every various pang calls up a various suffusion of splendor.* Even the common stickleback of our ponds and ditches can put on its colors to picture its emotions. There is, it seems, a mighty amount of ambition, and a vast deal of fighting sheerly for conquests' sake, among the myriads of this pygmy little fish

---

* The description of Falconer must be familiar to every reader, but I cannot resist quoting it. It shows how minutely the sailor poet must have observed. Byron tells us how

> "Parting day
> Dies like the dolphin, whom each pang imbues
> With a new color, as it gasps away,
> The last still loveliest, till — tis gone, and all is gray."

Falconer, in anticipating, reversed the simile The huge animal, struck by the "unerring barb" of Rodmond, has been drawn on board, and

> "On deck he struggles with convulsive pain ;
> But while his heart the fatal javelin thrills,
> And flitting life escapes in sanguine rills,
> What radiant changes strike the astonished sight !
> What glowing hues of mingled shade and light !
> Not equal beauties gild the lucid West
> With parting beams o'er all profusely drest ;
> Not lovelier colors paint the vernal dawn,
> When Orient dews impearl the enamelled lawn;
> Than from his sides in bright suffusion flow,
> That now with gold empyreal seem to glow ;
> Now in pellucid sapphires meet the view,
> And emulate the soft celestial hue ,
> Now beam a flaming crimson on the eye,
> And now assume the purple's deeper dye.
> But here description clouds each shining ray —
> What terms of art can Nature's powers display ? "

which inhabit our smaller streams; and no sooner does an
individual succeed in expelling his weaker companions from
some eighteen inches or two feet of territory, than straight
way the exultation of conquest converts the faded and
freckled olive of his back and sides into a glow of crimson
and bright green. Nature furnishes him with a regal robe for
the occasion. Immediately on his deposition, however, —
and events of this kind are even more common under than
out of the water, — his gay colors disappear, and he sinks
into his original and native ugliness.*

But of color, as I have said, though thus important, the
ichthyologist can learn almost nothing from Geology. The
perfect restoration of even a Cuvier are blank outlines. We
just know by a wonderful accident that the Siberian elephant was red   A very few of the original tints still remain
among the fossils of our north country Lias. The ammonite,

---

* "In the *Magazine of Natural History*," says Captain Brown, in
one of his notes to White's *Selborne*, " we have a curious account of
the pugnacious propensities of these little animals   ‘ Having at various times,' says a correspondent, ‘ kept these little fish during the spring
and part of the summer months, and paid close attention to their habits
I am enabled from my own experience to vouch for the facts I am about
to relate. I have frequently kept them in a deal tub, about three feet
two inches wide, and about two feet deep. When they are put in for
some time, probably a day or two, they swim about in a shoal, apparently exploring their new habitation   Suddenly one will take possession
of the tub, or, as it will sometimes happen, the bottom, and will instant-
ly commence an attack upon his companions , and if any of them
venture to oppose his sway, a regular and most furious battle ensues.
They swim round and round each other with the greatest rapidity,
biting, (their mouths being well furnished with teeth,) and endeavor-
ing to pierce each other with their lateral spines, which, on this occasion, are projected   I have witnessed a battle of this sort which lasted

when struck fresh from the surrounding lime, reflects the prismatic colors, as of old ; a huge Modiola still retains its tinge of tawny and yellow; and the fossilized wood of the formation preserves a shade of the native tint, though darkened into brown. But there is considerably less of color in the fossils of the Old Red Sandstone. I have caught, and barely caught, in some of the newly disinterred specimens, the faint and evanescent reflection of a tinge of pearl ; and were I acquainted with my own collection only, imagination, borrowing from the prevailing color, would be apt to people the ancient oceans, in which its forms existed, with swarthy races exclusively. But a view of the Altyre fossils would correct the impression. They are enclosed, like those of Cromarty, in nodules of an argillaceous limestone. The color, however, from the presence of iron, and the absence of bitumen, is different. It presents a mixture of gray, of pink, and of

---

several minutes before either would give way; and when one does submit, imagination can hardly conceive the vindictive fury of the conqueror, who, in the most persevering and unrelenting way, chases his rival from one part of the tub to another, until fairly exhausted with fatigue. From this period an interesting change takes place in the conqueror, who, from being a speckled and greenish-looking fish, assumes the most beautiful colors , the belly and lower jaws becoming a deep crimson, and the back sometimes a cream color, but generally a fine green, and the whole appearance full of animation and spirit I have occasionally known three or four parts of the tub taken possession of by these little tyrants, who guard their territories with the strictest vigilance, and the slightest invasion brings on invariably a battle. A strange alteration immediately takes place in the defeated party: his gallant bearing forsakes him, his gay colors fade away, he becomes again speckled and ugly, and he hides his disgrace among his peaceable companions. ' ”

brown ; and on this ground the fossil is spread out in strongly contrasted masses of white and dark red, of blue, and of purple. Where the exuviæ lie thickest, the white appears tinged with delicate blue — the bone is but little changed. Where they are spread out more thinly, the iron has pervaded them, and the purple and deep red prevail. Thus the same ichthyolite presents, in some specimens, a body of white and plum-blue attached to fins of deep red, and with detached scales of red and of purple lying scattered around it. I need hardly add, however, that all this variety of coloring is, like the unvaried black of the Cromarty specimens, the result, merely, of a curious chemistry.

CHAPTER XIV.

THE curtain rises, and the scene is new. The myriads of the lower formation have disappeared, and we are surrounded, on an upper platform, by the existences of a later creation. There is sea all around, as before ; and we find beneath a dark-colored, muddy bottom, thickly covered by a dwarf vegetation. The circumstances differ little from those in which the ichthyolite beds of the preceding period were deposited ; but forms of life, essentially different, career through the green depths, or creep over the ooze. Shoals of *Cephalaspides*, with their broad, arrow-like heads, and their slender, angular bodies, feathered with fins, sweep past like clouds of crossbow bolts in an ancient battle. We see the distant gleam of scales, but the forms are indistinct and dim : we can merely ascertain that the fins are elevated by spines of various shape and pattern ; that of some the coats glitter with enamel ; and that others — the sharks of this ancient period — bristle over with minute thorny points. A huge crustacean, of uncouth proportions, stalks over the weedy bottom or burrows in the hollows of the banks.

(243)

Let us attempt bringing our knowledge of the present to bear upon the past. The larger crustacea of the British seas abound most on iron-bound coasts, where they find sheltering places in the deeper fisures of sea-cliffs covered up by kelp and tangle, or under the lower edges of detached boulders, that rest unequally on uneven platforms of rock, amid forests of the rough-stemmed cuvy. We may traverse sandy or muddy shores for miles together, without finding a single crab, unless a belt of pebbles lines the upper zone of beach, where the forked and serrated fuci first appear, or a few weed-covered fragments of rock here and there occur in groups on the lower zones. In this formation, however, the bottom must have been formed of mingled sand and mud, and yet the crustacea were abundant. How account for the fact? There is, in most instances, an interesting conformity between the character of the ancient rocks, in which we find groups of peculiar fossils, and the habitats of those existences of the present creation which these fossils most resemble. The fisherman casts his nets in a central hollow of the Moray Frith, about thirty fathoms in depth, and draws them up foul with masses of a fetid mud, charged with multitudes of that curious purple-colored zoophyte the sea-pen, invariably an inhabitant of such recesses. The graptolite of the most ancient fossiliferous rocks, an existence of unequivocally the same type, occurs in greatest abundance in a finely-levigated mudstone, for it, too, was a dweller in the mud. In like manner, we may find the ancient Modiola of the Lias in habitats analogous to those of its modern representative the muscle, and the encrinite of the Mountain Limestone fast rooted to its rocky platform, just as we may see the Helianthoida and Ascidioida of our seas fixed to their boulders and rocky skerries. But is not analogy at fault in the present instance?

Quite the reverse. Mark how thickly these carbonaceous impressions cover the muddy-colored and fissile sandstones of the formation, giving evidence of an abundant vegetation. We may learn from these obscure markings, that the place in which they grew could have been no unfit habitat for the crustaceous tribes.

There is a little, land-locked bay on the southern shore of the Frith of Cromarty, effectually screened from the easterly winds by the promontory on which the town is built, and but little affected by those of any other quarter, from the proximity of the neighboring shores. The bottom, at low ebb, presents a level plain of sand, so thickly covered by the green grass-weed of our more sheltered sandy bays and estuaries, that it presents almost the appearance of a meadow. The roots penetrate the sand to the depth of nearly a foot, binding it firmly together; and as they have grown and decayed in it for centuries, it has acquired, from the disseminated particles of vegetable matter, a deep leaden tint, more nearly approaching to black than even the dark gray mudstones of Balruddery. Nor is this the only effect: the intertwisted fibres impart to it such coherence, that, where scooped out into pools, the edges stand up perpendicular from the water, like banks of clay; and where these are hollowed into cave-like recesses, — and there are few of them that are not so hollowed, — the recesses remain unbroken and unfilled for years. The weeds have imparted to the sand a character different from its own, and have rendered it a suitable habitat for numerous tribes, which, in other circumstances, would have found no shelter in it. Now, among these we find in abundance the larger crustaceans of our coasts. The brown edible crab harbors in the hollows beside the pools; occasionally we may find in them an overgrown lobster, studded with parasitical shells and zoophytes — proof that the creature, having attained its full size, has ceased to cast its plated covering. Crustaceans of the smaller varieties abound. Hermit crabs traverse the pools, or creep among the weed; the dark green and the dingy, hump-backed crabs occur nearly as frequently; the radiata cover the banks by thousands. We find occasionally the remains of dead fish left by the retreating tide; but the living are much more numerous than the dead; for the sand-eel has suffered the water to retire, and yet remained behind in its burrow; and the viviparous blenny and common gunnel still shelter beside their fuci-covered masses of rock Imagine the bottom of this little bay covered up by thick beds of sand and gravel, and the whole consolidated into stone, and we have in it all the conditions of the deposit of Balruddery — a mud-colored, arenaceous deposit, abounding in vegetable impressions, and enclosing numerous remains of crustaceans, fish, and radiata, as its characteristic organisms of the animal kingdom.   There would be but one circumstance of difference : the little bay abounds in shells ; whereas no shells have yet been found in the mudstones of Balruddery, or the gray sandstones of the same formation, which in Forfar, Fife, and Moray shires represent the Cornstone division of the system.

Ages and centuries passed, but who can sum up their number ? In England, the depth of this middle formation greatly exceeds that of any of the other two ; in Scotland, it is much less amply developed ; but in either country it must represent periods of scarce conceivable extent. I have listened to the controversies of opposite schools of geologists, who, from the earth's strata, extract registers of the earth's age of an amount amazingly different. One class, regarding the geological field as if under the influence of those principles of perspective which give to the cottage in front more than the bulk and altitude of the mountain behind, would assign to the present scene of things its thousands of years, but to all the extinct periods united merely their few centuries; while with their opponents, the remoter periods stretch out far into the bygone eternity, and the present scene seems but a narrow strip running along the foreground.   Both classes appeal to facts; and, leaving them to their disputes, I have gone out to examine and judge for myself.   The better to compare the present with the past, I have regarded the existing scene merely as a *formation* — not as superficies, but as depth; and have sought to ascertain the extent to which, in different localities, and under different circumstances, it has overlaid the surface.

The slopes of an ancient forest incline towards a river that flows sluggishly onwards through a deep alluvial plain, once an extensive lake.   A recent landslip has opened up one of the hanging thickets.   Uprooted trees, mingled with bushes, lie at the foot of the slope, half buried in broken masses of turf; and we see above a section of the soil, from the line of vegetation to the bare rock.   There is an under belt of clay, and an upper belt of gravel, neither of which contains any thing organic; and overtopping the whole we may see a dark-colored bar of mould, barely a foot in thickness, studded with stumps and interlaced with roots.   Mark that narrow bar: it is the geological representative of six thousand years. A stony bar of similar appearance runs through the strata of the Wealden: it, too, has its dingy color, its stumps, and its interlacing roots; but it forms only a very inconsiderable portion of one of the least considerable of all the formations · and yet who shall venture to say that it does not represent a period as extended as that represented by the dark bar in the ancient forest, seeing there is not a circumstance of difference between them ?

We descend to the river side. The incessant action of the current has worn a deep channel through the leaden-colored silt; the banks stand up perpendicularly over the water, and downwards, for twenty feet together, — for such is the depth of the deposit, — we may trace layer after layer of reeds, and flags, and fragments of driftwood, and find here and there a few fresh-water shells of the existing species. In this locality, six thousand years are represented by twenty feet. The depth of the various fossiliferous formations united is at least fifteen hundred times as great.

We pursue our walk, and pass through a morass. Three tiers of forest trees appear in the section laid open by the stream, the one above the other. Overlying these there is a congeries of the remains of aquatic plants, which must have grown and decayed on the spot for many ages after the soil had so changed that trees could be produced by it no longer; and over the whole there occur layers of mosses, that must have found root on the surface after the waters had been drained away by the deepening channel of the river. The six thousand years are here represented by that morass, its three succeeding forests, its beds of aquatic vegetation, its bands of moss, and the thin stratum of soil which overlies the whole. Well, but it forms, notwithstanding, only the mere beginning of a formation. Pile up twenty such morasses, the one over the other; separate them by a hundred such bands of alluvial silt as we have just examined a little higher up the stream; throw in some forty or fifty thick beds of sand to swell the amount; and the whole together will but barely equal the Coal Measures, one of many formations.

But the marine deposits of the present creation have been,

perhaps accumulating more rapidly than those of our lakes, forests, or rivers? Yes, unquestionably, in friths and estuaries, in the neighborhood of streams that drain vast tracts of country, and roll down the soil and clay swept by the winter rains from thousands of hill-sides; but what is there to lead to the formation of sudden deposits in those profounder depths of the sea, in which the water retains its blue transparency all the year round, let the waves rise as they may? And do we not know that, along many of our shores, the process of accumulation is well nigh as slow as on the land itself? The existing creation is represented in the little land-locked bay, where the crustacea harbor so thickly, by a deposit hardly three feet in thickness. In a more exposed locality, on the opposite side of the promontory, it finds its representative in a deposit of barely nine inches. It is surely the present scene of things that is in its infancy! Into how slender a bulk have the organisms of six thousand years been compressed! History tells us of populous nations, now extinct, that flourished for ages: do we not find their remains crowded into a few streets of sepulchres? 'Tis but a thin layer of soil that covers the ancient plain of Marathon. I have stood on Bannockburn, and seen no trace of the battle. In what lower stratum shall we set ourselves to discover the skeletons of the wolves and bears that once infested our forests? Where shall we find accumulations of the remains of the wild bisons and gigantic elks, their contemporaries? They must have existed for but comparatively a short period, or they would surely have left more marked traces behind them

When we appeal to the historians, we hear much of a remote antiquity in the history of man a more than twilight gloom pervades the earlier periods: and the distances are exaggerated, as objects appear large in a fog. We measure,

24

too, by a minute scale. There is a tacit reference to the threescore and ten years of human life, and its term of a day appears long to the ephemera. We turn from the historians to the prophets, and find the dissimilarity of style indicating a different speaker. Ezekiel's measuring-reed is graduated into cubits of the temple. The vast periods of the short-lived historian dwindled down into weeks and days. Seventy weeks indicated to Daniel, in the first year of Darius, the time of the Messiah's coming. Three years and a half limit the term of the Mohammedan delusion. Seventeen years have not yet gone by since Adam first arose from the mould; nor has the race, as such, attained to the maturity of even early manhood. But while prophecy sums up merely weeks and days, when it refers to the past, it looks forward into the future, and speaks of a thousand years. Are scales of unequally graduated parts ever used in measuring different portions of the same map or section — scales so very unequally graduated, that, while the parts in some places expand to the natural size, they are in others more than three hundred times diminished? If not, — for what save inextricable confusion would result from their use, — how avoid the conclusion, that the typical scale employed in the same book by the same prophet represents similar quantities by corresponding parts, whether applied to times of outrage, delusion, and calamity, or set off against that long and happy period in which the spirit of evil shall be bound in chains and darkness, and the kingdom of Christ shall have come? And if such be the case — if each single year of the thousand years of the future represents a term as extended as each single year of the seventeen years of the past — if the present scene of things be thus merely in its beginning — should we at all wonder to find that the formation which represents it has laid down merely its few first strata?

The curtain again rises. A last day had at length come to the period of the middle formation; and in an ocean roughened by waves, and agitated by currents, like the ocean which flowed over the conglomerate base of the system, we find new races of existences. We may mark the clumsy bulk of the *Holoptychius* conspicuous in the group; the shark family have their representatives as before, a new variety of the *Pterichthys* spreads out its spear-like wings at every alarm, like its predecessors of the lower formation; shoals of fish of a type more common, but still unnamed and undescribed, sport amid the eddies; and we may see attached to the rocks below substances of uncouth form and doubtful structure, with which the oryctologist has still to acquaint himself. The depositions of this upper ocean are of a mixed character: the beds are less uniform and continuous than at a greater depth. In some places they consist exclusively of sandstone, in others of conglomerate; and yet the sandstone and conglomerate seem, from their frequent occurrence on the same platform, to have been formed simultaneously. The transporting and depositing agents must have become more partial in their action than during the earlier period. They had their foci of strength and their circumferences of comparative weakness; and while the heavier pebbles which composed the conglomerate were in the course of being deposited in the foci, the lighter sand which composes the sandstone was settling in those outer skirts by which the foci were surrounded. At this stage, too, there are unequivocal marks, in the northern localities, of extensive denudation. The older strata are cut away in some places to a considerable depth, and newer strata of the same formation deposited unconformably over them. There must have been partial upheavings and depressions, corresponding with the partial character of the depositions; and, as a necessary consequence, frequent shiftings of currents. The ocean, too, seems to have lessened its general depth, and the bottom to have lain more exposed to the influence of the waves. And hence one cause, added to the porous nature of the matrix, and the diffused oxide, of the detached, and, if I may so express myself, churchyard character of its organisms.

Above the blended conglomerates and sandstones of this band a deposition of lime took place. Thermal springs, charged with calcareous matter slightly mixed with silex, seem to have abounded, during the period which it represents, over widely-extended areas; and hence, probably, its origin. An increase of heat from beneath, through some new activity imparted to the Plutonic agencies, would be of itself sufficient to account for the formation. I have resided in a district in which almost every spring was charged with calcareous earth; but in cisterns or draw-wells, or the utensils in which the housewife stored up for use the water which these supplied, no deposition took place. With boilers and tea-kettles, however, the case was different. The agency of heat was brought to operate upon these; and their sides and bottoms were covered, in consequence, with a thick crust of lime. Now, we have but to apply the simple principles on which such phenomena occur, to account for widely-spread precipitates of the same earth by either springs or seas, which at a lower temperature would have been active in the formation of mechanical deposits alone. The temperature sunk gradually to its former state; the purely chemical deposit ceased; the waters became populous as before with animals of the same character and appearance as those of the upper conglomerate; and layer after layer of yellow sandstone, to the depth of several hundred feet, were formed as the period passed. With this upper deposit the system terminated.

Though fish still remained the lords of creation, and fish of apparently no superior order to those with which the vertebrata began at least three formations earlier, they had mightily advanced in one striking particular. If their organization was in no degree more perfect than at first, their bulk at least had become immensely more great. The period had gone by in which a mediocrity of dimension characterized the existences of the ancient oceans, and fish armed offensively and defensively with scales and teeth scarcely inferior in size to the scales and teeth of the gavial or the alligator, sprung into existence It must have been a large jaw and a large head that contained, doubtless among many others, a tooth an inch in diameter at the base. I may remark, in the passing, that most of the teeth found in the several formations of the system are not instruments of mastication, but, like those in most of the existing fish, mere hooks for penetrating slippery substances, and thus holding them fast. The rude angler who first fashioned a crooked bone, or a bit of native silver or copper, into a hook, might have found his invention anticipated in the jaws of the first fish he drew ashore by its means; and we find the hook structure as complete in the earlier ichthyolites of the Old Red Sandstone as in the fish that exist now. The evidence of the geologist is of necessity circumstantial evidence, and he need look for none other; but it is interesting to observe how directly the separate facts bear, in many examples, on one and the same point. The hooked and slender teeth tell exactly the same story with the undigested scales in the fœcal remains alluded to in an early chapter.

In what could this increase in bulk have originated? Is there a high but yet comparatively medium temperature in

24*

which animals attain their greatest size, and corresponding
gradations of descent on both sides, whether we increase the
heat until we reach the point at which life can no longer
exist, or diminish it until we arrive at the same result from
intensity of cold ? The line of existence bisects on both sides
the line of extinction.   May it not probably form a curve,
descending equally from an elevated centre to the points of
bisection on the level of death ?   But whatever may have
been the cause, the change furnishes another instance of
analogy between the progress of individuals and of orders.
The shark and the sword-fish begin to exist as little creatures
of a span in length ; they expand into monsters whose bodies
equal in hugeness the trunks of ancient oaks ; and thus has
it been with the order to which they belong.   The teeth,
spines, and palatal bones of the fish of the Upper Ludlow
Rocks are of almost microscopic minuteness ; an invariable
mediocrity of dimension characterizes the ichthyolites of the
Lower Old Red Sandstone ; a marked increase in size takes
place among the existences of the middle formation ; in the
upper the bulky *Holoptychius* appears ; the close of the system ushers in the still bulkier *Megalichthys* ; and low in the
Coal Measures we find the ponderous bones, buckler-like
scales, and enormous teeth of another and immensely more
gigantic *Holoptychius* — a creature pronounced by Agassiz
the largest of all osseous fishes *   We begin with an age of
dwarfs — we end with an age of giants.   The march of Nature
is an onward and an ascending march ; the stages are slow,
but the tread is stately ; and to Him who has commanded,

---

* There have been fish scales found in Burdie House five inches in
length, by rather more than four in breadth   Of the gigantic *Holoptychius* of this deposit we have still much to learn.   The fragment of
a jaw, in the possession of the Royal Society of Edinburgh, which

and who overlooks it, a thousand years are as but a single day, and a single day as a thousand years.*

We have entered the Coal Measures. For seven formations together — from the Lower Silurian to the Upper Old Red Sandstone — our course has lain over oceans without a visible shore, though, like Columbus, in his voyage of discovery, we have now and then found a little floating weed, to indicate the approaching coast. The water is fast shallowing. Yonder passes a broken branch, with the leaves still unwithered ; and there floats a tuft of fern. Land, from the mast-head ! land ! land ! — a low shore, thickly covered with vegetation. Huge trees, of wonderful form, stand out far into the water. There seems no intervening beach. A thick hedge of reeds, tall as the masts of pinnaces, runs along the deeper bays, like water-flags at the edge of a lake. A river of vast volume comes rolling from the interior, darkening the water for leagues with its slime and mud, and bearing with it, to the open sea, reeds, and fern, and cones of the pine, and immense floats of leaves, and now and then some bulky tree, undermined and uprooted by the current We near the coast, and now enter the opening of the stream. A scarce penetrable phalanx of reeds, that attain to the height and well nigh the bulk of forest trees, is ranged on either hand. The bright and glossy stems seem rodded like Gothic columns; the pointed leaves stand out green at every joint, tier above tier, each tier resembling a coronal wreath or an ancient crown, with the rays turned outwards; and we see a-top

---

belonged to an individual of the species, is $18\frac{1}{2}$ inches in length ; and it is furnished with teeth, one of which, from base to point, measures five inches, and another four and a half.

* See, on this subject, the introductory note to the present edition, and note p. 154.

what may be either large spikes or catkins. What strange
forms of vegetable life appear in the forest behind! Can
that be a club-moss that raises its slender height for more
than fifty feet from the soil? Or can these tall, palm-like
trees be actually ferns, and these spreading branches mere
fronds? And then these gigantic reeds! — are they not
mere varieties of the common horse-tail of our bogs and morasses, magnified some sixty or a hundred times? Have we
arrived at some such country as the continent visited by Gulli-
ver, in which he found thickets of weeds and grass tall as woods
of twenty years' growth, and lost himself amid a forest of
corn, fifty feet in height? The lesser vegetation of our own
country, reeds, mosses, and ferns, seems here as if viewed
through a microscope · the dwarfs have sprung up into giants,
and yet there appears to be no proportional increase in size
among what are unequivocally its trees. Yonder is a group
of what seem to be pines — tall and bulky, 'tis true, but
neither taller nor bulkier than the pines of Norway and
America; and the club-moss behind shoots up its green,
hairy arms, loaded with what seems catkins above their topmost cones. But what monster of the vegetable world comes
floating down the stream — now circling round in the eddies,
now dancing on the ripple, now shooting down the rapid? It
resembles a gigantic star-fish, or an immense coach-wheel,
divested of the rim. There is a green, dome-like mass in the
centre, that corresponds to the nave of the wheel, or the
body of the star-fish; and the boughs shoot out horizontally
on every side, like spokes from the nave, or rays from the
central body The diameter considerably exceeds forty feet:
the branches, originally of a deep green, are assuming the
golden tinge of decay; the cylindrical and hollow leaves
stand out thick on every side, like prickles of the wild rose on
the red, fleshy, lance-like shoots of a year's growth, that will

be covered, two seasons hence, with flowers and fruit. That strangely formed organism presents no existing type among all the numerous families of the vegetable kingdom.* There is an amazing luxuriance of growth all around us. Scarce can the current make way through the thickets of aquatic plants that rise thick from the muddy bottom; and though the sunshine falls bright on the upper boughs of the tangled forest beyond, not a ray penetrates the more than twilight gloom that broods over the marshy platform below. The rank steam of decaying vegetation forms a thick blue haze, that partially obscures the underwood; deadly lakes of carbonic acid gas have accumulated in the hollows; there is silence all around, uninterrupted save by the sudden splash of some reptile fish that has risen to the surface in pursuit of its prey, or when a sudden breeze stirs the hot air, and shakes the fronds of the giant ferns or the catkins of the reeds. The wide continent before us is a continent devoid of animal life, save that its pools and rivers abound in fish and mollusca, and that millions and tens of millions of the infusory tribes swarm in the bogs and marshes. Here and there, too, an insect of strange form flutters among the leaves. It is more than probable that no creature furnished with lungs of the more perfect construction could have breathed the atmosphere of this early period, and have lived.

Doubts have been entertained whether the limestone of Burdie House belongs to the Upper Old Red Sandstone or to the inferior Coal Measures. And the fact may yet come to be quoted as a very direct proof of the ignorance which obtained regarding the fossils of the older formation, at a time when the organisms of most of the other formations, both above and below it, had been carefully explored. The Limestone of Burdie House is unequivocally and most characteristically a Coal Measure limestone. It abounds in vegetable

* See Note O.

remains of terrestrial or lacustrine growth, and these, too, the vegetables common to the Coal Measures — ferns, reeds, and club-mosses. One can scarce detach a fragment from the mass, that has not its leaflet or seed-cone enclosed, and in a state of such perfect preservation, that there can be no possibility of mistaking its character. If in reality a marine deposit, it must have been formed in the immediate neighborhood of a land covered with vegetation. The dove set loose by Noah bore not back with it a less equivocal sign that the waters had abated. Now, in the Upper Old Red Sandstone none of these plants occur. The deposit is exclusively an ocean deposit, and the remains in Scotland, until we arrive at its inferior and middle formations, are exclusively animal remains. Its upper member, " the yellow sandstone," says Dr. Anderson, of Newburgh, " does not exhibit a single particle of carbonaceous matter — no trace or film of a branch having been detected in it, though, if such in reality existed, there are not wanting opportunities of obtaining specimens in some one of the twenty or thirty quarries which have been opened in the county of Fife in this deposit alone." No two bordering formations in the geological scale have their boundaries better defined by the character of their fossils than the Old Red Sandstone and the Coal Measures.

We pursue our history no further. Its after course is comparatively well known. The huge sauroid fish was succeeded by the equally huge reptile — the reptile by the bird — the bird by the marsupial quadruped; and at length, after races higher in the scale of instinct had taken precedence in succession, the one of the other, the sagacious elephant appeared, as the lord of that latest creation which immediately preceded our own. How natural does the thought seem which suggested itself to the profound mind of Cuvier, when indulging in a similar review ! Has the last scene in the

series arisen, or has Deity expended his infinitude of resource,
and reached the ultimate stage of progression at which perfection can arrive? The philosopher hesitated, and then decided in the negative, for he was too intimately acquainted
with the works of the Omnipotent Creator to think of limit-
ing his power; and he could, therefore, anticipate a coming
period in which man would have to resign his post of honor
to some nobler and wiser creature — the monarch of a better
and happier world. How well it is, to be permitted to indulge
in the expansion of Cuvier's thought, without sharing in the
melancholy of Cuvier's feeling — to be enabled to look forward to the coming of a new heaven and a new earth, not in
terror, but in hope — to be encouraged to believe in the system of unending progression, but to entertain no fear of the
degradation or deposition of man! The adorable Monarch
of the future, with all its unsummed perfection, has already
passed into the heavens, flesh of our flesh, and bone of our
bone, and Enoch and Elias are there with him — fit representatives of that dominant race, which no other race shall
ever supplant or succeed, and to whose onward and upward
march the deep echoes of eternity shall never cease to
respond.

ICHTHYOLITES OF THE OLD RED SANDSTONE.

FROM

AGASSIZ'S "POISSONS FOSSILES."

₊ The synonymes here — now supplanted, however — with the names of a few doubtful or fictitious species, are given in *Italics*, — the former opposite the names ultimately adopted, the latter immediately under the names of the determined species.

Acanthodes pusillus.
Actinolepis tuberculatus.
Asterolepis Asmusii. — Syn. *Chelonichthys Asmusii*
    "   apicalis.
    "   granulata.
    "   Hœninghausii.
    "   Malcolmsoni
    '   minor. — Syn. *Chelonichthys minor.*
    "   ornata.
    "   speciosa.
    "   *concatenatus.*
    "   *depressus.*
Bothriolepis favosa. — Syn. *Glyptosteus favosus.*
    "   ornata   "   "   *reticulatus*
Byssacanthus arcuatus.
    "   crenulatus.
    "   lævis.
Cephalaspis Lewisii.
    "   Lloydii.
    "   Lyellii.
    "   rostratus.

25

Cheiracanthus microlepidotus.
"　　　minor.
"　　　Murchisoni.
Cheirolepis Cummingiæ.
"　　Traillii.
"　　Uragus.
"　　*splendens.*
"　　*unilateralis.*
Chelyophorus pustulatus.
"　　　Verneuilii.
Cladodus simplex.
Climatius reticulatus.
Coccosteus cuspidatus.
"　　decipiens — Syn. *latus.*
"　　maximus.
"　　oblongus.
Cosmacanthus Malcolmsoni.
Cricodus incurvus. — Syn. *Dendrodus incurvus*
Ctenacanthus ornatus.
"　　　serrulatus
Ctenodus Keyserlingii.
"　　marginalis.
"　　parvulus.
"　　Worthii.
"　　*radiatus.*
"　　*serratus.*
Ctenoptychius priscus.
Dendrodus latus.
"　　minor.
"　　sigmoides
"　　strigatus.
"　　tenuistriatus.
Diplacanthus crassispinus.
"　　　longispinus.
"　　　striatulus.
"　　　striatus.
Diplopterus affinis.

Diplopterus oorealis. — Syn. *Agassizii.*

"   macrocephalus.

Dipterus macrolepidotus.

" *arenaceus.*

" *brachypygopterus.*

" *macropygopterus.*

" *Valenciennesii.*

Glyptolepis elegans.

"   leptopterus.

"   microlepidotus.

Glyptopomus minor. — Syn. *Platygnathus minor.*

Haplacanthus marginalis.

Holoptychius Andersoni.

"   Flemingii.

"   giganteus.

"   Murchisoni.

"   nobilissimus.

"   Omaliusii.

Homacanthus arcuatus.

Homothorax Flemingii.

Lamnodus biporcatus. — Syn. *Dendrodus biporcatus.*

" hastatus. — Syn. *Panderi Dendrodus hastatus, compressus.*

" sulcatus.

Narcodes pustilifer.

Naulas sulcatus.

Odontacanthus crenatus. — Syn. *Ctenoptychius crenatus.*

"   heterodon.

Onchus heterogyrus.

" semistriatus.

" sublævis.

Osteolepis arenatus.

" macrolepidotus

" major.

" microlepidotus.

" *intermedius.*

" *nanus.*

Pamphractus Andersoni.

Pamphractus hydrophilus. — Syn. *Pterichthys hydrophilus*
Parexus recurvus.
Phyllolepis concentricus
Placothorax paradoxus.
Platygnathus Jamesoni
    "   paucidens.
Polyphractus platycephalus.
Psammosteus arenatus. — Syn. *Placosteus arenatus.*
    "   mæandrinus. "   "   *mæandrinus.*
    "   paradoxus. "   *Psammolepis paradoxus.*
    "   undulatus. "   *Placosteus undulatus.*
Pterichthys arenatus.
    "   cancriformis.
    "   cornutus.
    "   major.
    "   Milleri.
    "   ·   latus
    "   oblongus.
    "   productus.
    "   testudinarius.
Ptychacanthus dubius.
Stagonolepis Robertsoni.

NOTES.

NOTE A, Page 18.

In the last edition of his "Elements" (1855), Sir Charles Lyell has considerably altered and amplified this description, for which he has been to a large extent indebted to the discoveries and publications of Mr. Miller. See "Elements of Geology," chap. xxvi.

NOTE B, Page 40

"And in the latter formation [Coal Measures] the first reptiles appear" This statement requires now to be slightly modified, in consequence of the discovery in 1851, by Mr Patrick Duff of Elgin, of a true reptile (Telerpeton Elginse) in the Upper Old Red of Morayshire The fact is referred to in "The Testimony of the Rocks," pages 46 and 104 See also Lyell's "Elements" for a figure and description of the creature The argument following the above quotation is not, however, in any way affected by this discovery It is right, however, to add, that up to a very recent period, Mr Miller was known to have expressed some doubts as to whether the rock in which the Telerpeton was found did not belong to a much higher formation than the Old Red Sandstone.

NOTE C, Page 54

For a more minute description of the head-plates of the Coccosteus, see "Foot-Prints of the Creator," pages 73 and 74. See also Plate ix.

NOTE D, Page 72.

See "Foot-Prints of the Creator," pages 75–80, where the structure of the head of the Osteolepis is fully described and figured.

NOTE E, Page 93

In "The Testimony of the Rocks" the flora of the Old Red is treated at great length. See pages 433–462. See also, on the same subject, "Foot-Prints of the Creator," pages 209–222.

NOTE E, (No 2) Page 126.

The genus *Cephalaspis* (Agas) has been confounded with the *Pteraspis* (Kner). *Cephalaspis rostratus* is a *Pteraspis*, and Professor Huxley and Mr Salter describe *Cephalaspis Lewisii* and *Lloydii* as *Pteraspides*. Sir P. de Grey Egerton has determined two new species of *Cephalaspis* (*C. Salweyi* and *C. Murchisoni*) — *Proc. Geol. Soc*, *August*, 1857.

NOTE F, Pages 128 and 143

Sixteen years ago, when "The Old Red Sandstone" was written, the Cephalaspis was little understood Since then, however, a few specimens have been found in the neighbourhood of Arbroath, which demonstrate that the animal was provided with a large and powerful tail, and with equally powerful pectorals, so that its impetus need not have been, as here stated, "comparatively slow" It is now also well ascertained that the peculiar "cutting-knife" or "bolt"-like shape of the head, so generally noticeable in the earlier specimens, was the result of accident A single cephalic shield of bone, thickly covered with discoidal bony plates of beautiful workmanship, was bent round the whole of the upper portion of the creature's head, including the sides, somewhat after the fashion of a lady's bonnet shade, with this difference, that, instead of the pointed ends, or "horns," being fastened, as in the case of the bonnet, they projected freely backwards in the fish. It was altogether, therefore, an armature of *defence*, and not partly of *offence*, as hinted at in the text. Of this Mr. Miller had long been quite aware, and, in consequence, had expressed himself approvingly of the restoration figured in Plate x. An Arbroath specimen, in the possession of Mr. Powrie of Reswallie, which shows the head in profile, has the cephalic shield bent round in the manner described. In the large majority of instances, however, the fish being found lying on its belly, the curvature of the shield has yielded to the pressure of the overlying stone, and the appearance of the head is consequently that of a perfectly flat crescent, as represented in Plate xiii. fig. 1.

NOTE G, PAGES 129 AND 137, — "Middle Empire."

Here, and elsewhere in these pages, the Forfarshire gray beds are spoken of as constituting the *middle* portion of the formation.

BALRUDDERY SPINES.

In "The Testimony of the Rocks," however, pages 452–455, Mr. Miller remarks, that "the evidence on the point is certainly not so conclusive as I deemed it fifteen years ago" (p. 452); and again (p. 455), "It must, however, be stated, on the other hand, that the crustaceans of the gray tilestones of Forfar and Kincardine not a little resemble those of the upper Silurian and red tilestone beds of England; and that, judging from the ichthyodorulites found in both, their fishes must have been at least generically allied. The crustaceans of the upper Silurian of Lesmahagow, too, seem certainly much akin to those of the Forfarshire tilestones." The spines figured in the accompanying cut, when compared with those in Sir R. Murchison's "Siluria," may help the scientific reader to determine the question.

ADDITIONAL NOTE, BY REV. W. S. SYMONDS. — In Worcestershire, in the neighborhood of Kidderminster, the *Cephalaspis Lyellii.* has been detected in beds that appear to be intermediate between the Tilestones and Cornstones and associated with other fossils supposed to be *characteristic of the Tilestones* Mr. Roberts of Kidderminster has found the *Pterygotus* of the Kington Tilestones and the *Pteraspis* of Mr. Banks in the same Gray Sandstones and Cornstones which contain *Cephalaspis Lyellii* and *Pteraspis ornatus* I exhibited these fossils at a meeting of the Geological Society of London, April 1857, in the presence of Sir P. Egerton, Sir R Murchison and Sir C. Lyell.

NOTE II, PAGES 133 AND 137

The correctness of the term "tail-flap," used by Mr. Miller when describing a peculiar-looking plate of the Balruddery lobster, has been questioned. Sir Charles Lyell and Mr Page both believe it to have been a jaw-foot Several fine specimens of this organism have been sent up to Mr. Salter of the Jermyn Street Museum, London, whose decision will probably definitely settle the matter

NOTE II, (No 2) PAGE 135 BY RLV W S SYMONDS

Near Ludlow, Hereford, and several other localities. the Upper Ludlow fish-bed has been traced over an extensive area; but in several places the fishes appear to be absent, and their places supplied by large Crustaceans, chiefly *Pterygotus Himantopterus, Eurypterus,* and *Pterygotus,* have been found by Mr Banks associated with *Pteraspides* and *Lingula cornea,* while Mr Roberts has *Pteraspis* and *Pterygotus* in the same beds as *Cephalaspis Lyellii.* The *Pterygotus* of Kidderminster seems identical with the Scotch *Seraphim.*

NOTE I, PAGES 142 AND 145.

This organism Mr Miller had some time ago definitely concluded to be vegetable See "The Testimony of the Rocks," p.

448, where he says, — " There now seems evidence enough to conclude that they are the remains, not of the eggs of an animal, but of the seed of a plant."

ADDITIONAL NOTE, BY REV. W. S SYMONDS — These fossils — *Parka decipiens* — now known to be the seeds of a plant, are abundant in the Kidderminster beds   See also Plate xii.

NOTE K, PAGE 149

For recent additions made to the flora and fauna of the English and Irish Old Red Sandstone, see *Siluria*, in "Lyell's Elements" and " The Geological Journal," vol. xii.

NOTE L, PAGE 156.

See " The Testimony of the Rocks," pages 247 and 248.   See also Plate xiv

NOTE M, PAGE 170.

See, in connection with this remark, the quotations in note G. May not the fact here mentioned of the Pterichthys occurring in the Caithness and Fifeshire beds, and *not* in the Forfarshire, be another argument for the greater antiquity of the latter ?

NOTE N, PAGE 196.

From the tenor of the remarks at p 453 of " The Testimony of the Rocks," it will be seen that Mr. Miller had come latterly to regard the conglomerate of the south of the Grampians as the analogue of that of Caithness.   In November 1856 he decidedly expressed this as his matured opinion, in conversation with the writer.

NOTE O, PAGE 257.

The organism here referred to is now ascertained to have been a *root*, and not an independent plant, — the root, namely, of the Sigillaria.   See " The Testimony of the Rocks," pages 65–7.

NOTE BY THE REV. W. S. SYMONDS.

A *Pterichthys* has been discovered by Mr. Baxter of Worcester in the yellow sandstone of the Clee Hill district, Salop. This yellow sandstone is below the carboniferous limestone of the Clees, and is the equivalent of the Cyclopterus Hibernicus sandstones of Ireland and the Dura Den beds of Scotland. The Pterichthys has not before been discovered in England, and is therefore an important addition to the Upper Old Red fossils of England. A new species of *Eurypterus* has also been described by the Rev. W. S. Symonds, in the " Edinburgh New Philosophical Journal," October 1857, from the Upper Cornstones of Herefordshire.

GEOLOGICAL PAPERS

READ BEFORE THE

ROYAL PHYSICAL SOCIETY OF EDINBURGH.

CONTENTS.

GEOLOGICAL EVIDENCES

IN FAVOR OF

REVEALED RELIGION.

THE following treatise was read by Mr. MILLER, on taking the chair, for the first time, as President of the Society, on 7th January, 1852:—

GENTLEMEN,—You have done me the honor of electing me, by a unanimous vote, to be one of the Presidents of the Royal Physical Society. I little thought, some two-and-thirty years ago, when, rather in obedience to a native instinct than with any ulterior object, I sought to acquaint myself with geological phenomena, that there awaited me any such honor. For, unaware at the time that there even existed such a science as Geology, or that the field which it opens has its many laborers, some of whom meet with less, and some with more success in their labors, I could not so much as imagine that distinction was to be achieved by studying the forms and structures of the strange organisms which I laid open amid rocks and in quarries, or in inquiring into the circumstances in which they had lived and died, or into the causes to which, in ages long gone by, they had owed their entombment in the stone. But it seems to be one of the characteristics of a true science, that it should promise little and perform much; and that for those who devote themselves to it simply for its own sake, it should reserve a class of favors of a purely exterior character, rarely vouchsafed to the suitors who make court to it for that dowry of the extrinsic and the adventitious which it occasionally brings.

It certainly *is* one of the characteristics of geological science, though in a far higher sense than that to which I have adverted, that it promises little and performs much. It contrasts strongly in this respect with those purely mental sciences still properly taught in our higher schools,—for they constitute the true gymnastics of mind, but, like other gymnastics, are to be regarded, not as actual work, but simply as a preparation for it. The use of the dumb-bells opens the chest and strengthens the muscles; but it is left to labor of quite another kind to supply the wants of the present, or to provide for the necessities of the future. And such appears to be the sort of relation borne by the purely mental to the natural sciences. How very different, however, the prospects which they seemed to open to the curious inquirer in the earlier ages of their history, or even in the earlier history of individual minds among ourselves! Mental science must have appeared to many of us, when we first approached it, as a magnificent gateway, giving access to a vast province, in which not only all knowledge regarding the nature of mind was to be acquired, but in which also, through the study of the intellectual faculties, we were to be introduced to the best possible modes of acquiring all other knowledge. But have we not been disappointed in our hopes? nay, from the doubts and uncertainties conjured up by the nice dialectics of the science, have we not had eventually to cast ourselves for escape on the simple instincts of our nature? and, ultimately, have we not gained well nigh as little through the process, so imperatively demanded by the metaphysician, of turning the mind upon itself, instead of exercising it on things external to it, as if we had been engaged in turning the *eye* upon itself, instead

of directing it on all the objects which it has been specially
framed to see, — among the rest, on other eyes, and the peculiarities of their structure? In both natural and physical
science, on the contrary, have we not often found, that while
the promise has been slight, the fulfilment has been ample far
beyond the reach of anticipation? When the boy James Watt
was playing, as Arago tells the story, with the steam of the
family tea-kettle, — now marking how its expansive force raised
the lid of the utensil, and now how, condensed into water, it
trickled powerlessly adown the sides of the cold china cup,
which he had inverted over it, — who could have imagined
that in these simple processes there lay wrapped up the principle of by far the mightiest agent of civilization which man has
yet seen, — an agent that, in a century after the experiment
of the boy, would have succeeded in giving a new character to
the arts both of peace and of war? Or who could have sur-
mised, when, at nearly the same period, the Philadelphian
printer was raising for the first time his silken kite in the
fields, that there was an age coming in which, through a knowledge of laws hitherto unknown, but whose existence he was
then determining, man would be enabled to bind on his
thoughts to the winged lightning, and to send them, with an
instantaneousness that would annihilate time and space, across
land and sea? Nor in that geological branch of natural science to which, with the cognate branches, our Society has
specially devoted itself, has performance in proportion to previous promise been less great. When it was first ascertained
by the father of English geology, William Smith, — a man
not yet more than twelve years dead, — that the Oolitic beds
of England have always a uniform order of succession, and
that this uniformity is attended by a certain equally uniform
succession of groups of fossils, could it be once inferred that
he was laying hold of a principle which, in the course of a

single age, was destined marvellously to unlock the past history
of our planet, and to acquaint us with God's doings upon it, as
the Creator of all, for myriads of ages ere he had first breathed
the spirit of life into human nostrils, or man had become a
living soul? It is one of the great marvels of our day, that
through the key furnished by geologic science we can now
peruse the history of past creations more clearly, and arrive at
a more thorough and certain knowledge of at least the struct-
ural peculiarities of their organisms, than we can read the
early histories of the old dynasties of our own species, that
flourished and decayed on the banks of the Euphrates or of
the Nile, or ascertain the true character of the half-forgotten
tyrants with whom they terminated, or from whom they began.

It seems scarce possible that, in at least the leading facts
of geologic history, we shall witness any very considerable
change. There is no truth more thoroughly ascertained than
that the great Tertiary, Secondary, and Palæozoic divisions
represent in the history of the globe, periods as definitely distinct and separate from each other as the modern from the
ancient history of Europe, or the events which took place previous to the Christian era from those that date in the subsequent
centuries which we reckon from it. All over the globe, too, in
the great Palæozoic division, the Carboniferous system is found
to overlie the system of the Old Red Sandstone, and that, in
turn, the widely developed Silurian system. It is not less certain, that in the Secondary division, the Triassic deposits are
overlaid by the Oolitic ones, and both by the Cretaceous; nor
yet, that in the Tertiary division, the beds of the Pliocene, with
their large per centages of existing shells, as exemplified in
the Red and Coraline Crags, belong to a greatly later period
than that old Eocene age represented by the extinct shells and
strange mammals of the Paris basin and the London clay
There is no human history more definitely ranged into centu-

ries than the geological into periods and epochas ; nor is the certainty less great, or the chance of transposition in any degree less slight in the one case than in the other. For, respecting at least the main geologic systems, their order of succession, and the organisms which they contain, the evidence is as positive and conclusive as it is regarding any piece of human history whatever. There are, however, certain geologic inferences very extensively adopted, which are founded rather on negative than on positive evidence ; and these must of necessity, be subject, during the course of discovery, to modification and change. And we find resting mainly on this department of the negative,—I should, perhaps, rather say of the assumptive, — two of the extremer schools of the present day, — that school which, founding on a certain progressive rise, in the course of the geologic periods, from lower to higher types, both animal and vegetable, would infer that what we term creation is in reality but development, — the low, in the lapse of un-measured ages, having passed, it is alleged, into the high ; and another school, represented by at least one very masterly geologist, which teaches that there has been no upward progress in creation, but that the earth, in all the periods of its history represented by the geologic systems, must have existed under the same great conditions in which it now exists, and have produced, mingled with inferior forms, plants of the same superior classes, and, if we except man himself, animals of the same high divisions of the vertebrata.

What, however, are the positive facts with which, as geologists, we are called on to deal ? In the Tertiary Flora we find great abundance of true dicotyledonous trees, — in its Fauna, frequent forms of the mammals, which, in at least the later ages of the division, are of high types. We pass into the great Secondary division, and find trees as abundant in its Flora, in at least some of the middle deposits, as in any of the Tertiary

beds; but we have not yet succeeded in detecting among them
a single dicotyledonous tree of the higher sub-classes, and only
a few dicotyledonous leaves.   They are all coniferous gymnospermæ, chiefly of the pine and araucarian families; and in
the Fauna associated with them, we find that the prevailing
forms are reptilian.   The reptile occupied as large a place in
these Secondary periods as that occupied by the mammal in
the Tertiary ones   So far, indeed, as we yet definitely know,
there existed during these herpetological ages only two species
of mammals, — a small marsupial and small insectivorous animal.   Again, in the Flora of the Palæozoic division, we still
find the pine and the araucarian, mixed, however, with extraordinary vegetable types, some of which have become wholly
obsolete, and some of which are linked by but faint analogies
to aught that now exists; but which, generally speaking, seem
to be, though high representatives of their kind, of a kind in
itself not high.   In the Fauna of the period, down till at least
the base of the middle Palæozoic system, fishes seem the dominant forms, — fishes, many of them of great size, formidably
armed, and uniting in their organization, reptilian to the ordinary ichthyic peculiarities, but in not a few of their number
destitute of an internal skeleton of bone.   True, during these
ages the reptile also existed, but in such scanty proportions,
that while the Coal Measures have yielded their ichthyic remains by thousands and tens of thousands, they have yielded
to the sedulous search of the geologist only three reptiles and
the trace of a fourth; and, while in single platforms of the
Old Red Sandstone there are perhaps as many fishes entombed
as are at present living on all the fishing banks of the country,
the entire system has furnished the remains of but one reptile
(if, indeed, the lacertian of Spynie in reality belong to it), and
the foot-tracks of a few others.   In the Lower Palæozoic formations, the trace of even the fish becomes unfrequent, and the

dominant organisms are crustaceans and molluscs. Now, such being the ascertained facts of our science, we are, I think, justified in still holding against the disciples of the one school to which I have referred, that there has been progress in creation from a lower to a higher level. So far as there exists any evidence on the subject at all, we must hold that, in at least the group, the Palæozoic existences were of a lower and humbler order than those of the Secondary ages, and those of the Secondary ages of a lower and humbler order than those of the periods of the Tertiary. As shown by the vertebrate remains of the geologic epochs, the balance, which greatly preponderated in the times of the Tertiary in favor of the mammals, greatly preponderated in the times of the Secondary in favor of the reptiles, and in the long evanished Palæozoic ages, in favor of the fishes. And so now, as before, these three great periods may be properly described as the periods of the fish, the reptile, and the mammal; nor do the late exceptional cases, in which traces of reptiles have been found among the Palæozoic fishes, or of mammals among the Secondary reptiles, interfere more with the justness of such designations than the existence in New Zealand of one small indigenous mammal of the rat family, among its some fifty or sixty ornithic species, interferes with the propriety of designating it a land of birds, or the existence among the some forty-six *pouched* species of Australia of a few mammals that are not pouched, with the propriety of designating it a land of marsupials. Let us be content, then, as geologists, to found our deductions, until our science shall have provided us with a new class of facts, on the facts which we already possess. No sooner were we introduced, through the discovery of his grace the Duke of Argyll, to a small Tertiary deposit in the island of Mull, than we found that it yielded in abundance leaves of the buckthorn and the plane. No sooner had our boulder clays and drift gravels begun to exhibit their organisms, than we found that what they submitted to our examination were tusks of the elephant and the mastodon, and bones of the rhinoceros, the ox, and the deer. If trees of the same dicotyledonous class as the plane and the buckthorn occurred in our Secondary or Palæozoic periods, in at least aught approaching to the recent or Tertiary proportions, how is it that amid their fossil woods, though they have yielded their specimens by thousands, not a single dicotyledonous specimen, save of the gymnospermæ, has yet been found? Or if the great Palæozoic period indeed abounded in mammals, such as the elephant and the deer, how is it that, while in the Palæozoic deposits of even our own neighborhood and country we have met with the remains of fishes by tens of thousands, and of molluscs by millions, all the Palæozoic systems of the world have hitherto failed to present us with a single mammalian tooth or bone? Or even if in these ancient deposits a few dicotyledonous woods or mammalian fragments *were*, after the search of years, to be found, what could we infer regarding the *proportions* in which either dicotyledons or mammals had existed in the periods which the deposits represented, save from the proportions in which we found their remains occurring in them? Nay, do we not find Sir Charles Lyell setting his imprimatur on an exactly similar style of induction as that upon which we found, when, in determining the various formations of the Tertiary division, he has recourse to his principle of per centages? He would assuredly not deem that a Pliocene or Miocene deposit among whose numerous organisms he had failed to find an existing plant or shell. In the geologic, as in other departments,

"What can we reason but from what we know."

The gulf between mental and geologic science is still too broad, and perhaps too carelessly surveyed on the theologic side, to permit us to judge of the influence which the discoveries of the geologist are yet to exercise on the ethical departments of literature. We can, however, already see that the vastly extended knowledge of God's workings of old which the science communicates, must exercise no slight influence upon certain departments of natural theology, and give a new tone to those controversies regarding the evidences of our faith which the Church has ever and anon to maintain with the world. Geology has already put an end to that old fiction of an infinite series of beings which the atheist was wont to substitute in his reasonings for the great First Cause through which all exists, nor does it leave other than very unsolid ground to the men who would fain find an equivalent for the exploded infinite series of their predecessors in a developing principle. Nay, I would ask such of the gentlemen whom I now address as have studied the subject most thoroughly, whether, at those grand lines of division between the Palæozoic and Secondary, and again between the Secondary and Tertiary periods, at which the entire type of organic being alters, so that all on the one side of the gap belongs to one fashion, and all on the other to another and wholly different fashion,—whether they have not been as thoroughly impressed with the conviction that there existed a Creative Agent to whom the sudden change was owing, as if they themselves had witnessed the miracle of creation? Further, may we not hold that that acquaintance with bygone creations, each in succession of a higher type than the one which preceded it, which geology enables us to form, must soon greatly affect the state of arguments employed on the skeptical side, which, framed on the assumption that creation is but a "singular effect,— an effect without duplicate,—have urged, that from that one effect only can we know aught regarding the producing Cause? Knowing of the Cause but from the effect, and having expe-

rience of but one effect, we could not rationally hold, it has
been argued, that that producing Cause could have originated
effects of a higher or more perfect kind.   The creation which
it had produced we knew; but, having no other measure of its
power, we could not, it was contended, regard it as competent
to the production of a better or nobler creation, or, of course,
hold that it could originate such a state of things as that perfect
future state which Faith delights to contemplate.   Now, it has
been well said of the author of this ingenious sophism, — by
far the most sagacious of the skeptics, — that if we admit his
premises, we will find it difficult indeed to set aside his conclusions.   And how, in this case, does geology deal with his
premises?   By opening to us the history of the remote past of
our planet, and introducing us, through the present, to former
creations, it breaks down that *singularity* of effect on which he
built, and for one creation gives us many.   It gives us exactly
that which, as he truly argued, his contemporaries had not, —
an *experience in creations*.   And let us mark how, applied to
each of these in succession, his argument would tell   There
was a time when life, animal or vegetable, did not exist on our
planet, and when all creation, from its centre to its circumference, was but a creation of dead matter.   To what effect in
that early age would have been the argument of Hume?   Simply to this effect would it have borne, — that, though the producing Cause of what appeared was competent to the formation
of earths, metals, and minerals, it would be unphilosophic to
deem it adequate to the origination of a single plant or animal.
— even to that of a spore or of a monad.   Ages pass by, and
the Palæozoic creation is ushered in, with its tall araucarians
and pines, its highly organized fishes, and its reptiles of a comparatively low standing.   And how now, and with what effect,
does the argument apply?   It is now found that in the earlier
creation the producing Cause had exerted but a portion of its

power, and that it could have done greatly more than it actually
did, seeing that we now find it to be a Cause adequate to the
origination of vitality and organization in two great types, —
the vegetable and the animal, — as exemplified in pines and
araucarians, in fishes and in reptiles. But still confining ourselves with cautious skepticism within the limits of our argument, we continue to hold that, as fishes of a high, and reptiles
of a low order, with trees of the cone-bearing family, are the
most perfect specimens of their respective classes which the
producing Cause has originated, it would be unphilosophic to
hold, in the absence of proof, that it would originate aught
higher or more perfect. And now, as yet other ages pass
away, the creation of the great Secondary division takes the
place of the vanished Palæozoic; and we find in its few dicotyledonous plants, in its reptiles of highest standing, and in
its some two or three comparatively humble mammals, that in
the previous, as in the earlier creation the producing Cause
had been, if I may so express myself, working greatly under
its strength, and that in this third creation we have a still
higher display of its potency. With some misgivings, however, we again apply our argument And now yet another
creation, — that of the Tertiary period, with its noble forests
of dicotyledonous trees, and its sagacious and gigantic mammals, — rises upon the scene ; and, as our experience in creation has now become very considerable indeed, and as we have
seen each in succession higher than that which preceded it, we
find that, notwithstanding our assumed skepticism, we had, —
compelled by one of the most deeply-seated instincts of our
nature, — been secretly anticipating the advance which the
new state of things actually realizes. But, applying the argument yet once more, we at least assume to hold, that as the
sagacious elephant is the highest example of animal life produced by the originating Cause, it would be unphilosophic to

deem it capable of producing a higher example; and, while we are thus reasoning, man appears upon creation, — a creature immeasurably superior to all the others, and whose very nature it is to make use of his experience of the past for his guidance in the future. And if that only be solid experience or just reasoning which enables man truly to anticipate the events which are to come, and so to make provision for them, and if that experience be not solid, and that reasoning not just, which would serve but to darken his discernment, and prevent him from correctly predicating the cast and complexion of coming events, what ought to be his decision regarding an argument which, had it been employed in each of the vanished creations of the past, would have had but the effect of arresting all just anticipation regarding the creation immediately succeeding, and which, thus reversing the main end and object of philosophy, would render the philosopher who clung to it less sagacious in divining the future than even the ordinary man? But, in truth, the existing premises, wholly altered by geologic science, are no longer those of Hume. The foot-print of his unhappy illustration does not now stand alone. Instead of one, we see many foot-prints, each in advance of and on a higher level than the print immediately behind it; and, founding at once on an acquaintance with the past, extended throughout all the periods of the geologist, and on that instinct of our nature whose peculiar function it is to anticipate at least one creation more, we must regard the expectation of "a new heavens and new earth, wherein dwelleth righteousness," as not unphilosophic, but as, on the contrary, altogether rational, and fully according to experience.

ANCIENT GRAUWACKE ROCKS OF SCOTLAND.

PART FIRST—HISTORICAL.

"From Portpatrick on the west coast, to St. Abb's Head on the east," says Dr. James Hutton, in his far-famed Theory of the Earth, "there is a tract of schistus mountains, in which the strata are generally much inclined, or approaching to the vertical situation ; and in these inclined strata," he adds, "geologists allege there is not to be found any vestige of organized body." But the opinion can be "proved," he further states, "to be erroneous." He himself, indeed, though he had been occasionally employed in examining the rocks of this "south Alpine country of Scotland" for more than forty years, had failed to find in them any traces of the organic ; but his distinguished friend Sir James Hall, when travelling, in the summer of 1792, between Noblehouse and Crook, had detected sea-shells in "an Alpine limestone" by the wayside, at Wrae Hill, in the parish of Broughton, and thus demonstrated, as the limestone is intercalated with the schistus rocks, the fossiliferous character of the deposit. Even geologists had not yet become palæontological ; and we find Sir James, in a passage quoted in the "Theory," describing the shells which he had detected simply as "forms of cockles."

He was greatly more exact, however, in his appreciation of
the mechanical peculiarities of the deposit, and his description of those strange convolutions of the strata which give to
the south of Scotland its series of axial lines, and its repeti-
tions of beds and bands that come ever and anon to the surface, and continue to render the place of at least its nether
groups of rock so obscure, is still approvingly referred to by
our higher geologists. To account for these strange foldings,
Sir James, in his paper in the "Transactions of the Royal
Society of Edinburgh," on the Vertical Position and Convolutions of certain Strata, and their relations with Granite,
broached that theory of lateral pressure applied by some unknown force outside the area of the foldings themselves, which
is still regarded as the best yet originated on this subject, and
illustrated it by his famous experiments of the bands of vari-
ously-tinted clays, and the layers of differently-colored cloths,
which he succeeded in pressing, by the application of lateral
force, from a horizontal into a convoluted position   His paper
did not appear in its completed form until the year 1812;
but as his theory had been originated more than twenty years
previously, when, on visiting, in the company of Dr. Hutton
and Professor Playfair, a portion of the east coast of Berwickshire, he found no fewer than "sixteen distinct bend-
ings of the strata in the course of about six miles," and as,
long ere the publication of his view and experiments, they
were well known to his scientific friends, I refer to them at
this early stage in my brief sketch of the history of geological discovery in our Scottish Grauwacke.

Dr Hutton had described the "Alpine Schistus" of the
South of Scotland as belonging to the Primary class of rocks,
and founded an argument for his theory on the fact that, in
direct opposition to the belief of geologists regarding the deposits of this special division, they yet do contain fossils.   In

1805, Professor Jameson published his " Mineralogical Description of Dumfriesshire ; " and to him must be assigned the merit of first determining that these ancient schists belong, not to the Primary, but to what Werner has termed the Transition or Grauwacke Series. He states in this work, that he had traced these Transition rocks in Scotland " from the northern extremity of the Pentland Hills, which is about six miles distant from the shores of the Frith of Forth, to Lang-robie, in Dumfriesshire, about three miles from the Solway Frith." We find him, too, giving very correctly the other limits of the system as developed in our southern counties, and classifying with much precision the mechanical and mineralogical peculiarities of the rocks which compose it. But when he comes to speak of its organisms, he is content to discuss the subjects in a single sentence, founded apparently, from its vague generality, less on his own observations in the field which he describes, than on the general conclusions of his master, Werner. After stating that " Transition or Grauwacke slates contain petrifactions," whereas " primitive clay slate " does not, he goes on to say that the " petrifactions found in transition rocks are of animals and plants of the lower orders, that probably no longer exist on the face of the earth." An anonymous critic, who in the succeeding year, 1806, reviewed his work in a London periodical (the " Literary Journal,") and who was evidently acquainted with the Grauwackes of Dumfriesshire, took up the subject, and regretted that the Professor had not been more specific. " Our author might have added," we find him saying, " that *vegetable* petrifactions are very common in the Grauwacke slates of Dumfriesshire. The omitting of this circumstance is rather unaccountable," it is added, " as he could not possibly have avoided making the observation. He has been very properly punished for the omission. The assertion that Grauwacke contains petri-

27*

factions has been denied, and our author has been challenged to produce a *single* petrifaction in the Grauwacke of Dumfriesshire. To us, who know perfectly well that vegetable petrifactions are very common in that Grauwacke, this challenge appears not a little bold." Thus far the reviewer. He seems to have observed for himself, but not very correctly. Mr. Harkness tells us, in a paper which appeared in the " Geological Journal " for 1851, that though the Dumfries Grauwackes contain their thick bands of anthracite, of apparently vegetable origin, there has been detected in them no vegetable remains whatever They abound, however, in graptolites ; and it was probably these leaf-like zoophytes, whose nature is still so imperfectly understood, that caught the eye of the reviewer, and constituted his " vegetable petrifactions." The Grauwacke of Scotland does, however, contain vegetable impressions apparently fucoidal ; though they are far from common in any of the rocks which I have yet seen, and yield no characters by which they can be distinguished from the simpler fucoids of the Old Red Sandstone. In one of the specimens now on the Society's table, derived from the shales of Girvan, there occurs a fucoidal stem of this latter description, associated with graptolites of the double-sided genus *diprion*, — a genus never found, it is said, save in the Lower Silurian.

In 1808, Professor Jameson published that third volume of his "System of Mineralogy, in which he fully developed his geological views, and described in language that has since become obsolete, the character and order of succession of the various formations. The work, however, added nothing to the previous knowledge of our Scotch Grauwacke, save perhaps, a very curious hypothesis regarding its convoluted strata, framed evidently to meet the theories of Hutton and Sir James Hall. " Very striking curvatures sometimes oc-

cur," said the Professor, "in Transition or Grauwacke slate.
The waved and concentric circular appearances *are the effects
of crystallization*, whereas other curved and angular appearances seem to be connected with the mode of deposition of
the strata, and may be traced either to inequalities of the
fundamental rock, or to irregularities in the deposition of the
strata themselves." We do not now expect so much from
crystallization, nor, when we see fossils spread out on a vertical plane, do we try to believe that, in defiance of the law
of gravitation, they had pasted themselves there of old, as
one pastes prints upon a screen: but as a fossil theory may
be in some instances scarce less curious than a fossil plant or
animal, the use of the extract will, I trust, be forgiven me.
About four years after the publication of Professor Jameson's
work, the late Mr. Thomas Allen of this city read a very able
paper before the Edinburgh Royal Society, on the Transition
Rocks of Werner, in which we find reference made to their
fossiliferous character in our southern Highlands. But there
are no new localities given. Over the one discovery of Sir
James Hall at Wrae Hill our Scotch geologists seem to have
hybernated for more than forty years. In truth, the great
controversy which then divided them into Plutonists and
Neptunians seems to have operated unfavorably on the progress of general discovery. In looking over our book-shelves
for some wanted volume, we soon come to find that we have
eyes for only it, and that all the other volumes fail to attract
notice or attention. And such seems to have been the case
with not a few of our Scotch geologists; they went out to
search among the shelves of that great geologic library in
which the early histories of the globe are stored up, for whatever could be made to tell in favor of their own hypothesis,
or to militate against that of their neighbors, and, engrossed
by this one object, they seem to have been indifferently suited

for the accomplishment of any other. In the various notices
of our Scotch Grauwacke which occur in the Transactions of
the Edinburgh scientific societies during the years in which
the battle raged between the two schools, I do not find trace
of a single discovery worthy of being introduced into a history of the system. Curious observers, however, outside the
area of the conflict, seem to have been now and then finding
in the deposit occasional traces of the organic. I have been
told by the late Mr. William Laidlaw (the trusted friend of
Sir Walter Scott), whose acquaintance I had the pleasure of
forming early in 1839, that on two several occasions, many
years before, he had found minute bivalves, and what he
deemed vegetable impressions, in the Grauwacke slates of
Peebleshire.

The second notice of fossils in our Grauwacke at all defi-
nite in its details, and which intimated original discovery, occurred long after the first, — at a time when geology had made
rapid strides towards the position which it at present occupies, — and was of a peculiar interest to Edinburgh geologists,
from the near neighborhood of the locality which it indicated
to the Scottish metropolis. In 1839, Mr. Charles Macklaren
published his "Geology of Fife and the Lothians;" and in
that ingenious work, — equally remarkable for the boldness
of its theories and the truthfulness of its observation, — geologists were first told that there exist fossils in the Grauwacke slate of the Pentlands. The organisms of the older
rocks are not unfrequently restricted to a single stratum:
even in the Lower Old Red Sandstone one may pass along
sections of the strata many hundred feet in thickness, without detecting a trace of aught organic, and then find in some
thin layer, perhaps not a foot in thickness, the fucoids, or
fishes, or minute bivalves, of the formation, congregated by
hundreds and thousands; and in the Scotch Grauwacke this

peculiar arrangement obtains in a still more marked degree. The organisms of a wide district of country are confined often to a single layer, occupying scarce half an inch, in a section thousands of feet in vertical extent. And such seems to be the arrangement among the ancient slates of the Pentlands. Mr. Maclaren found his fossils near Deerhope-foot, at the side of a small stream that falls into the North Esk, and he describes them, in the portion of his work devoted to the geology of the Pentland range, as of two kinds. In one, fragments of what seem minute trilobites are congregated together in thin layers ; in the other, there are the distinctly marked impressions of what appear to be orthoceratites. I owe two of those Pentland fossils to the kindness of Mr. Maclaren. The one, apparently a portion of an orthoceratite, exhibits a side view of what seem to be five of the septa , the other greatly resembles that curious and still but imperfectly understood vegetable of the Coal Measures, *Sternbergia approximata :* but it is in all probability not a vegetable, but an animal organism, — very possibly an orthoceratite also. One of these specimens bears on the label the date of its discovery (7th of April 1834), — a date five years anterior to that of the publication of Mr. Maclaren's volume, and forty-two years posterior to the discovery of Sir James Hall. The fact that by much the greater part of half a century should have intervened between the first and second discoveries of organic remains in our Grauwackes, — for, waving the claim of Mr. Laidlaw, whose discovery seems never to have been recorded, and can now be associated with neither locality nor date, Mr. Maclaren's *is* decidedly the second, — is a fact of itself sufficient to show that our Scotch schools were in those days not zealously palæontological; and we know from other sources, that arguments were sought after within their precincts, with much more avidity than fossils. But the error has been seen and in part corrected; and the future of Scotch Geology bids fair to be characterized by the doing of more and the saying of less.

In the same year in which Mr. Maclaren published his "Geology of Fife and the Lothians," the "Silurian System" of Sir Roderick Murchison appeared,—one of those great works which form eras in the history of science, and from which, as from the charts of some distinguished voyager, after explorers have learned to shape their course aright, and to recognize as familiar and easily definable, tracts previously unnamed and unknown. In both the old world and the new, the great divisions first laid down in this work by Sir Roderick have been detected and identified, and an introductory book added to the organic history of our planet, from the rich and varied materials which they supply. For, however, several years after its publication, our Scottish Grauwacke continued to remain a *terra incognita*, as before; for though there appeared from time to time truthful descriptions of the deposit itself, its place in the scale was still doubtful. Two years after (1841), Mr. James Nicol,—now Professor of Geology in Queen's College, Cork—produced his Prize Essay on the Geology of Peeblesshire; and to an accurate description of the mineralogical components of the Grauwacke of that county added a new locality for its fossils, in Grierston, near Traquair, where, in a slate quarry, there occur thin but continuous layers of graptolites, often in a state of the most exquisite keeping. Some of the finest Scottish specimens of this ancient organism which I have yet seen I have derived from this Grierston deposit. We also find Mr. Nicol referring, in his Essay, to that limestone quarry of Wrae Hill in which Sir James Hall had found his fossil shells; but its lime, when he wrote, had been exhausted, or so covered up by the rubbish of the workings, that its organisms could be

detected no longer. "It strikes one as a melancholy reflection," we find him saying, "when leaving this deserted quarry,
where the wild whistle of the mountain sheep shows how
seldom their solitude is invaded, that these relics of former
creations, which, if preserved to science, might have added
an interesting page to the world's history, should have thus
perished by the hand of man at so recent a period, after having remained safely stored up in the cabinet of nature for so
many ages, and throughout so many awful revolutions." I
may here add, however, that shells have since been detected
in the limestones of the Wrae Hill, both by Mr. Nicol himself, and by Mr. Robert Chambers, and the discovery of Sir
James fully verified. In 1842, one of the members of our
Royal Physical Society, Mr. William Rhind, published his
brief but interesting treatise on the "Geology of Scotland."
And in referring, in a general notice, to our Grauwacke deposits, we find him stating, that the "formation" to which
they belong "corresponds to some of the beds of the Cambrian
system, as existing in Wales;" and that in graptolites discovered in the Grauwacke slates of Innerleithen, "the first indications of organized fossils appear." He adds, that "distinct specimens of these lay before him as he wrote, which
had been presented to him by the discoverer, Mr. James
Nicol." In 1845, Mr. Nicol published his "Guide to the
Geology of Scotland," — a work which I have ever since
carried about with me in my geologic rambles, and which,
in every instance in which its author has described from his
own observations, I have found correct. In this useful work
we find him again referring to the graptolites of Grierston and
the shells of Wrae Hill; and, further, briefly intimating yet
another Grauwacke locality rich in fossils, though he was evidently in doubt regarding its true place in the scale. "In
a limestone below the coal near Girvan," he remarks, "Silu-

rian fossils are said to occur," — a circumstance not unfrequent," it is added, "in the Mountain Limestone of Scotland." No one, however, is now more thoroughly convinced than Professor Nicol, that the Silurian organisms of Girvan are not organisms of the Carboniferous series; that, on the contrary, they definitely determine the place and age of the deposits in which they occur as Lower Silurian; and further, that they throw more light on the history of this ancient system, in its development in the southern Highlands, than the fossils of all our other Scottish localities put together.

In January 1848, Mr. Nicol, at that time Assistant Secretary of the London Geological Society, read before that body a paper on the Silurian Rocks of the Valley of the Tweed, which was afterwards published in the Journal of the Society. Even at a period so recent he could properly state, in his introduction, "that there is perhaps no extensive formation in the British islands of which we possess less certain geological knowledge than of the rocks constituting the great mountain chain which crosses the southern counties of Scotland from east to west." His paper, however, served to add considerably to the little previously known regarding the deposit. Among the fossils by which it was illustrated, Mr. Salter recognized the fragments of five genera of trilobites, and an equal number of genera of shells, chiefly brachipods, all of a character indicative of the Lower Silurian group. About the same time a collection made from the Grauwackes of the shores of Kirkcudbright was submitted to the London Geological Society by Lord Selkirk, and was found to be of an Upper Silurian character; indeed, as appeared from the identity of some of the fossils, of the age of the Wenlock shale. In the May of the same year in which Professor Nicol submitted his paper to the public, the subject was still further elucidated in a valuable memoir, by Mr. Carrick Moore, Secretary to the Geological

Society, on the Silurian Rocks of Ayr and Wigtonshire, which added yet further to our knowledge of the fossils of these ancient rocks, and in which, in its published form, the first Scottish Maclurea was figured and described, though somewhat doubtfully, from the imperfect state of keeping of the specimen, and under another name. At the meeting of the British Association held in this city in 1850, Professor Sedgwick read a paper on the Geological Structure and Relations of the Frontier Chain of Scotland, which derived a peculiar value from the previous labors of that great geologist in the older Silurian rocks of England, and in which he divided our Grauwackes, though with much hesitation, especially with respect to both the earlier and later beds, into five great divisions, — four of them belonging to the Lower, and the fifth *probably*, as he stated, to the Upper Silurian. In comparing the Scottish with the Cambrian chains, he remarked that the lowest and oldest fossils of both appear to be graptolites ; and in a paper on the Graptolites of the Black Slates of Dumfriesshire, by Mr. R. Harkness, which appeared in the " Geological Journal" of last year, we find a minute description, accompanied by good figures, of these earliest inhabitants of what is now Scotland. They are judged to have been zoophites, akin in some of their forms to our modern Pennatuladæ, and in others, it is supposed, to the Sertularia ; but the relationship of these last is deemed less clear. It is, I suspect, remote in both cases. Some of my Girvan specimens of *Graptolithus foliaceus*, — one of the species deemed akin to the Pennatuladæ, — exhibit the central axis prolonged beyond its double row of cells, but, unlike our common sea-pen (*Pennatula phosphorea*), always at the upper end ; and in specimens of *Graptolithus tenuis*, derived from the same neighborhood, and which is one of the species regarded as akin to the Sertularia, though some of the stems seem fringed on both sides with short, oblique, alternate cells, somewhat

resembling those of the common *Sertularia halecina*, we find,
on examination, that they are in reality restricted to one side,
and that the apparent fringes of the other are but mere notches
in the stem.   In one respect, however, judging from the rocks
in which we usually find them, these organisms must have resembled the sea-pens.   There is a deep submarine ravine, which
runs for some distance along one of the middle reaches of the
Moray Frith, and at the steep edges of which the water deepens
suddenly from about twelve to about thirty fathoms.   The
bottom on either side is gravelly and hard, whereas the ravine
is charged with a dark adhesive mud, abounding in fish bones,
and which intimates to the sense of smell, when brought to the
surface, that there must have entered into its composition no
small portion of organized matter.   Now, this muddy ravine
abounds with sea-pens.   When not a specimen can be procured
on the hard ground on either side, the fisherman's lines, when
his boat drifts across the hollow, becomes charged with them :
every muscle bait brings up attached to it what the fishers of
the Frith term its " sea-tree ; " so that specimens may be procured by the hundred.   And from the dark-colored, finely-
grained, semi-bituminous character of the slates in which the
graptolites chiefly occur, it is apparent that they also loved a
muddy habitat

I have now to refer to but two other papers on our Scotch
Grauwacke.   In 1849, Professor Nicol made the Silurian
deposits of the south-east of Scotland the subject of yet another
very able memoir, in which he specified several new localities
for its fossils, and added to the previous list at least one new
fossil more, — a hitherto undescribed species of Graptolite.
He bestowed much care, too, in ascertaining the general direction of the beds and mountain ranges of our southern Highlands ; and found it coincident, on an average drawn from no
fewer than sixty-six several observations, with the direction of

the continuous band of clay-slate which, running diagonally from sea to sea, reclines, at a steep angle on the northern side of the great Lowland valley of Scotland, against the flanks of the Grampians. And, — to conclude the purely historical portion of my subject, — in 1851 Sir Roderick Murchison contributed a paper on the Silurian Rocks of the South of Scotland, accompanied with descriptions and figures of its characteristic fossils (especially of those of the Girvan deposits), which gives us to know, on certainly the highest authority, that whilst the true place of those apparently older members of the Lower Silurian system in Scotland which, represented by what are the first and second of Professor Sedgwick's five great divisions, is, as the Professor himself observes, exceedingly doubtful, there can be scarce any doubt entertained, that in the deposits of Girvan and Kirkcudbright we possess the analogues and representatives of the middle and upper members of the Lower Silurians of England, and the lowest member of its Upper Silurians. For many years we have been accustomed to regard our Scotch Grauwackes and Grauwacke slates as remarkable for their paucity in organisms. Sir Roderick seems, on the contrary, to have been struck by their abundance, and the distinctness with which they tell the story and exhibit the character of the deposits which inclose them. " Fossils abound," says this first of geologists, in describing Mulloch Hill, in the neighborhood of Girvan, "and for the most part their shells are so well preserved, that great was my astonishment when I cast my eye over the surfaces of this rock, and thought of the long time which had elapsed before such unequivocal and really beautiful Silurian types had been made known in Scotland." The perusal of Sir Roderick's paper greatly excited my curiosity. I had visited, nearly seven years before, — guided by the descriptions of his "Silurian System," — the rich deposits of middle England, the Wenlock limestones and shales of

Dudley, and the Upper Ludlow and Armistry deposits of Sedgley and its neighborhood; and I was now desirous to decipher, under his guidance, the characters of those added pages to the geologic history of our country, from which his paper had led me to expect so much. And, availing myself of a pause in my professional labors, towards the close of last May, when the two General Assemblies were sitting, and when all our abler clergy were speaking articles in the form of speeches, and so rendering it unnecessary that I should write any, I set out, in the middle of a tract of very delightful weather, for Girvan.

PART SECOND — DESCRIPTIVE.

As the traveller passes downward along the valley of the Girvan, the scenery, which had been hitherto of a pleasing but purely Lowland character, begins to assume somewhat bolder features. The hills on either side heighten into heath-covered mountain ranges; and we remember that Scotland has its southern as certainly as its northern Highlands. "The mountainous country in the south-western borders of Scotland," says Sir Walter Scott, in one of his novels, "is called *Iheland*, though totally different from the much more mountainous and more extensive district of the north, usually accented *Highland*" The bottom of the valley, however, which these hills overlook, is of a soft and pastoral character, with perhaps more of wood than is common in a Lowland valley, but laid out into rich fields that recline along the lower slopes, and occupied by a quiet stream, — the Girvan. Within a few miles of where it opens into the sea, we see on its northern side, high over field and meadow, a steep prominent range of gray crags, that at once remind us of those pale-tinted mural rocks of Silurian Limestone which form so striking a feature in the scenery of Dudley

and its neighborhood. And they, too, like the English precipices, are composed of a Silurian Limestone, rich in fossils.
Far beneath, however, and in what at first seems an inferior
position, we see rising among the trees the peculiar groups of
buildings, with their tall chimneys and long armed engines,
that indicate a coal-producing district, and mark on a sloping
hill-side, immediately over a thick wood, a slim column of smoke
ascending out of the ground, — where one of the seams beneath
has been burning for years, — like the smoke of some subordinate volcano. The valley of the Girvan forms a deep and
very irregular basin, composed of Silurian rocks, but occupied
for several miles by a small though not unproductive patch of
the Coal Measures, which abuts unconformably against the
older deposits, and lies so low in the system as to be overlaid
by the Mountain Limestone The explorer, in passing downwards, should strike off to the north from the public road at
the pleasant village of New Dailly, and rise on the hill-side,
after crossing the stream and passing the Castle of Dalquhar-
ran, towards the older rocks, turning first, however, by the way,
to visit the coal-workings immediately above the Castle, and
then, a little further on, to examine, in a chance opening among
the trees, the overlying fossils of the Carboniferous Limestone.
He would do well, however, if desirous to economize time, and
make himself sure of seeing all in the district that is worthy
of being seen, to secure the services of Mr. Alexander M'Callum, the ingenious fossil collector of Girvan, under whose guidance he will learn more in a day than he could perhaps find
out for himself in a week. Under the intelligent direction of
Mr. M'Callum, whose services Sir Roderick Murchison has
deemed worthy of special acknowledgment in his paper, I struck
up from the coal-works and overlying limestone and shale, in
which well known fossils, such as *Productus giganteus* and
Productus Martini, may be detected, and reached the steep

28*

side of a rocky hill overhung by wood, in which several quarries have been opened, chiefly for the repair of roads. The rock, a dingy, olive-tinted sandstone, which in color and quality reminded me of some of the Caradoc sandstones, abounds in fossils, — at one place, where a deeply-shaded and rarely-trodden road has been cut into it, chiefly corals, apparently of the species *Favosites fibrosus.* But though, from their light color, conspicuous on the dark rock, their state of keeping is usually bad. In a deserted quarry a little further on I found the Silurian forms in great abundance, — trilobites, orthoceratites, crinoidal stems, brachipods of the ancient genera orthis, and atrypa, a large Maclurea, a bellerophon, casts of what seem to be turritella, a large trochus, and corals of the genus petraia, and of another more composite genus which was wholly unfamiliar to me, but which I find figured by Murchison as a nidulites. I found in this quarry a unique-looking univalve, somewhat resembling a trochus, which, if not encrusted by some mat-like coral, that has imparted to it a style of ornament not its own, must be new; and the remains of more trilobites, shells, and corals, than I had at one time supposed all the Grauwacke deposits of the south of Scotland could have furnished The place, long deserted apparently by the quarrier, — rich in mosses and herbaceous plants that love the shade, and shut in on every side by a thick wood, — is one in which the geologist might profitably pass many hours in a solitude not unfavorable to thought, and rarely indeed interrupted by the foot of man.

On ascending yet further towards the hill-top, and exchanging for the gloom of the wood a lone and somewhat dreary heath, I found the organic remains of the rock becoming still more numerous. Shells occur in beds and layers; and not in the rich limestone beds of Dudley have I seen them lie more thickly. The stone here is of a firmer texture than in the

quarry, and, where unweathered, of a darker gray, and, as
the organisms which it encloses yield more readily on expo-
sure than the surrounding matrix, they exist upon the surface
as mere darkened casts, but in the fresh fracture are of a pearly
white.   And here, also, trilobites and corals occur among the
shells.   A little further on, the rock assumes yet a different
hue; it abounds in iron, which imparts to it in some places a
deep red, in others a buff-yellow hue, and the fossils, converted
into a bright yellow ochre, present, when broken, an almost
golden aspect, and are of great, though from their state of
extreme oxidization, of short-lived beauty.   I have rarely seen
anything richer in appearance than the bright yellow trilobites
on a deep red ground which I laid open in one of the higher-
lying quarries of the hill.   They reminded me of the trilobites in the collection of a certain noble lord, now deceased,
who became eccentric as he grew old, and, to improve their
appearance, got them gilded and burnished.   Sheets of festi-
nella of the same bright hue, that, when first exposed by the
hammer, resemble pieces of gold lace, mingled with sprigs of
golden coral, and deeply sulcated golden petraia, also occur in
great abundance; with bronze-looking shells by the million,
chiefly of the genera orthus, atrypa, and terebratula.   So
thickly do these lie in some of the beds, as to give to the otherwise solid rock a fissile character.   One of the most remaka-
ble-looking fossils of the group, is, however, a large trilobite,—
an Illænus, furnished with a caudal shield as large as that
which covers its head, and of a decidedly Lower Silurian type,
as are almost all the other accompanying organisms, though
some of them have a wide range in the system, and occur in
the lower beds of its upper division.   I may mention, that I
found here, at the height of many hundred feet over the sea, the
boulder clay, with its characteristic pebbles scored and polished, and in most cases bearing their striæ in the line of their

longer axes; that, in general correspondence with the average color of the rocks of the district, it was of a deep gray color; and that its boulders were chiefly of Silurian rocks, charged with the characteristic fossils of the system.

Quitting the upper part of the hill, with its richly fossiliferous quarries, and striking downwards to the west and south, I passed through a series of corn-fields, and, on reaching a little stream which flows through a valley nearly parallel to that of the Girvan, found the rock partially exposed along its course. It consists here, not, as in the hill above, of an indurated sandstone, but of a gray rubbly shale, much broken by transverse *dies* and fractures, and which, though its relations to the sandstone are not clearly seen, seems, as premised by Sir Roderick Murchison, to rest over them. In localities to the south of the Girvan, as at Ardwell, Piedmont-Glen, and Peawhapel-Burn, it is rich in orthoceratites, and contains numerous beds of graptolites; in this locality, known as the farm of Drummuck, it abounds in trilobites. Mr. M'Callum had wrought out the exposed front, to which he introduced me, until arrested by a field-fence, on which he was not permitted to encroach. But though I could procure, in consequence, no specimens for myself, I acquired several very interesting ones from Mr. M'Callum, which, with many others, he had dug out of this front; and I certainly at one time never expected to see a group of these curious crustaceans at once so ample and so characteristic, from the Grauwacke slates of Scotland. *Calymene Blumenbachii*, the well-known Dudley trilobite, is the prevailing form of the deposit, — a form abundant, as its common English name testifies, in the lower deposits of the Upper Silurians of England, but which in North Wales also occurs in the Lower Silurians. I found, associated with this trilobite, in the same fragment of shale, what seems to be a Forbesia, — hitherto exclusively an Irish form; and was lucky enough to procure a complete *Cheirurus gelasinosus*, — a species of which Sir Roderick figures from this deposit a detached head, and which, though I find no trace of it in his "Silurian System," is described by M'Coy as a not rare trilobite in the Silurian rocks of Kildare. It is a circumstance not unworthy of notice, that the Scottish Silurian fossils are more completely identical with those of the Irish than with those of the English group. They are *Celts*, if I may so speak, rather of the old Scoto-Irish than of the old Welsh type. I have said that to the south of Girvan these trilobite shales are rich in graptolites and orthoceratites. The graptolites are usually of that double fringed section (*diprion*), with an axis in the centre, to which the typical *Graptolithus foliaceus* belongs ; the only exceptional species, so far as I know, being *Graptolithus tenuis*, a member of that single fringed section (*monoprion*) represented by the typical *Graptolithus Ludenses*. Associated with these, but rarely, we sometimes find a large dark-colored lingula, probably the *Lingula ovata* of M'Coy, also a Kildare species ; and *Orbicula crassa*, a finely striated shell, bearing usually the same dark hue, as if both organisms had been covered by an epidermis, which had alone survived when their shelly substance had been absorbed in the rock. The orthoceratites of the deposit exist in a peculiar state of keeping They have been converted, with the filling of all their chambers, into a pure chocolate-colored lime ; whilst the gray shale in which they lie is so little calcareous as to remain impassive under the strongest acids. Many of them seem to have been broken across ere they were committed to the rock, and exist as detached though very entire fragments, consisting of from six to ten chambers a-piece. It is stated by Sir Roderick Murchison, that one of the largest of the Girvan orthoceratites being of a kind unknown to him, he referred it to M. Barrande, then on a visit to our country, who recognized it as a Bohemian species, occurring in the lower part of the Upper Silurian division. Sir Roderick adds, as further remarkable, that on submitting to the Continental geologist some of the shales and nodules in which these Ayrshire shells are imbedded, "he declared to him that he might produce our Scottish rocks as Bohemian specimens." The Bohemian species of orthoceratite has, of late, I may mention, been found in Ireland by M'Coy.

Taking leave of the interesting shale deposit at Drummuck, I scaled the southern side of the little valley in which it occurs, and came down upon the range of bold limestone cliffs, whose picturesque appearance, rising high over the woods, had, at the distance of several miles, attracted my notice, in the valley of the Girvan. The relations of this limestone to either the indurated sandstones or the trilobite shales, is, from the covered character of the ground, not distinctly traceable; but its fossils belong to the Lower Silurian group, and it is identical in structure and appearance with a limestone which crops out in several localities to the south of the valley, and which, underlying the sandstone, is evidently the oldest deposit in the district. It is an exceedingly hard sub-crystalline stone, and looks as if an outburst of the trap rocks which rise around it, and at certain points send out enormous dikes into its substance, had given it, for the purposes of the palæontologist, rather too much of the fire. And so, though it abounds in fossils, — corals, trilobites, and shells, — they are rarely sufficiently distinct enough to be identified. Occasionally, however, on the argillaceous surfaces of the thick beds of which the rock consists, we find a trilobite or shell impressed with characters sufficiently legible; and its more massive corals and encrinal stems are, from their lighter color, and the trace which they still retain of internal structure, usually distinguishable enough in the body of the stone. It is a curious circumstance, that not only in the group do the fossils of this rock resemble

those of the Silurians of Canada and the United States, but
that some of its organisms not yet found in England seem to
be even identical with those of the other side of the Atlantic.
It contains a terebratula indistinguishable from a Canadian
species, and a Maclurea determined by M'Coy to be the *Maclurea magna* of the United States. This last massive genus,
which resembles that of Euomphalus, save that its whorls lie
in nearly the same plane, is by no means rare in the limestones
of the Girvan district, but so much so in the Silurians of the
sister kingdom, that it does not appear in Murchison's great
work. Some of our graptolites are also identical, it is said,
with American species; and, on lately exhibiting my small
collection of Scoto-Silurian fossils to a geologist of the United
States, he told me that none of the organisms which he had
yet seen in the museums of our country so reminded him,
from their general appearance, of those of his own. It is
surely not uninteresting thus to find the hitherto little known
Silurian deposits of Scotland connecting its geology, by links
not elsewhere found in Britain with the geology of Bohemia
on the one hand, and with that of the New World on the other.
I need scarce add, that our Old Red Sandstone, in its Holopty-
chii and Asterolepi, furnishes similar links that connect it with
the Old Red Sandstones of Russia and the American colonies.
Both systems, — though deemed, at a comparatively recent
time, so poor in the organic, that in the one, according to Hutton, "geologists alleged there was not to be found any vestige
of organized body," and that in the other, according to Murchison, geologists contended there were no organisms, at least
peculiar to it as a deposit, — are now recognized as not only
important depositories of the geologic records of the country,
that fill up vast periods in its physical history which would
have otherwise remained unsatisfactory blanks, but as also
establishing, by their remains, the identity of its character, in

the remote ages of primæval life, with other and widely-distant regions of the globe. I have said, that the limestone cliffs of this deposit are singularly picturesque. At one point we find them traversed by a broad dyke of compact greenstone, which has been followed by the quarrier into the very bowels of the hill; and so, for several hundred feet together, we can see the yawning rent in the earth's surface which it had so lately filled, with its corresponding angles and its answering protuberances and inflections, existing as it must have existed when first torn asunder by the convulsion to which it owed its origin, and ere the molten matter had come boiling through it from the abyss. It is a wild recess, tapestried by mosses and overhung by brush-wood, and, from where it opens into the richly fossiliferous rock, in which lie entombed by millions the organisms of perhaps the earliest creation, the eye glances adown a noble val-ley, bosky with green woods, and checkered with smiling fields, and marks, where it opens to the broad Atlantic, a busy sea-port town, or rests far beyond on the dim cloud-like Arka When I last stood in its opening, at the close of a long sum-mer's day delightfully spent, the broad sun, then resting on the far horizon, was casting its last red gleam on bush, and crag, and brown hill-top, and the deep slant shadows of evening lay stretched along the bottom of the valley. And then, as the light declined, the moon, in her first quarter, began to show her slender form through the dappled cloudlets, like a silver scimitar, and I saw her brightening image as I passed, reflected on the stiller pools of the Girvan. How widely different must not the scene have been when those organisms of the rock lived at the bottom of their old Palæozoic ocean, and the light of that sun and moon, — mayhap the only unchanged objects on which the eye rested, — was caught by the many-sided eyes of the trilobite, or guided the carnivorous orthoceratite to its prey! Let me indulge for a brief space, ere I conclude, in an attempted restoration of the probable scenes and events of the period, in what is now Scotland.

For many ages, a wide ocean, from which the eye fails to see any shore, or the sounding-lead to find any bottom, rolls over what is now our country. Its profound depths, wrapped up in darkness, sink beneath the zero line of animal or vegetable life; and the fine gray mud, or light micaceous sand, that settles upon its unseen bottom, as the impalpable dust that mottles the sunbeam sinks on the floor of some deserted hall or old haunted chamber, scarce forms, after the lapse of years, a layer as thick as the roofing slate into which, in these latter times, we find it consolidated. Gradually, however, and persistently, the deposition goes on. Besides, under the deep-seated impulsions of the Plutonic forces, vigorous in their early youth, there is a general rising of the platform. At length the light of day reaches it through the lessening space, in a dim green twilight, and it becomes a scene of organic existence. Vast fields of nameless algæ, still represented amid the rocks by our anthracite bands, embrown for many leagues the ocean bottom; and millions of zoophytes, not higher in the scale than the modern pennatuladæ, which they not a little resemble, crowd every square rood of surface. And here, at wide intervals, some ancient terebratula fastens its fleshy cable to the rock, or there some lingula stands erect, flower-like, in its horny stem. There are changes taking place, now gradual, anon abrupt. At one time death itself serves but to furnish fresh platforms for new life; at another, through some subsidence in the general floor, the zero line of vitality is again reached, and over perished myriads, the dead, sluggish strata settle down. At length, when unreckoned centuries — mayhap hundreds of centuries — have passed, the middle ages of the Lower Silurian period are ushered in; and when the Llandeilo flags and Bala limestones are in the course of deposition in what is now the

principality of Wales, the transition limestones of Ayrshire
are also gradually forming, in no small part, — so abundant has
life now become in the waters, — of massive corals, and of the
stony exuviæ of encrinites and molluscs. But to the period
of this calcareous deposit, — so vastly prolonged, that the massive corals of its later ages grow upon rock formed of the remains of their early predecessors, — there comes a last day :
a sandy deposit begins to be cast down over it, and, in the
altered circumstances, many of the corals die, to re-appear no
more. But life in other forms is not less abundant than in the
previous time. The sedentary brachipods, — pentamerus, with
its strange internal partitions, — terebratula, with its perforated
umbone, — orthis, spirifer, and atrypa, with their long tendril-
shaped arms, — lie so thickly upon the arenaceous bottom, that
their remains, as they yield to the inexorable law of death, form
no inconsiderable proportion of the ever-rising platform on
which their successors spend also their determined day, and
yield, in turn, to the destroyer. And thus, during the earlier
and middle ages of the Caradoc Sandstones, stratum after stratum is laid down, each, in succession, a home for the living and
a burying-ground for the dead. And then yet another change
takes place. The arenaceous deposit is succeeded by a deposit
of gray argillaceous mud : the fauna, too, alters in at least its
aspect, in the proportions borne in it by families and genera.
Though in one certain bed, and for a comparatively short
period, a small species of terebratula abounds, the brachipods
generally greatly decrease, — a consequence, mayhap, of the
altered nature of the bottom, now considerably softer than before ; but, on the other hand, the cephalopoda, represented
chiefly by the orthoceratites, very much increase, and the trilobites attain to their numerical maximum. Scales of fishes,
somewhat resembling the bony plates on the sides of the sturgeon, have been found by Mr. M‘Coy in the Silurians of Ire-

land, in a deposit at least as old as these shales; whereas the system in Scotland has hitherto failed to yield any trace of the vertebrata. But though not yet prepared to demonstrate that fishes swam in this corner of the ancient Scoto-Silurian ocean over the argillaceous shales, these must have been traversed by many a restless mollusc and crustacean, — the one-chambered bellerophon, and the many-chambered orthoceratites, — by Calymene, Cheirurus, and Phacops, with their nicely-adjusted armor of many joints, and by the massive Illænus, with its double buckler. With this upper formation of the Lower Silurian division, deposition in the earlier Palæozoic period seems to have ceased in this district. Farther to the south, however, on the shores of the Solway, the shales, in a somewhat altered form, pass into the lower beds of the Upper Silurian, and exhibit some of its characteristic fossils. And with these the Old Grauwacke record, as a record of life and death, abruptly closes in Scotland, and a chapter of purely physical revolution begins, — a chapter perplexed by passages of doubtful meaning, and by many different readings, but which tells, in every page, of widely-extended convulsion and upheaval, and of the operations of deeply-seated forces of a power incalculably great.

During the ages of either the Upper Silurian or the inferior Old Red Sandstone, the deposits of the Lower Grauwacke division in Scotland seem to have been the subject of enormous lateral pressure, which raised their strata into many folds and ridges over wide districts, and, as there is reason to believe, elevated them above the sea level. Sir Roderick Murchison reckoned in the neighborhood of Girvan from five to six axial lines in a section of less than eight miles; and on the east coast, in the instances made so famous by Sir James Hall, axial lines are, as I have already had occasion to state, still more numerous. Nay, the great difficulty which lies in the way of determining the true place of the older rocks of our southern

Highlands arises from the inability geologists have hitherto
experienced of drawing, amid the perplexities of these convolutions, a base line for the whole, and from the further circumstance that, for great distances together, so completely vertical
are the strata, that the ascending cannot be distinguished from
the descending direction.   On visiting the Pentland range of
hills for the first time, many years ago, there was nothing which
so impressed me as that vertical position in which I invariably
found the Grauwacke slates of the district.   Forming the fundamental rock on which all the other rocks, sedimentary or
igneous, had been in succession cast down or erupted, I saw it
assuming the appearance of a foundation of piles, and presenting to even the very oldest of them, — the Old Red conglomerate, — its upturned edges.   This vertical Grauwacke, I said,
must have assumed its present character and position, — nay,
must have presented all its present marks of great antiquity, —
at a time when the materials of the conglomerate existed at
the bottom of an Old Red Sandstone ocean, as beds of un-
fixed water-rolled pebbles, mixed with loose sand.   Nor is it
easy, surely, to affix limits to the tremendous potency of the
earth-tempest that must have originally raised it, over so extensive an area. from the horizontal to the vertical position.
Unacquainted at the time with the experiments of Sir James
Hall, I was reminded, during my visit, of a phenomenon which
I had witnessed when a boy. many years before, but which now
came to assume in my memory a new character as an illustration   A severe long protracted frost had just broken up, and
the lower reaches of the Cromarty Firth were covered by immense floats of ice, which had formed in its upper flats and
shallows : when one of those dead calms which in our climate
in the winter season so frequently herald a storm was disturbed
by a smart breeze from the south-east. and the loose floats borne
oceanwards by the tide were drifted back, from between the

Sutors, into an inflection of the shore which intervenes between
the town and the hill of Cromarty. When the tide fell, and
the bottom of the bay was laid bare, we found it occupied for
many acres by the stranded ice, mass crowded upon mass, so
that scarce an interstice could be seen between them, and all
occupying the horizontal position of their original formation
As the tide rose, however, and the night fell, the gale freshened
into a hurricane; the ice, jambed against the steep shore on
the one hand, and exposed to the heavy roll of the waves on
the other, began to *pack*, not so much by rising, as in a choked
up river, mass over mass, as by rising on edge; and in the
morning, when the tide had again fallen, we found it occupying,
not the whole, as before, but only the inner portion of the bay,
and uptilted on edge, for roods together, like, in short, the uptilted Granwacke slates of the Pentlands. And may not, I
asked, as the scene rose fresh in memory amid the recesses of
the hills, — may not I be now witnessing the somewhat similar
results of some tremendous earth-storm, in which the molten
waves of the abyss first broke up the consolidated but still comparatively thin crust of our planet, as ice is broken up under
the joint operations of storm and thaw; and then packed into
this corner, as the ice-floats were packed into the little bay,
those ruins of the surface which, while yet unbroken, and in
the horizontal position, must have extended over a much greater
space? It does seem, from the appearance of many of our
more dislocated and older formations, that there came a time
in the history of the globe in which there was, if I may so
speak, no longer room to spread them out, and they had to be
compressed, in consequence, into many a fold and wrinkle.
Are we to infer that these ancient robings of the earth, with
their many convolutions, which, as it were, hang loose about it,
indicate a shrinking in its general bulk? or are they merely
but locally too large for the portions of surface which they oc-

cupy? We are, I suspect, not yet in circumstances to answer the question. But to conclude, — I have said it is probable that our convoluted Grauwackes were raised at a very early period over the level of the sea. At least, in the beds of Red Sandstone which rest unconformably over their lower slopes, and along their deeper valleys, we detect the first traces in the south of Scotland of a terrestrial flora. The fauna is decidedly that of the Upper Old Red Sandstone, and, mingled with scales of *Holoptychius Nobilissimus*, and plates of *Pterichthys major*, there occur what seem to be fragments of calamites, and what are unequivocally the fronds of a fern. And though shadow and darkness still envelop the land upon which they grew, we may be permitted to indulge at least in the provisional belief, that its framework was formed of our convoluted Lower Silurians, already existing as solid rock, and charged, as now, with the remains of a creation that had perished, that it was encircled by an Old Red Sandstone ocean, inhabited by fishes of uncouth form and gigantic size; and that it presented on its sloping hill-sides its primæval denizens of the vegetable kingdom, now to the dews of the night, and anon to the light of day. Who would not wish to know somewhat regarding the geography, and the organisms, vegetable and animal, of this ancient land of the Lammermoors, — this Scotland emphatically of the olden time? But, save in a few tattered fragments, its chronicles have perished, and we can but darkly surmise, from the existing evidence, that such a land there once was.

RED SANDSTONE, MARBLE, AND QUARTZ DEPOSITS OF ASSYNT;

WITH THEIR SUPPOSED ORGANISMS AND PROBABLE ANALOGUES.

In hurriedly journeying, two years ago, through the upper parts of Assynt, on my way to Loch Invei, I was so struck by the appearance of the stratified limestone deposit to which the marble beds of that locality belong. that I returned last season to examine it more at my leisure, and to trace, if possible, its relations to the other rocks of the country: I had been impressed, in the passing, both by its peculiar aspect, and its occurrence in the same wild tract with a remarkable system of sandstone mountains, unique in the British islands, which have been represented by M'Culloch as formed of the *Old Red* Sandstone, and which, from the nearly horizontal disposition of their strata, he regarded as hills of denudation It is impossible, he argued, carefully to examine these widely-separated mountains, formed of thin nearly horizontal beds of ripple-marked sandstone, that rest unconformably on the fundamental gneiss of the district, without coming to the conclusion that they are but the mere fragments of a once continuous sandstone bed, from one to three thousand feet in thickness, of which by much the greater part has been washed away by the waves and currents of unreckoned ages. But if this sandstone belong in reality to the Old Red system, what, I asked, are these apparrently associated beds of stratified limestone and shale? Are they not the representatives, though mayhap in an altered state, of those Old Red ichthyolitic beds which, overlying the great conglomerate, exist in Ross, Cromarty, and Moray, as alternating layers of lime, clay, and sandstone, and occur in Caithness as the extensively developed flagstones so well known in commerce as Caithness flag? And it was chiefly in the hope of finding some data on which to determine the true answer to the query that I last autumn visited Assynt.

I had examined, in the previous year, the Old Red Sandstone of Ru-Store and Durness, and satisfied myself that it is the same rock which is developed in these localities that forms the insulated hills of Sulven, Coul-beg, and Coul-more, and which occurs at Gairloch in Ross-shire, in the southern parts of Skye, and in the island of Rum; and further, that in Sutherland, as in Ross and Iverness-shires, it rests unconformably on a base of gneiss. I now fixed on Inch-na-damph, near the head of Loch Assynt, as the best possible centre for examining the *associated* deposits of the district. It lies within less than two hours' walk of both the upper and lower beds of the great system to which all the upper rocks of Assynt belong, and is in the immediate neighborhood of a range of noble precipices, — the crags of Stronchrubie, — which present a magnificent section of the stratified limestone. Beginning with these, I traced them upwards from near their base to the deposit which rests over them (an immense bed of quartz rock, that forms by much the greater part of one of the loftiest of the Sutherlandshire hills, — Benmore); and then, reversing my course, traced them downwards, with the deposits which lie under them, until I reached the fundamental gneiss of the country. Without, however, detailing the results of single excursions, let me attempt briefly describing the entire system in the ascending order, from the base upwards.

The gneiss upon which the system rests is exactly the same fundamental deposit here that we find it to be in the Highlands of Scotland generally. It is of the ordinary mineralogical composition, too, and mixed up, as elsewhere, with the usually associated rocks and minerals, existing in the character of veins, beds, and included masses. It presents, however, a peculiarity in the cast of its scenery, — shared also by the gneiss districts of Wester Ross, — which renders what I may term its pictorial aspect widely different from that of the gneiss of the central and eastern Highlands. Our gneiss hills generally are squat, truncated, confluent, massive prominences, traversed by wide straths, and open glens, and, though imposing often from their vast proportions, they are somewhat monotonous when spread over a wide tract, from their obtuse and rounded outlines, and and from their lack of height in proportion to their great breadth of base. Ben Weavis in Ross-shire, that rises to an altitude of little more than three thousand feet from a base some five or six miles either way, and on whose flat summit another hill as tall as itself might be set down, may be regarded as a some-what extreme but characteristic specimen of the class. And such, over an area of some seven or eight thousand square miles, is the ordinary scenic character of our gneiss hills. The gneiss hills of Assynt, with those of the adjoining districts, — Eddrachilles on the one hand, and Wester Ross on the other, —are, on the contrary, not massive, and rarely confluent: they never rise more than a few hundred feet in height; they are seldom traversed by continuous valleys; and they are extremely abrupt and rugged in their outline. Seen from one of their summits, the appearance presented is that of a rough cockling sea; while in travelling among them, so thickly do they stand together, and so perplexing is the intricacy, that I felt as if I had got into a *forest* of hills, and was in danger of losing my way. From the imperfect drainage occasioned by the want of continuous valleys, the district abounds in mossy swamps and little shallow lakes, or rather lochans, remarkable for the vast number of water-lilies that, in the flowering season, mottle their surface, and relieve, by their quiet beauty, the general ruggedness of the scenes in which they occur. A brown and scanty vegetation, much interrupted by gray precipices, partially clothes the hill-sides; and, among the groups of turf cottages which the traveller occasionally sees embosomed in solitary recesses beside their scanty patches of corn, he may find the last lingering remains of rude and primitive contrivances that have become obsolete in every other part of the British islands. Those small cottage-mills, — the immediate successors of the hand-mill, — in which the water-wheel moves horizontally, and which, when laid open by the antiquary in some encroaching moss or drifted sand-hill, he regards as the relics of a remote time, — are still extant and in use in this rugged gneiss region.

The Red Sandstone of the district rests immediately over the gneiss, but belongs to a widely different epoch. The gneiss we find uptilted in every direction, as if it had been operated upon by the disturbing forces from many centres, and for many ages; whereas the sandsone which rests unconformably over it presents a series of unbroken strata, reclining usually at low angles, and which had no share in the deep-seated convulsions which uptilted and broke up the rocks below. Along the coast, — as in Durness in the Cape Wrath district, at Ru-Store, and on towards Loch Broom, Gairloch, and Applecross, it presents very much the scenic character of the Old Red Sandstone on the east coast; and nothing can be more striking than the change which takes place in the landscape, in passing from the wild ruggedness of a gneiss region, to the level fields, swelling moors, and long undulating ridges of a sandstone one. But in the interior of the country, where the sandstone occurs chiefly in detached hills, it lends to the prospect features of surpassing boldness and grandeur. Rising over a basement of rugged gneiss hills, that present the appearance of a dark tumbling sea, we descry a line of stupendous pyramids from two to three thousand feet in height, which, though several miles distant in the background, dwarf, by their great size, the nearer eminences into the mere protuberances of an uneven plain. Their mural character has the effect of adding to their apparent magnitude. Almost devoid of vegetation, we see them barred by the lines of the nearly horizontal strata, as edifices of man's erection are barred by their courses of dressed stone; and, while some of their number, such as the peaked hill of Suilvein, rise at an angle at least as steep and nearly as regular as that of an Egyptian pyramid, in height and bulk they surpass the highest Egyptian pyramid many times. Their color, too, lends to the illusion. Of a deep red hue, which in the light of the setting sun brightens into a glowing purple, they contrast as strongly with the cold gray tone of the gneiss tract beneath as a warm-colored building contrasts with the earth-tinted street or roadway over which it rises. The stone of which they are composed is a hard, compact, arenaceous rock, usually of a chocolate tint, and varying in grain from an ordinary sandstone to a conglomerate. But the pebbles which it encloses, and which usually occur in thin beds, are greatly smaller than those of the Great Old Red conglomerate on the east coast, — ranging in bulk from the size of a pea to that of an egg. They are almost all water-rolled, — usually quartzose or feldspathic in their composition, though in considerable pro-portion jasperous; and, as I have often remarked of the peb-bles of the Great Conglomerate, the prevailing color among

them is red, in a proportion which no longer obtains among
the primary rocks of the country. I detected in this sandstone, in the island of Rum, thin beds of a gray stratified clay,
resembling the clay of the ichthyolite beds of Ross and Cromarty; but, though they inclose occasional nodules, I failed to
discover in them aught organic. The Old Red Sandstone of
the west coast, like its probable analogue the Great Conglomerate of the east, is, so far as we yet know, an unfossiliferous
deposit. I may here mention, that I found at Gairloch in
Ross-shire, nearly thirty years ago, a variety of this sandstone
of a finer and closer grain than ordinary, which yielded freely
to the chisel, and made, — what is by no means common in the
formation, — an excellent hewing stone. M'Culloch had not
yet published his geological map of Scotland; and the limits
of the various rock-systems in the more inaccessible parts of
the country were scarce at all known, when I was despatched,
in advance of a party of workmen engaged to erect a dwelling-
house on the shores of Gairloch, to find some suitable quarry
for the rubble-work, — a sort of commission which it was
thought, though I was but a mere lad at the time, my habit at
looking at rocks might qualify me to execute. I was struck,
on my arrival, by the flatness of the promontory which forms
the northern barrier of the loch, and the general softness of its
outline, compared with that of the rugged gneiss region around,
and, immediately setting out to ascertain what sort of a rock
entered into its composition, I found, somewhat to my surprise,
that it consisted entirely of red sandstone. But, though I procured in abundance ashlar and corner-stones for our purposed
building, my discovery did not stand my master, the contractor,
so much in stead as it might; as, in despair of finding sandstone in Gairloch, he had previously freighted a vessel with
stones for the hewn work from the quarries of Burghead in
the Moray Frith. As I have already incidentally remarked,

M'Culloch estimates the thickness of the Old Red of the west coast, in his description of the hills scooped out of it by the denuding agencies, at from one to three thousand feet.

Above the Red Sandstone there occurs a bed of quartz rock, several hundred feet in thickness, which bears in some of its layers a pure white, in others a flesh-colored tint. It is a stratified rock, but less regularly so than the sandstone which it overlies, and, though hard, splinty, and indestructible in all its strata, it is decidedly mechanical in its composition. This indurated deposit must have at one time existed as a quartzose sand, — at another as an ordinary sandstone. Its upper strata are of a red color, mottled with white; and in one of these the white portions take the form of minute cylinders, vertically arranged across the stratum, like jars in a case. Where exposed to the weather, the red parts of the stone waste from around these, leaving them standing up over the surface, as the little pipes in the cistern of a shower-bath stand up over the plane of the bottom; and these curiously relieved cylinders M'Culloch regarded as probably organic. I could, however, find no grounds whatever for the conclusion, as in their mechanical structure they differ in no respect from the red matrix which incloses them. They serve, however, to remind one of similar appearances in the Old Red Sandstone of the east coast. This bed of quartz rock forms some of the more picturesque mountains of Assynt. Seen from the inn at Inch-na-damph, the tall hill of Spike-an-Quenaig, which is entirely composed of it, is one of the most remarkable in a landscape which, for the bold grace of its features, is scarcely surpassed in Scotland An outline of flowing curvature divests it of the stiffness necessarily associated with the perfectly conical form. It swells slightly outwards where the architect would place his cornice, and then terminates in a horizontal table of small extent, resembling the plane of a pedestal. The entire hill is in truth a

noble pedestal, on which some colossal statue, vastly greater
than that of Rhodes, might be advantageously placed, to form,
like the memory of some great man in the history of a people,
the central object of the landscape, and when I first looked
upon its fine proportions, relieved against the bright amber-
tinted clouds of a gorgeous sunset, and marked how its summit
seemed, according to the poet, "to kiss the sky,' I felt I could
have understood, had it been told that some hoary seer had, in
ancient times, ascended from its top into the heavens, how the
legend had originated.

On this quartz bed the stratified limestone rests, with its
associated marbles. Less bold in its features than the other
rocks of the district, apparently because of a texture less suited
to resist the denuding and weathering influences, we find its
place marked, amid the brown heaths which lie over the Red
Sandstones, or amid the stony nakedness of the quartz-rock
regions, by the rich green of the verdure which covers it. All
the more valuable farms of Assynt lie on the limestone. At
one point, however, on the farm of Stronchrubie, in the immediate neighborhood of Inch-na-damph, it presents a magnificent
range of precipices, a full mile in length by about three hundred feet in height, which rises immediately above the road,
and forms at this point the most striking feature in the prospect. The steep face of the range is barred horizontally by
the strata, black, red, and gray, and relieved and softened
by the bright green verdure that waves over its shelves and
ledges, and bristles from every recess and crany. As we pass
on to the west, the precipitous range flattens into a gentle slope,
still, however, lined longitudinally by the projecting strata,
which, easier of access than in the precipices, can here be
examined in detail. Though chiefly calcareous, the rock presents, from its decidedly flaggy structure, so much the appearance of Caithness flagstone (which, however, in some of its

beds is also calcareous), that, on laying open some of the
masses with the hammer, my first impulse was to examine
them for the characteristic ichthyolites.   In brief, the stone of
not a few of the subordinate beds of this deposit cannot be distinguished from Caithness flagstones of the more rubbly kind,
and are totally unlike any primary rock with which I am acquainted.   We find them associated, however, with other rocks
of a widely different character, such as traps of the porphyri-
tic and green-stone series ; but though these assume, in conformity with the general arrangement of the deposit, the form
of strata, they are in all probability mere plutonic injections
into the body of the deposit, and newer, not only than the
strata over which they rest, but also than the strata by which
they are overlaid.   In some instances, these trap beds cross
the line of stratification.   There occur, however, in the lower
parts of the limestone division, intercalated strata of quartz
rock, mechanical in its structure, which must be regarded as of
the same age as the calcareous beds with which it alternates.
The limestone is of various colors and qualities , and we find
each stratum retaining its peculiar character and tint for great
distances together.   Some of the strata are earthy, and of a
chocolate brown approaching to red ; some minutely crystalline, and of various tints of gray ; some nearly white, on at
least their weathered surfaces ; and some, as on the farm of
Auchmore, about a mile from the parish church, well nigh
black, and, like the limestones of the ichthyolite beds of the
east coast, strongly bituminous.   Like the limestone of most
other localities, and of almost all ages, this calcareous deposit
is a cavernous rock.   There occur in it in this neighborhood
several picturesque caves by the side of a tumbling stream,
within less than half an hour's walk of Inch-na-damph ; and
the famous cave of Smoo, at Durness, so graphically described
by Sir Walter Scott, is hollowed in what appears to be the

same deposit. It is remarkable, too, for the singular copious-
ness and number of its springs,—equally, I may mention, a
peculiarity of the ichthyolite beds of Cromarty and Ross.
Where the highway runs along the base of the tall limestone
escarpment of Stronchrubie, we see that every hollow has its
little stream of sparkling crystalline water, that comes leaping
to the light from amid the lower strata of the precipices; and
on the farm of Auchmore we find a spring — perhaps the largest in Scotland — which constantly discharges a current of
four cubic feet of pure water, and goes roaring down the hill
in its rocky channel, rapid and copious as the water of a mill-
lade just as the miller has raised the sluice. It is really a fine
object,— finer and more imposing than I had previously supposed a mere *spring* could be. It comes bursting up out of
the earth, a little river, very clear, and in summer very cool,
though in winter it feels warm to the hand, and during hard
frosts smokes, as if heated over a fire; and rank aquatic plants
of richest green, never scathed by the frosts of winter, spring
up in a broad fringe along its edges.

It is with this great limestone deposit that, as I have
already intimated, the marbles of Assynt are associated.
Though unstratified themselves, they usually occur in the
deposit as detached strata, or beds rather. more or less continuous for considerable distances. They are of various colors, each bed bearing its own, such as, of a pure white, or a
white mottled with a delicate greenish yellow, or white clouded
with gray, or altogether of a diffused light gray tint, or of a
deep gray streaked with red; and they were wrought for orna-
mental purposes in two several places about thirty years ago,
by a Mr. Jopling from Newcastle. "But owing principally,"
say the Messrs. Anderson of Inverness, in their admirable
"Guide Book," "to the disadvantages arising from the want
of roads fit for the conveyance to the coast of the weighty

blocks, the speculation did not succeed; and although this chief obstacle has since been removed, no attempt has been made to renew the undertaking." One of the old workings occurs in the neighborhood of the parish church, where a large block, operated upon by the saw, may still be seen in the hollow whence it was excavated. The marble here is of the dark gray variety, streaked and veined with red; but, as shown by the dressed surfaces of the mass left behind by the workers, it seems but indifferently suited to resist the action of the weather, in at least a climate such as that of Assynt. In little more than a quarter of a century the marks of the tool have almost entirely disappeared from the stone; and the sparry substance which fills the red veins has sunk considerably beneath the level of the darker portions which it traverses. At the other old working, near Ledbeg, about six miles higher up the valley, the white and gray varieties of marble occur; and bare rounded masses may be seen from the road, rising over the brown heath or peaty soil, like those wasted and partially soiled wreaths of snow that mottle at midsummer the upper zones of our higher hills. It formed a subject of complaint to the workmen, that the rock in this locality is so traversed by cracks and flaws, that they failed to procure from it blocks at once solid throughout, and of a size sufficient for such purposes as the manufacture of table-slabs or large chimney-lintels, and I have been informed that the noble proprietrix of the county at the time,— the late Countess Duchess of Sutherland,— desirous to procure for the ancient family seat of Dunrobin a fine specimen of the native marble of the district, in the form of a chimney-piece for one of the public rooms, had to content herself, instead, from this cause, with simply a chimney-piece for one of the smaller bed-rooms. As the workings, however,— prosecuted for but a short time,— were but mere scratchings of the surface, it is probable that

30*

the masses at a greater depth are greatly more sound, and that — as is common in marbles — what occurs as a flaw within the influence of the percolating rains and penetrating frosts, may exist, removed beyond their reach, as merely a streak or vein. I find it stated by Mr. Carmichael, in an elaborate essay on the Limestone Quarries of Scotland, which received the prize of the Highland Society, that no real marble has ever been found in this country,— no stone, at least, fitted to stand what he terms the three criteria of a true marble, viz., susceptibility of a high polish, chemical composition, and compact homogeneous structure. He states that Sutherland marble leaves three per cent. of residuum when subjected to the testing muriatic acid, whereas Carrara marble leaves none; and that every attempt to polish Scotch marbles has shown them to be " coarse, dissimilar in their texture, full of flaws, and of a dull lustre, even when smoothed to the best advantage." To the flaws of the Assynt marble I have already referred as probably of a surface character; with regard to its chemical composition, I may venture to remark, that a marble may surely be less pure by three per cent. than that of Carrara, and yet be a real marble notwithstanding, and with respect to the polish of which the Sutherland marble is susceptible, it may be enough to state, that though pieces which I attempted polishing for myself are, as may be seen from specimens on the Society's table, dull in their lustre, those beside them, which I submitted to a marble cutter, bear quite as high a gloss as most of the finely variegated marbles of the Continent.

Above this great limestone bed there occurs a second more than equally great deposit of quartz rock, generally of a white color, but in some of its strata tinged with red. It is truly a vast formation; forming, though laid along the surface at a low angle, by much the greater part of some of the loftiest

hills of the country,— such as Glasveen, Ben-Uic, and Benmore.   Even where most indurated, it is everywhere, like the
resembling bed which underlies the limestone, purely mechanical in its structure,— an indurated, indestructible sandstone,
in short ; and how very indurated and indestructible it is, the
gray and hoary nakedness of the massive eminences composed
of it serves very conclusively to show.   It never resolves into
soil . the only tracts of soil which occur over it are of a peaty
character, formed simply through the agency of water, and of
that low vegetation which, in a weeping climate, water can of
itself sustain.   Where the hill-sides, formed of this deposit,
rise steeply, they admit of no covering at all,— not even of a
crust of moss or of lichen ; and their summits gleam white and
bright to the summer sun, as if overlaid by a continuous layer
of snow.   I may add that, from its great durability, it bears
with singular distinctness, in this region, marks of the old glacial action.   High above the sorely weathered limestones, that
retain not a trace on their surface save of the recent storms
that last washed them, we find the white quartz rock still as
smoothly polished, as distinctly grooved, as sharply lined and
furrowed, as if the great ice-river which produced the phenomena had grated over them but yesterday.   This upper deposit
of quartz enters largely into the composition of some of the
wildest and most desolate scenery of Assynt   In looking up
the dark narrow lake which takes its name from the district,
we see the broad bases and naked storm-riven summits of
Benmore and the neighboring mountain Glasveen, forming the
back-ground of the landscape.   The ancient castle of Ardvo-
rack, and the old mansion-house of Eddrachalda,— both broken
and roofless ruins, situated within a few hundred yards of
each other,— the one shattered by lightning, the other scathed
by fire,— comprise, from one interesting point of view, the
only human dwellings visible in the prospect : solitude broods

around; the distant hills, bald, verdureless, and hoary, seem
the hills of a worn-out and desolate planet, and harmonize
well with the deserted ruins and the dark, lonely lake beneath;
and altogether so impressive and unique is the scene, that,
when I first looked upon it through the lurid haze of a stormy
evening, it seemed suggestive of universal death and extinction, and the lifeless old age of creation.   According to the
poet,—

> "The sun's eye had a lightless glare,
> The earth with age was wan."

I have already referred to M'Culloch's supposed organisms
of the bed of quartz rock which underlies the Limestone.
Other supposed organisms of, as has been thought, a less
equivocal character, also occur in the deposit, though I failed
to detect them in this neighborhood, where, however, they are
said to be found, though more rarely than on the northern
coast of Sutherland, on the shores of Loch Eriboll.   I visited
that locality in the previous year, mainly that I might acquaint
myself with what at the time were deemed the most ancient of
Scottish fossils,—these supposed organisms, but though, under the intelligent guidance of Mr. Clark, of Eriboll, I succeeded in finding them, I found the evidence regarding both
their place and character of a very unsatisfactory kind.   They
occur not *in situ*, but in detached boulders spread over a limestone district, though derived apparently from the neighboring
quartz rock.   Unlike, however, the quartz rock of Assynt, the
stone yields to the weather, in consequence, it would seem, of
a considerable admixture of iron in its composition.   In breaking open a boulder, we see an oxydized, discolored ring running parallel to its outer surface; and it is almost always in
the discolored ring that the supposed fossils occur.   They are
small tubular bodies, from one to three lines in length, by
about half a line in breadth, of a grayish or brownish-white

color, non-calcareous,— for they do not effervesce on the application of the most powerful acids,— and containing usually a
brown oxydized substance in their interior. In the better, at
least more distinct, specimens, they somewhat resemble fragments of serpula, or those segments of dentalia which one occasionally finds in the boulder-clay of Caithness, but they are
in all probability not the remains of either annelid or mollusc,
but mere effects of the oxydization, under peculiar circumstances, that has discolored the matrix in which they lie. Iron
pins or nails we find not unfrequently represented on sea-
beaches where wrecks have taken place, or near some dock-
yard or harbor, by mere oxydized tubes, hollow within; and it
is not improbable that to minute, pin-like crystals of some mineral or metal now represented by only the oxydized substance
enclosed within the hollow, do these little tubes owe their origin. I at least wholly failed to satisfy myself that they are
organic in their character, nor do I suppose that they would
be by any means the oldest of Scottish fossils, even if they
were.

This upper quartz rock forms the highest and most modern
deposit of the marble districts. Taking the summit of Benmore as its apex, a shaft sunk on the top of that noble hill, to
the depth of perhaps eight or ten thousand feet, would pass in
succession through the first or upper quartz, through the limestone with its associated marbles and flagstones, through the
second or lower quartz, through the red sandstone, with its
conglomerate beds; and finally, it would reach the unconformable gneiss, on which the whole system rests; for as one
system must these four great deposits be regarded. Where,
among the other systems of Scotland, I ask, are we to seek for
its analogue and representative?

Let me first remark, that the Lower Old Red Sandstone of
the east coast of Scotland, as developed in Inverness, Ross,

Cromarty, Sutherland, Caithness, and the Orkney Islands, consists of exactly the same number of great divisions as this system of the western coast. That subordinate Red Sandstone of the western system which has been colored as *Old Red* in every geological map of Scotland ever published, and which extends, in an interrupted belt, from Eilan Garbh, beyond Cape Wrath, to the Island of Rum, a distance of more than a hundred and twenty miles, corresponds in place to the Great Conglomerate of the east coast,— a deposit equally continuous. The lower quartz bed which overlies the red sandstone we find occupying exactly the place of a thick arenaceous bed, by which, on the east coast, the Great Conglomerate is overlaid. The stratified limestones, with their associated flagstones and marbles, occupy exactly the place of the flagstones and associated limestones of Caithness, and the stratified, semicalcareous, nodule-bearing clays of Cromarty and Ross. And, finally, we see the vast upper quartz deposit of the west occupying exactly the place of that thick deposit of sandstone, red, white, and yellow, which overlies the ichthyolitic flagstones and stratified clays of the east, and which may be found immensely developed in the Ward-hill of Hoy, and in the promontories of Dunnet-head, Cannisbay, and Tarbet-ness. Bed for bed, the two systems correspond not only in number, but in character and place, for even the quartz-rock beds that are altered most cannot be regarded as other than indurated beds of quartzose sandstone. Let me further remark, that both systems rest unconformably on the same ancient rock,— the fundamental gneiss of the country. Were the systems not identical, we would have to account for the curious fact, that, resting on apparently the same rock, the number, character, and relative position of their beds should also be the same,— a contingency, regarded simply as such, that would exhaust many chances. Why, for instance, should the stratified limestone and flagstone bed, which occupies, in Caithness and elsewhere on the east coast, the second place in the system reckoned from the top downwards, and the third from the bottom upwards, occupy exactly the same place in Assynt, and not the place of any of the other beds? Or why should the red, rough-grained sandstone, with its included pebbles, which occupies the first place in the system of the east coast reckoning upwards, occupy also the first place, reckoning upwards, in that of the west coast, and not the place of any of the three beds which overlie it? Or, further, why should the place of the two great sandstone beds of the east-coast system, in their position as second and fourth, be occupied in the west-coast system by arenaceous beds also second and fourth in the series, instead of being occupied by beds not arenaceous? The number of the chances against such thorough coincidences as that exemplified here, regarded simply as chances, are so great, that they will be found to occur in no two British systems not identical. The probability, so to speak, that an unaltered system which in one locality is fossiliferous in one of its beds and non-fossiliferous in any of the others, should in another locality be slightly altered in all its beds, and, in consequence, non-fossiliferous in them all, is a probability which must be regarded as having many more chances in its favor.

Let me also remark, that the Old Red system of the east coast, which rests, as I have said, on the unconformable gneiss, is overlaid in several localities, as at Eathie and Shandwick, by beds of the Liassic formation. A wide gap occurs in the geologic scale in these northern districts: the Carboniferous, Permian, and Triassic systems, are wanting, and along the northern side of the Moray Frith generally the Old Red Sandstone forms the immediate base of the Lias,—a formation which, though it barely appears on the edge of the land there, is apparently largely developed under the bed of the German

Ocean. And it is worthy of being noted, as bearing on our
question, that the Scottish Lias of the Atlantic holds — as at
Broadford and Applecross — exactly the same relation to the
Red Sandstone of the west coast that the Scottish Lias of the
German Ocean does to the *Old* Red Sandstone of the east.
Both Red Sandstone deposits may be equally described as
resting on the gneiss and overlaid by the Lias. Further, I
may be permitted to ask, to what system known to the geologist does the Red Sandstone of our north-western coasts
belong, if not to the Old Red System? Quartz rock, in all its
various modifications, from a purely mechanical to a purely
crystalline stone, is of common occurrence in what are known
as the primary districts, a bed of mica-schist is not unfrequently found to pass almost imperceptibly, by gradually
dropping its mica, into a true quartz rock; nor are such tran-
sitions unfrequent in gneiss deposits; but the only true Red
Sandstone I ever yet met in a so-called primary district is the
Red Sandstone of the north-western coast of Scotland. It
must represent, with the overlying quartzose and calcareous
beds, an enormously extended period. Where, among the primary rocks of the southern Highlands, for instance, or of any
other region, shall we look for the deposits representative of
the same age? Regarded as primary, it forms an intercalated
period in the geologic history of this north-western tract of
country, which we find unrepresented in every other district.
I may add, that the quartz-rock formation, which runs diagonally athwart the kingdom in detached patches, from Islay on
the west to Banff and Aberdeen shires on the east, and which
holds geologically a middle position between the gneiss and the
mica-schist, is an altogether different deposit from the quartz-
rock of Assynt.

Both Dr. M'Culloch and the late Mr. Cunningham of Edinburgh have stated, that a great formation of gneiss in the

northern parts of Sutherland is found overlaying its quartz rock; and "this relation of quartz rock of undoubted mechanical origin to highly crystalline gneiss is a fact," remarks Professor James Nicol, in his " Guide to the Geology of Scotland," "of considerable importance, though merely what might have been anticipated on the metamorphic theory." I visited, two years ago, the district near Whiton Head, in which the sections occur that are said most thoroughly to demonstrate this superiority of the gneiss to the quartz rock, but was prevented from examining them by a tract of wet and very boisterous weather. There seems, however, to be a link wanting in the evidence, in its bearing on the matter specially in hand,—the position of the Assynt deposits. The gneiss of the Moin,—a dreary waste, that stretches between Loch Eriboll and the Kyle of Tongue,—*does* seem to overlie the quartz rock of Whiton Head, just as in many other localities genuine gneiss holds, on the small scale, a superior position to genuine quartz rock; but it has, perhaps, still to be shown that the quartz rock here is at all of the same age, or occupies relatively the same place, as that which in Assynt overlies the calcareous flagstones, and forms the summit of Ben More. The nearest Red Sandstone to the gneiss and underlying quartz rock of Whiton Head is that of Craig na Vrechan, at Tongue, and *it* very decidedly *overlies* the gneiss. But this special point I do not profess to have examined.

In conclusion let me remark, that while, from the reasons adduced, I have been led to conclude that the sandstone deposit of the west of Sutherland, with its associated quartz rock and limestone beds, represents the Lower Old Red Sandstone of the eastern coast, I do not regard the conclusion as founded on other than merely a strong probability. In speculating on the true place of a deposit in which fossils do not occur, and whose stratigraphical relations to the well-known

31

fossiliferous rocks cannot be traced, we must, I suspect, be content with simply the probable. For my own part, the occurrence in one of the flagstones of Strongchrubie, of the spine of a Cheiracanthus, or of a few scales of Dipterus, or of the plates of a Coccosteus, would satisfy me more thoroughly than all the arguments ever derived from mineralogical character, or from the occurrence, in a certain order, of certain peculiarly marked beds. But while I must regard the identity of the Red Sandstone of the north-eastern and north-western coasts of Scotland as by no means fully established, I am at least strongly of opinion that, as they are essentially the same in their aspect, order, and components, they represent also the same period in the history of the globe. From finding the strata of the Old Red Sandstone upturned against our primary mountains, and truncated atop, and from those detached fragments of the system which occur as insulated hills far in the Highland interior, I was led to conclude, many years ago, that this deposit had at one time overlaid all the primary rocks of Scotland, from the southern flanks of the Grampians to the northern boundary of Sutherland,— a conclusion to which Sir Charles Lyell, in the later editions of his "Elements," has approvingly referred, as coincident with views on the subject entertained by himself. And these arenaceous rocks of Assynt, with their associated limestones and marbles, I must regard as in all probability a portion of this once continuous system, hardened by metamorphic action, and which having, in consequence, resisted the denuding agencies that swept away the contemporary beds, still continue to wrap over the contorted and broken gneisses and granites of the district, and to form its most elevated mountains. It is the surviving fragment of a covering of which almost all the other portions have crumbled away piecemeal and disappeared.

CORALS OF THE OOLITIC SYSTEM OF SCOTLAND.

CORALS are extremely rare in the Lias. Messrs. Milne-Edwards and Haime figure, in their elaborate "Monograph of the British Fossil Corals," only three Liassic species, two of them exceedingly minute *Turbinolidæ*, and the third apparently a *Cyathophyllum*, of doubtful lineage, and very probably, it is stated, a misplaced palæozoic specimen. In the Lias of the eastern coast of Scotland, at Eathie, Nigg, and Shandwick, I have not succeeded, after the search of years. in finding a single coral, in that of Skye, however. I have been more fortunate. When examining, nearly eight years ago, the Liasic deposit at Broadford, — by far the most extensive development of this formation in Scotland, for it runs across the island from sea to sea, in a belt from two to four miles in breadth, — I came, near the base of the formation, and at a little distance from where it leans against the so-called Old Red Sandstone of Slate, on what seemed to be a dark-colored bed of concretionary limestone, of very irregular surface, and varying from three to four feet in thickness. The seeming concretionary masses were separated by what appeared to be a gray, indurated mud, which wrapped them round, concealing their true character; but where the edge of the bed was exposed to the lashings of the surf, the hardened mud had been washed away from the calcareous nuclei, and I was not a little surprised to find, that the seeming concretions were massive corals, apparently all of one species, and evidently of the family Astreidæ. The masses in this unique bed, each a corallum, are of irregular form, but usually flat and oblong, and vary in size, from nine or ten inches in length by six or eight in breadth, to from three to four inches in length by from two or three in breadth; while in thickness they vary from about two-and-a-half inches to less than an inch. They are thickly covered on all sides by shallow polygonal calices, irregular both in size and form, for they vary from nearly half an inch to little more than a line and a-half in breadth, and present from four to six sides. The dividing walls are thin, and not prominent, and each calice is traversed by from thirty to sixty septa of unequal size. A coral of the Inferior Oolite, *Isastrea tenuistriata*, resembles this Isastrea of the Lias more closely than any other fossil species yet figured; but in the Oolitic Isastrea the calices seem to be more equal in size, and more regular in form, and, from the smallness and fragmentary character of the specimen given in the monograph, I was unable to determine whether it possessed what seemed to be the most marked characteristic of the Skye coral In all the other species of Isastrea I have yet seen, each corallum has a determinate base, from which the coralites radiate; whereas in the Liassic species they seem congregated together on all sides of the corallum (which appears to have had no base), like the cells in a honeycomb, and even cover wen-like protuberances on the general surface, in a way that precludes the possibility of their having radiated from any common axis or centre.

The history of this coral bed of Skye, so unique in the Lias, seems to be simply as follows: In what is now the Inner Hebrides, as in other parts of the British islands, the Liassic deposit appears to have been a muddy one, and unfavorable, in consequence, to the growth of corals. Comparatively early in the period, however, a pause took place in the process of deposition, massive corals began to form at the bottom of a clear sea; the term of rest was protracted for ages, as one corallum died, another formed over it, until at length the bed had become several feet thick, and then the deposit suddenly returned to its old conditions. An arenaceous mud began to be cast down, which insinuated itself into all the interstices of the bed, as the run lime of the mediæval builders insinuated itself among the loose stones with which they filled up the interior portions of their walls. In circumstances so ungenial the coralites died, stratum after stratum, — not a few of these richly charged with the peculiar shells of the Lias, — ammonites, belemnites, and the characteristic gryphæa incurva, — were heaped over them to the depth of several hundred feet. In a few of the overlying strata the same coral again appeared, but only in small and unfrequent specimens, and, so far as we yet know, not until the times of the Lower Oolite did corals in any considerable abundance again live in the seas of the Scottish Oolitic system

The Lower Oolite, as developed in the neighborhood of Helmsdale, on the north-eastern coast of the kingdom, is comparatively rich in corals; at least, if species be not numerous, individual specimens are far from rare. I stated to the Society on a previous occasion, that on examining, some years since, a heap of materials collected along the beach in that neighborhood for burning into lime, I found that about two-thirds of the whole consisted of fossil wood, and the remaining third of a massive fossil coral. This coral, also an Isastrea, is of great size: I have seen specimens which a strong man could scarce raise from the ground; and a specimen on the table of the Society, selected, however, rather for its fine form than for its bulk, measures full eighteen inches in length, by about a foot in height. Its coralites, unlike those of the Liassic species, are very tall, extending in some specimens from the base to the upper surface. Its calices, however, are considerably smaller, and of more equal size, averaging about two lines across. Their walls, which are thick and well-defined, stand up abruptly, with mural erectness, over the central depression, which varies from a line to a line and a-half in depth. They are divided by from twenty to twenty-four septa, of which, however, more than the one-half are rudimentary, leaving but from four to eight of their number to meet in the centre of the visceral cavity. In the thickness of its walls and the character of its septa, this Helmsdale Isastrea greatly resembles the *Isastrea oblonga* of the superior Oolite, — a species which has been found hitherto only at Tilsbury, Wiltshire. It also resembles, however, though in a less degree, *Isastrea Richardsoni*, — a coral of the Lower Oolite; but it is possibly a new species. I have found in the same beds, though much more rarely, what seemed to be a different species of Isastrea, though closely allied to the one described. The corallum, massive like that of the other, is always greatly smaller. The calices, however, are considerably larger, and rather thinner in the walls, which do not stand up so abruptly over the central hollows; the septa vary from about twenty to twenty-four in number; and, where they meet in the centre, they rise in many of the calices into a protuberant knob, like the termination of a true columella, which, however, like all the other species of the extinct genus Isastrea, it wants. A Thamnastrea is also found in the same beds, but always hitherto in a state of bad keeping. Unlike any of the Oolitic Thamnastrea figured by Messrs. Milne-Edwards and Haime, the corallum forms a mere incrustation on rocks and stones of older deposits than the Oolite, and is in some specimens less than half a line in thickness; the calices are small and shallow, and rather thickly set. The circular elevation, which corresponds in this genus to the inclosing wall of Isastrea, is very apparent in weathered specimens, but, as in *Thamnastrea Lyelli*, only faintly visible in those that are less worn; while, as in the species *Thamnastrea scita*, the columella, if it at all possessed one, was rudimentary. I have usually found this species encrusting masses of indurated Old Red Sandstone of the flagstone formation, which must have been as ancient a looking rock in the times of the Oolite as it is now, and, when laid open by the waves along the beach, must have exhibited its ichthyolitic remains in their present state of keeping. In fine, in its rocks and stones this beach of the Oolite on what is now the eastern coast of Sutherland must have resembled that of the neighboring county of Caithness in the present day. And, as on the latter shore, as we approach the line of extreme ebb, we find rolled masses of dark gray flagstone, partially covered with pale-colored nulliporite encrustations, there would have been found, had there been an inquiring eye to prosecute the search, similar dark gray masses, bearing their encrustations of Thamnastrea, along the old shores of the Oolite.

But while the framework of the scenery must have been thus the same in both eras, and the same incalculably ancient sea must have broken in both against the same old fossil-bearing rocks, how entirely different must not the vital scenery of the two periods have been! Where we now see microscopic Lepralia and dwarfish Sertularia, huge Isastrea, embroidered by their flower-like polypes, and wide-spreading sheets of Thamnastrea, similarly mottled, must have gleamed white through the green depths of the water, as their existing representatives may be seen gleaming from the quiet recesses of tropical lagoons in the present day; the ammonite and belemnite must have careered over and around them amid the sheen of ganoidal scales; and, where the seal now disports, the plesiosaurus must have gambolled, and the goggle-eyed ichthyosaurus have darted along the tracts now traversed by the porpoise and the whale.

The Oolitic deposits in the neighborhood of Helmsdale consist mainly of beds of a laminated, dark-colored, arenaceous shale (charged with ammonites and belemnites, serpula and terebratula), which alternate with beds of a rough conglomerate, formed chiefly, as has been already intimated, of Old Red Sandstone materials. The corals, especially those of the genus Isastrea, occur both in the shales and the conglomerates, but it is amid the rocky masses of which the latter are composed that they seem to have grown; and in the shale we not unfrequently find them overturned, as if they had been torn with violence from their proper habitats on some stony ridge or hard bottom, and buried head-downwards in the mud. Corals, apparently of two different species, occur at Broia, but in so defective a state of keeping, that little else can be said regarding them than that they are said to belong to the genus Thecosmilia. In both, the corallum is composite and dendroid; but in the one the branches strike off at more acute angles than in the other. Its calices, too, are more rounded at their edges, and its septa less simple, more flexuous, and more prominently denticulated. So imperfect is their state of preservation, that neither species exhibits the exterior coating or epitheca characteristic of the genus. The place in the system in which they occur is higher than that of the beds at Helmsdale, but not higher than the base of the Great Oolite. And such are all the corals of the Oolitic system in Scotland with which the explorations of years have brought me acquainted.

The other subject to which I purpose directing for a brief space the attention of the Society has a connection, rather incidental than direct, with the fossil corals of our country. On first acquainting myself, about ten years ago, with the massive

Isastrea of Helmsdale, whose resemblance to *Isastrea oblonga*
I have pointed out, I remarked that not a few of the larger
specimens had been perforated, apparently in the recent state,
by circular openings, resembling those made by our recent pho-
ladæ, and which were usually filled up by a grayish-colored
grit, identical with that which formed the uniting cement of the
conglomerate in which the corals occurred. I at once attributed their formation to lithodomous shells of the Oolite, and
ventured to describe, in the *Witness* for 1843, one of my first-
found specimens as "a curious fragment of coral perforated by an
ancient pholas." "The cavtiy," I continued in my description,
"exactly resembles those cavities of the existing lithodomous
shells which fretted so many of the calcareous masses that lay
scattered on the beach on every side of the specimen, but it is
shut firmly up by the coarse gritty sandstone in which the coral
itself had lain buried; and a fragment of carbonized wood lies
embedded in the entrance. The cave is curtained across by a
wall of masonry immensely more ancient than that which converted into a prison the cave of the Seven Sleepers." Several
years, however, elapsed from this time ere I succeeded in detecting the shells by which the cavities had been formed; and
not until two years ago did I find specimens sufficiently entire
to admit, and that still but imperfectly, of description. They
seem to have been slim wedge-shaped bivalves, greatly resembling modiola, but belonging evidently to the genus Lithodomus.
Sir Roderick Murchison, in his great work on the Geology of
Russia, figures a Lithodomus of the Oolite of that country under the specific name *Lithodomus Eramanus;* but it is a greatly
smaller shell than the Scotch one, measuring little more than
a quarter of an inch in length, whereas the Helmsdale species measures, in my larger specimens, two inches and a line in
length. The Russian species, however, in proportion to its
general size, seems to have been a massier and broader shell.

An Oolitic bivalve figured in the same work as *Mytilus vicin-alis*, very much resembles, both in size and form, save that it also is proportionally a massier shell, one of my smaller specimens. Some of the larger masses of the Helmsdale Isastrea are much fretted by this busy excavator. In one of the smaller fragments of coral on the table we find the fossil remains of three individual shells that had burrowed in it, and the cell of a fourth; and in the massive corallum beside it there are no fewer than four-and-twenty of these excavations now filled with grit, but doubtless once tenanted by a borer a-piece. If, as is probable, it was living at the time when the excavators were at work within it, and possessed, what is more questionable, the sense of feeling, it must have been wofully subject to stomach complaints and fits of griping in the bowels.

Though these lithophagi of the Oolite occur chiefly in the corals of the period, they are not exclusively restricted to them. I have found them, though rarely, in Old Red flagstones of the conglomerate, and have ascertained that, had there been naturalists in those days to differ and dispute, the question might as certainly have been raised as now, whether the stone-boring shells made their way into the masses which they inhabited by mechanical means, or through the agency of some acidulous solvent. The corals, in their recent state, were of course calcareous, and, in consequence, dissolvable by an acid; and the flagstones which the borers usually selected also contain a good deal of calcareous earth; but their prevailing material is so largely aluminous and quartzose, that it seems scarce likely that a mere solvent could have perforated them.

I venture in conclusion, two general remarks. First, the corals of the Oolitic system in Scotland, massive in size, and occurring in some localities in very considerable abundance, resemble in these respects no recent corals of the higher latitudes. The corals of the higher latitudes are, we find, either diminutive or few. Groups of large corals are characteristic of the intertropical seas, or at least of seas of either hemisphere that border on the tropics. I have seen an Isastrea of Helmsdale that measured about two feet and a half in length by about eighteen inches in breadth, and which, as I have said, a strong man could scarce raise from the ground; and arborescent masses of *Thecosmila annularis* have been found in the Coral Rag of England, that measured from a foot and a-half to two feet in height. There occur no such corals now in seas which lie between the fiftieth and sixtieth degrees of latitude, whether to the south or north of the equator. And though I would not found much on one or two exceptional species, I do think that, seeing we would at once pronounce a similar group of recent corals to be the product of seas greatly warmer than our own, we might, I think, be permitted to infer, — reasoning from what we know, — that the Oolitic seas of what is now Scotland were of a higher temperature than our Scottish seas of the present day; and that, in short, in the corals of the Scotch Oolite we have one of many evidences that in this early period these northern regions enjoyed a greatly more genial climate than they do now. I may add, however, that in the same beds, mingled with fronds of cycas and zamia, and the stems of gigantic horsetails, — all now the productions of a warm climate, and that seem to give evidence to the same fact as the corals, — there occur numerous fragments, and occasionally whole trunks, of fossil pines, that apparently testify, by their annual rings of small size, indicative of slow growth, to a climate as ungenial and severe as that of Sweden or Norway. The evidence which they yield can, however, be scarce said to be of a conflicting character with that of the corals and the cycadites. If the Oolitic land was a lofty one, a very few miles might have served to separate a genial from a severe climate; and the pines might have been brought down by rivers from

an elevated and bleak interior, as different in its temperature
and productions from the sea-coast, as the pine-covered sides
of the Alps, where they rise towards the snow line, are different in *their* temperature and productions from the rich vine-
bearing valleys which they overlook.

I remark, in the second place, that the occurrence in the
Oolite of those boring shells of which I have laid specimens
before the Society is not without interest, as in some measure
illustrative of that unity of plan on which the Creator has
wrought in all the geologic periods, and which serves so strikingly to indicate the identity of the Worker.   Those four master ideas embodied in the animal kingdom which furnished
Cuvier with his principles of classification, each forming the
centre of a great division, seem to have been equally the master
ideas of all the geologic creations.   So far as we know, animal
life existed at all times, when it existed at all, in its four master
types, and no more ; and these in the Oolitic ages, — life radiating round a centre, as in the Isastrea, — life lodged within a
series of rings, as in the annelids and the crustacea, — life
combined with a duality of corresponding parts, as in the cut-
tle-fishes and the clams, — and life associated with a brain and
vertebral column, as in fishes and reptiles, — were not less
prominently developed than now.   Had a Cuvier then existed
to write the history of animated nature, the various classes
would have occupied very different proportional spaces in his
" Animal Kingdom " from that occupied by those of the present
time ; but the master divisions, — vertebrata, mollusca, articu-
lata, and radiata, — would have been the same.   For of all
the creations, I repeat, in the leading idea there has been no
change.   Two of these we find exemplified before us in single
specimens. — those in which the lithodomi lie sepultured in
cavities hollowed in Isastrea, and we are enabled to trace this
identity of idea into yet minuter ramifications, when we thus

find that, along these old Oolitic shores of Scotland, as along
the shores of our country in the present day, the rocks were
inhabited by their hermit shells, — the *Edomites* of the molluscous world, as a modern naturalist poetically terms them, —
that spent silent lives in excavating for themselves cells in the
stone, in which they watched in patience for the food brought
them by wavelet and current, and which, like the cells of so
many other anchorites and recluses, were ultimately to prove
their sepulchres. The idea that stones and rocks should be
thus inhabited is an idea old as eternity: it must have had being *as an idea* ere the existence of rock, or coral, or molluscous
life; for He from whom it emanated saw the end from the
beginning, and makes no accessions to his fund of thought; and
to be permitted thus to trace it towards its source, and to detect
it embodied in a creation whose last surviving organism perished
myriads of ages ago, enables us in some degree to conceive of
the fact, and to conceive also of the fixed character, of that
Master Existence, the Author of all, who said, in a long posterior age, when revealing Himself to man, " I am the Lord ;
I change not."

32

THE

FOSSILIFEROUS DEPOSITS OF SCOTLAND.

THE following address was read by Mr. MILLER, on his resigning the President's Chair of the Society:—

GENTLEMEN,—It is customary for the retiring President, in taking leave of the chair, to address the members on some general subject connected with the objects which our Society has been instituted to carry out, and in conforming to the practice, I shall take the liberty of stating, as briefly as possible, the results at which I have arrived, in recently arranging the specimens of a collection perhaps more adequately representative of the Geology of Scotland than any other that has yet been made. There are other collections which, though more partial in their character, excel it in particular departments; but none which I have yet seen sweep so completely the entire scale of our Scottish formations; and as such of its divisions as are most defective indicate, negatively at least, by the blanks on their partially filled shelves, the deposits on which we have still to direct our energies, it may be well that your attention should be specially called to these, as fields in which work has still to be done, and in which the reward of fresh and interesting discovery awaits the patient laborer. I am not sure that we need warmly congratulate ourselves on the fact,— but certainly a fact it is,— that the geologic section of our Society is in no danger of exhausting its work at home for a very considerable time to come. We have still much to do in acquainting ourselves with the extinct productions of our country in those remote pre-Adamic periods of its history when it existed, now as a group of Pleistocene islands,— now as a land covered by the Oolitic forests, and washed by seas tenanted by the ammonite and the nautilus,— now, ere yet its existing mountains had arisen from the abyss, as a series of dark plains and steaming morasses, brown with the rank and dusky vegetation of the Carboniferous period,— now as an extended sea-bottom, muddy or arenaceous, swum over by the strange ganoids of the Old Red Sandstone, and with here and there a minute island, green with, so far as it is yet known, the earliest ferns and the oldest trees,— and now as the bottom of a sea profounder still,— a sea without visible shore, inhabited by the minute brachipods and unique crustaceans of the earlier Silurian ages. That history of Scotland which, omitting the human period as too modern, stretches backwards from the recent shells of the old-coast line to the olenus and lingula beds of Girvan, and which is still unwritten, save in the rocks, will give our younger members work enough thoroughly to decipher and transcribe for perhaps a quarter of a century to come.

On first setting myself, about fourteen years ago, to add to my collection a set of Silurian fossils, I had to content myself with specimens derived chiefly from England and America. All the organisms detected at that time in the great Silurian deposits of Scotland,— though Sir James Hall had found shells in the Wrae Hill limestone nearly half a century previous, and Mr. Charles Maclaren in the Silurians of the Pentlands at least *six* years previous,— would scarce have half-filled a single shelf. Now, however, our old obstinate Grauwackes are yielding their organisms,—Dumfries, Galloway, and Peebles-shire their graptolites, and Girvan and its neighborhood its tri-lobites and its shells. The shores of the Solway near Kirkcud-bright are furnishing, though still inadequately, their fossils of the *Upper* Silurian; and it seems not improbable that the Gir-van locality may be yet found to furnish characteristic speci-mens of all the various deposits of the *Lower* Silurian, from those emphatically ancient beds beneath which only a single organism has yet been detected, up to those superior deposits of the Lower division in which the Dudley Trilobite (*Caly-mene Blumenbachii*) occurs, and which Sir Roderick Murchi-son regards as occupying the same, or nearly the same, horizon as the *Upper Caradoc*. I am informed by our accomplished brother member, Professor Wyville Thomson, that in a recent visit to Girvan, he found, in an ancient Conglomerate to the south of the town, specimens of a small lingula and olenus, identical, so far as he could judge from their state of keeping, with the fossils of unquestionably the same genera which mark, in the sister kingdom, the primeval zone of life. It would be interesting to find in our own country, as has already been found in North America, England, and Scandinavia, a base line,—representative, apparently, of the earliest age of organ-ized being,—from whence to commence the geologic history of what our fathers used to term, without quite knowing all that was implied in the epithet, *old* Scotland. But whether this base line of the oldest fossiliferous system be found in our country or no, the system itself, especially as developed within the southern and western districts, must be held to possess a peculiar interest, from the circumstance that, though some of its more curious fossils have not yet been found in the amply developed and well-sought Silurians of England, they occur in those of Bohemia on the one hand, and of Canada West and the United States on the other. They thus form in the general history of the globe a connecting link between deposits considerably more than four thousand miles apart. I may add that, during the last few years, I have been able to place in my little museum, beside its Silurian fossils of America and England, a not less ample collection of the Silurian fossils of our own country, which, though still inadequate, contains several rare organisms, with which, so far as is yet known, the English deposits could not have supplied me. Still, however, much remains to be done in this curious field. I was shown only a few weeks ago, by a gentleman from the neighborhood of Lesmahagow, a fossil crustacean, derived, he said, from the Grauwacke of that neighborhood, which, so far as I could judge, in its rather indifferent state of preservation, is new to Scotland, and which very considerably resembles that Hymenocaris of North Wales which Sir Roderick describes in his "Siluria" as a true primordial fossil. And where the crustacean occurs, it is more than probable that other organisms will yet be found.

The Lower Old Red Sandstone of Scotland has been more thoroughly wrought out than perhaps any of the other formations of the country, and it occupies, in consequence, a larger space in my collection. I have not yet found fossils in the Great Conglomerate, which forms its base; nor, perhaps, could organisms, save of the most robust structure, be expected in a rock formed of great water-rolled pebbles, which, ere they could have assumed their present rounded forms, must have been tossed by the storms of ages. In the pebbles themselves, however, we have curious glimpses afforded us of the old metamorphic rocks of Scotland; which were, we find, considerably different in the group from the rocks of similar origin that in the present age of the world compose our great Highland nucleus. The schistose gneisses, now the prevailing metamorphic rocks of the kingdom,—for they occupy nearly ten thousand square miles of its area,—were then but feebly developed, compared with its many-colored porphyries, its granites, and its quartz-rocks. In the Forfarshire Conglomerate, the prevailing rocks are hard porphyries, of an infinite variety of hue, and indistinguishable in their composition from the porphyries of Ben Nevis and Glencoe; in the Conglomerate of Cromarty and Ross, a decaying granite, red like that of Peterhead, but as finely grained as that of Aberdeen, blent with red quartz-rock and red granitic gneiss, is the prevailing stone; in that of Orkney, as exhibited in the neighborhood of Stromness, the prevailing rock is also a red granite, somewhat larger in its grain, and more durable, than the Cromarty one. The stone which composes many of these inclosed pebbles can no longer be found *in situ;* and a good representative collection of at least the classes of the rocks which they exemplify would serve to show the nature of the framework of that ancient unknown land to whose existence the Great Conglomerate bears evidence; and which — as over many thousand square miles the pebbles present the worn and rolled character — must have been exposed, zone after zone, during a protracted period of gradual depression, to the incessant wear of the ocean. The Conglomerate seems to have been exposed in an after period to intense heat. We find many of its hardest pebbles bent and indented, as if they had been reduced to the consistency of dough, or distorted by miniature faults, which scored their lines of fracture with the ordinary *slicken-sided* markings, when they were in a state viscid enough to re-unite. The fact would have been deemed a great one during the heat of the controversy waged in this city between the antagonistic schools of Hutton and Werner, but it is not less interesting now, when it can be looked at more quietly, and so I have given to a series of the pebbles which illustrate it a place in my collection.

Above the upper beds of the Great Conglomerate, at distances varying from forty to a hundred and sixty feet, the fishes of the Lower Old Red Sandstone appear,—curious, as the most ancient ganoids known to the geologist, and further, from the circumstance that, while the still older placoids of the Upper Silurian system exist merely as detached teeth, spines, and shagreen points, these Old Red fishes exhibit in the better specimens the entire outline of the original animals, with not a few of their anatomical peculiarities. It is from this formation that our knowledge of the oldest skulls, of the oldest vertebral columns, and of the oldest pelvic and thoracic arches, anywhere preserved, is to be derived. With the fish we sometimes find associated, though not often, specimens illustrative of what seems to be our most ancient terrestrial Flora,—club-mosses, —reed-like casts and impressions, streaked longitudinally, like the interior of the calamite, but apparently without joints,— what appear to be ferns,—and, in at least one unique specimen, a true wood of the araucarian family,—the oldest which has yet presented its structure to the microscope. In some localities, such as Cromarty, Thurso, and perhaps Moray, the various ichthyic species of the formation seem to have been pretty nearly ascertained and collected: for several years I have not succeeded in discovering from the several Cromarty deposits a single new species; and my friend Mr Dick, though permanently resident on the spot, has had a similar experience at Thurso. Species of the rarer kinds may, however, long elude very assiduous search, and yet turn up at last, and in the course of the present twelvemonth I have received from a tract of shore near Cromarty, which I have walked over many hundred times, an ichthyic species,—the *Diplacanthus crassispinus*,—of which my collection had possessed no previous specimen. I owe it to the kindness of Miss Catherine Allardyce,—a lady who, to a minute knowledge of not a few other branches of natural science, adds an intimate acquaintance with the fossils of our northern formations, and whose skill in zoophytology the late lamented Dr. Landsborough has acknowledged in his interesting "History of British Zoophytes." Further, it is worthy of remark that, just as the naturalist cannot now acquaint himself with all the animals or plants of Scotland in any single locality, so all the fossil species of any one formation cannot be exhausted in any one limited field or district, but must be sought for in various districts ere the list can be regarded as tolerably complete. The old Devonian species of fishes, like those of the present day, seem to have had their favorite haunts and feeding or spawning grounds, and must now be sought for where they congregated of old. The *Diplacanthus striatus*, for instance, is one of the commonest of the Cromarty Old Red fishes, and the *Dipterus* and *Asterolepis* very rare; whereas at Thurso, Mr. Dick, after years of exploration, never found a single spine of *Diplacanthus*, but not a few noble specimens of *Asterolepis*, and finely preserved skulls and jaws of *Dipterus*. And in a neighboring locality, Banniskirk, *Dipterus* is the prevailing fish, and may be found by scores. Again, the Old Red of Caithness generally is poor in specimens of *Pterichthys*,— the rocks of Thurso have not yet furnished a single specimen; whereas in those of Moray the genus is not rare; and in a quarry a few miles to the northeast of Stromness it is more abundant than any of its contemporaries. I mention these facts to show how necessary it is to the Palæontologist who sets himself to exhaust the organisms of a formation within even a single country, that he should either be a sedulous traveller, or have a widely-located circle of friends engaged with him as fellow-laborers in the work.

No ichthyic species of this Lower formation of the old Red Sandstone has yet been detected in Scotland to the south of the Grampians. In the great belt of Old Red which traverses the island diagonally, from the coasts of Kincardine and Forfarshire on the east, to those of Renfrew and Ayr on the west, the fossils, — restricted very much to the gray sandstones of the deposit, — are of an entirely different group. Here, as in the immensely developed Cornstones of England, the prevailing and most characteristic organism is the *Cephalaspis*; which has now been found in Forfar and Kincardineshires by Sir Charles Lyell, Mr. Webster, and others; in Sterlingshire by our ingenious brother member Mr. Alexander Bryson, and in Ayr by the late Dr. Brown of Longline; — all the specimens, however, in the same gray beds of micaceous sandstone, represented by what is known as the Arbroath pavement, which, like the red deposits that lie over and under them, run from side to side of the kingdom. While the fossils of the Lower Old Red Sandstone are more adequately represented in my collection than those of any other Scottish formation, the fossils of this Middle Old Red are almost the *least* adequately represented. And in this respect it resembles every other collection yet made, except that of Mr. Webster, now, I understand, in the possession of Lord Kinnaird. There is perhaps no Scottish formation in which the Palæontologist has still so much to do as in this Middle Old Red Sandstone. Our respected President Dr. Fleming called attention, a full quarter of a century ago, to some of its plants, and again took up the subject no further back than last year, in an interesting paper read before our Society; and Agassiz has figured and described some of its fishes, and more partially and incidentally, at least one of its crustaceans. But much still remains to be done. From what I have seen of Mr. Webster's collection, I should infer that materials have been already accumulated sufficient for the restoration of its great crustacean, — one of the most gigantic of its family, whether recent or extinct; and, as the Den of Balruddery has furnished of itself nearly a hundred specimens of *Cephalaspis* (still a comparatively rare ichthyolite elsewhere), most of which are now in the hands of Lord

Kinnaird, it would be well that some ichthyologist had access
to the collection, in order to determine whether in Scotland, as
in England, we have more than one species of this singular
genus. Dr. Fleming found in this Middle Old Red formation
an apparent fern, with kidney-shaped leaflets; and it yielded
several years ago, near Clockbriggs, in Forfarshire, a large specimen of *Lepidodendron*, which exhibits the internal structure.
I owe a fragment of this fossil to an intelligent geologist, Mr.
William Miller, banker, Dundee; but so imperfect is its state
of preservation, that, though it presents to the microscope the
large irregularly-polygonal cells of its genus, it bears none of
the nicer specific marks which might serve to distinguish it
from the several greatly more modern species which occur in
the Coal Measures.

Above this Middle formation lies the Upper Old Red Sandstone, with its peculiar group of organisms, chiefly fishes. And
of it, too, much remains to be known. Save that it has not
yet produced a *Coccosteus*,—a genus which seems restricted
to the oldest ichthyic group of the system,—its fishes more
resemble those of the Lower than of the Middle Old Red. It
has its three species of *Pterichthys*, its *Diplopterus*, and apparently its *Dipterus*, and its Celacanths, chiefly of the Holopty-
chian genus, represent not inadequately the Celacanths of the
genera *Asterolepis* and *Glyptolepis*, which occur chiefly, though
not exclusively, in the Lower formation. The two formations
appear, however, to have no *species* in common. In looking
over the fine collection of Mr. Patrick Duff, derived chiefly
from the Scat Craig, in the neighborhood of Elgin, I found
only a single ill-preserved gill-cover,—seemingly that of a
Dipterus,—which I could not at once determine to be specifically different from aught produced by the inferior deposit.
Rocks of this Upper formation have not yet been detected in
Scotland to the north of the Moray Frith; and its richest Brit-

ish deposits are to be found in Moray, Perthshire, Fife, Berwickshire, and Ayr. In the collection of fishes from Dura Den, exhibited four years ago before the British Association, then assembled at Edinburgh, I saw several Celacanths that have not yet been described; and a good deal has still to be done in fixing and restricting some of the genera of the formation already named and figured It will be found, for instance, that Agassiz's genus *Placothorax*, and his two species *Coccosteus maximus* and *Pterichthys major*, will ultimately all resolve themselves into the latter species alone. — *Pterichthys major;* of which, by the way, vast numbers have recently been found, though in a broken state. in the Upper Old Red Sandstone of the "Heads of Ayr." We may of course expect, however, to see more species and genera added to the group than subtracted from it. I must mention, ere concluding this part of my subject, a curious fact connected with the flora of the formation. When visiting last spring the Museum of Economic Geology in Jermyn-street, under the friendly guidance of the late Professor Edward Forbes, he pointed out to me an interesting group of plants, in a fine state of keeping, which had been derived from the Old Red Sandstone of Ireland. The genera seemed identical with those of the Coal Measures, but all the species were different. I marked, among the others, an elegant Cyclopterus, — *Cyclopterus Hibernicus*, — of which Sir Roderick Murchison figures a single pinna in his recently published "Siluria." The Professor also introduced me to the only ichthyic organism that had been found in the Irish deposit, with the plants, a ganoidal fish, apparently a Celacanth, and very much of the type of those of the Upper formation, though I failed to identify the species with any of those already known. Professor Forbes, in return, visited my collection here only a few weeks ago; and, in a fern of this Upper deposit, laid open by our ingenious member, Mr. John Stewart, in Prestonhaugh quarry near Dunse, he recognized his Irish Cyclopterus. As Mr. Stewart found the Scotch specimen associated with plates of *Pterichthys major* and scales of *Holoptychius Nobilissimus*,— two of the most characteristic ichthyolites of the Upper formation,— there can be no hesitation in assigning to it its place in the scale, and, of course, its position as an Upper Old Red fossil in Scotland may be held to determine that of the interesting group to which it is found to belong on the Irish side of the channel.

With respect to the true place of that deposit of pale quartzose sandstone which overlies the Upper Old Red in Moray, and has become famous in geology for its reptilian foot-tracks, its unique *Stagonolepis*, and its well-marked curious little reptile the *Telerpeton Elginense*, we are not yet provided with any determining evidence. No species common to the Upper Old Red and this rock has yet been discovered in either deposit. Mr. Patrick Duff, to whose labors we owe both the *Stagonolepis* and the *Telerpeton*, is in possession (with the exception of the reptilian foot-prints detected by Captain Brickendon) of all the few fossils found in the superior rock, and of a very ample collection of those of the underlying one; but I have seen nothing in the two sets in the least resembling each other. The late Dr. Mantell supposed, indeed, he had traced a considerable resemblance between the scales of *Stagonolepis* and those of a ganoid of Dura Den,—the *Glyptopomus*. They bear, however, a much closer resemblance to the scales of the *Mystriosaurus Muensteri*, a reptile of the Lias of Munich, of which I exhibited a good print to this Society about three years ago, the use of which I owed to the kindness of Sir Charles Lyell. When visiting a quarry in this northern deposit several years since, I was informed by the workmen that they frequently came upon foot-tracks like those found by Captain Brickendon. The only other remains of the deposit is that of the reptile *Telerpeton;* and, when we take into account the fact that in this northern locality outliers of the Lias and Oolite are not unfrequently found resting conformably on the Old Red Sandstone, and that the vertebrate organisms of these deposits are preponderatingly reptilian, it seems at least as probable that it belongs to that Secondary period of the world's history during which reptiles were abundant, as to that middle Palæozoic period during which, though fishes were largely developed, reptiles were exceedingly rare. But the final determination of the point must be regarded as awaiting the researches of the future.

The Carboniferous deposits in Scotland have, from their economic importance, been longer wrought than those of any of its other systems, and yet all their fossils, animal and vegetable, are still far from being adequately known. During the last few years I have found the remains of both plants and animals in Carboniferous deposits, not many miles removed from our Scottish capital, that have still to be figured and named; and much remains to be done in the work of restoring from suites of specimens organisms of the system, both vegetable and animal, already known in part. It is only within the last two or three years that trace of reptiles has been detected in our Scotch Coal Measures. The *Probatrachus colei* of Owen has been found in the coal-field near Carluke; and the footprints of a much larger reptile detected in our Dalkeith coalfield by Mr. Henry Cadell, the experienced and intelligent mineral surveyor of his Grace the Duke of Buccleuch. I refer to these interesting facts to indicate the direction in which there is encouragement to press our researches. We have hitherto had little experience in Scotland of that style of exhaustive research of which the Palæontographical Society of England is presenting us with so admirable an example. Curiously enough, however, old David Ure, one of our earliest collectors

of the carboniferous fossils, gave, in his "Natural History of
Rutherglen," published more than sixty years ago, an example
of this exhaustive style, perhaps as complete as was possible
at the time.   He seems to have figured, and, after a sort, described, every fossil of both the Coal and the Mountain Limestone, which he succeeded in dis-interring during what, in an
age in which there were few to sympathize in his labors, must
have been a very sedulous course of research.   The magnificent sections of our neighborhood give peculiar facilities in exploring the Coal Measures and their contents, — facilities which
geologists who have resided for a season amid the soil-covered
flats of central England would well know how to appreciate.
There are few finer sections of the Coal deposits anywhere in
Britain than those laid open along the shores of Granton, Mus-
selburgh, and Prestonpans; and the section of the Mountain
Limestone exposed in the ravine at Dryden is, so far as I have
yet seen, the most extensive in Scotland.   By those who hold,
as is done by some of the geologists of our western capital, that
this formation is wanting as a base to the Scottish Coal-field, a
visit to this section might be found very instructive.   It does
not exhibit that great thickness of limestone for which the corresponding formation in England is so remarkable, but presents,
for several hundred feet together, in its encrinal bands, intercalated amid shales and sand-tone, evidence of a marine origin;
and its upper calcareous beds, laden with spirifers and producta,
and of very considerable thickness, show that a tolerably profound sea must have covered the field shortly ere the formation
of our older beds of workable coal.

My collection contains no specimens of the New Red Sandstone of Scotland, — the scene of those discoveries of the late
Dr. Duncan of Ruthwell from which that division of geologic
science known as Ichnology took its rise.   Nor are at least
sets of its specimens to be found in any of the Scotch museums

I have yet seen; but as Sir William Jardine is understood to be still engaged in figuring and describing its various footprints, — the only traces of former existence which it has been found to contain, — we bid fair to be acquainted, at no distant date, with all that it produces. It could be wished, however, that we had the result of Sir William's labors conveyed to us in that cheap but yet adequate form of outline engraving in which Professor Hitchcock has figured the foot-tracks, reptilian or ornithologic, of the New Red Sandstones of the Connecticut.

In the Lias and Oolite of Scotland a good deal still remains to be accomplished. Some of their richest deposits lie scattered among the inner Hebrides, and along lochs and creeks of the Western Highlands, rarely visited by the tourist, and far from inns; and this difficulty of access has served to lock up in these solitudes many a curious fossil, that may be regarded as held in safe keeping, to reward the enterprise of our younger geologists. My collection contains not a few curious specimens, derived from these Hebridean recesses during a desultory voyage in the Free Church yacht Betsey, made about ten years ago, — reptilian remains, fossil wood, and the teeth of placoidal fishes from the Oolite of Eigg, and pinnæ, ammonites, and massive corals from the Lias of Pabba and Skye. It may serve to show that we are no more to argue an entire identity of the Oolitic deposits of Scotland with those of England, than of its Silurian with the Silurians of that country, — that corals, which are of exceeding rarity and minute size in the English Lias, form entire beds of great extent and several feet in thickness in the Lias of Skye. I can, however, only indicate the *locale* of some of the deposits in which these rarities may be found, — simply referring, in the passing, to the localities already indicated by Sir Roderick Murchison in his earlier papers, — such as the Oolites in the neighborhood of Portree, the Oolitic beds of Raza, and the Liassic strata of Applecross; as also to the curious fresh-water or estuary deposit of Loch Staffin, described in the "Geological Journal" for 1851, by the late Professor Edward Forbes. There is a patch of Lias on the shores of Loch Alme, exceedingly rich in some of the characteristic organisms of the formation, which I would fain have examined with some care, but wanted the necessary opportunity. From deposits partially overflown by the Trap of Mull, and which crop out along the eastern shores of that Island, I have exhumed specimens that bear in the group an Oolitic aspect; and in spending a few hours in the Island of Pabba, when the yacht, my home for the time, was cruising in the offing, I found in it such promise of a rich fossil harvest, that when a young friend, — Mr. Archibald Geikie, — requested me last year to point out to him some one or two centres from which I thought he might best acquaint himself with our Scottish Lias of the western coast, I ventured to recommend the latter island, and the southern portion of the neighboring Bay of Broadford, as two of the most promising. Mr. Geikie, — in whom our Society may, I trust, recognize a future member, — found his way to Pabba, — introduced himself to the sole family resident on the island, — slept, I believe, in a barn, — lived on potatoes and milk, — and brought away with him an interesting suite of fossils. And after this manner must the Hebrides, and the Western Highlands be explored. The Oolitic beds of the eastern coast are considerably more accessible than those of the west. The Lias of Eathie, near Cromarty, is one of the richest deposits in animal remains which I have anywhere seen; and it has yielded several unique fossils, — such as the broad-spiked leaflets of some ancient tree attached to a stem of a twelvemonth's growth, that yields to the microscope, in a prepared section, the coniferous tissue, — cones of unique structure, — a well-marked frond of Zamia of an undescribed species, — numerous ammonites in a fine state of preservation, — and one of the com-

pletest sets of Liassic belemnites yet collected. What have been
deemed corresponding deposits, which, however, I am disposed
to refer to a higher horizon, occur in the neighborhood of the
northern Sutor; and near the base of one of these, at Caanrie,
there is a seam of coal or lignite very much resembling that of
Biora, and flanked by a bed of fresh water shells and Perna,
the last identical in species, so far as I have been able to determine the point, with that of the Perna bed described by the
late Mr. Robertson of Woodside as flanking the Biora seam.
Above the coal there occurs a rubbly stratum, also like one at
Brora, charged with vast numbers of the *Belemnite sulcatus;*
and in an upper stratum I found a well-marked specimen of
Ammonites perarmatus; likewise a species of the Brora coal-
field.   In short, I am disposed to hold, — both from the identity
of many of its fossils, and its general appearance, — that this
supposed Liassic deposit is in reality an Oolitic one, and that
its coal occupies a horizon not much removed from that of the
coal at Brora.   I may here mention, that the Lias of Eathie
was the scene, only two years ago, of a disastrous coal-boring
speculation, on which much good money was expended.   The
unlucky speculator, — an industrious and respectable man, whom
I would fain have dissuaded from an undertaking so hopeless,
but who, as he had no faith in geology, simply thanked me for
my advice, and wrought on. — dug a wide pit in the Liassic
shales, to the depth of more than a hundred feet, and found in
abundance ammonites and belemnites, with a few well-preserved
vertebral joints of Ichthyosaurus, and unfortunately here and
there fragments of cone-bearing trees, with their trunks converted into jet, but, of course, no coal.   The hole was made
large and deep enough to prove the sepulchre of several hundred pounds; but I console myself by reflecting that the inev-
itable expense of the excavating operations was incurred in
defiance of all that I could say; and I would now urge on **my**

friends the anti-geologists, that they should much rather attempt making shillings by lecturing against the science, than run the risk of losing the shillings already made by becoming *miners* in its despite.

The Oolite of Sutherland, — famous for containing the only seam of coal in this formation, at least in Britain, which could have been wrought for years without much positive loss, — was elaborately described many years ago by Sir Roderick Murchison, in a memoir that gave rich earnest of his after contributions to geologic science. It is impossible, however, to exhaust a great formation otherwise than slowly; and not a few fossils have been added of late years to the list appended to Sir Roderick's memoir. It is from the vegetable organisms of this deposit that we can now form our most adequate conceptions of the Oolitic Flora of Scotland. As in England and America, it had its numerous cycadaceæ, — its ferns of simple undivided frond, unique in their venation, but resembling in their forms the hart's-tongue genus (Scolopendra), its thuyites, its pines; and though they occupied a scarce appreciable space in the group, its dicotyledonous plants. When, after glancing over some of the vegetable productions of the system, such as its cycadaceæ, now restricted to the warmer climates, or over its massive corals, which attained to a size seldom rivalled in the present state of things, save in the intertropical seas, I have then examined some of its woods externally gnarled, and stunted, and marked internally by minute annual rings, as small as those of a Scotch fir or Norwegian pine that had grown on some exposed hill-side, it has occurred to me that some of the Oolitic districts in what is now Scotland must have had their lofty mountain ranges, which, while a genial climate prevailed at their bases, rose, mayhap, to nearly the snow-line, and bore on their bleak ridges the stunted slow-growing trees. The framework of this ancient land was composed — as we learn from its conglomerates, and in some instances from the fragments of rock still locked fast amid the roots of its trees — of Old Red flagstones, identical with those of Caithness, and evidently bearing at the time marks of as high an antiquity as they do now. Many of these flagstone masses, sorely water-rolled, occur in an Oolitic paste; and we find in strange neighborhoods shells of the Oolite inclosed in the paste, and fishes of the Old Red in the pebbles which it envelops. I have found a pebble which bore inside an Old Red *Osteolepis* encrusted with an Oolitic *Thamnastrea;* and another pebble occupied by an Old Red fucoid that was partially perforated by an Oolitic lithodomus shell. It is surely not uninteresting thus to catch, as it were, glimpses, through the high antiquity of a Secondary age, of a Palæozoic age vastly more ancient still, — to see long withdrawing vistas opening, through the remote times of the Oolite, into the incalculably more remote times of the Lower Old Red Sandstone.

Those outliers of the Weald, or rather of a fresh-water or estuary Oolite, which occur in Morayshire, are adequately represented in only a few local collections, — the completest set of these fossils which I have yet seen being that in the possession of Mr. Patrick Duff of Elgin, who, living in the immediate neighborhood of the rich deposits at Linksfield, and animated by an ever fresh zeal for the interests of natural science, has been concentrating his exertions for years on these detached deposits, and on the not less rich formations of the Old Red Sandstone on which they rest. Their organisms, — constituting a link in the geologic history of Scotland which no other locality has yet supplied, — consist of the dorsal spines of a new species of *Hybodus*, — the teeth of an *Acrodus* and *Spenonchus*, — the scales, and, at least in one instance, an entire specimen, of a *Lepidotus*, which Agassiz has identified as the *Lepidotus minor* of the English Weald, — bones and teeth of

Plesiosaurus, a well-marked chelonian femur, — shells, both marine and fresh-water, such as *Unio Planorbis Paludina,* — what seem to be an *Astarte* and a small *Ostrea,* — and whole strata formed of a minute *Cyprus.* There are appearances connected with the Linksfield deposit that date from a comparatively recent period, which are at least as extraordinary as aught that the beds themselves contain. They form there a small hill, about from forty to fifty feet in height, and several hundred feet in extent either way; while beneath lies a thick deposit of the Old Red cornstones, wrought in this locality for lime. Interposed, however, between this hill of the Weald and the calcareous cornstones, there is a bed of the ordinary boulder clay of the district, charged not only with the fragments of the rock on which is lies, but also of the well-marked Wealden strata which overlie it; and, more curious still, the cornstone bears on its surface, so far as the quarriers have yet penetrated, the ordinary glacial markings characteristic of the boulder clay. It would seem as if during the glacial period this hill had been so shifted or raised from its foundations, that the agent, whatever its nature, which during the icebergal period dressed and grooved the rock-surfaces of the country, was enabled to dress and groove the cornstone on which the hill now rests. The appearances, — suggestive of the operations of some incalculably enormous force, — are suited to remind one of that sublime simile employed by Milton, in describing the effect of the stroke under which the rebel angel reeled and fell : —

> " As if on earth
> Winds underground, or waters forcing way
> Sidelong, had pushed a mountain from his seat,
> Half-sunk, with all its pines "

With these detached outliers we take leave in Scotland of the Secondary formations, in their character as original deposits,

whose strata still occur in the order in which they were first
laid down. We find, however, in Banff and Aberdeenshires,
and more partially in Caithness, remains of the Cretaceous
system, occurring in some localities in the character of re-for-
mations. A deposit at Moreseat, near Cruden, elaborately described by Mr. William Ferguson, late of Glasgow, seems to be
almost exclusively a re-formation of the Greensand, and on
the Hill of Dudwick, near Ellon, there are vast accumulations
of flints, in which the Rev. Mr. Longmuir of Aberdeen, who
has carefully explored the locality, detected many of the characteristic Cretaceous fossils furnished by the chalk of England.
I have examined beds of gravel a few miles to the south of
Peterhead, in which there occurs merely a per centage, though a
not inconsiderable one, of these chalk flints; but I have been informed by our ingenious corresponding member, Mr. Peach,
with whom I saw several of the Cretaceous organisms of the
locality, that, had I set myself to examine in a different direction, more to the north and west, I would have found thick
gravel beds composed of chalk flints almost exclusively. The
best collections yet made of the organisms of this denuded system, of which only the broken fragments survive, are those of
Mr. Longmuir, representative of the Scottish Chalk, and of
Mr. Ferguson, representative of the Scottish Greensand. Both
are inadequately represented in my collection; and what it
possesses I owe chiefly to the kindness of Mr. Longmuir, and
to that of Mr. Dick, the original discoverer of the Chalk in
Caithness, where it occurs, however, merely in detached fragments in the boulder clay. Much need not be expected from
the organic remains of a deposit so broken and scattered. I
have seen in its flints, however, finer and more delicately preserved specimens of a Flustra, that not a little resembles our
existing *Flustra foliacea*, than any I have yet succeeded in
detecting in those of England; and the group, however frag-

mentary and incomplete, must be regarded as possessing a certain interest of its own, in its character as a portion of the fossil records of a country whose *later* geologic history, like her civil one both late and early, is meagre in its authentic materials, and, in consequence, unsatisfactory in its details.

With but one baiting place,—that furnished by his Grace the Duke of Argyle's discovery of Miocene leaf-beds in the Island of Mull,—we have to stride, in Scotland, wholly across the Tertiary divisions, and find our first footing on the deposits of the Pleistocene. I have not yet seen the leaf-beds represented in any collection, save the great British one in Jermyn Street. They must, however, be regarded as possessing peculiarly a *Scotch* interest, not merely from the glimpse which they yield us of those old dicotyledonous forests of our country which succeeded, after the lapse of unreckoned ages, the coniferous forests of the Oolite, but also from the circumstance of their irrefragably demonstrating that, up till a comparatively late period, Scotland had its great outbursts of Trap. A thick bed of rudely columnar basalt overlies the most modern of these beds; and deposits of trap tuff, in which his Grace detected rolled chalk flints, overlie the older ones; thus showing, that long after the times of the Chalk, and when trees allied to the yew, the plane, and the buckthorn, grew in our forests, those deluges of molten matter from the abyss which had obtained throughout the earlier geologic ages, had not yet ceased, but were, on the contrary, potent enough to overspread wide areas to the depth of from twenty to forty feet. From these times of fire we at once pass, in this northern part of the island, to a period of ice,—to the ages represented by grooved and polished surfaces, travelled rocks, boreal shells, and the boulder clay. Though geologically the period was one, it yields, I am disposed to think, evidence of three distinct successive stages.

The Boreal shells of Banffshire (which occur at Gamrie in a finely stratified sand, two hundred and thirty feet over the sea, and at Castleton King-Edward in a similar deposit of very considerable elevation, and at least six miles inland), lie deep, —though exposed laterally in sections,—in the Pleistocene deposit. At Castleton I found the shells within a few feet of the underlying Grauwacke rock, and an immense deposit of beds of sand and clay, and over all a thick bed of partially consolidated ferruginous gravel lying above them. At Gamrie, though, from the great slope of the ground, the fact is less certain, they also seem to lie low; and further, both from their littoral aspect, and the circumstance that we find no trace of a littoral terrace where they occur, I cannot avoid the conclusion that they mark the line where a *shore* of the country existed for a time, when the country was in a state of subsidence, and ere yet the higher lying boulder clay was formed. The only peculiarity of the shells themselves, viewed in the group, is their intensely boreal character. The sole species of Astarte which I have yet found at either Gamrie or Castleton King-Edward,—and I have now visited these deposits five several times,—is the Greenland shell, *Astarte Arctica; Natica clausa,* —a shell of Spitzbergen and the North Cape,—is the prevailing Natica; and the most abundant shell, of at least the Gamrie deposit, is a bivalve not yet found living in our seas, but common ten degrees further to the north, *Tellina proxima.* Even the great size to which the latter shell attained in this locality is not without its bearing on the question "The few specimens which have been dredged [dead] in Britain," says the late Professor Forbes, in his admirable history of the British Mollusca, "are much smaller than the exotic ones, none which we have seen exceeding three-quarters of an inch in length, and about half an inch in breadth." The mollusc is one of those which attain to their fullest development amid the

frosts and snows of the higher latitudes; and it is a curious
fact, that in the Gamrie and Castleton deposits we find it of a
considerably greater size than anywhere else in Scotland.   My
largest specimens from the Clyde beds hardly exceed an inch
in length; whereas my largest Gamrie specimens are nearly
two inches long, and their *breadth* very considerably exceeds
the length given as British by Professor Forbes.

Most of the boulder clays,—especially the higher lying
deposits,—I regard as more modern than these Banffshire
beds.   They mark a period when the land sat low in the
water, and existed as but a group of wintry islands.   To the
south of the Grampians, their organisms are but few; they
have yielded at wide intervals horns of the rein-deer, and tusks
of the northern elephant; but, save in an insulated patch in
Wigtonshire, no shells.   The boulder clay in Caithness is, on
the other hand, rich in shells.   They excited the attention of a
mineral surveyor, who flourished about the beginning of the
present century,— old John Busby,— more than fifty years
ago; they also attracted the notice of the late Sir John Sinclair; and in one of my Caithness journeys, I was told by my
friend Mr. Dick, that one of the hills on which they occur has
borne from a still more early period the name of "*Buckie's
Hill;*" but to Mr. Dick himself, and to Mr. Cleghorn of Wick,
has the working out of the deposit been mainly left.   And so
effectively has it been done, that Mr. Dick, as he informs me,
has not for a considerable time past succeeded in finding in it a
single new shell.   The prevailing molluses of the deposit are
Cyprina, Islandica, and *Turritella communis,* especially the
former; the prevailing Astarte, though the *Arctica* also occurs,
is *Astarte elliptica;* the prevailing Tellina, *Tellina Solidula.*
Tellina proxima is of smaller size than in the Gamrie beds;
and *Natica clausa* less common.   Still the deposit is very
decidedly a boreal one in its shells, and in its mechanical phe-

nomena the most decidedly boreal of the group. Every rock-surface on which it rests is grooved and striated, almost every softer pebble which it encloses is scratched and furrowed, usually in the line of its longer axis; all its larger shells exist as broken fragments, often rounded as if by attrition, and bearing in their lines and scratches marks of the same agents that dressed the rocks and scored the pebbles; nay, the very substance and color of its prevailing clays show that it is mainly composed of the dressings of the rocks on which it rests,—all giving evidence, apparently, of a time when our half-foundered country sat from eight hundred to a thousand feet lower in the water than it does now, and vast packs of grinding icebergs went careering over what are now its lower hills and its higher table-lands.

The Clyde beds and their contents belong apparently to a still later time. Their largest shells are usually in a state of great entireness and fine keeping. I had the pleasure of laying open, two years ago, at Fairlie, on the Ayrshire coast, a virgin deposit unknown before, in which I found continuous scalps of *Pecten Islandicus* still occupying the place in which they had lived and died, and with their upper valves covered with large balanæ, such as we now dredge up from the outer limits of the laminarian zone, and all fresh and unbroken. Huge *Panopæa* were there sticking fast in an unctuous clay, with their open siphuncular ends turned upwards; and entire specimens of *Cyprina Islandicus* and *Modiola Modiolus*, with their valves still connected by the sorely decayed ligament. *Tellina proxima* was abundant, but reduced in size to little more than half the Gamrie dimensions. I found *Astarte elliptica* the prevailing Astarte; and groups of younger Cyprina huddled together in the character — which they do not now assume on our coasts — of gregarious shells. No crushing iceberg had passed over this deposit: a grooved and polished rock of Old Red Sandstone

lies beneath, overlaid by a thin stratum of red clay, apparently
derived from it, but the higher-lying gray stratum in which
the shells occur had a different origin : it is simply the partially
consolidated mud of a quiet sea-bottom ; and though its group
of organisms manifest decidedly the boreal character, I cannot
doubt that they lived at a time when, either from some change
in the currents of the coast, or from the elevation of the protecting islands outside,— an effect of a general rising of the
land,— the sea was no longer an exposed one. They in all
probability mark that later stage of the wintry period to which
the last-formed group of our local glaciers belonged, and in
which our gradually-emerging country presented, age after age,
a broader and yet broader area, won from the deep.

One period more, and I shall have completed my survey.
All the shells which have hitherto been found beneath our latest terraces of upheaval still exist on our coasts. They represent a time, perhaps not greatly in advance of the earlier
historic ages, when the country had begun to exist under its
present climatal conditions. Some of these modern shells are,
however, found to occur in very different proportions, in certain localities, from what they do now. The only specimens of
Pholas candidus which I have been able to procure from the
Lower reaches of the Cromarty Frith occur in a clay-bed of
the old coast period which underlies an arable field in the
Lones of Fern, a full mile from the sea. My only specimens
of *Scrobicularia piperata* from the Frith of Forth have been
derived from the brick clays behind Portobello, more than a
quarter of a mile beyond the reach of the tide. My first
found Scotch specimens of *Thracia convexa* I collected last
year from a raised sea-bottom near North Queen-ferry. The
upheaval of the land seems to have altered the conditions, in
certain localities, favorable to the production of shells such as
Scrobicularia and *Pholas ;* and *Thracia convexa,* though it

still lives in the Frith of Forth, — which furnished me in the
course of last summer with two specimens, that, from their
appearance, must have died within the twelvemonth, — seems
to be a greatly less abundant shell in the locality now than during the ages of the old-coast line, and appears, unless, indeed,
it has been hitherto strangely missed by our dredgers, to be
dying out.   The old sea-bottom at Queensferry, little more
than half an acre in extent, furnished me with full three dozen
specimens, though in a state more or less broken, — an extraordinary number for what has been well described in the history
of the Mollusca as one of our rarest British shells.   Of these
recent shells of the ancient coast line we find older and newer
beds.   The *Scrobicularia* of Portobello, for instance, were the
inhabitants of a muddy estuary, which ran along what is now
the flat, winding, willow-skirted valley that runs inland towards
the village of Easter Duddingstone ; but ere the last upheaval
of the land they must have been dead for ages ; for how can
we otherwise interpret their position in the brick-clay, with from
six to eight feet of an argillaceous deposit, of apparently slow
formation, resting over them.   The *Pholas* bed of the *Lones*
of Fern exists in similar conditions.   It, too, was deeply silted
over ere the last rise of the land , whereas the shells of Granton, and of many other localities on the coast, must have been
beach-shells at the time of the upheaval ; and not a few of them
were, mayhap, living scarce half a year before.   In some of
these old estuary deposits, — such as that of Portobello, — we
find interesting remains of the aboriginal trees of the country,
— boles of oak, birch, alder, the Scotch fir, and the yew, — with
handfuls of sorely blackened hazel-nuts, and the trunks and
branches of a dwarfish hawthorn, converted into a glossy substance, nearly resembling jet.   They yield us curious glimpses
of those mighty woods which covered the country ere it had
become a home of man, or during those earlier ages of his in-

habitancy, when he was yet too unskilful to commence its history.

Such is a view, all too inadequate, and yet, I fear, not a little tedious, both of the several fields in which our geologic members have still much labor before them, and of what a Scottish museum, truly national, should represent. Though the breaks and hiatuses are many, there are still noble materials within the limits of our country for the composition of its pre-Adamic history, — that history of which the record is in the rocks, and of which organisms are the significant and impressive characters. The very gaps which occur in the long chronicle serve all the more strongly to divide it into periods, each furnished with its own independent group of being, specifically unlike that which went before, or that which followed after, and suited to remind us all the more emphatically in consequence, that to every species that ever lived in the old geologic ages there came a "last day." We have been long accustomed to recognize the inexorable reign of death in its relation to individuals, and to regard it as one of the most assured and certain of all things, that as all who have lived upon our earth during the ages of the past have died, so it is "appointed for all" who now live upon it "once to die." The same experience which leads us to anticipate that the sun will rise and set to-morrow, just because the sun has risen and set during all the many days of the past, leads us also to anticipate that all the individual creatures which now inhabit the earth will die, just because all the individual creatures which inhabited the earth in the bygone ages *have* died. And now we find geology extending this uniform experience of death from individuals to species, and compelling us to believe, on the strength of the argument to which we so unhesitatingly yield in the other cases, that as all the *species* of the past have died, so it is destined for all the species of the present also to die. The theologian had to contend in the last age with a class of skeptics who,—their skepticism assuming, as is not very uncommon, the form of credulous belief,—used to argue that there had been an infinite series of men upon earth, and, of course, if the race had no beginning, could it be held in consistency that it was to have an end? We now absolutely know, as geologists, not only that a beginning there was, but that the beginning was a comparatively recent event; and further, founding on the unvarying experience of the past, we also know that the race, in at least its existing character and condition, is to have an end. There are peculiarities, too, in the visitations of the present time, suited to suggest many a pregnant thought in connection with this curious and surely not unimportant subject. I travelled by railway, in middle autumn, two years ago, for about a hundred miles, through a series of well-cultivated fields; and found almost all their potatoes, constituting about one-fifth of the entire produce of the district, killed by a mysterious disease, and exhaling a heavy odor of death and decay, that infected the air mile after mile. There were perhaps as many individual plants of this useful vegetable lying brown and dead in the extensive area through which I passed as the entire species would have consisted of had it not been so sedulously and extensively cultivated by man; and the appearance of the blackened and fetid fields suggested to me how, in at least some of the instances, species may have died. A disease similarly extensive is devastating at the present time the vineyards of the south; and it is said that, should it continue its ravages for a year or two longer, the generous *Madeira* of the wine-drinker will become as much a mere tradition in consequence as the extinct wines of the ancients. Nay, during the present age have we not seen a new and terrible disease, quite as mysterious in its character and origin as any of those which have fallen on the vegetable kingdom, sweeping away greatly more than a hundred millions of our own species?

Read in the light of geologic history, with its irrefragable evidence of the often-repeated extinction of entire creations, these visitations of the age assume a peculiar significancy. But the subject is one which I must not pursue. The same time which, in its sure course, conducts both individuals and species to their last day, has brought round the last day of my occupancy of this chair. Accept, gentlemen, ere I leave it, my best thanks for the marked kindness and courtesy which I have on every occasion received at your hands, — for the tolerance which has overlooked my many shortcomings, — and for the attention and respect with which my various communications have been received. I trusted to have had the honor of resigning it to a gentleman who, fifteen years ago, was one of the most active and zealous members of the Royal Physical Society ; and who had, since that time, achieved for himself in natural science in general, and in geology in especial, a reputation co-extensive with the civilized world.* But, alas! Death reigns. This distinguished man, in the full blow of his fame, and in the mature prime of vigorous manhood, has passed suddenly away ; and wherever in either hemisphere physical science is cultivated, or the bypast history of our globe excites the legitimate interest, his early death will be felt and deplored as a heavy loss. The spoiler has broken abruptly off many a train of ingenious thought, — cut short many a course of sedulous inquiry, — arrested, just ere its formation, many a profound induction, — and scattered hoards of unrecorded knowledge, the adequate re-gathering of which many years to come may fail to witness. But our idle regrets can neither restore the dead nor benefit the living. Let us rather manifest our regard for the memory of our illustrious brother, — taken so unexpectedly from among us, — by making his disinterested devotion to science our example, and by striv-

---

* It had been proposed, at the previous meeting of the Society, to call to the vacant Presidential Chair the late Professor Edward Forbes.

ing to catch the tone of his frank and generous spirit. And seeing how very much he succeeded in accomplishing within the limits of a life that has, alas! fallen short by more than thirty years of the old allotted term, let us diligently carry on, in the love of truth, our not unimportant labors, remembering that much may be accomplished in comparatively brief space if no time be lost, and that to each and all that "night cometh" at an uncertain hour, under whose dense and unbroken shadow "no man can work."

The End.

Diary and Correspondence OF THE LATE AMOS LAWRENCE. Edited by his son, WM. R. LAWRENCE, M. D. Octavo, cloth, $1.25; also, royal 12mo. ed., cl., $1.00.

Kitto's Popular Cyclopædia OF BIBLICAL LITERATURE. 500 illustrations. One vol., octavo, 812 pages. Cloth, $3.

Intended for ministers, theological students, parents, Sabbath-school teachers, and the great body of the religious public.

Analytical Concordance of the Holy SCRIPTURES; or, The Bible presented under Classified Heads or Topics. By JOHN EADIE, D. D. Octavo, 836 pp. $3.

Dr. Williams' Works.
Lectures on the Lord's Prayer — Religious Progress — Miscellanies.

☞ Dr. Williams is a profound scholar and a brilliant writer. — *New York Evangelist.*

Modern Atheism. Considered under its forms of Pantheism, Materialism, Secularism, Development and Natural Laws. By JAMES BUCHANAN, D. D., LL. D. 12mo. Cloth, $1.25.

The Hallig; or the Sheepfold in the Waters. A Tale of Humble Life on the Coast of Schleswig. From the German, by Mrs. GEORGE P. MARSH. 12mo. Cl., $1.

The Suffering Saviour. By Dr. KRUMMACHER. 12mo. Cloth, $1.25.

Heaven. By JAMES WM. KIMBALL. 12mo.

Christian's Daily Treasury. Religious Exercise for every Day in the Year. By Rev. E. TEMPLE. 12mo. Cloth, $1.

Wayland's Sermons. Delivered in the Chapel of Brown Univ. 12mo. Cl., $1.00.

Entertaining and Instructive Works FOR THE YOUNG. Elegantly illustrated. 16mo. Cloth, gilt backs.

The American Statesman, Life and Character of Daniel Webster. — *Young Americans Abroad;* or Vacation in Europe. — *The Island Home;* or the Young Cast-aways. — *Pleasant Pages for Young People.* — *The Guiding Star.* — *The Poor Boy and Merchant Prince.*

THE AIMWELL STORIES. Resembling and quite equal to the "Rollo Stories." — *Christian Register.* By WALTER AIMWELL. *Oscar;* or the Boy who had his own way. — *Clinton;* or Boy-Life in the Country. — *Ella;* or Turning over a New Leaf. — *Whistler;* or The Manly Boy. — *Marcus;* or the Boy Tamer.

WORKS BY Rev. HARVEY NEWCOMB. *How to be a Lady.* — *How to be a Man.* — *Anecdotes for Boys.* — *Anecdotes for Girls.*

BANVARD'S SERIES OF AMERICAN HISTORIES. *Plymouth and the Pilgrims.* — *Romance of American History.* — *Novelties of the New World,* and *Tragic Scenes in the History of Maryland and the old French War.*

God Revealed in Nature and in CHRIST. By Rev. JAMES B. WALKER, Author of "The Philosophy of the Plan of Salvation." 12mo. Cloth, $1.

Philosophy of the Plan of Salvation. New enlarged edition. 12mo. Cloth, 75 c.

Christian Life: SOCIAL AND INDIVIDUAL. By PETER BAYNE. 1.mo. Cloth, $1.25.

All agree in pronouncing it one of the most admirable works of the age.

Yahveh Christ; or the Memorial Name. By ALEX. MACWHORTER. With an Introductory Letter, by NATH'L W. TAYLOR, D. D., in Yale Theol. Sem. 16mo. Cloth, 60 c.

The Signet Ring, AND ITS HEAVENLY MOTTO. From the German. 16mo. Cl., 31 c.

The Marriage Ring; or How to Make Home Happy. 18mo. Cloth, gilt, 75 c.

Mothers of the Wise and Good. By JABEZ BURNS, D. D. 16mo. Cloth, 75 c.

☞ A sketch of the mothers of many of the most eminent men of the world.

My Mother; or Recollections of Maternal Influence. 12mo. Cloth, 75c.

The Excellent Woman, with an Introduction, by Rev. W. B. SPRAGUE, D. D. Splendid Illustrations. 12mo. Cloth, $1.

The Progress of Baptist Principles IN THE LAST HUNDRED YEARS. By T. F. CURTIS, Prof. of Theology in the Lewisburg University. 12mo. Cloth, $1.25.

Dr. Harris' Works.
The Great Teacher. — The Great Commission. — The Pre-Adamite Earth. — Man Primeval. — Patriarchy. — Posthumous Works, 4 volumes.

The Better Land; OR THE BELIEVER'S JOURNEY AND FUTURE HOME. By Rev. A. C. THOMPSON. 12mo. Cloth, 85 c.

Kitto's History of Palestine, from the Patriarchal Age to the Present Time. With 200 Illustrations. 12mo. Cloth, $1.25.

An admirable work for the Family, the Sabbath and week-day School Library.

The Priest and the Huguenot; or, PERSECUTION IN THE AGE OF LOUIS XV. From the French of L. F. BUNGENER. Two vols., 12mo. Cloth, $2.25.

This is not only a work of thrilling interest, but is a masterly Protestant production.

The Psalmist. A Collection of Hymns for the Use of Baptist Churches. By BARON STOW and S. F. SMITH. With a SUPPLEMENT, containing an Additional Selection of Hymns, by RICHARD FULLER, D. D., and J. B. JETER, D. D. Published in various sizes, and styles of binding.

This is unquestionably the best collection of Hymns in the English language.

☞ In addition to works published by themselves, they keep an extensive assortment of works in all departments of trade, which they supply at publishers' prices. ☞ They particularly invite the attention of Booksellers, Travelling Agents, Teachers, School Committees, Librarians, Clergymen, and professional men generally (to whom a liberal discount is uniformly made), to their extensive stock. ☞ To persons wishing copies of Text-books, for examination, they will be forwarded, per mail or otherwise, on the reception of *one half* the price of the work desired. ☞ Orders from any part of the country attended to with faithfulness and dispatch.

IMPORTANT NEW WORKS.

THE TESTIMONY OF THE ROCKS: or, Geology in its Bearings on the two Theologies, Natural and Revealed. By HUGH MILLER. "Thou shalt be in league with the stones of the field." — *Job*. With numerous elegant illustrations. 12mo, cloth, $1 25

The completion of this important work employed the last hours of the lamented author, and may be considered his greatest and in fact his life work.

MACAULAY ON SCOTLAND. A Critique. By HUGH MILLER, Author of "Footprints of the Creator," &c. 16mo. flexible cloth, 25c

When we read Macaulay's last volumes, we said that they wanted nothing but the fiction to make an epic poem, and now it seems that they are not wanting even in that — PURITAN RECORDER

He meets the historian at the fountain head, tracks him through the old pamphlets and newspapers on which he relied, and demonstrates that his own authorities are against him. — BOSTON TRANSCRIPT.

THE GREYSON LETTERS. Selections from the Correspondence of R. E. H. GREYSON, Esq. Edited by HENRY ROGERS, Author of "The Eclipse of Faith." 12mo, cloth, $1 25.

"Mr Greyson and Mr Rogers are one and the same person. The whole work is from his pen; and every letter is radiant with the genius of the author of the 'Eclipse of Faith'" It discusses a wide range of subjects in the most attractive manner. It abounds in the keenest wit and humor, satire and logic It fairly entitles Mr Rogers to rank with Sydney Smith and Charles Lamb as a wit and humorist, and with Bishop Butler as a reasoner

If Mr Rogers lives to accomplish our expectations, we feel little doubt that his name will share, with those of Butler and Pascal, in the gratitude and veneration of posterity — LONDON QUARTERLY.

Full of acute observation, of subtle analysis, of accurate logic, fine description, apt quotation, pithy remark, and amusing anecdote . . . A book, not for one hour, but for all hours, not for one mood, but for every mood, to think over, to dream over, to laugh over. — BOSTON JOURNAL

A truly good book, containing wise, true and original reflections, and written in an attractive style. — Hon GEO S HILLARD, LL D, in *Boston Courier*

Mr Rogers has few equals as a critic, moral philosopher, and defender of truth . . This volume is full of entertainment, and full of food for thought, to feed on — PHILADELPHIA PRESBYTERIAN.

The Letters are intellectual gems, radiant with beauty and the lights of genius, happily intermingling the grave and the gay — CHRISTIAN OBSERVER

ESSAYS IN BIOGRAPHY AND CRITICISM. By PETER BAYNE, M A, Author of "The Christian Life, Social and Individual." Arranged in TWO SERIES, OR PARTS 12mo, cloth, each, $1 25

This work is prepared by the author exclusively for his American publishers. It includes eighteen articles, viz:

FIRST SERIES — Thomas De Quincey — Tennyson and his Teachers — Mrs Barrett Browning — Recent Aspects of British Art — John Ruskin — Hugh Miller — The Modern Novel, Dickens, &c. — Ellis, Acton, and Currer Bell — Charles Kingsley

SECOND SERIES — S T Coleridge — T B Macaulay — Alison — Wellington — Napoleon — Plato — Characteristics of Christian Civilization. — Education in the Nineteenth Century. — The Pulpit and the Press.

LIFE AND CHARACTER OF JAMES MONTGOMERY. Abridged from the recent London, seven volume edition By Mrs H. C KNIGHT, Author of "Lady Huntington and her Friends, &c With a fine likeness and an elegant illustrated title page on steel 12mo, cloth, $1 25

This is an original biography prepared from the abundant, but ill-digested materials contained in the seven octavo volumes of the London edition The great bulk of that work, together with the heavy style of its literary execution, must necessarily prevent its republication in this country At the same time the Christian public in America will expect some memoir of a poet whose hymns and sacred melodies have seen the light of every household This work, it is confidently hoped, will fully satisfy the public need. It is prepared by one who has already won distinguished laurels in this department of literature

Lightning Source UK Ltd.
Milton Keynes UK
UKOW05f1133201117
313028UK00004B/589/P